The World Book Complete Word Power Library

THE
WORLD BOOK COMPLETE
WORD POWER
LIBRARY

Volume One

A Guide to Writing and Speaking

A Word User's Treasury of Useful Quotations

Published by
World Book–Childcraft International, Inc.
A subsidiary of The Scott & Fetzer Company
Chicago   London   Paris   Sydney   Tokyo   Toronto

The World Book Complete Word Power Library

Copyright © 1981 by
World Book–Childcraft International, Inc.
Merchandise Mart Plaza, Chicago, Illinois 60654

Printed in the United States of America

ISBN 0-7166-3110-5

Library of Congress Catalog Card No. 80-53648

Welcome to word power

Probably the single most difficult task facing each and every one of us on a daily basis is effective communication. How can we express to others the feelings, ideas, and information we wish to communicate? How can we do this in ways that make it likely our meaning will be fully understood? And, on the other hand, how can we improve the chances that we will understand as fully as possible the messages others are attempting to communicate to us?

The primary method of communication between people is words. Words are the collections of sounds and symbols we have assigned to describe our experiences, emotions, and ideas. Words are abstract labels that may be arranged and rearranged to communicate a variety of meanings in a variety of ways.

Words may be used to communicate meanings in either a written or a spoken way. Because even the most common, everyday communication is an extremely complex activity, various rules for using words have developed over the many years words have served as a method of communication.

Indeed, without rules and guidelines, words could not be used to communicate clearly. For effective communication to take place, all participants must understand what each word stands for and what each group of words means when arranged in a certain way.

The World Book Complete Word Power Library has been developed specifically to help you increase your overall ability to use words. "Word power," the collection of skills and techniques that enable a person to communicate effectively, is perhaps the most vital area for personal growth that you will ever encounter. Success in school, efficiency on the job, enjoyment of social interaction, and warmth in personal relationships—all depend greatly on the extent of your ability to use your word power.

The World Book Complete Word Power Library gathers, from many different sources, the skills and techniques you need to develop your ability to use both the written and the spoken word. Usually the various kinds of information presented in this publication can only be found by searching through many different books and pamphlets. Yet here all the material has been organized in an easy-to-use format in two handy volumes.

The two volumes of *The World Book Complete Word Power Library* are divided into four largely self-contained parts. Each part features information you need to improve some specific facet of your personal word power.

Part 1, "A guide to writing and speaking," is a veritable gold mine of strategies, tips, and guidelines to help you communicate more efficiently in both writing and speaking. Presented here in an easy-to-read, easy-to-understand, nontechnical way are the basic rules that govern the proper use of the English language.

"A guide to writing and speaking" has been prepared under the direction of the editors of *The World Book Encyclopedia.* The guidelines for effective writing presented here are based on knowledge and experience gained through years of producing publications noted for clarity and readability.

While Part 1 is designed to provide you with a thorough foundation in the rules governing correct writing, the emphasis throughout is on the practical. Part 1 is loaded with tips, examples, and advice for the kinds of writing we all encounter at some time in our lives.

Effective written communication is important to you. But most people spend much more time engaged in spoken communication. This important area has not been overlooked. Part 1 includes tips for improving your spoken communication in both formal and conversational situations.

Every section includes activities that will help you to practice the skills presented in that section. Write your answers to these activities on a separate piece of paper (*not* in the book itself). Then the activities can be used again later for review. And all members of your family can continue to use the activities to develop their communication skills for years to come.

"A word user's treasury of useful quotations," Part 2 of *The World Book Complete Word Power Library,* is a collection of noteworthy statements made throughout history by both major and minor figures from literature, the arts, politics, business—virtually all areas of important human activity. The statements have been collected and categorized according to subject matter by the World Book editors.

Use of Part 2 should help you to make both your written and spoken communication more interesting and informative. There is nothing like a wisely chosen, hard-hitting quotation to arouse interest or to drive home an important point.

Knowing the correct and most effective ways in which to use words is only half the story of developing personal word power. In addition to gaining word use skills, you must also increase the storehouse of words you know how to use.

Part 3, "A word builder guide," features strategies and techniques to help you expand and enliven your vocabulary. Vocabulary development should be an active, ongoing process. To help you in this process, "A word builder guide" emphasizes "Self-help" exercises and activities.

"A word builder guide" has been created with the cooperation of Dr. Joseph O'Rourke, Research Associate in the College of Education, The Ohio State University; and Dr. Edgar Dale, Emeritus Professor of Education, The Ohio State University. Both are well-known and highly respected figures in the field of vocabulary development.

Another way to increase your storehouse of words is using a thesaurus. A thesaurus can help you use words precisely and add variety to your writing and speaking. A *thesaurus* is basically a list of synonyms. By presenting groups of words with similar meanings, a thesaurus enables you to choose a word that says exactly what you want to say. A thesaurus also offers you a variety of ways to communicate essentially the same message.

Part 4, "A word finder thesaurus of selected words," has been compiled exclusively for *The World Book Complete Word Power Library*. The contributor of Part 4 is Walter D. Glanze, noted word expert.

This is a thesaurus with a difference. "A word finder thesaurus of selected words" is based entirely upon words that have been identified as part of the living vocabulary we all use in our day-to-day communication. Antiquated and obscure terms have been omitted. Technical terms have been avoided. This publication represents one of the first efforts to prepare a thesaurus based upon the English language as it is actually used today.

Taken together, the four parts of *The World Book Complete Word Power Library* provide you with the basic resources for improving virtually every area of word use. Here in two volumes is much of the information you will need to become a more effective communicator and, therefore, to help improve your efficiency in school, at home, and on the job.

Staff

Editorial director
William H. Nault

Editorial

Executive editor
Robert O. Zeleny

Managing editor
Dominic J. Miccolis

Editors
Seva Johnson
Gail Rosicky

Editorial assistant
Janet T. Peterson

Writers/editors
Patricia K. Kummer
David L. Murray
Ann B. Poole

Index editor
Jean Babrick

Art

Senior art director
William Hammond

Art director
Joe Gound

Design director
Ronald A. Stachowiak

Designer
Harry Voigt

Design production
Bernard Arendt

Photo editor
Paul Quirico

Photographer
Steve Hale

Product production

Executive director
Philip B. Hall

Research and development
Henry Koval

Manufacturing
Joseph C. LaCount

Pre-press services
J. J. Stack

Product control
Barbara Podczerwinski

Composition
John Babrick

Film separations
Alfred J. Mozdzen

Contents

Volume One

Volume Two

Contents of Volume One

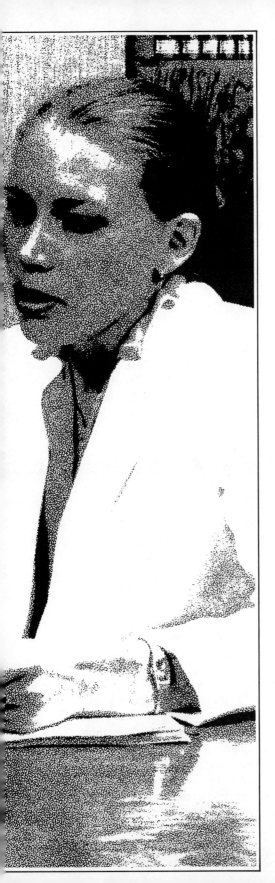

Part 1

A guide to writing and speaking

Introduction

"A guide to writing and speaking" presents a wealth of information to help you communicate more effectively in all aspects of your life. No matter who you are or what you do, the way you communicate with others plays a significant role in determining your success. Your ability to communicate affects whether you are understood or misunderstood; whether your ideas are listened to or ignored; whether you are effective or ineffective—in school, at home, in the community, on the job.

"A guide to writing and speaking" has been designed to serve two basic purposes. First, the guide serves as a *reference* tool for finding the fundamental rules and conventions governing the use of the English language. When you need to refresh your memory on any of these basic rules, the guide serves as a source to which you can turn to quickly find what you need. Second, the guide serves as a *learning* tool to help you practice and develop your communication skills. It offers advice and suggestions for specific kinds of writing and speaking situations you may encounter throughout life.

Section 1, "Knowing the basics," reviews the fundamentals of writing. It offers a "Table of spelling rules," along with tips for avoiding common spelling problems. It reviews the parts of speech and the basic sentence parts and explains how to structure effective sentences.

Section 2, "Rules of style," provides the rules governing the technical matters of writing. There are clear, concise lists of rules for capitalization and punctuation. The accepted titles used to address government officials and other dignitaries are listed. And there are sections on preparing footnotes and bibliographies.

"Commonly misused words, phrases, and constructions," section 3, explains how to correct frequently made errors in grammar and word use. Specific words and phrases are listed alphabetically for easy reference. This section also offers a list of clichés to avoid in your writing and tips for correcting common grammatical errors.

Section 4, "Tips about everyday writing," explains how to plan, organize, and write both business and personal letters. People in the business world can benefit from the suggestions for preparing clear, concise business reports and memorandums. And there is information on writing résumés and cover letters, along with advice for filling in forms.

Section 5, "Model letters for selected occasions," includes more than 20 business and personal letters for a variety of purposes and occasions, such as order letters, complaint letters, thank-you notes, invitations. The model letters, combined with specific guidelines for writing each kind of letter, can give you ideas for putting your own letters together.

"Writing for school situations," in section 6, offers sound advice for students of all ages, at all levels. It presents the steps for carefully planning, researching, organizing, and writing school papers—including specific suggestions for short reports and term papers. A section on taking written examinations explains how to prepare for tests and how to improve test-taking skills.

Section 7, "Speaking before a group," can help you be a more confident speaker. It outlines the six steps in preparing and practicing a speech and suggests specific techniques for delivering a speech. Even if you never give a formal speech, the techniques offered can help you present your ideas—and yourself—more effectively through the spoken word.

Section 8 considers those communication skills used in speaking "Face to face and over the phone." It presents tips for having better conversations, for using the telephone wisely, for improving your listening skills, and for making a good impression in formal interviews.

Also included in "A guide to writing and speaking" is a list of "10,000 Commonly used words." This list serves as a quick reference for finding the spelling, hyphenation, and syllable breaks in the words you probably use most often.

To help you practice the skills offered in "A guide to writing and speaking," each section ends with activities called "Use what you know." An answer key to these activities is provided so that you can check your progress. An index at the end of Part 1 will help you quickly find the many kinds of information presented in this guide.

1 Knowing the basics

Do you make a lot of spelling errors? Have you forgotten how some parts of speech function? Are your sentences well-structured and easily understood? If you have a weakness in any of these areas, your written work—letters, reports, and papers—is probably not as effective as it could be.

The way you write is a reflection on you. If your sentences are poorly structured and hard to understand, people will notice your errors instead of what you have to say. But good, clear writing tells people that *you* are careful and accurate—and that your ideas are worth reading.

This section provides the foundation: the background knowledge you need to write clear, correct sentences. It reviews the rules for spelling and the functions of the parts of speech. It describes how sentences are structured and offers suggestions for writing sentences that are more effective. You can refer back to this section whenever you have a question on these basic points of writing.

Rules for spelling

Accurate spelling is a small but important part of your writing. Misspelled words can detract from your letters, reports, and papers. Misspellings give the impression that you have not been careful in your work. All writers have trouble spelling some words and need to check their spelling to be sure that their writing is precise.

Why is spelling difficult for many people? One reason is that many words in the English language are not spelled the way they sound. For example, *phoenix* is pronounced *feniks*. Thus, sounding out a word does not guarantee that you will properly spell the word. You can look a word up in the dictionary if you have some ideas about where to look for it. When you know how a word sounds but don't know how it is spelled, check the Table of Spellings of English Sounds. There you will find some possible spellings of the sounds in the word. Then you can check those possible spellings in the dictionary to find the correct spelling.

Common spelling problems

Table of spellings of English sounds

The sound	as in	may be spelled	as in
short *a*	h*a*t	*ai*	pl*ai*d
		au	l*au*gh
long *a*	*a*pe	*ai*	*ai*d
		ay	pl*ay*
		ea	br*ea*k
		ei	*ei*ght
		ey	th*ey*
short *e*	s*e*t	*a*	m*a*ny
		ai	s*ai*d
		ay	s*ay*s
long *e*	sh*e*	*ae*	C*ae*sar
		i	mach*i*ne
		ie	bel*ie*ve
short *i*	h*i*m	*ee*	b*ee*n
		o	w*o*men
		u	b*u*sy
		y	h*y*mn
long *i*	*i*ce	*ai*	*ai*sle
		ei	h*ei*ght
		y	st*y*le
short *o*	l*o*t	*a*	w*a*tt
long *o*	*o*pen	*ew*	s*ew*
		oa	m*oa*t
		oe	h*oe*
		oo	br*oo*ch
		ou	s*ou*l
		ow	sl*ow*

The sound	as in	may be spelled	as in
short *u*	c*u*p	*o*	c*o*me
		ou	d*ou*ble
yü	*yu*le	*eu*	f*eu*d
		ew	f*ew*
		u	*u*se
		ue	c*ue*
f	*f*un	*gh*	enou*gh*
		ph	*ph*oto
g	*g*o	*gh*	*gh*ost
		gu	*gu*est
		gue	ro*gue*
j	*j*ar	*dg*	ri*dg*e
		g	fra*g*ile
m	*m*e	*lm*	ca*lm*
		mb	cli*mb*
n	*n*o	*gn*	*gn*at
		kn	*kn*ow
		pn	*pn*eumonia
ng	thi*ng*	*n*	thi*n*k
r	*r*un	*rh*	*rh*yme
		wr	*wr*ong
s	*s*ay	*c*	*c*ent
		ce	ri*ce*
		ps	*ps*ychology
sh	*sh*e	*ch*	ma*ch*ine
		ci	spe*ci*al
		ti	na*ti*on
t	*t*ell	*ed*	dropp*ed*
z	*z*oo	*s*	de*s*ert
		sc	di*sc*ern
		ss	de*ss*ert
		x	*x*ylophone

Another reason for misspelling some words is mispronunciation. If you mispronounce words by adding or omitting letters or syllables, you will probably also misspell them. Words like *mischievous, government,* and *environment* when mispronounced might be misspelled as *mischievious, goverment,* and *envierment.*

Guidelines for spelling

How, then, can you avoid misspelling words? First, keep a dictionary close by when you are writing. When in doubt about the spelling or pronunciation of a word, look up the word in the dictionary. After you have looked up the word, try to study the word in the following ways:

1. Write the word clearly and neatly.
2. Spell the word out loud.
3. Divide the word into syllables.

4. Pronounce the word out loud.
5. Study the difficult parts of the word.
6. Read and learn the definition of the word.
7. Make up a sentence using the word with its proper meaning.
8. Close your eyes and try to remember how the word looks.
9. Use the word whenever possible in writing and conversation.

Even when you know how to spell a word, spelling problems can still arise. That usually happens when you change a word—when you want to make it plural, or change the tense, or add a prefix or suffix. The following Table of Spelling Rules will help you avoid some of these problems. There are, of course, exceptions to almost every rule. Look over the rules and their exceptions in this table. Then refer to it when you have a spelling problem.

Table of spelling rules

Problem	Rule	Some exceptions
Words with *i*'s and *e*'s: *believe, deceit*	Use *i* before *e* except after *c* or when sounded like *a* as in *neighbor* and *weigh*.	*ancient, financier, counterfeit, either, foreign, height, leisure, seize, weird*
Words ending in *cede: precede*	The root *cede* is always spelled this way except in four words and their various forms.	*supersede, exceed, proceed, succeed* and their other forms (*superseded, exceeding, proceeds, succeeder*)
Words ending in *c: traffic*	Insert *k* when adding an ending that begins with *e, i,* or *y: trafficked.*	*arced*
Words ending in soft *ce* or *ge: peace, advantage*	Retain the final *e* before adding *able* or *ous: peaceable, advantageous.*	
Words ending in silent *e: desire*	Drop the final *e* before suffixes beginning with a vowel: *desirable.*	*mileage*
Words ending in silent *e: love*	Retain the final *e* before suffixes beginning with a consonant: *lovely.*	*acknowledgment, argument, duly, judgment, ninth, wholly*
Words ending in *ie: tie*	Change *ie* to *y* when adding *ing: tying.*	
Words ending in *oe: hoe*	Retain the final *e* before a suffix beginning with any vowel except *e: hoeing* but *hoed.*	

Problem	Rule	Some exceptions
Words ending in *y* preceded by a consonant: *occupy*	Change *y* to *i* before a suffix unless the suffix begins with *i: occupies* but *occupying*.	
Adjectives of one syllable ending in *y: dry*	Retain *y* when adding a suffix: *drying*.	
Words of one syllable and words accented on the last syllable, ending in a consonant preceded by a vowel: *glad, repel, occur*	Double the consonant before a suffix beginning with a vowel: *gladden, repelled, occurred*.	*crocheting, ricocheted, filleted, transferable* (but *transferred*). Also, if the accent shifts to the first syllable when a suffix is added, the final consonant is not doubled: *preferred*, but *preference*.
Words ending in a consonant preceded by more than one vowel: *boil, reveal*	Do not double the consonant before a suffix beginning with a vowel: *boiled, revealing*.	
Words ending in more than one consonant: *work, conform*	Do not double the final consonant: *worked, conforming*.	
Words not accented on the last syllable: *benefit*	Do not double the final consonant: *benefited*.	
Words ending in *l: horizontal*	Retain the *l* before a suffix beginning with *l: horizontally*.	Words ending in *ll* drop one *l* before the suffix *ly: hilly, fully*.
Prefixes and suffixes ending in *ll: all-, -full*	Omit one *l* when adding these to other words: *almost, grateful*.	
Prefixes *dis-, il-, im-, in-, mis-, over-, re-, un-*	Do not change the spelling of the root word: *dissimilar, illegal, immoral, innumerable, misspell, overrun, reedit, unnerve*.	
Words ending in a double consonant: *possess, enroll*	Retain both consonants when adding suffixes: *possessor, enrolling*.	
Nouns ending in *f* or *fe: handkerchief*	Form the plural by adding *s: handkerchiefs*.	Some nouns ending in *f* or *fe* form the plural by changing the *f* or *fe* to *ve* and adding *s: knives, elves, halves, leaves, loaves, shelves, wives*.
Nouns ending in *y* preceded by a consonant: *lady*	Form the plural by changing *y* to *i* and adding *es: ladies*.	Proper nouns ending in *y* form the plural by adding *s:* "Three *Garys* work in my office."
Nouns ending in *ch, sh, s, x, z: gas, church, brush, glass, fox, topaz*	Form the plural by adding *es: gases, churches, brushes, glasses, foxes, topazes*.	

Problem	Rule	Some exceptions
Nouns ending in *o* preceded by a vowel: *cameo*	Form the plural by adding *s:* *cameos.*	
Nouns ending in *o* preceded by a consonant: *potato*	Form the plural by adding *es:* *potatoes.*	*dittos, dynamos, silos* For some nouns, either *s* or *es* is correct: *buffalos* or *buffaloes, volcanos* or *volcanoes.*
Compound nouns: *major general, notary public, sister-in-law*	Make the modified word plural: major *generals,* *notaries* public, *sisters*-in-law.	
Nouns ending in *ful: cupful*	Form the plural by adding *s* to *ful: cupfuls.*	
Letters, numbers, dates, signs, and words referred to as words	Form the plural by adding *'s:* six *b's,* two *5's,* the *1970's,* *%'s, but's.*	

Now you have some guidelines and rules to help you improve your spelling. As you work on your spelling problems and refer to these rules, you might wish to make a list of the words that you frequently misspell. Keep the list in your dictionary.

Parts of speech

The various parts of speech (noun, verb, pronoun) are pieces that, when put together correctly, make whole and complete sentences. When you are reading or writing, you probably don't think about which part of speech the individual words belong to. And you usually don't need to. But you *do* need to find and correct errors in your own writing. If you understand how the parts of speech function, you can more easily recognize errors. And you will better understand how to use the methods and rules for correcting those errors. Understanding grammar, therefore, gives you specific ways to make your writing clear and precise.

Traditional grammar books usually list eight parts of speech: nouns, pronouns, adjectives, verbs, adverbs, prepositions, conjunctions, and interjections. Every word belongs to one of these parts of speech. Some words belong to more than one part, depending on how they are used. For example, *snap* is a noun: "The *snap* on her jacket broke." *Snap* is also a verb: "Twigs *snap* underfoot in autumn." And *snap* is an adjective: "The boss made a *snap* decision."

This section reviews the parts of speech, explains how they function, and gives you advice for using them properly in your writing.

Nouns

Nouns name persons, places, and things. Everything you can give a name to is a noun: *Joe, woman, country, France, house, Buckingham Palace, book.* There are two kinds of nouns: proper and common. Proper nouns name particular persons, places, and things: *Abraham Lincoln, Elizabeth Tudor, Illinois, Africa, Magna Carta, The New York Times.* Proper nouns are always capitalized. Common nouns name kinds or types of persons, places, or things: *girl, executive, lake, mountain, tree, desk.* Common nouns are not capitalized.

Nouns are further divided into three groups: concrete, abstract, and collective. Concrete nouns name things that you can see, hear, smell, taste, and touch: *car, music, flowers, bread, piano.* Concrete nouns can be singular or plural: *window, windows; lady, ladies; lake, lakes.* You can use the articles *a, an,* or *the* before concrete nouns: *a* cat, *an* apple, *the* boy.

Abstract nouns name ideas, actions, and qualities that you cannot experience through your senses: *anger, betrayal, courage, curiosity, intelligence, strength. The* is used most of the time before abstract nouns: "He had *the strength* of ten people."

Collective nouns name groups or collections of persons or things: *family, class, congregation, crowd, people, set, team.* Collective nouns are singular in form and usually take a singular verb. "The *family was* eating dinner." "The *set* of dishes *was* broken." Sometimes a collective noun is followed by a plural verb when the individuals are emphasized rather than the group. "The *people were* running in different directions."

Pronouns

Pronouns take the place of nouns. They help you avoid the monotonous repetition of nouns. Read the following sentence:

> Margaret called David and asked David if David would be able to bring David's car to Margaret's house so Margaret could use David's car.

Isn't that an awkward sentence to read! By using pronouns in place of some nouns, the sentence would read more smoothly.

> Margaret called David and asked *him* if *he* would be able to bring *his* car to *her* house so *she* could use *it.*

Each pronoun in that sentence had an *antecedent*—a noun that the pronoun stood for. A pronoun must always refer back to some noun.

There are five kinds of pronouns: personal, relative, interrogative, demonstrative, and indefinite.

Personal pronouns. A pronoun that substitutes for the name of a person, place, or thing is a personal pronoun. The seven personal pronouns are *I, you, he, she, it, we, they.* They substitute for nouns when nouns are used as subjects. These pronouns *do* things. Any one of them will complete this sentence: ". . . ran toward the lake." Each of these pronouns also has an object form: *me, you, him, her, it, us, them.* As objects, they receive some kind of action—something is *done* to them. Any personal pronoun in the object form will complete this sentence: "The waves engulfed. . . . "

Most problems with personal pronouns arise because personal pronouns take different forms as subjects and objects in sentences. This is not true of nouns; nouns keep the same form regardless of whether they are used as subjects or objects. Both of the following sentences are correct. "The *man* met the *woman.*" "The *woman* met the *man.*" If you used pronouns to replace *man* and *woman,* you would have to say *"He* met *her"* or *"She* met *him."* You couldn't say *"Him* met *her"* or *"She* met *he."* In sentences using the linking verb *to be* and its many forms *(is, are, am, was, were),* always use the *subject* form of the personal pronoun after the linking verb. "It is *I.*" "I am *she.*"

Choosing the correct pronoun to follow a preposition can also cause problems. Use the *object* form of the pronoun after a preposition. "She is going *with* Jane and *me.*" "This dispute is *between* you and *him.*"

Personal pronouns also have a *possessive* form: *my, mine; your, yours; his; her, hers; its; our, ours; their, theirs.* "The book is *hers,* not *yours.*" *"Our* house is smaller than *theirs.*"

Reflexive pronouns are formed by adding *self* or *selves* to the personal pronouns: *myself, yourself, herself, himself, itself, ourselves, yourselves, themselves.* They are called *reflexive* because the action of the verb is directed back toward the subject: "He hurt *himself.*" These pronouns can also be *intensive* when they give emphasis to the subject. "The teacher *herself* led the protest to the principal's office."

Do not use reflexive pronouns when a simple personal pronoun will do. It is wrong to say, "Jane and *myself* went to school." Instead say, "Jane and *I* went to school."

Relative pronouns. Relative pronouns *relate* back to a noun or pronoun in a preceding clause, and they connect the two clauses. *Who* is used to refer to persons. *Which* is used to refer to things or to a group of persons treated as a group. *That* is used to refer to persons or things.

The man *who* lives next door broke his leg. [*who* refers back to *man*]
The refrigerator *which* had just been delivered needed cleaning. [*which* refers back to *refrigerator*]

The team *which* won the tournament was presented a trophy.
[*which* refers back to *team*]
The book *that* I bought was on sale. [*that* refers back to *book*]
The woman *that* I met was very rude. [*that* refers back to
woman]

Interrogative pronouns. These pronouns are used to ask
questions: *who, which,* and *what.*

Who rang the doorbell?
Which of you wants to help?
What are you doing with the hammer?

Demonstrative pronouns. These pronouns point out and
identify particular persons or things. The demonstrative
pronouns are *this, that, these,* and *those.* They answer the
question "Which?"

This is the way to do the job.
That is the wrong way.
These are my gloves; *those* by the door are yours.

Indefinite pronouns. Indefinite pronouns like demonstrative
pronouns answer the question "Which?" But they do not refer
to definite persons or things.

Someone moved into the apartment next door.
Several were hired this month.
Neither can come to work today.

Other indefinite pronouns are *another, any, anyone, anything, both,
each, everybody, everyone, everything, few, many, nobody, none, one, some,
something.*

Adjectives

Adjectives modify nouns and pronouns. That is, they describe,
limit, or in some other way give a more exact meaning to a
noun or pronoun. Descriptive adjectives indicate a quality or
condition of the noun: a *long* trailer, a *happy* dog, a *slippery* road.
Limiting adjectives point out the exact noun referred to or
show quantity: *this* desk, *those* children, *five* dollars, *the* boy.
Notice that articles *(a, an, the)* and demonstrative pronouns *(this,
that, these, those)* can be used as adjectives.

Phrases may also act as adjectives: "The car *with the racing
stripes* stalled." Adjectives also modify phrases that are used as
nouns: *"Walking to work* [noun phrase] was *difficult* [adjective]."

Verbs

Verbs are very important words. Without a verb, there can be
no sentence. "Mary the party" doesn't tell us much. But by
adding a verb, you create a sentence: "Mary *enjoyed* the party."

Verbs allow us to make statements, ask questions, and give commands.

The boy *ran* home. [statement]
Why *run* home? [question]
Run home, quickly! [command]

Verbs can express action or a state of being.

The dog *grabbed* the stick. [action]
The dog *is* quiet now. [state of being]

Action verbs may express physical action *(talk, push, fall, drink)* or mental action *(believe, think, hope, decide)*. Most verbs are action verbs. Those that are not are either linking verbs or auxiliary verbs.

Linking verbs link the subject of the sentence to another word, in order to make a statement: "Jack *became* furious." The verb *became* links the subject *Jack* with the word *furious,* to make a statement about Jack. Some common linking verbs are *appear, be, feel, grow, look, remain, seem, smell, sound, stay,* and *taste.*

Auxiliary verbs (sometimes called *helping verbs*) are used with other verbs to change tense, voice, or mood. Forms of the verbs *be, do, have, can, may, shall,* and *will* are auxiliary verbs. A verb's *tense* tells when the action occurred: present, past, or future. The present tense *runs* becomes the future tense *will run* by adding the auxiliary verb *will* to *run.*

The *voice* of a verb—active or passive—tells the relation of the subject to the verb. When the subject does the acting, the verb is in the *active* voice: "The children *made* their beds." When the subject receives the action, the verb is in the *passive* voice: "The bed *was made* by the children." The passive was formed by adding the auxiliary verb *was* to *made.* When choosing whether to use active or passive voice, decide whether the doer of the action *(children)* or the receiver of the action *(bed)* is important. Then make the more important idea the subject of the sentence.

Verbs also have different moods: indicative, subjunctive, imperative. Verbs in the *indicative mood* make a statement of fact: "Grandfather and I *took* a walk." The *subjunctive mood* deals with things that might be or could be: "If Father had been home, we *would have taken* a walk." Once again, auxiliary verbs *(would* and *have)* were used to change the mood of the verb. In the *imperative mood,* verbs give a command or make a plea. "Go away!" "Please, go away."

Verbs may be either transitive or intransitive. A *transitive* verb transfers the action from one noun to another noun. A transitive verb always has an object. An *object* receives the action of the verb or completes the meaning of the verb:

"Mary accepted the *invitation.*" The object *invitation* receives the action of the verb *accepted.*

Intransitive verbs do not transfer action; thus, they do not have objects: "The chair *broke.*" *Broke* is intransitive because it needs nothing to complete its meaning. Many verbs may be either transitive or intransitive, depending on the meaning of the sentence. For instance, the verb *broke* would be transitive in the sentence "The chair *broke* the glass."

Adverbs

Adverbs, like adjectives, are modifiers. They give a more exact meaning to verbs, adjectives, other adverbs, or whole sentences. Adverbs answer the questions *how? when? where? why?* or *to what extent?*

	modifies	answers the question
The team played *well.*	verb *(played)*	how?
I will *never* sing for you.	verb *(will sing)*	when?
The giant had *thunderously* loud footsteps.	adjective *(loud)*	how?
Father drove *very* slowly through the storm.	adverb *(slowly)*	to what extent?
She walked *outside.*	verb *(walked)*	where?

Most words ending in *ly* are adverbs: *badly, hardly, nearly, quietly.* Other words commonly used as adverbs are *always, fast, very, well, soon, now.*

Phrases may also act as adverbs: "The car drove *over the cliff.*" The phrase *over the cliff* modifies the verb *drove* and tells where.

Some adverbs act as conjunctions. *Conjunctive adverbs* join two sentences and modify one of the sentences: "We liked the house; *nevertheless,* we are not going to buy it." Other conjunctive adverbs are *hence, however, moreover, otherwise, still, therefore, thus.* When you use a conjunctive adverb to join two sentences, put a semicolon before the conjunctive adverb and a comma after it.

Prepositions

Prepositions precede nouns and pronouns and show the relationship of the noun or pronoun to some other word in the sentence.

That man *in* the last row ran *to* the door *before* me.

The relationships shown in this sentence are—

Position—*in* the last row
Direction—*to* the door
Time—*before* me

The prepositional phrase *in the last row* is used as an adjective because it tells something about the *man*. The phrases *to the door* and *before me* are used as adverbs since they modify the verb *ran*. They tell *where* the man ran and *when* he ran.

A preposition may be a single word or a group of words. Here are some common prepositions:

about	except	alongside
above	for	concerning
across	from	notwithstanding
at	out	throughout
beneath	over	underneath
beside	under	as to
by	up	because of
down	upon	contrary to
during	with	in spite of

Conjunctions

Conjunctions join together words, phrases, clauses, or sentences. There are three kinds of conjunctions: coordinating, subordinating, and correlative.

Coordinating conjunctions join together words or groups of words that are grammatically the same.

They ate pancakes *and* sausages. [*and* connects two nouns]
I will get up, *but* I won't work. [*but* connects two main clauses]

Other coordinating conjunctions are *for, or, nor, so, yet.*

Subordinating conjunctions connect subordinate clauses to main clauses: "Many cars were on the highway *because* it was a holiday." The subordinating conjunction *because* introduces the subordinate clause "because it was a holiday" and joins it to the main clause "Many cars were on the highway." A subordinating conjunction may also introduce a subordinate clause that comes *before* the main clause: "*If* Mary studies very hard, she will probably pass the test." Other subordinating conjunctions include *although, as, before, since, so that, unless, while.*

Correlative conjunctions are two coordinating conjunctions that are used as a pair: *both . . . and, either . . . or, neither . . . nor, though . . . yet.*

You should wear *both* your mittens *and* your scarf.
Either go to school *or* stay in bed.

Interjections

Interjections express emotion. They are an unusual part of speech because they have *no* grammatical connection with the other words in a sentence. They usually stand alone or are set off by commas.

> *Ouch!* I hurt my thumb.
> *Oh,* you're here!

Because interjections show emotion, they add spice to writing: *bravo, hurrah, hush, tsk-tsk, whoops.* But remember: Just as food can be overspiced, so can writing.

The sentence: parts and structure

A sentence is a group of words that contains a subject and a predicate and expresses a complete thought. You probably remember this definition from previous studies about sentence structure. If you fully understand this definition, you'll probably write better sentences. Let's analyze some terms in this definition.

A subject and a predicate. Every sentence must have a subject and a predicate. The *subject* is the person or thing about which a statement is made. The *predicate* is the word or group of words that makes a statement about the subject.

> My neighbor built a deck in his backyard.

In this sentence, *neighbor* is the simple subject and *my neighbor* is the complete subject. The predicate is *built a deck in his backyard.* The predicate must have a verb *(built)* and may have words or groups of words that modify or complete the meaning of the verb. In the example sentence, *a deck* is an object, which receives the action of the verb *built.* And *in his backyard* modifies *built* by telling where.

A complete thought. Besides requiring a subject and a predicate, a sentence must express a complete thought. If any of those three requirements is missing, you will have an incomplete sentence, called a *sentence fragment.* Here are some examples of sentence fragments you should avoid:

> **Fragment:** The house on the hill, being abandoned for twenty years. [no predicate]

This fragment has no predicate because it contains no verb; *being abandoned for twenty years* is a modifier, not a verb.

> **Fragment:** Was run down and inhabited by rats. [no subject]

This fragment clearly has no subject; it does not tell *what* was run down.

Fragment: Because the owners had died in an accident.
    [incomplete thought]

This fragment is a subordinate clause. Even though a
subordinate clause has a subject and a predicate, it does *not*
express a complete thought. Therefore, a subordinate clause
cannot stand alone; it must be joined to a main clause to
complete its meaning. This fragment does not tell us what
happened *because the owners had died in an accident.* We would have
to join this subordinate clause to a main clause in order to
express a complete thought.

Sentence: The house on the hill was run down *because the
    owners had died in an accident.*

Of course, a sentence can have more than one thought. But
the thoughts within one sentence should be closely related.
Look at the following sentence:

After Mr. and Mrs. Smith died, their house stood abandoned
because their daughter couldn't decide whether to rent out
the house or sell it.

There are several thoughts in this sentence: *Mr. and Mrs. Smith
died; their house stood abandoned;* and *their daughter couldn't decide.*
These thoughts express a related sequence of events: the
Smiths' deaths and the daughter's indecision led to an
abandoned house. When you put more than one idea in a
sentence, be sure that you properly connect the ideas. If you
are joining sentences together, use a conjunction, a semicolon,
or subordinate clauses. But when thoughts are *not* closely
related, you should state them in separate sentences.
    If a sentence doesn't sound correct after you have written it,
ask yourself the following questions.

1. Does the sentence have a *subject?*
2. Does the sentence have a *predicate?*
3. Does the sentence express a *complete thought?*
4. Are the *thoughts* in the sentence *closely related?*

Up to this point, we have dealt with the basic parts of the
sentence: the subject and the predicate. Now we will look at
some *word groups* that are important in writing sentences. You
don't usually write sentences one word at a time. You think
and write in groups of related words. These groups of related
words are called phrases and clauses.

Word groups in sentences

Phrases. Phrases are groups of related words that do not
contain both a subject and a predicate. Phrases can act as a
single part of speech—as a noun, adjective, adverb, or verb.

Here are some examples of *noun phrases:*

Marching in the St. Patrick's Day Parade was the group's goal.
[noun phrase used as a subject]
Kathy wanted *to memorize the poem.* [noun phrase used as an
object]

Adjective phrases modify nouns and pronouns.

The band *marching at the end of the parade* was out of step.
[adjective phrase modifying the noun *band*]
Tired from a hard day at play, he fell asleep quickly. [adjective
phrase modifying the pronoun *he*]

Phrases that modify verbs, adjectives, or other adverbs are
called *adverb phrases.*

He ran *to catch the last train.* [adverb phrase modifying the
verb *ran*]
At the last second, he jumped *on the train.* [adverb phrases
modifying the verb *jumped*]

Verb phrases are groups of words that act as verbs. They consist
of a main verb and auxiliary verbs, or of a verb and its
modifiers.

By the end of the week, the report *will have been completed.*
[main verb and auxiliary verbs]
Good dressmakers *sew carefully, precisely, and neatly.* [verb and
its modifiers]

Clauses. Clauses are groups of related words which have both
a subject and a predicate. There are two kinds of clauses: main
clauses and subordinate clauses. *Main clauses* are sometimes
called independent clauses because they can stand alone and
make complete sense.

I hurried to work because I was late.

I hurried to work is a main clause. It makes complete sense by
itself and could become a sentence with the addition of a
period.

Subordinate clauses, sometimes called dependent clauses, are not
able to stand alone. Though they contain a subject and a verb,
they do not express a complete thought. They depend on the
rest of the sentence for their meaning. Certain words, called
linking words, join subordinate clauses to main clauses. Some
linking words are *what, that, who, whom, which, than, when, after,
although, since,* and *because.* Like phrases, subordinate clauses can
act as nouns, adjectives, and adverbs. The following sentences
show how various subordinate clauses are used:

	Type of clause	How used
What he said was insulting.	noun	subject
Joe wrote *that you were visiting him.*	noun	object
The little boy was afraid of *what the big dog would do.*	noun	object of preposition
The remark *which he made* was insulting.	adjective	modifies *remark*
The people *who live next door* went on vacation.	adjective	modifies *people*
The blue pen was the one *that she wanted.*	adjective	modifies *one*
The Johnsons bought a new car *because Mrs. Johnson received a raise.*	adverb	modifies *bought*
The girls swam faster *than the boys did.*	adverb	modifies *faster*
Mary is taller *than Kathy is.*	adverb	modifies *taller*

Sometimes subordinate clauses do not have a linking word; the linking word is understood. We all understand that *She is a woman I admire* is the same as *She is a woman that I admire.*

Appositives. Appositives are nouns that identify or describe another noun or a pronoun. An appositive may be a single noun, a noun phrase, or a noun clause.

My sister *Margaret* got married. [appositive identifying *sister*]
The neighbor's dog, *a roly-poly little mutt,* ran away. [appositive describing *dog*]

Phrases, clauses, and appositives can be either restrictive or nonrestrictive. If they are *restrictive,* they are necessary to the meaning of the sentence. That is, they *restrict* the meaning of the sentence by identifying a definite person or thing. *Nonrestrictive* phrases, clauses, and appositives merely add description to an already identified person or thing. They can be omitted without changing the meaning of the sentence. Here are some examples of restrictive and nonrestrictive phrases, clauses, and appositives:

Restrictive	Nonrestrictive
The man *sitting beside her* was her father.	My father, *combing his hair,* was getting ready for work.
The composer *that I like best* is Beethoven.	Beethoven, *who wrote nine symphonies,* is my favorite composer.
Our neighbor *John* gave us some fish.	Our neighbor to the south, *John Jones,* gave us some fish.

Nonrestrictive phrases, clauses, and appositives are set off by commas. Restrictive phrases, clauses, and appositives are *not* set off by commas because they are essential to the meaning of the sentence.

Sentence structure

One way of classifying sentences is by their structure—by the kind of clauses contained in a sentence. The four kinds of sentence structure are *simple, compound, complex,* and *compound-complex.*

Simple sentences. A simple sentence is made up of one main clause. It has one subject and one predicate and expresses one main thought.

> Robins are a sure sign of spring.
> Why are you going to the store?

The simple sentence may contain a compound subject or a compound verb, or both a compound subject and a compound verb.

> Mary and John walked up the drive and entered the house.

The compound subject is *Mary* and *John,* and the compound verb is *walked* and *entered.*

Compound sentences. A compound sentence contains two or more main clauses that are equally important and closely related in thought.

> Reading a book is fun but writing one is hard work.
> Jane fixed the main course, and Kate made the dessert.
> You enjoy the beach; I prefer the mountains.

The main clauses of a compound sentence can be connected by a conjunction alone, by a comma and a conjunction, or by a semicolon.

Complex sentences. A complex sentence has one main clause and one or more subordinate clauses.

> 　　　subordinate　　　　　　　　　main
> *Although Jack studied all night,*　he still failed the test.
>
> 　　subordinate　　　　　　main　　　　　subordinate
> *After I left the office,*　I bought the book　*that you recommended.*
>
> 　　　　　　　　subordinate　　　　　　　　main
> Students　*who achieve high marks*　are usually well-organized.

Notice in the last example that the subordinate clause appears in the middle of the main clause; the subordinate clause modifies the subject of the main clause, *Students.*

Compound-complex sentences. A compound-complex sentence is made up of two or more main clauses and one or more subordinate clauses.

subordinate   main

If we take our vacation in July,   we'll go to Minnesota;

subordinate   main

if we wait until December,   we'll go to California.

subordinate   main

Since the day was warm and sunny,   the children played

main

and I weeded the garden.

The sentence: kinds and use

Sentences may be classified in several different ways. In the previous section, we classified sentences according to their clause structure. We studied the grammatical parts that make up simple, compound, complex, and compound-complex sentences. In this section, we will study the sentence from the standpoint of content: what sentences do and how words and ideas are arranged in them.

A sentence can have one of four purposes:

What sentences do

1. State a fact or make an assertion.
2. Ask a question.
3. Give a command or make a plea.
4. Express strong feeling.

A sentence that states a fact or makes an assertion is a *declarative sentence.* These sentences end with a period. Most of the sentences that you write are probably declarative sentences. Look at these examples:

I am going away.
The mail was not delivered today.
After the people finished working, they went home.

An *interrogative sentence* asks a question and is followed by a question mark (?). The word order in a question is usually different from the word order in a declarative sentence. In most questions, the subject comes in the middle of the verb phrase.

When are you going away?
Why wasn't the mail delivered today?
How many people went home after they finished their work?

The *imperative sentence* gives a command or makes a plea. In an imperative sentence the subject is usually not written—it is understood. *You* is the understood subject of imperative sentences. Commands may be followed by a period or an exclamation point (!); pleas end with a period. The following are examples of imperative sentences:

Go away!
Please, cut the grass today.
Finish your work and go home.

An *exclamatory sentence* expresses strong feeling. It exclaims! Exclamatory sentences end with an exclamation point. Some exclamatory sentences have an understood subject or predicate, as in a command.

How surprised we were!
What a game! [*it was* is understood]

Exclamatory sentences should be kept short so that they have greater impact on the reader.

Since most of your writing is in declarative sentences, you can vary your writing with the appropriate and effective use of interrogative, imperative, and exclamatory sentences. You can also vary the sentence structure. Notice the different kinds of sentences that are used in the following paragraph.

1. What a glorious day it is! 2. The birds are chirping, the sun is shining, and the air smells fresh. 3. Now that we've had breakfast, we can start working in the yard. 4. First, weed the garden. 5. I'll plant the tulip bulbs. 6. After that's finished, you can cut the grass and I'll wash the car. 7. Do I hear thunder? 8. Oh, no, it's starting to rain! 9. I guess we'll just read the paper and wash the dishes.

Look at the different types of sentences used in that paragraph: 1. simple exclamatory; 2. compound declarative; 3. complex declarative; 4. simple imperative; 5. simple declarative; 6. compound-complex declarative; 7. simple interrogative; 8. simple exclamatory; 9. complex declarative.

How words are arranged in sentences

Subject-verb order. The usual order of words in sentences is subject-verb-object (S-V-O). Here are some typical sentences:

S V   O
I drove the car.

      S   V   O
The girls were playing softball.

     S   V   S   V   O
Snow was on the ground although the calendar said spring.

Sometimes new life can be given to ordinary sentences by inverting the order of the subject and verb. Look at this sentence which uses typical subject-verb order:

    S   V   S   V
When love walked out the door, my happiness was gone.

This sentence can become more dramatic when the subject-verb order is inverted:

    V   S   V   S
Gone was my happiness when out the door walked love.

Though inverted sentences add impact to your writing, use them sparingly. If you overuse inverted sentences, your writing will be difficult to read.

Loose sentences. In loose sentences, the main idea is given first and then details follow.

> I'm moving to Arizona because I'm tired of the snow here and bored with my job.
> The woman dragged the case of stolen jewels slowly and carefully up the back stairs.

Loose sentences are written after the manner of most of our speech. They are direct and easy to follow. Too many loose sentences in succession, however, can be boring. By changing the order of the ideas, you can add variety to your writing.

Periodic sentences. In periodic sentences, the complete meaning of the sentence does not come until the end—until the *period.* Placing the main idea at the end can give that idea stronger emphasis.

> Because I'm tired of the snow here and bored with my job, I'm moving to Arizona.

Periodic sentences can even keep the reader in suspense until the final words are read. For example:

> Up the back stairs, slowly and carefully, the woman dragged the case of stolen jewels.

The case of stolen jewels is what the sentence was all about. But you had to wait until the end to find out. Since periodic sentences can keep the reader hanging, don't use them too often. Also, use periodic sentences only when the idea in the sentence is significant and deserves such strong emphasis. For example:

> Because the United States tries to be all things to all people, its reward is often ingratitude and distrust.

Balanced sentences. A balanced sentence contains two or more equally important ideas; each idea is expressed in a distinct part. The parts are balanced in that they are of about the same length and have the same grammatical structure (such as parallel phrases or parallel clauses). This balanced word structure is especially useful when you want to emphasize similarities or contrasts between ideas.

> Father was dead, mother was dying, and I was wounded.
> The brave never complain in adversity; the cowardly complain in prosperity.

Balanced sentences have a definite beat. Used occasionally, they have a dramatic effect. But if you use too many of them together, your writing will develop a singsong rhythm.

Loose, declarative sentences are the main pattern for your writing. When you want to emphasize a point or catch the reader's attention, vary this pattern. Vary the word order by writing inverted, periodic, or balanced sentences. Vary the function of the sentence by using imperative, interrogative, or exclamatory sentences. You should use these variations on the loose, declarative sentence for emphasis or effect. If you use these variations too often, they lose their impact.

Use what you know

These activities have been designed to help improve your use of the spelling and writing skills presented in this section. Answers to the activities can be found in the **Answer Key** that begins on page 270.

Spelling words correctly

Rewrite the following singular nouns in plural form. If you are unsure, refer to the Table of Spelling Rules.

Example: lady   **Answer:** ladies

1. army
2. Larry
3. bush
4. class
5. box
6. crutch
7. radio
8. tomato
9. mother-in-law
10. teaspoonful
11. wolf
12. staff

Join each word in column A with the prefix or suffix in column B. If you are unsure, refer to the Table of Spelling Rules.

Example: occupy   -ed   **Answer:** occupied

A	B
13. outrage	-ous
14. manage	-able
15. endure	-able
16. panic	-y
17. try	-ing
18. ready	all-
19. fill	full-
20. mortal	im-
21. spell	mis-
22. literate	il-

Identifying parts of speech

In the following sentences, identify the part of speech of each italicized word as it is used in the sentence.

Example: *You* will *find desks,* chairs, *and* blackboards *in every* classroom.

Answer: pronoun, verb, noun, conjunction, preposition, adjective

1. *Oh,* my *leg,* I *think* I *broke* it!
2. *The argument* began *loudly but ended* quietly.
3. *If* you take *me to* this *great* movie, I'll *be* your friend *forever.*
4. *During* the *Vietnam* era, *demonstrations against* the war *were* staged *on* many *college* campuses.
5. *Many* were *invited* but *few* people came.
6. *Good grief! This* car won't *start* for *anyone.*
7. The *sturdily* built chair was *surprisingly comfortable.*

Analyzing parts of sentences

In the following sentences, locate and label the noun phrases, adjective phrases, and adverb phrases.

Example: Reading the newspaper relaxes me after work.
Answer: Reading the newspaper—noun phrase
after work—adverb phrase

1. I'll meet you in the lobby before the concert.
2. Puffing and hissing, the steam engine finally arrived.
3. The customers waiting in line were getting impatient.
4. Finding the right home can take months.

In the following sentences, decide whether the italicized clause is a main clause or a subordinate clause.

Example: *If you can't take the heat,* stay out of the kitchen.
Answer: subordinate clause

5. Herbert Hoover was the first President *who was born west of the Mississippi River.*
6. Everyone has dreams, *but some people don't recall them.*
7. Many people believe *that we can learn to communicate with dolphins.*
8. Though he is best known for his painting, *Leonardo da Vinci was also a scientist and inventor.*

In the following sentences, locate the subordinate clauses; then label them as noun clauses, adjective clauses, or adverb clauses.

Example: What you need is a watch that keeps good time.
Answer: What you need—noun clause
that keeps good time—adjective clause

9. The people who lived next door moved because their house was too small.
10. What I want is a juicy hamburger dripping with tomatoes.
11. My brother, who is a serious student, prepared for weeks to take the bar exam.
12. If you write the report on Sunday, you can meet the deadline.

Decide if each of the following items is a complete sentence or a sentence fragment.

Examples: a. Being rich, he does whatever he wants.
b. Because I've never been there before.
Answers: a. sentence
b. fragment

13. Grown in the coastal lowlands, sugar cane is Puerto Rico's most important crop.
14. Even though he made every effort to complete the work.
15. Search and rescue teams of rangers that are trained to find people lost in forests, caves, or mountains.
16. How delighted they were to finally arrive at home.

Writing effective sentences

One way to learn how to write better is by reading good writing. Well-written periodic sentences and balanced sentences can be found in the works of many famous writers and speakers. Read some of Edgar Allen Poe's mysteries and tales; they abound with periodic sentences. Abraham Lincoln's Gettysburg Address and John F. Kennedy's Inaugural Address are full of well-constructed balanced sentences.

After you have read from the sources suggested, try to use some periodic sentences and balanced sentences in your next piece of writing. The only way to improve your writing is by actually writing.

2   Rules of style

Do you always know when and what to capitalize? Is your use of punctuation clear and correct? If you had to write a research paper or report, would you be able to construct a bibliography and footnotes? All these are matters of style.

In this section, rules of style for capitalization and punctuation are reviewed. Some ways for properly addressing officials and dignitaries are listed. And some standard forms for preparing footnotes and bibliographic entries are explained. You can use this section as a quick reference whenever you have a question on these matters of style.

Capitalization

Capital letters act as signals to readers. They distinguish proper nouns and adjectives from common nouns and adjectives. They announce new sentences and the beginning of direct quotations. Knowing when to use capital letters and when to use lower-case letters can sometimes be confusing. The following list gives you some general rules to observe for capitalization.

1. Capitalize proper nouns.

James Smith   San Francisco   Declaration of Independence

2. Capitalize proper adjectives. Proper adjectives are adjectives that are formed from proper nouns, and proper nouns that are used as adjectives.

American tourist	Shakespearean drama	Chinese art
Iowa farmers	New England states	Texas chili

3. Do *not* capitalize the following words; even though they are derived from proper nouns, their use is now considered common enough that they are no longer capitalized.

anglicize	manila envelope
arabic numerals	pasteurized milk
bohemian life style	plaster of paris
brazil nut	platonic friendship
chinaware	quixotic
derby hat	roman numerals
dutch oven	russian dressing
frankfurter (hot dog)	scotch plaid
french fries	turkish bath
india ink	venetian blinds
japan (varnish)	vienna bread
macadam road	vulcanize

4. Capitalize the pronoun *I* and the interjection *O.*

Rejoice, O ye people, for I bring you glad tidings.

5. Capitalize words that show family relationships when they are used instead of a name or as part of a name.

I asked Mother if Uncle John was coming.

Do *not* capitalize these words when they are preceded by a possessive, such as *my, your, their.*

My mother and uncle visited your grandfather.

6. Capitalize nicknames and other identifying names.

Babe Ruth   the Sun King   Richard the Lion-Hearted

7. Capitalize special titles when they immediately precede a personal name.

General Patton   Governor Ella Grasso   Pope John Paul II

Do *not* capitalize them when they do not precede the name.

Ella T. Grasso, governor of Connecticut
George S. Patton was a great American general.

8. Capitalize professional titles and their abbreviations when they follow a personal name.

John Smith, M.D.   Jane Doe, Doctor of Philosophy
Maria Ames, R.N.

9. Capitalize personified nouns.

She was called by Destiny to clear a path for Justice.

10. Capitalize brand names.

Comet (cleanser)   Cougar (car)   Rice Krispies

11. Capitalize specific political and geographical locations (and the adjectives derived from them).

Chicago   Cook County   Asia   Asian

12. Capitalize the names of all nationalities, races, and tribes (and the adjectives derived from them).

German   Japanese   Sioux   Nordic   Caucasian

13. Capitalize words of direction when they are used to designate a specific place.

North Pole   Far East   Middle West   the South

Do *not* capitalize *north, south, east,* and *west* when they refer to a direction or a section of a state.

We live west of Chicago and vacation in northern Michigan.

14. Capitalize the names of specific geographic features and the common nouns that are part of the proper names.

Mississippi River   Rocky Mountains   Pacific Ocean

But:

the Mississippi and Ohio rivers   the falls of the Niagara

15. Capitalize the names of buildings, monuments, streets, bridges, parks, and other specific locations, and the common nouns that are part of the proper names.

White House	Statue of Liberty	Fifth Avenue
Grant Park	Brooklyn Bridge	U.S. Route 34

16. Capitalize the names of organizations, business firms, and institutions.

League of Women Voters	General Foods Corporation
Northwestern University	Burnsville High School

17. Capitalize the names of political parties and religious denominations and their members.

Republican Party	Roman Catholic	Islam
Democrat	Presbyterian	

18. Capitalize the names of sacred writings and of specific creeds, confessions of faith, and prayers.

the Bible	the Talmud	the Koran
Apostles' Creed	Hail Mary	the Lord's Prayer

19. Capitalize nouns and pronouns that refer to a specific Supreme Being.

God   Allah   Jehovah   Lord   Zeus
Trust in Him for He is good.

But:

The Romans believed in many gods.

20. Capitalize specific cultural and historical events, wars, treaties, laws, and documents.

Reign of Terror	World War II	Treaty of Versailles
Homestead Act	Articles of Confederation	

21. Capitalize the names of historical and cultural periods.

Renaissance   Roaring Twenties   Era of Good Feelings

But:

colonial period   Elizabethan drama

22. Capitalize the names of specific branches, departments, and other divisions of government.

House of Commons	Department of State	Supreme Court
Chicago Park District	Library of Congress	

But:

traffic court   the city council

23. Capitalize the names of specific awards and prizes.

Nobel Peace Prize   Academy Award   Medal of Honor

24. Capitalize the names of specific trains, planes, ships, satellites, and submarines. (These specific names are also italicized or underlined.)

Orient Express   Spirit of St. Louis
Lusitania   Skylab   Nautilus

25. Capitalize the names of stars, planets, constellations, and other astronomical designations. But lower-case *sun* and *moon*.

Big Dipper   Milky Way   North Star
Mars   Ursa Major   Earth

But:

the earth

26. Capitalize the days of the week, months of the year, and holidays. Lower-case the seasons of the year.

Tuesday   October   Memorial Day
spring   fall   summer   winter

27. Capitalize the first word of a sentence or a word or phrase that has the force of a sentence.

The children are running across the street.
Stop!   Wow!

28. Capitalize the first word of a direct quotation.

"We're leaving tomorrow," said Mary.
Jane replied, "Have a good trip."

29. Capitalize the first word of a complete statement following a colon (:).

Here is my decision: You will not be promoted.

30. Capitalize the first word in the salutation and the first word of the complimentary close of a letter.

Gentlemen: Yours truly,
. Dear Sir: Sincerely yours,
My dear Ellen: With love,

31. Capitalize the first word and all important words in the titles of works of art, books, magazines, newspapers, poems, songs, articles, television shows, plays, reports, and other writing.

The Thinker   The Last Supper   A Christmas Carol
The Saturday Evening Post   Sun-Times   "The Raven"
The Skin of Our Teeth   "The Waltons"

32. Capitalize the parts of a book when reference is made from one part to another of the same book.

The sources for this information are listed in the
Bibliography.

But:

A bibliography is a list of sources.

Punctuation: kinds and use

Punctuation has one purpose: to make writing clear. The
correct use of punctuation makes your writing more effective,
expresses your thoughts clearly, and shows the relation of
your thoughts to one another. The punctuation marks and
their most common uses are presented here.

A period is used —

1. At the end of complete declarative sentences and of
commands given without emphasis.

The sun was shining.   Please, wash the car.

2. After each number or letter that begins a heading in an
outline.

Why I Like Sports
I. A way to improve my health
    A. By exercising indoors
        1. Weight training

3. After initials, abbreviations, and after each part of some
abbreviations.

E. W. Smith, Inc.   Dr.   ft.   Mrs.   U.S.   C.O.D.

The abbreviations for some organizations and government
agencies do *not* use periods.

FBI   VISTA   ABC   IBM

A question mark is used —

At the end of direct questions, statements ending with a
question, or words or sentences that indicate a question.

Why did you buy that dress? That was silly, wasn't it?
You're leaving now? Why?

An exclamation point is used —

1. After a word, phrase, or sentence expressing strong feeling.

Yuch! That tastes awful.   What a beautiful day!

2. To emphasize a command or a strong point of view; or to show amusement, sarcasm, or irony.

Go away!   Okay, I'll forget about it!
I'm supposed to fix supper while you read the paper!

A colon is used —

1. After a complete sentence followed by a list.

Executives carry many things in their briefcases: reports, newspapers, and brown-bag lunches.

2. After a statement followed by a clause that further explains the statement.

Working women often find themselves with a double workload: They have an income-producing job and the housework.

3. After the salutation of a business letter.

Dear Sir: Gentlemen: Dear Ms. Williams:

4. To separate hours from minutes, parts of a citation, or parts of a book's title.

6:30 A.M.   Genesis 1:15   *Germany: A Modern History*

A comma is used —

1. To separate long coordinate clauses of a compound sentence.

She could go to college now, but she would rather wait a year.

2. Between words, phrases, or clauses in a series.

Jane carried her coat, hat, and gloves.
I washed the dishes, Joe dried them, and Sam put them away.

3. To set off phrases and dependent clauses preceding the main clause of a sentence.

By taking the tollway, we saved fifteen minutes.
Although the children were tired, they continued playing.

4. To set off phrases, clauses, or appositives that are not essential to the meaning of the sentence.

The nurses, kind as they were, couldn't replace Mother.
Mr. Garcia, the office manager, is well-organized.

5. To set off coordinate phrases modifying the same noun.

Her hair is as long as, but darker than, mine is.

6. Between parts of a sentence suggesting contrast or comparison.

> The more time you take now, the less you'll have later.

7. To indicate the omission of one or more words.

> The eggs were runny; the bacon, greasy; and the toast, burnt.

8. To separate identical or similar words in a sentence.

> Walk in, in groups of three.

9. To separate words that might be mistakenly joined when reading a sentence.

> Soon after, the bridge was closed for repairs.

10. To set off words that introduce a sentence *(first, second, yes, no, oh);* and to set off words that suggest a break in thought *(however, namely, of course).*

> No, I can't do that.   First, write down your name.
> The car broke down, of course, before I got to work.

11. To set off the name of a person spoken to.

> Kevin, your bicycle is across the street.
> Your bicycle, Kevin, is across the street.

12. To set off a short quotation from the rest of the sentence.

> "I'll order the drapes today," Mother said.
> "I wish," John mused, "that this lecture would end."

13. After the greeting of an informal letter and after the complimentary close of any letter.

> Dear Mom and Dad,   With love,   Sincerely yours,

14. Before any title or its abbreviation that follows a person's name.

> J. E. Lopez, M.D.   Janet Brown, Dean of Students

15. To separate the parts of a date, an address, or a geographic location.

> May 31, 1969   Christmas Day, 1976
> We once lived at 5615 Martin Drive, Milwaukee, Wisconsin.
> Disneyland is in Anaheim, California.

16. To set off groups of digits in large numbers.

> 6,780   42,536   103,789,450

17. To separate unrelated numbers in a sentence.

> In 1979, 37,000 doctoral degrees were granted.

The semicolon is used —

1. Between parts of a compound sentence when they are not joined by the conjunctions *and, but, for, nor,* or *or.*

> I want to finish the report now; I'll go to lunch later.

2. To separate independent clauses when the clauses are long or when the clauses already contain commas.

> Because the visibility was good, we planned to visit the observation floor of the Sears Tower; but since the elevators were not working, we toured the lobby.

3. After each clause in a series of three or more clauses.

> Lightning flashed; thunder roared; and rain poured down.

If the clauses in the series are short, you may use either semicolons or commas. Your choice depends on how much you want to separate the clauses; semicolons create a greater pause than do commas. If the clauses are long, it is usually better to use semicolons.

4. Before words like *hence, however, nevertheless, therefore,* and *thus* when they connect two independent clauses.

> Today is a holiday; *therefore,* the mail will not be delivered.

5. To separate items in a list when commas are used within the items.

> Attending the council meeting were Mr. Sloan, the grocer; Mrs. Bates, the banker; and Mr. Green, the florist.

6. Before explanatory expressions such as *for example, for instance, that is,* and *namely* when the break in thought is greater than that suggested by a comma.

> People prefer to own a home for several reasons; *namely,* the privacy of a backyard, the storage space of a basement or an attic, and the spacious room sizes.

The dash is used —

1. To indicate a sudden change or break in thought.

> The best way to finish that—but no, you don't want my opinion.

2. To suggest halting or hesitant speech.

> "I—er—ah—can't seem to find it," she mumbled.

3. Before a repeated word or expression.

> He was *tired—tired* of running away from himself.

4. To emphasize or define a part of a sentence.

Marge Smith—that well-organized woman in the office—was promoted to assistant manager.

5. Before a summarizing statement introduced by *all, this,* or similar words.

Fame, fortune, and position—*these* are the rewards for hard work.

To indicate a dash, use one line (—) when writing by hand; when typing, two hyphens (- -) are used for a dash.

The apostrophe is used —

1. To form the possessive of a noun.

Singular possessive	Plural possessive
the tree's leaves	the boys' bicycles
Mary's hat	the Johnsons' car
Charles's book	Tom and Bob's mother

2. To show omission of one or more letters, words, or numbers.

didn't (did not)   '79 (1979)
one o'clock (one of the clock)

3. To show plurals of numbers, letters, and words discussed as words.

two 4's   some *B*'s   too many *and*'s

The hyphen is used —

1. When spelling out compound numbers between 21 and 99.

twenty-three   sixty-one   twenty-ninth

2. When writing out fractions used as modifiers, but *not* when fractions are used as nouns.

two-thirds majority   *but:* Two thirds were counted present.

3. To avoid confusion of words that are spelled alike.

re-cover the sofa, *but* recover from the loss
re-lay a carpet, *but* a relay race

4. In some words, to avoid the awkward joining of letters.

semi-invalid   anti-intellectual   *but* cooperate

5. After a prefix when the root word begins with a capital letter.

pre-Columbian   anti-American   mid-Victorian

6. After the prefixes *all-, ex-, quasi-,* and *self-* (in most cases).

all-inclusive   ex-husband   quasi-legal   self-help

7. Between parts of a compound adjective when it appears before the word it modifies.

up-to-date news   hard-working man   well-known person
But: She is well known. It is up to date.

8. Between parts of some compound nouns.

father-in-law   stay-at-home   great-grandmother
But: coat of arms   man in white

9. To divide a word at the end of a line.
   You may divide a word only between syllables—but *not* between all syllables in all words. There are some places where you should not divide a word, even where there is a syllable break. Here are some general guidelines for deciding where you should or should not divide words at the end of lines.
   a. Place the hyphen at the end of the line, not at the beginning of the next line.

The bill passed through Congress, but the President vetoed it.

b. Do *not* divide words of one syllable, numbers expressed in figures, contractions, or abbreviations.

thought   width   give   prayer (*not* pray-er)
3,416,521 (*not* 3,416-512)
shouldn't (*not* should-n't)
UNICEF (*not* UNI-CEF)

c. Do *not* divide a word if either part of the hyphenation is a word by itself and the hyphenation could cause confusion.

piety (*not* pie-ty)   tartan (*not* tar-tan)

d. Divide the word as it is pronounced. But do not divide one-letter syllables or unpronounced *ed* from the rest of the word.

amend-ment (*not* a-mendment)   at-tached (*not* attach-ed)

e. Divide a word after a prefix or before a suffix. But do not carry over a two-letter suffix to the next line.

trans-portation *or* transporta-tion (*not* transpor-tation)
mostly (*not* most-ly)

f. Divide compound words between their main parts. And divide hyphenated compounds at the hyphen.

home-coming (*not* homecom-ing)
self-respect (*not* self-re-spect)

g. Divide between double consonants. But divide after double consonants if the root word ends in the double consonant.

bab-ble   run-ning   mis-sion
pull-ing   miss-ing

Be aware that there are some exceptions to some of the rules for hyphenating prefixes and compound words. Check your dictionary whenever you are unsure about hyphenating words—whether dividing a word at the end of a line, adding a prefix, or using a compound word.

You can also refer to the list of 10,000 Commonly Used Words (which begins on page 218). That list indicates if a word contains a hyphen; it also shows the syllable divisions for all the words listed. But remember that you cannot always divide a word at every syllable break shown. Once you find what the syllables in a word are, follow the guidelines given here to decide whether or not you can divide the word—and where.

Quotation marks are used —

1. To enclose all parts of a direct quotation.

"I think you should condense this," said the editor, "because we're running out of space."
"Daddy's home, Daddy's home!" the children shouted.

2. To enclose quoted words or phrases within a sentence.

My father always told me to "get a good night's sleep and eat a hearty breakfast."

Enclose a quotation within a quotation in single quotation marks.

"When I asked my father for advice, he said, 'Get a good night's sleep and eat a hearty breakfast,'" Jane explained.

3. To enclose the titles of short works of music and poetry.

"The Yellow Rose of Texas"   "O Captain! My Captain!"

4. Around the titles of lectures, sermons, pamphlets, chapters of a book, and magazine articles.

"The Way of the Just" in *The Self-Made Man in America* deals with social responsibility.

5. To enclose a word or phrase explained or defined by the

rest of the sentence, a technical term in nontechnical writing, and slang, irony, or well-known expressions.

To "blue-pencil" an article is to edit it.
The "pagination" in this book is out of order.
The "joy of motherhood" is not found in doing diapers.

6. Before the beginning of each stanza of a quoted poem and after the last stanza.

7. Before each paragraph of continuous quoted material and after the last paragraph. They are not used at the end of intermediate paragraphs. Often quotation marks are not used with indented, single-spaced quotes set off from the text.

8. Commas and periods are placed *inside* closing quotation marks.

"I will go now," she said, "and be back in an hour."

9. Semicolons and colons are placed *outside* closing quotation marks.

She said, "I'll go to the store"; but then she stayed home.
"To be or not to be": this is one of Shakespeare's most famous lines.

10. Question marks and exclamation points are placed *inside* the closing quotation marks if they belong to the quotation.

"What book are you reading?" he asked.
"Go now!" she ordered.

But if they are *not* part of the quotation, question marks and exclamation points go *outside* the quotation marks.

Did they sing "America the Beautiful"?
I was shocked when she said, "I've been fired"!

Parentheses are used —

1. To enclose explanatory material in a sentence when this material has no essential connection with the rest of the sentence.

George Washington (1732–1799) was our first President.

2. To enclose sources of information within a sentence:

Cain was jealous of his brother Abel and killed him (Genesis 4:5–8).

3. Around numbers or letters that indicate subdivisions of a sentence.

There are three wedding promises: (1) to love, (2) to honor, and (3) to cherish.

4. Around figures which repeat a number.

I wrote the check for twenty-one dollars and five cents ($21.05).

Brackets are used —

1. To enclose parenthetical matter within parentheses.

Shakespeare's most difficult tragedy (*Hamlet* [about 1600]) has been performed numerous times.

2. To correct a mistake in a direct quote.

"The chocolate mous[s]e was delicious," wrote the gourmet.

3. To indicate your own explanations or comments within direct quotations.

Kathy said, "When I get older [about six years old], I'm going to buy a dog."

4. To indicate stage and acting directions in plays.

MARY [seated, with face in her hands] I am so depressed!

Ellipses are used —

With direct quotations to indicate that a word or words have been omitted. Use three spaced dots to indicate that words have been omitted at the beginning or within the quotation.

The plants were healthy because Roger ". . . took care of them devotedly."
"The gardener . . . took care of them devotedly."

(Both these quotes omit words from the complete quote "The gardener loved the plants and shrubs and took care of them devotedly.")

To indicate words omitted at the end of a sentence, use four spaced dots (the first dot is the period).

"The gardener loved the plants and shrubs. . . ."

The virgule (slant line or slash) is used —

1. Between two words to indicate that the meaning of either word could apply.

My son and/or my daughter will be home.

2. As a dividing line in dates, fractions, and abbreviations.

5/29/68   5/8   c/o (in care of)

3. With a run-in passage of poetry to indicate where one line ends and another begins.

"All the world's a stage,/ And all the men and women merely players./ They have their exits and their entrances;/ And one man in his time plays many parts,/ His acts being seven ages."

Italics or underlining is used —

1. For the titles of books, plays, long poems, magazines, and newspapers.

Gone with the Wind   Hamlet   Paradise Lost
Newsweek   The Tuscaloosa News

2. For titles of paintings and other works of art.

The Blue Boy   Venus de Milo

3. For names of specific ships, planes, trains, and satellites.

Titanic   Spirit of St. Louis   Orient Express   Sputnik

4. For any foreign word that is not commonly used in English. These words have labels (such as *Latin, French,* or *Italian*) in the dictionary.

Jimmy was an *enfant terrible.*
The commencement speaker went on *ad infinitum.*

5. For any words, letters, or numbers considered as words.

A, an, and *the* are articles.
Cross your *t*'s and dot your *i*'s.
The *7*'s in multiplication were hard, but the *10*'s were easy.

Remember that these words appear in italics when set in type (as in books or magazines); they are underlined when writing by hand or typing.

Proper forms of address

The following list includes some officials and dignitaries whom you might have occasion to address in speaking or writing. Not all possible dignitaries are included; nor are the forms of address given necessarily the only correct ones. The forms given under "In speaking" are the titles that should be used when speaking in person to these officials. The forms listed under "Writing the address," "Salutation," and "Closing" should be used when writing business letters to officials. Address forms for women are the same as for men, except where indicated.

President of the United States

In speaking: Mr. President *or* Sir
          Madam President *or* Madam
Writing the address: The President
          The White House
          Washington, D.C. 20500
Salutation: Dear Mr. *or* Madam President:
Closing: Respectfully,

Vice-President of the United States

In speaking: Mr. Vice-President *or* Sir
          Madam Vice-President *or* Madam
Writing the address: The Vice-President
          Executive Office Building
          Washington, D.C. 20501
Salutation: Dear Mr. *or* Madam Vice-President:
Closing: Respectfully,

Cabinet Members (except Attorney General)

In speaking: Mr. Secretary *or* Mr. Green
          Madam Secretary *or* Miss, Mrs., *or* Ms. Smith
Writing the address: The Honorable John Green
          Secretary of State
Salutation: Dear Mr. *or* Madam Secretary:
          or Dear Secretary Green:
Closing: Sincerely yours,

Attorney General

In speaking: Mr. *or* Madam Attorney General
Writing the address: The Attorney General
Salutation: Dear Mr. *or* Madam Attorney General:
Closing: Sincerely yours,

Chief Justice of the United States

In speaking: Mr. *or* Madam Chief Justice
Writing the address: The Chief Justice of the United States
          Supreme Court Building
          Washington, D.C. 20543
Salutation: Dear Mr. *or* Madam Chief Justice:
Closing: Sincerely yours,

Associate Justices of the Supreme Court

In speaking: Mr. *or* Madam Justice
          or Mr. *or* Madam Justice Green

Writing the address: Mr. *or* Madam Justice Green
Salutation: Dear Mr. *or* Madam Justice:
　　　　　　 or Dear Mr. *or* Madam Justice Green:
Closing: Sincerely yours,

United States Senators

In speaking: Senator Green
Writing the address: The Honorable Mary Green
　　　　　　　　　　United States Senate
　　　　　　　　　　Washington, D.C. 20510
Salutation: Dear Senator: *or* Dear Senator Green:
Closing: Sincerely yours,

United States Representatives

In speaking: Mr., Miss, Mrs., *or* Ms. Smith
Writing the address: The Honorable Mary Smith
　　　　　　　　　　House of Representatives
　　　　　　　　　　Washington, D.C. 20515
Salutation: Dear Mr., Miss, Mrs., *or* Ms. Smith:
　　　　　　 or Dear Representative Smith:
　　　　　　 or Dear Congressman *or* Congresswoman Smith:
Closing: Sincerely yours,

United States Ambassadors

In speaking: Mr. *or* Madam Ambassador
Writing the address: The Honorable John Green
　　　　　　　　　　Ambassador of the United States of America
Salutation: Sir: *or* Madam: *or* Dear Mr. *or* Madam Ambassador:
Closing: Very truly yours, *or* Sincerely yours,
(Although it is permissible to refer to a United States
ambassador as an "American Ambassador," it is best not to do
so, because other Western Hemisphere ambassadors are also
conscious of being Americans.)

Governors

In speaking: Governor Smith
Writing the address: The Honorable Mary Smith
　　　　　　　　　　Governor of Tennessee
Salutation: Sir *or* Madam: *or* Dear Governor Smith:
Closing: Respectfully, *or* Sincerely yours,

State Senators and Representatives

State legislators are addressed in the same manner as United
States senators and representatives.

Mayors

In speaking: Mayor Green *or* Mr. *or* Madam Mayor
Writing the address: The Honorable John Green
Salutation: Sir: *or* Madam: *or* Dear Mayor Green:
Closing: Sincerely yours,

Judges

In speaking: Mr. *or* Madam Justice
Writing the address: The Honorable Mary Smith
Salutation: Sir: *or* Madam:
Closing: Sincerely yours,

Governor General

In speaking: Your Excellency
Writing the address: His *or* Her Excellency
　　　　　　The Right Honourable John Green
　　　　　　Governor General of Canada
　　　　　　Government House
　　　　　　Ottawa, Ontario K1A OA1
Salutation: Sir: *or* Madam: *or* Dear Sir: *or* Dear Madam:
Closing: Respectfully,

Canadian officials

Prime Minister

In speaking: Your Excellency *or* Mr. *or* Madam Prime Minister
Writing the address: The Right Honourable Mary Smith, P.C., M.P.
　　　　　　Prime Minister of Canada
　　　　　　Ottawa, Ontario K1A OA2
Salutation: Sir: *or* Madam: *or* Dear Sir: *or* Dear Madam:
Closing: Very truly yours, *or* Sincerely yours,

Senators

In speaking: Sir *or* Madam *or* Senator Green
Writing the address: The Honourable John Green
　　　　　　The Senate
　　　　　　Ottawa, Ontario K1A OA4
Salutation: Dear Sir *or* Madam:
Closing: Yours sincerely,

Members of the House of Commons

In speaking: Sir *or* Madam *or* Mr., Mrs., Miss, *or* Ms. Green
Writing the address: Mary Green, M.P.
　　　　　　House of Commons
　　　　　　Ottawa, Ontario K1A OA6

Salutation: Dear Sir *or* Madam:
Closing: Yours sincerely,

Foreign officials in the United States

Foreign Ambassadors to the United States

In speaking: Mr. *or* Madam Ambassador
Writing the address: His *or* Her Excellency
                The Ambassador of Australia
Salutation: Sir: *or* Madam: *or* Dear Mr. *or* Madam Ambassador:
Closing: Yours very truly,

Secretary-General of the United Nations

In speaking: Mr. *or* Madam Secretary-General
Writing the address: His (*or* Her) Excellency
                John Green
                Secretary-General of the United Nations
Salutation: Sir: *or* Madam: *or* Dear Mr. *or* Madam Secretary-General:
Closing: Yours very truly,
(For ambassadors and representatives to the United Nations, use the form "Representative of Brazil to the United Nations.")

Members of the clergy

The correct form for closing most business letters to the clergy is "Respectfully yours" and for closing social letters, "Sincerely yours."

Bishops

In speaking: Bishop Green
Writing the address: The Reverend John Green
                Bishop of Chicago
Salutation: Dear Bishop Green:
(Episcopal bishops often use "The Very Reverend." Roman Catholic bishops often use "The Most Reverend." Greek Orthodox bishops often use "The Very Reverend.")

Cardinals

In speaking: Your Eminence
Writing the address: His Eminence
                John Cardinal Green
                Archbishop of Chicago
Salutation: Dear Cardinal Green:
Closing: I have the honor to be,
        Your Eminence, respectfully yours,

Ministers

In speaking: Reverend Green *or* Doctor Green
Writing the address: The Reverend John Green
                        The Reverend Mary Smith
Salutation: Dear Reverend Green: *or* Dear Dr. Green:

Rabbis

In speaking: Rabbi Green *or* Doctor Green
Writing the address: Rabbi John Green
Salutation: Dear Rabbi Green:

Priests

In speaking: Father Green
Writing the address: The Reverend John Green
Salutation: Dear Father Green:

President or Chancellor of a university

Other forms

In speaking: President Green *or* Chancellor Smith
Writing the address: President John Green
                        Chancellor Mary Smith
Salutation: Dear President Green:
        Dear Chancellor Smith:
Closing: Very truly yours, *or* Sincerely yours,

Professors

In speaking: Professor Smith *or* Doctor Smith
Writing the address: Professor Mary Smith
                        Department of Music
                        University of Oklahoma
Salutation: Dear Professor Smith:
Closing: Very truly yours, *or* Sincerely yours,

Preparing footnotes

Footnotes are important in any writing that uses information from various sources—books, magazines, newspapers, pamphlets, or encyclopedias. Footnotes give credit to your sources and establish the authority for your statements. Always use footnotes when you use direct quotes from sources, when you rephrase someone's opinions or ideas, and when you present facts or figures that might be questioned.

Footnotes are placed at the bottom or foot of the page. They are numbered consecutively throughout the paper. The number of the footnote appears slightly above the line, after the sentence, fact, or quotation you are presenting in the paper. Then that same number appears at the bottom of the page, slightly above the line, before the footnote itself, which gives the source of the information.

Footnotes should follow a consistent format and style. Commas appear between the parts of a footnote, and a period is placed at the end. The first line of each footnote is indented; the second and following lines are flush with the left margin. Lines within a footnote are single-spaced, but you double-space between footnotes that appear together. The content of footnotes varies somewhat depending on the type of source you are citing. In the following paragraphs, the raised numbers refer you to sample footnotes for various kinds of sources.

When the source is a book, the footnote includes the author's name, the book title, and the number of the page(s) on which the information can be found.[1] The author's name is written first name first, and the book title is underlined.

> [1] Theodore M. Bernstein, Bernstein's Reverse Dictionary, pp. 37–39.

When the source is a magazine article, the footnote includes the author's name (if it is given), the title of the article, the magazine, the volume number, the date of the issue, and the page number(s).[2] The article title is in quotation marks, and the magazine name is underlined. If no author is given, begin with the title of the article.[3]

> [2] Rudolf F. Graf, "Build an Electronic Guard to Foil Car Thieves," Popular Science Monthly, vol. 193, October 1968, p. 140.

> [3] "The Righting of Writing," Time, vol. 115, May 19, 1980, p. 88.

For a later reference to a previously cited source, shorten the form of the footnote. A shortened form may contain only the author's last name and the page number.[4] (If you have used more than one book by the same author, you'll need to include the title in the shortened footnote.) If the source is the same work and page as the immediately preceding footnote, use *Ibid.* in place of a full footnote.[5] If the source is the same work but a different page from the immediately preceding footnote, use *Ibid.* followed by a comma and the page number.[6] *Ibid.* is the abbreviation of the Latin word *ibidem,* which means "in the same place." Underline *Ibid.* and place a period after it.

> [4] Bernstein, p. 41.

> [5] Ibid.

> [6] Ibid., p. 52.

The following are examples of footnotes for an encyclopedia article,[7] a newspaper article,[8] a work by more than one author,[9] and an edited work.[10]

[7] "How to Do Research," The World Book Encyclopedia, Vol. 22, p. 27.

[8] "Mayors Seek Greater U.S. Effort Against Drugs," The New York Times, May 6, 1971, p. 19.

[9] William Strunk, Jr., and E. B. White, The Elements of Style, p. 64.

[10] Thomas S. Kane and Leonard J. Peters, eds., Writing Prose: Techniques and Purposes, p. 220.

Citations placed together at the end of a paper, article, chapter, or book are called *end notes*. They are constructed in the same way as footnotes except the number preceding the source is on the line and followed by a period.[11]

11. "The Righting of Writing," Time, vol. 115, May 19, 1980, p. 88.

Be aware that there are several standard formats for footnotes that have slight variations from one another. The format given here will be appropriate in most kinds of writing you will do. If your instructor, school, or place of work requires a particular format, use it. Whatever format you use, be sure to use it consistently throughout your paper or report.

Preparing a bibliography

Your bibliography lists all the sources—books, magazines, encyclopedias, newspapers—that you used in preparing your research paper or report. The bibliography shows your reader the number and types of sources you used. It also shows your reader where to find more information on your topic.

Bibliographic entries have standard forms. The information included differs somewhat from that in footnotes. Like footnotes, a bibliographic entry contains the author and title, but it also includes facts about the publication of a source. The style of bibliographic entries differs from footnotes in that authors are listed last name first, and periods separate the three main parts of the entry (author, title, and facts of publication).

Following are examples of the content and format for various types of entries. Notice the information included and the punctuation used in each type of entry; then follow those formats in your own bibliography.

A bibliographic entry for a book contains the author, title, and facts of publication. The facts of publication include the city of publication (followed by a colon), the publisher (followed by a comma), and the year of publication. Here is an example of an entry for a book, along with sample entries for an edited book and a second (or third, etc.) edition of a book.

A book:
Bookchin, Murray. Our Synthetic Environment. New York: Harper & Row, 1974.

An edited book:
Kane, Thomas S., and Peters, Leonard J., eds. Writing Prose: Techniques and Purposes. New York: Oxford University Press, 1965.

A second edition:
Fowler, H. W. A Dictionary of Modern English Usage. 2d ed. New York: Oxford University Press, 1965.

Following are examples of entries for articles from a magazine, a newspaper, and an encyclopedia. The page numbers given are the pages for the entire article.

A magazine article:
Ellis, William S. "Canada's Highway to the Sea." National Geographic, vol. 157, May 1980, pp. 594–623.

A newspaper article:
Romero, Jack. "Panthers Finish First." Prairie Gazette, May 18, 1980, sec. 3, p. 4.

An encyclopedia article:
"How to Do Research." The World Book Encyclopedia (1976), Vol. 22, pp. 27–29.

Sometimes information—date, publisher, place of publication—cannot be found because a book is quite old. In that case, place an abbreviation in brackets—such as [n.d.] for "no date"—to show that the omission was not an oversight on your part. You do *not* need to make such a notation when no author is given for a newspaper or magazine article. It is generally understood that often no author is mentioned in newspapers and magazines.

Bibliographic entries are arranged alphabetically according to the last names of the authors—or according to the titles when authors are not listed. If a bibliography has more than one work by the same author, list those entries together and order them alphabetically by title. Use a long line where the author's name would appear in any entries following the first one.

Bibliographic entries are not numbered. Start each entry at

the left margin. Indent any additional lines. Single-space within each entry, and double-space between entries.

Here is a short sample bibliography:

Bernstein, Theodore M. Bernstein's Reverse Dictionary. New York: Quadrangle/The New York Times Book Co., 1975.

_____. The Careful Writer: A Modern Guide to English Usage. New York: Atheneum, 1978.

Ellis, William S. "Canada's Highway to the Sea." National Geographic, vol. 157, May 1980, pp. 594–623.

"The Righting of Writing." Time, vol. 115, May 19, 1980, pp. 88–91.

Strunk, William, Jr., and White, E. B. The Elements of Style. 2d ed. New York: Macmillan Publishing Co., 1972.

As with footnotes, there are several variations of format for bibliographies. The format here would be appropriate in most of your writing. If you are asked to use a different format, do so. Remember to use one format consistently in your bibliography.

Use what you know

These activities have been designed to help you review the rules of style presented in this section. Answers to the activities can be found in the **Answer Key** that begins on page 270.

Reviewing capitalization and italics

Find and capitalize all the words that should be capitalized in the following paragraph. Also find the words that should be in italics (or underlined).

1. last summer, bill, mary, joe, and i vacationed in central wisconsin and northern minnesota. 2. we started our trip one bright sunday morning in august. 3. the vega, running smoothly, brought us into the wisconsin dells about lunchtime. 4. i had a julienne salad with russian dressing, a piece of french bread, and a glass of iced lipton tea. 5. that night we watched the indian ceremonial dances at standing rock. 6. arriving in minneapolis the next day, we visited aunt alice. 7. then we toured the minneapolis institute of arts where rembrandt's lucretia hangs and where a tudor-style room has been reconstructed. 8. since the guthrie theater was closed that day, we weren't able to see hamlet. 9. after spending the night at the home of an old friend from burnsville high school, we headed for gull lake. 10. we took u.s. route 371, which goes through little falls, minnesota— home of charles lindbergh, pilot of the spirit of st. louis.
11. finally, we arrived at the lake. 12. mary and joe were thrilled to see their minnesota cousin, mike. 13. and bill and i were glad to talk to my sister and her husband. 14. mother and dad drove in a few minutes later. 15. the children yelled, "grandma, grandpa!"

Reviewing punctuation

Write the following sentences, adding all necessary punctuation. Underline all words that should be in italics.

1. Go sky diving Never Id rather live to be a hundred than live dangerously today said John.
2. I got up at 520 this morning finished reading James A Micheners book Hawaii and went to work
3. There are several ways to have a green yard spread grass seed roll sod or lay Astro Turf
4. Strolling up Main Street we found a lovely restaurant a gift shop and a grocery store but on turning the corner we saw an ugly factory
5. Are we going to the park Why of course we are First put on your jacket
6. Jan Smith PhD is married to Dr Robert Jones a surgeon at St James Hospital
7. In 1978 or was it 1979 we had over 100 inches of snow
8. David Rockefeller Nelsons brother runs the Chase Manhattan Bank

Using proper forms of address

Imagine that you have been invited to attend an important civic function. Decide how you should address the following officials as you are introduced to them:

Harry Redford, the mayor
Margaret Woodson, a U.S. senator
Roberta Brown, a state representative
Joseph O'Leary, a Catholic priest
Andrew Smithfield, an Episcopal bishop

Writing footnotes and bibliographic entries

Choose a book, an article from a magazine, and an article from a newspaper. Construct a bibliographic entry and two footnotes for each of the three sources.

3

Commonly misused words, phrases, and constructions

Have you ever read something that bothered you because it did not sound quite right? The writing may have suffered from incorrect use of words or from a misused grammatical construction. Maybe the writing contained clichés or misspellings.

This section presents many of the most commonly misused words, phrases, and constructions. It also suggests ways for you to correct and avoid these problems in your own writing.

Correct word use

Some words and expressions that are acceptable in casual conversation are not acceptable in formal speaking or writing. You should follow the standards of correct word use in all your formal speaking and writing—whether it be papers for school, or business letters and reports, or a speech to a group in your community. Using words and expressions correctly is a sign of a careful, thoughtful writer.

The following list contains some of the most commonly misused words and expressions. Read through the list now. Then refer back to it whenever you doubt the correct use of a word or expression.

a, an. *A* is used before words beginning with consonant *sounds; an,* before words beginning with vowel *sounds* (regardless of what the initial letter is).

> *a* table   *a* hat   *a* used car
> *an* apple   *an* hour   *an* oven

accept, except. *Accept* means "to receive willingly"; *except* means "to exclude." As a preposition, *except* means "other than."

> I will *accept* the first part of your proposal, but I must *except* the second part.
> I jog every day *except* Sunday.

advice, advise. *Advice* is a noun; *advise,* a verb. Do not use *advise* to mean "inform" or "tell"; save it for "give notice" or "warn."

> She gave me good *advice* when she *advised* me not to hitchhike.

affect, effect. *Affect* is a verb meaning "to influence." *Effect,* as a verb, means "to cause, bring about, or accomplish"; as a noun *effect* means "a result or an accomplishment."

> His presence *affected* the mood of the party.
> A treaty was *effected* after many months of meetings.
> The symphony had a wonderful *effect* on the audience.

aggravate, irritate. *Aggravate* means "to make an already troubled situation worse, or more serious." *Irritate* means "to annoy, exasperate, or chafe."

> Sitting in a draft *aggravated* my stiff neck.
> Some detergents can *irritate* your skin.

all the farther, all the faster. Do not use these expressions when you mean *as far as* or *as fast as.*

allude, elude, illude. *Allude* means "to make an indirect reference to something." *Elude* means "to avoid or evade." *Illude* means "to deceive or trick." And don't confuse *allude* with *refer: refer* is "to make a direct reference to a specific thing."

He *alluded* to a time in the past when he was young and happy.
The instructor *referred* us to page 20 in the text.
The refugees *eluded* the border patrol.
He *illuded* us into thinking he was a British earl.

among, between. Use *among* to show the relation of more than two persons or things; use *between* when dealing with two things (or more than two things if each is considered individually).
We are *among* friends.
I was standing *between* the sofa and the table.
The railroad runs *between* Chicago, Milwaukee, and Minneapolis.

amount, number. *Amount* is used with a unified bulk or lump sum; *number* suggests separate, countable units.
The *amount* of money you have depends on the *number* of coins and dollars.

and etc. Do not use this expression; *etc.* already means "and so forth." Adding *and* is redundant.

anticipate, expect. Use *anticipate* when you mean "to prepare for something." Use *expect* when you mean "to think something will occur."

They *anticipated* the storm by going to a safe place.
We *expect* the mail will be delayed.

anxious, eager. *Anxious* suggests anxiety or worry; *eager* means "looking forward to or wanting to."

We are *anxious* about the safety of the hostages.
I am *eager* to start my vacation.

anyways, anywheres. These are not acceptable in formal writing. Use *anyway* and *anywhere.*

apt, liable, likely. *Apt* suggests fitness or suitability; *liable* suggests obligation; and *likely* indicates probability.

She is an *apt* musician.
They were held *liable* for the damages.
The rain is *likely* to arrive here this evening.

awhile, a while. *Awhile* is an adverb; *while* (as in *a while*) is a noun. Use *a while* after prepositions (for *a while*, after *a while*).

Work *awhile* longer, and I'll help you.
She stood there for *a while.*

bad, badly. *Bad* is an adjective; *badly,* an adverb. Use *bad* after linking verbs *(is, feels, tastes).*

He was a *bad* boy today.
The engine misfired *badly.*
She feels *bad* about missing the concert.

beside, besides. *Beside* means "alongside of"; *besides* means "in addition to."

He sat *beside* me.
Besides the mortgage, I have car payments to make.

biannual, biennial. *Biannual* means "twice a year"; *biennial* means "once every two years."

Bursted, bust, busted. Never use *bursted;* the past tense of *burst* is *burst. Bust* and *busted* are slang uses of *burst;* they should not be used in formal writing.

The pipe *burst* today.   The pipe *is bursting* now.
The pipe *burst* yesterday.   This pipe *has burst* before.

can, may. *Can* means "is able to." *May* means "has permission to."

You *can* sketch well when you take your time.
After you have put everything away, you *may* leave.

capital, capitol. Use *capital* (with an *a*) when referring to money, upper-case letters, a city in which a government is located, or crimes punishable by death. Use *capitol* (with an *o*) only when referring to a building where legislatures meet.

Capitol has a *capital* C if it means the building in which the Congress of the United States meets.

contact, contacted. Much overused business terms. Try to replace them with *call, consult, telephone, see,* or *write.*

credible, creditable, credulous. *Credible* means "believable." *Creditable* means "worthy of esteem or praise." *Credulous* means "gullible."

His account of the situation was *credible.*
He made a *creditable* contribution to the project.
Credulous people believe everything that they are told.

data. *Data* is the plural form of the Latin word *datum.* It can be used as a collective singular noun when referring to a body of information as a unit.

The *data* [information] was available to everyone.
The *data* [figures] in this chart are confusing.

different than, different from. The preferred use is *different from.*

Rich people are *different from* you and me.

disinterested, uninterested. *Disinterested* means "unbiased"; *uninterested,* "having no interest in."

The dispute was settled by a *disinterested* party.
I am *uninterested* in your dispute.

doubt but, help but. Do not use these expressions in formal writing.

due to, because of. Do not use *due to* for *because of, owing to,* or *on account of. Due to* is correct after a linking verb, or as an adjective following a noun.

Wrong: *Due to* heavy traffic, I was late.
Correct: *Because of* heavy traffic, I was late.
          My tardiness was *due to* heavy traffic.

each . . . are. An error in agreement. *Each* implies one and takes a singular verb. Plural words used in phrases that modify *each* do not change the number of the verb.

Each woman *was* promoted.
Each of the women *was* promoted.

emigrate, immigrate. *Emigrate* means "to move out of a country"; *immigrate,* "to move into a country."

They *emigrated* from Ireland.   She *immigrated* to Canada.

enthuse. Do not use the verb *enthuse* in formal writing. Use *showed enthusiasm* or *was enthusiastic.*

Wrong: He *enthused* about the new project.
Correct: He *showed enthusiasm* about the new project.
          He *was enthusiastic* about the new project.

etc. Avoid using this expression in formal writing. Instead use *and so forth, and the like,* or a similar phrase. Or say specifically what you mean.

Wrong: Use books, magazines, etc., to do your research.
Correct: Use books, magazines, and the like to do your research.
Use books, magazines, and other library materials to do your research.

farther, further. Use *farther* to suggest a measurable distance. Use *further* to show a greater degree, extent, quantity, or time. *Further* also means "moreover" and "in addition to."

We walked *farther* than we had to.
We can discuss this matter *further* tomorrow.

fewer, less. *Fewer* applies to things that can be numbered or counted. *Less* applies to things in bulk, in the abstract, or in degree and value.

There are *fewer* houses here because there is *less* land.

formally, formerly. *Formally* means "in a formal manner"; *formerly* means "in the past."

Jan Smith, *formerly* of Jones, Brown, and Little, was *formally* attired for the opening of Smith, Green, and Wilson.

good, well. *Good* is an adjective; *well,* an adverb. *Well* acts as an adjective only when describing someone's health.

I had a *good* time; the dinner had been planned *well.*
She felt *good* about the project, but she did not feel *well* enough to go to work.

had best, had better, had ought. Use *ought to* or *should.*

hanged, hung. Criminals are *hanged;* things (pictures, clothes, drapes) are *hung.*

hardly, scarcely. *Hardly* means "done with difficulty" or "barely able to." *Scarcely* refers to an insufficient quantity.

I could *hardly* push the power mower; I had *scarcely* any energy left.

have got. Use just *have.* "I *have* it [not I've *got* it]."

imply, infer. *Imply* means "to suggest or hint at"; *infer* means "to draw a conclusion."

He *implied* that the company was not doing well.
After reading the article, I *inferred* that there is a recession.

in, into. *In* suggests being inside; *into* suggests the act of entering.

When I walked *into* the room, she was sitting *in* my chair.

inside of, off of, outside of. When used in prepositional phrases, the *of* is not necessary.

I keep my wallet *inside* my purse.
He stood *outside* the door.

irregardless, disregardless. Do not use either of these words. Use *regardless*.

is when, is where. Do not use these phrases when writing definitions or explanations.

Wrong: Writing *is when* you put your thoughts on paper.
Correct: Writing *is* putting your thoughts on paper.

its, it's. *Its* is the possessive of *it; it's* is the contraction for *it is*.

It's sad that the dog broke *its* foot.

kind, sort, type. These are singular nouns and must be modified by singular adjectives.

this kind   *but*   these kinds
that type   *but*   those types

kind of a, sort of a, type of a. The *a* is incorrect. And do not use *kind of, sort of,* or *type of* in place of *somewhat, rather,* or *almost*.

What *kind of* material are you using?
I'm *somewhat* undecided.

leave, let. *Leave* means "to depart" or "to allow to remain in a certain condition." *Let* means "to allow, enable, or not interfere with."

I will *leave* the room and *let* you come in.
Leave the window open.

lie, lay. *Lie* means "to recline"; the principal parts of the verb *lie* are *lie, lay, lain, lying. Lay* means "to put or place"; the principal parts of *lay* are *lay, laid, laid, laying*.

lie	lay
Lie down and rest.	Will you *lay* the tile?
I *lay* down yesterday to rest.	I *laid* the tile yesterday.
I *had lain* down to rest.	I *have laid* tile before.
I *was lying* on the couch.	We *are laying* the tile.

like, as. *As* is a conjunction; use *as* to join clauses. *Like* is a preposition; *like* + a noun or pronoun forms a prepositional phrase.

I did the assignment *as* I was instructed to do it.
My sister looks *like* me. I look *like* Aunt Ruth.

loan, lend. *Loan* is a noun; *lend* is a verb.

I will *lend* you the money, but this *loan* must be paid in full.

lots, lots of, a whole lot. Use *many, much,* or *a great deal* in place of these expressions.

of. Used incorrectly for *have* after auxiliary verbs.

Wrong: would *of,* could *of,* should *of*
Correct: would *have,* could *have,* should *have*

perform, preform. Perform means "to carry out or to give a performance"; *preform* means "to form or shape beforehand."

The orchestra *performed* beautifully.
The patio is made of *preformed* concrete.

practicable, practical. *Practicable* means "capable of being put into practice"; *practical* means "being useful or successful."

The proposed plan seemed *practicable.*
She always finds *practical* solutions for our problems.

principal, principle. *Principal* as a noun refers to a sum of money, or a person or thing of first importance; as an adjective, *principal* means "first, chief, or main." *Principle* is a noun meaning "a law, code, doctrine, or rule."

The *principal* of the loan was $70,000.
Our *principal* is Ms. Smith.
She is a woman of high *principles.*

raise, rise. *Raise* is a transitive verb requiring an object; its principal parts are *raise, raised, raised, raising. Rise,* an intransitive verb, does not require an object; its principal parts are *rise, rose, risen, rising.*

I *raised* tomatoes and corn.
Please *rise* when the judge enters.

real, really. *Real* is an adjective meaning "genuine or having reality." *Really* is an adverb meaning "actually or truly."

The stone looked like a *real* diamond, but it *really* was a fake.

reason is because. Do not use this construction. Instead, say *reason is* or *reason is that.*

> **Wrong:** The *reason* why I am late *is because* the car stalled.
> **Correct:** The *reason* why I am late *is that* the car stalled.

respectfully, respectively. *Respectfully* means "in a respectful manner." *Respectively* means "each in the order given."

> I am *respectfully* submitting this report for your approval.
> In the 1930's, Naziism, Fascism, and Communism were political movements in Germany, Italy, and the Soviet Union *respectively.*

seen, saw. The principal parts of *see* are *see, saw, seen, seeing.*

> **Wrong:** I *seen* them at the store.   We *have saw* the movie.
> **Correct:** I *saw* them at the store.   We *have seen* the movie.

shall, will. Use *shall* with *I* and *we* in the future tense, and in legal papers and directives. Use *will* with *he, she, it,* and *they,* and with *I* and *we* when expressing a promise.

> I *shall* go to work; she *will* go to school.
> The buyer *shall* have clear title to the property.
> I *will* do all that I can to help you.

sit, set. *Sit* means "place oneself"; *set* means "to put or place something."

> *Sit* down and rest awhile. I will *set* the box on the floor.

so. Do not use *so* in place of *so that, therefore,* or *thus.* And do not use *so* to mean "very" in formal writing: *so* kind, *so* terrible.

that, which. *That* is used chiefly to begin restrictive clauses (clauses that are essential to the meaning of the sentence). *Which* is used to begin nonrestrictive clauses (clauses that are not essential, but simply provide additional information); but *which* is also used in some restrictive clauses.

> The house *that* I liked was not for sale. [restrictive]
> My house, *which* is old, needs many repairs. [nonrestrictive]
> The book *which* I ordered has arrived. [restrictive]

then, also. These words are adverbs. Do not use them instead of conjunctions.

> **Wrong:** He ate breakfast, *then* went to work.
>   We enjoy skiing, *also* skating.
> **Correct:** He ate breakfast *and* then went to work.
>   We enjoy skiing *and* skating.

there, their, they're. *There* means "in or at that place." *Their* is a possessive pronoun. *They're* is a contraction for *they are.*

> I parked the car *there.*
> *Their* house was custom-built.
> *They're* going to leave soon.

to, too, two. *To* is a preposition (*to* the store) and the sign of an infinitive (*to* walk). *Too* is an adverb meaning "also" or "more than what is proper or enough." *Two* is the number (*two* cats).

try and. Do not use *try and* in formal writing. Use *try to.*

> **Wrong:** I will *try and* finish the painting today.
> **Correct:** I will *try to* finish the painting today.

type. Do not use as a substitute for *type of.*

> **Wrong:** I would like to buy this *type* dress.
> **Correct:** I would like to buy this *type of* dress.

unique. *Unique* means "the only one of its kind" or "without equal." Do not use *more* or *most* with *unique.*

very. *Very* is an overused adverb. Try to use more specific modifiers, or use words that are strong in themselves. This same advice applies to *so, surely, too, extremely, indeed.*

> **Weak:** She sings *very* well.
> **Improved:** She sings *beautifully.*
>   She is a *talented singer.*

while. *While* means "during the time that." Do not use *while* in place of *although, and, but,* or *whereas.*

> **Wrong:** The days were hot, *while* the nights were cool.
> **Correct:** The days were hot, *but* the nights were cool.
>   *While* you were on vacation, we redecorated your office.

who, whom. Use *who* as a subject. Use *whom* as an object.

> That is the boy *who* threw the rock. [*who* is the subject of *threw*]
> The girl for *whom* I bought the gift was delighted. [*whom* is the object of the preposition *for*]
> My mother, *who* is often late, came early. [*who* is the subject of *is*]

Commonly misspelled words

There are probably some words that often cause spelling problems for you. Misspelling words such as *referred, desirable,* and *deceit* stems from forgetting some of the rules for spelling (see pages 5–9). Other words—*ecstasy, grammar, separate*—have to be memorized; their spellings do not follow any particular rules. Sometimes you can make up ways to help you remember the spelling of a word, such as "There is *a rat* in sep*arat*e." By using this device, you will put the *a*'s in the correct places in *separate*.

Here is a list of words that are commonly misspelled. After looking through the list, work on the words that cause spelling problems for you. If you are keeping in your dictionary a list of words that you frequently misspell, you might want to add some words from this list.

acceptance	beneficiaries	conspicuous
accessible	benefited	copyrighted
accessories	bookkeeper	correspondent
accidentally	bureau	courageous
accommodation	cancellation	currency
accompanying	canvasser	deceased
achievement	capacity	definitely
acknowledgment	carburetor	description
acquaintance	casualties	desirable
advantageous	ceiling	differed
advisable	census	dilapidated
aggregate	centennial	dilemma
aggressive	changeable	dimensions
allege	chargeable	disappearance
allotment	collateral	disappointment
all right	colonel	disastrous
analysis	commission	disbursement
anesthetic	commitment	discrepancy
anxiety	committee	discretion
apartment	commodities	disease
apparatus	comparatively	disseminate
appearance	compel	distributor
approximately	competent	division
ascertain	conceivable	duly
athletics	concession	ecclesiastical
attacked	condemn	ecstasy
attorneys	confectionery	elementary
authoritative	congratulate	eligible
auxiliary	conscience	eliminate
battalion	conscious	embarrassment
believed	consensus	embodying

encouragement
encumbrances
enforceable
entitled
equipment
equipped
exaggerate
exceed
excel
exercised
exhilarating
exhort
existence
exorbitant
extension
extraordinary
facilities
facsimile
fallacy
familiar
fascinating
foliage
forcibly
foreclosure
forty
foundries
fourteenth
freight
fundamental
gauge
government
grammar
grateful
grievance
guarantee
harass
hindrance
horticulture
hygiene
hypocrisy
identify
imitation
improvement
incidentally
indebtedness
indemnity
independent
innocuous

inoculate
intention
interference
interfering
irrelevant
itinerary
judgment
knowledge
laboratories
leisure
license
lieutenant
likelihood
likely
maintenance
maneuver
manual
millennium
miscellaneous
mislaid
misspell
misstatement
mortgage
necessarily
ninety
ninth
notarize
noticeable
occasionally
occur
occurrence
offered
omission
omitted
ordinarily
outrageous
pamphlet
parallel
partner
peculiar
permanently
persistent
personnel
phenomenal
pneumonia
possession
preferable
preferred

preparatory
prescription
pretension
privilege
procedure
proceedings
professional
proffered
promissory
prophecy
prophesied
protocol
psychology
publicly
pursuing
quantity
questionnaire
receivable
recommend
reign
relevant
rendezvous
repetition
rhyme
rhythm
sacrilegious
satisfactorily
scarcely
schedule
scissors
seizure
separate
serviceable
similar
skiing
souvenir
specialty
specifically
specimen
strictly
substantially
succeeded
sufficient
superintendent
supersede
susceptible
symmetrical
sympathy

syndicate	undoubtedly	vegetable
temperament	unforeseen	veil
thorough	unnecessarily	weight
tomorrow	until	weird
traceable	vacillate	wholly
tragedy	vacuum	wrapper
transferable	vague	yield
transferred	variable	zoological

Misused constructions

Writing can also suffer from the misuse of grammatical constructions: incorrect subject-verb agreement, faulty pronoun references, incomplete or run-on sentences, or misplaced modifiers. These errors confuse the reader. They hide the writer's thoughts. Or even worse, they can completely change the writer's meaning.

This section explains some of the most serious problems in grammatical constructions.

Problems of agreement

Subject-verb agreement. A verb must agree with its subject in number and person.

> **Number:** The *paper was* at the door. [singular]
> The *papers were* on my desk. [plural]

	Singular	**Plural**
Person:	*I am* at home.	*We are* at home.
	You are at home.	*You are* at home.
	He, she, it is at home.	*They are* at home.

Here are some additional reminders about subject-verb agreement.

1. When other parts of a sentence come between the subject and the verb, these parts do not change the person or the number of the verb.

> The *boys* who had a good time at the party *are* now playing softball.
> The *report* about leases and contracts *was* distributed.

2. Inverting the order of the subject and verb does not affect agreement.

> In the trunk *were piles* of money. [*Piles were. . . .*]

3. Some nouns are plural in form but are singular in meaning and therefore take singular verbs: *news, measles, United Nations.*

> The *news was* bad.
> The *United Nations is* located in New York.

Some nouns are plural in form but may be either singular or plural, depending on their meaning in the sentence. Some of these nouns are *economics, athletics, politics, ethics.*

Politics is the art of the possible.
His *politics are* constantly changing.

4. Two or more subjects joined by *and* take a plural verb.

The *baby* and the *dog love* attention. [They love. . . .]

If the two subjects form a single idea or are thought of as a unit, they should take a singular verb.

Macaroni and *cheese is* my favorite dish. [It is. . . .]

5. Singular subjects joined by *or* or *nor* take a singular verb.

Either the *house* or the *garage is* on fire.

If the subjects joined by *or* or *nor* differ in number or person, the verb agrees with the subject nearer the verb.

Neither the *lamp* nor the *bulbs were* working.
Either the *trees* or the *lawn needs* cutting.

6. A collective noun takes a singular verb when the group is regarded as a unit. But a collective noun takes a plural verb when emphasis is placed on the individual members of the group.

The *audience was* applauding. [*applauding* together]
The *audience were* arriving. [*arriving* separately]

Pronoun agreement. We have already seen that pronouns used as subjects must agree with their verbs. Pronouns must also agree with their antecedents. Here are some rules for making pronouns agree with their verbs and their antecedents.

1. When using indefinite pronouns as subjects be careful to choose the correct form of the verb.

These indefinite pronouns are considered to be singular and take singular verbs: *each, either, neither,* and all pronouns ending in *-body* or *-one.*

Everyone is here.   *Nobody wants* to be sick.
Each of these apples *is* spoiled.

These indefinite pronouns are considered to be plural and take plural verbs: *both, few, many, several.*

Both of you *are* going to succeed.
Many are called, but *few are* chosen.

All, any, most, none, and *some* may be either singular or plural, depending on their meaning in the sentence. When the pronoun refers to one thing or to a quantity as a whole, use a singular verb. When the pronoun refers to a number of individual items, use a plural verb.

Some of the money *was* missing. [singular]
Some of their friends *were* there. [plural]
All of my hope *is* gone. [singular]
All of you *are* invited. [plural]

2. When the subject is a relative pronoun *(who, which, that),* the verb should agree with the pronoun's antecedent.

She is the editor *who speaks* Spanish. [editor speaks]
The dogs *that were barking* are quiet now. [dogs were barking]

3. A pronoun agrees with its antecedent in gender, number, and person.

The *woman* picked up *her* briefcase.
The *women* picked up *their* briefcases.

Be especially careful when the pronoun's antecedent is an indefinite pronoun. Follow the rules given above for deciding if the indefinite pronoun is singular or plural; then make the other pronoun agree with the indefinite pronoun.

Neither of the girls is wearing *her* coat.
All of the girls are wearing *their* coats.

4. When the antecedent is a collective noun, the pronoun is either singular or plural—depending on whether the collective noun is singular or plural in the sentence.

The *board* made *its* decision.
The *board* discussed the matter among *themselves.*

Faulty pronoun references

Every pronoun must have an antecedent. Place pronouns as close as possible to their antecedents so that it is clear what word the pronoun refers back to.

1. Avoid confusing references. A reader will be confused if a sentence contains two possible antecedents for a pronoun.

Confusing: After Michael talked to Bill, *he* was angry.
Clear: After Michael talked to Bill, Bill was angry.
     or Michael was angry after he talked to Bill.

2. Avoid vague references. Vague references occur when the antecedent of a pronoun is not actually stated. Using *they, this, that,* and *which* to refer to an entire statement (rather than to one noun) is a common form of vague reference.

Vague: I had not finished the report, *which* irritated Mr. Brown.

Clearer: The fact that I had not finished the report irritated Mr. Brown.

My failure to finish the report irritated Mr. Brown.

3. Avoid the indefinite use of *it, they,* and *you.*

Confusing: In the first act, *it* shows Hamlet's character.
Clearer: In the first act, Hamlet's character is shown.

In the first act, Hamlet shows his character.

Shifts in point of view

In writing, the point of view should be as consistent as possible. Shifts in point of view include changes in number, subject, tense, and voice. Of course, there are times when you do need to change the point of view. But frequent and unnecessary shifts are confusing.

1. Avoid unnecessary shifts in number (singular and plural).

Wrong: *Plants are* decorative, but *it requires* much care.
Correct: *Plants are* decorative, but *they require* much care.

2. Avoid unnecessary shifts in the subjects in sentences.

Wrong: If *you* do your research, *it* will be a good paper.
Correct: If *you* do your research, *you* will write a good paper.

3. Avoid unnecessary shifts in tense (present, past, future).

Wrong: Jack *came* home and *took* off his jacket. He *walks* to his room and *changes* clothes. Ten minutes later, he *was* ready to eat dinner.
Correct: Jack *came* home and *took* off his jacket. He *walked* to his room and *changed* clothes. Ten minutes later, he *was* ready to eat dinner.

4. Avoid unnecessary shifts in voice (active and passive).

Wrong: He *did* good work, but no raise *was received.*
Correct: He *did* good work, but he *received* no raise.

Improper parts of speech

Words that belong to one part of speech are sometimes *incorrectly* used as another part of speech. Here are some examples of using the incorrect part of speech:

Nouns incorrectly used as verbs: *author* a book, *host* a program
Adjectives incorrectly used as adverbs: played *good, real* pretty

Sentence faults

Sentence faults occur when you write sentences that are incomplete or when you improperly run sentences together. (If you would like to review basic sentence structure, see "The sentence: parts and structure" on pages 16–21.)

Sentence fragments. A sentence fragment is the error of

writing an incomplete sentence. If you put a period at the end of a phrase or a subordinate clause, you will have a fragment. Phrases and subordinate clauses cannot stand alone.

You can correct a sentence fragment by joining it to a sentence.

Fragment: *After going to college for four years.* I was ready to teach.
Correct: After going to college for four years, I was ready to teach.
Fragment: I was late for work. *Although I awoke earlier than usual.*
Correct: I was late for work, although I awoke earlier than usual.

Sometimes you can add words or change the wording to make the fragment a complete sentence in itself.

Fragment: Watching the election results all night.
Correct: I was watching the election results all night.
Fragment: One of my friends who lost her ring in the swimming pool.
Correct: One of my friends lost her ring in the swimming pool.

Run-on sentences. A run-on sentence is the error of writing two or more sentences together without properly connecting them. A comma alone cannot properly join sentences together. These are run-on sentences because only a comma appears between the two clauses:

Run-on: The managers from the New York office toured the plant, they made a favorable report.
Run-on: The board is scheduled to meet tomorrow, it has many matters to discuss.
Run-on: Classes started on September 5, however, I did not register until September 7.

Run-on sentences can be corrected in several ways:

1. Make two separate sentences.

The managers from the New York office toured the plant. They made a favorable report.

2. Use a semicolon between the clauses.

Classes started on September 5; however, I did not register until September 7.

3. Use a conjunction between the clauses (such as *and, but, or,* or *nor*).

The managers from the New York office toured the plant, *and* they made a favorable report.

4. Make one of the statements into a phrase or a subordinate clause.

Scheduled to meet tomorrow, the board has many matters to discuss.

Another error is to run sentences together with no punctuation at all between them. These run-together sentences must also be separated or properly connected.

Wrong: I spent $54.00 for this dress I like the style.
Correct: I spent $54.00 for this dress. I like the style.
    I spent $54.00 for this dress because I like the style.
    I spent $54.00 for this dress; I like the style.

Wrong: Why are you leaving now wait I'll walk home with you.
Correct: Why are you leaving now? Wait! I'll walk home with you.
    Why are you leaving now? Wait and I'll walk home with you.

Split constructions

Sometimes writers unnecessarily split infinitives, separate subjects from verbs, or separate parts of a verb phrase. When writers do any of these things, they are splitting constructions. The following list contains examples of split constructions. Avoid them in your writing.

1. Avoid split infinitives. An infinitive is *to* + a verb *(to walk, to think)*. Putting other words between *to* and the verb is often awkward.

Awkward: To be or *to* not *be:* that is the question.
Better: To be or not *to be:* that is the question.
Awkward: We had *to* without any preparation or warning *pack* our belongings.
Better: We had *to pack* our belongings without any preparation or warning.

2. Avoid unnecessarily separating a subject and its verb or a verb and its object. Keeping these basic sentence parts together usually makes your writing clearer.

Awkward: *Mary,* in one bounding leap, *cleared* the fence. [subject and verb separated]
Awkward: Mary *cleared,* in one bounding leap, *the fence.* [verb and object separated]
Better: *Mary cleared the fence* in one bounding leap.

3. Do not separate a preposition from its object.

Awkward: He walked *into,* since he was in the neighborhood, *the museum.*

Better: Since he was in the neighborhood, he walked *into the museum.*

4. Do not separate the parts of a verb phrase.

Awkward: Mary *has,* although you would not think so, *been* ill.

Better: Mary *has been* ill, although you would not think so.

Awkward: I *might have,* if you had not opposed me, *bought* the stocks.

Better: If you had not opposed me, I *might have bought* the stocks.

Faulty parallel constructions

Parallel construction means expressing two or more related ideas in the same grammatical form. To make a pair of ideas parallel, you would state both ideas in the same structure—in the same kind of words, phrases, clauses, or sentences. You should also use parallel structure in a series of items joined by *and* or *or.* Here are some examples of parallel structure:

Words: *Working* and *playing* are both important.
Phrases: Both *at home* and *at the office* she is well organized.
Clauses: I will cut the grass *when my back is better* and *when the mower is repaired.*
Sentences: *My neighbor to the south has a brick house and a well-maintained lawn. My neighbor to the north has a stucco house and a weedy lawn.*

Here are some examples of faulty parallelism, along with some ways to correct them:

Wrong: *To write* was easier for her than *talking.*
Correct: *Writing* was easier for her than *talking.*
Wrong: He enjoys playing *golf, tennis,* and *to play softball.*
Correct: He enjoys playing *golf, tennis,* and *softball.*
Wrong: *Having checked our bags* and *since we had said good-bye,* we boarded the plane.
Correct: Since we *had checked our bags* and *had said good-bye,* we boarded the plane.
Wrong: The homeowners association *maintains the entrances* and *is conducting a mosquito abatement program.*
Correct: The homeowners association *maintains the entrances* and *conducts a mosquito abatement program.*

Problems with modifiers

Whenever you use modifying words, phrases and clauses, be sure that the relationship between the modifier and the word it modifies is clear. Avoid the following common problems with modifiers.

Dangling modifiers. Adjective phrases and clauses that are not connected to any word or phrase in the sentence are called *dangling modifiers.* These danglers cause confusion; the reader does not know what they modify. Following are examples of dangling modifiers, along with some ways to correct them.

Dangling: *Hanging the curtains,* the rod slipped and hit him on the head.

Correct: When *he was hanging the curtains,* the rod slipped and hit him on the head.

Dangling: *Young and alone,* the city can be a frightening place.

Correct: *Young and alone, she* was frightened by the city.
Young and alone, a person can be frightened by the city.

Dangling: *To complete the project on time,* the typewriter must be repaired.

Correct: *To complete the project on time, I* must have the typewriter repaired.
If the project is to be completed on time, the typewriter must be repaired.

Squinting modifiers. An adverb that is placed between two verbs—both of which it could modify—is called a *squinting modifier.*

The hammer that he was waving *menacingly* fell to the floor.

Look at *menacingly* one time, and it seems to refer to *was waving;* look at it again, and it seems to refer to *fell.* In other words, the modifier, *menacingly,* squints at both verbs. The writer probably meant:

The hammer that he was *menacingly* waving fell to the floor.

Misplaced modifiers. These are phrases or clauses that are not placed close enough to the word they modify. Thus they may appear to modify some other word, rather than the word they are intended to modify. Of the three incorrect modifier constructions, the misplaced modifier is the easiest one to correct. Look at the following groups of sentences. The first sentence in each group has a misplaced modifier; the second has the modifier in the correct place.

Misplaced: Mary admitted to her mother *with a sad face* that she had failed the chemistry examination. [seems to modify *mother*]

Clear: With a sad face, Mary admitted to her mother that she had failed the chemistry examination.

Misplaced: He keeps the awards he won *at school in his bedroom.*

Clear: *In his bedroom,* he keeps the awards he won *at school.*
The awards he won at school are kept in his bedroom.

Clichés to avoid

Clichés are expressions that have lost their original impact
because they have been overused. Many similes are clichés: *red
as a rose, eyes like stars, hungry as a bear*. Clichés are also found in
business letters and reports and in academic papers: *this will
inform you, that is to say*.

Writers who use clichés have not bothered to think clearly
about what *they* want to say. If you are tempted to use a
cliché, try to rephrase the idea so that *your* thought comes
through in your own words.

The following list contains some clichés—there are many
more—that you should avoid:

a bolt from the blue	cooperate together
a long-felt want	deadly earnest
a month of Sundays	depths of despair
abreast of the times	doomed to disappointment
according to Hoyle	each and every
according to our records	enclosed herewith
aching void	epic struggle
acid test	equal to the occasion
acknowledging your letter	every fiber of her being
after all is said and done	fair sex
all in all	familiar landmark
along the same line	few and far between
and like that	first and foremost
artistic temperament	fly off the handle
as luck would have it	footprints on the sands of time
at a loss for words	force of circumstances
attached hereto	free as the breeze
bathed in tears	get down to brass tacks
bitter end	goes without saying
blood is thicker than water	goodly number
brilliant performance	green as grass
budding genius	green with envy
busy as a bee	heartfelt gratitude
by and large	heart's content
by leaps and bounds	heated argument
captain of industry	holds promise
center of attention	holy bonds of wedlock
checkered career	holy state of matrimony
clinging vine	ignorance is bliss
close to nature	in one fell swoop
compares favorably	in response to your favor
conspicuous by his absence	in terms of
contents carefully noted	in the bag
cooked his goose	in the last analysis

in the neighborhood of

in this day and age

iron will

irony of fate

it should be understood

it stands to reason

knock the tar out of him

last but not least

last straw

like a bull in a china shop

like an old shoe

looking for all the world like

mantle of snow

method in his madness

needs no introduction

nipped in the bud

no one in his right mind

none the worse for wear

paramount issue

pending merger

picturesque scene

pleasing prospect

powers that be

promising future

proud possessor

pursuant to your request

race, color, or creed

reigns supreme

relatively new to the field

revolutionary development

right and proper

sad to relate

sadder but wiser

safe to say

sea of faces

self-made man

sigh of relief

significantly reduced

skeleton in the closet

strong as an ox

strong, silent type

struggle for existence

stubborn as a mule

sturdy as an oak

take my word for it

taken into custody

talk is cheap

than meets the eye

thanking you in advance

the bottom line

the happy pair

the plot thickens

the thrill of victory

the time of my life

the weaker sex

the worse for wear

thereby hangs a tale

thunderous applause

time marches on

tired but happy

to all intents and purposes

too funny for words

upset the applecart

venture a suggestion

walk of life

we wish to state

wedded bliss

wends its way

wheel of fortune

where angels fear to tread

widespread use

with bated breath

without further delay

words fail me

words fail to express

wrought havoc

wry smile

yesterday's darling

Use what you know

These activities have been designed to review your understanding of the commonly misused words, phrases, and constructions presented in this section. Answers to the activities can be found in the **Answer Key** that begins on page 270.

Recognizing correct word use

From each pair given in parentheses, choose the word or phrase that expresses the best word use.

1. I was *(sitting, setting)* *(besides, beside)* my husband.
2. When I walked *(in, into)* the living room, she *(rose, raised)* from the sofa.
3. He *(accepted, excepted)* the contract and will *(try to, try and)* finish the project earlier than is *(expected, anticipated)*.
4. I am *(kind of, somewhat)* short of money. Could you *(loan, lend)* me $20.00 until Monday?
5. They *(enthused, were enthusiastic)* about the *(creditable, credulous)* speech she had given.
6. She was received *(formerly, formally)* by the president and her request was listened to *(respectfully, respectively)*.
7. *(A, An)* uninterested person is *(different than, different from)* *(a, an)* disinterested person.
8. The reason why the *(principle, principal)* is *(aggravated, irritated)* *(is because, is that)* we failed *(bad, badly)*.

Correcting misspelled words

The following words are misspelled; write the correct spelling
for each word.

1. batallion
2. familier
3. sacreligious
4. siezure
5. itinarery
6. priveledge
7. vascilate
8. questionaire
9. souvener
10. alledge
11. copywrited
12. protacol
13. superceed
14. appearence
15. extasy

Correcting misused constructions

Each of the following sentences contains one or more misused
constructions. Identify the problems—for example, subject-
verb agreement, run-on sentence, or misplaced modifier. Then
rewrite the sentence to correct the problems.

1. A recent test on rats show that certain dyes causes cancer.
2. Each girl received their diploma.
3. Before we could put the car in the garage, it had to be
   repaired.
4. I went to the window, and you could feel the wind
   blowing.
5. The children toured the museum, they learned many new
   things.
6. When the plane landed in the storm. The passengers
   disembarked.
7. While driving on Eighth Street, an accident occurred.

Avoiding clichés

Rewrite the following paragraph, using your own wording in
place of the clichés.

   We were sure that we had wrapped up the deal because our
contact had said that it was in the bag. We had not lain back
in the weeds but had jumped at the opportunity. We were,
however, doomed to disappointment. After all is said and
done, each and every one of our proposals was shot down. We
were left up a creek. None the worse for wear, however, we
chalked the whole thing up to experience and began to look
for greener pastures.

4   Tips about everyday writing

Do you put off writing personal letters? Are your business reports and letters poorly organized? Do you think that filling forms and writing résumés are a waste of time? When you know the form, content, and purpose of these various types of communication, you will probably be more at ease when you need to do such writing.

This section shows you how to plan before you write. It also explains the purpose and format of various kinds of letters, forms, and reports. And it describes how to most effectively arrange the content of your letters and reports.

Plan before you write

You probably have to do some kind of writing at least once a week, and maybe more often than that. This writing may be a letter, a school or business report, or maybe something as simple as a short note asking someone to do a chore or a favor for you.

If you are like most of us, you almost certainly feel a twinge of panic when you actually put pencil to paper. You may ask yourself, "Now, what am I going to say? How should I say it? Can I be sure a reader will understand my meaning?" These questions, and others like them, are a sure sign that you have not planned your writing.

How often have you heard someone say, "My project failed because I did not take the time to plan it out properly"? Well, a piece of writing can also fail to communicate its message if it was poorly planned, or not planned at all, to begin with.

The very first thing in any writing plan is to identify the audience. Before you begin to write, you must identify whom you are writing to.

Identifying your audience

This sounds simple enough. But it is one of the most frequently ignored writing rules. Most people write to please themselves. That is why sentences, letters, whole reports are often perfectly understandable to the people who wrote them but make little or no sense to the people who are trying to read them.

Because anything you write as a means of communication is directed at a specific audience, you should know as much about that audience as possible. You should know in general the age level, sex, educational background, occupation, and likely interests of your audience. This information will give you some understanding of the possible likes and dislikes of your audience. And this understanding will help you to adjust your writing style and content to your audience.

If you are communicating with a friend, relative, or business associate, part of your problem has been solved. You know these people. You probably communicate with them regularly. You should have a very good idea of the words you must choose and the style you must use to communicate your meaning.

But if you are communicating in writing to persons you have never met, how can you find out about them? What can you do to try to make sure that your meaning will be understood?

If you have already received some kind of written communication from the person, you have an advantage. Remember, most people write to please themselves. The content and style of almost every piece of writing is full of clues about its writer.

For example, the person's name may tell you the person's sex. The intent of the piece of writing may give you some clue about the person's occupation. Vocabulary, structure, and spelling may tip you off to level of education. The actual subject may help you to pinpoint some of the person's interests.

Once you have a feeling for *who* your audience is, you should begin to consider *what* your message is going to be. Is this a business communication or a personal communication? Do you wish to deliver your message in a formal or in an informal manner?

Make a list of the topics that you could cover. Now review the list and consider both who your audience is and what you wish your message to be. Eliminate the topics that you think would either not interest your audience or would be inappropriate. Of the topics that remain, decide in what order you wish to present them.

For example, you may be writing an informal letter to a close friend who lives in a distant city. You know your friend enjoys music but is bored by sports. If you have planned your letter, you would probably describe in detail any records or tapes you may have purchased recently but would probably not mention that extra-inning baseball game you attended. You have identified your audience and have planned your writing to suit the reader. In this way you have helped to guarantee that your message will be communicated.

Your mother might want to hear about your records and tapes, the baseball game, the weather, and the neighbor's new baby. If that is the kind of letter she likes to receive, that is the kind of letter you should write to her. In both cases, remember to arrange the topics into some logical order and try to make some connection between topics.

Another example of matching writing to the intended audience might be that of an engineer who is writing a formal report about a new automobile engine. If the report is to be sent to the stockholders of an automobile company, the engineer would not use technical language. Instead, the report would probably stress how the new engine would enable the company to make a larger profit. But if this report was to be read by other engineers at the company, the writer would probably describe in detail how the engine works.

Always keep in mind the fact that you are writing to communicate a message. If your writing fails to do this, the message may just as well not have been written. You must always have your audience in mind as you write if clear, concise communication is your goal.

After you have identified your reader, you must determine *why* you are writing. That is, you must identify the main purpose of the report or letter. Do you want to *complain* about a product, to *invite* your cousin for the weekend, or to *persuade* the board of directors to acquire another company.

When you have determined your main purpose for writing, ask yourself if the letter or report has other purposes. Another purpose in a letter of complaint might be to have a defective product repaired. A second purpose of a report to persuade might also be to present factual information. In almost every kind of written communication, an underlying purpose might be to motivate some kind of action on the part of the reader.

When you are planning the purpose of your letter or report, you should decide what *tone* your message will have. Will it be humorous, apologetic, sympathetic, informative, questioning, or urgent? The way you word your message is as important as the message itself. If you are humorous when you should be apologetic, your reader will probably be angry. If you are sarcastic when you should be understanding, your reader will probably be hurt.

Identifying your purpose before you start to write is as important as identifying your audience. Knowing what your purpose is will help you to choose exactly the right words and use exactly the right tone to deliver your message.

Personal letters

The personal letter is also known as the *friendly* letter. It is the kind of letter you might write to a member of your family or to an acquaintance. Even though the personal letter is written to someone you know, it has certain forms you should follow.

There are five parts to a personal letter: (1) the heading, (2) the salutation, (3) the body, (4) the complimentary close, and (5) the signature. An explanation of each part follows:

1. *The heading* is placed in the upper right-hand corner of your letter. The heading features information the reader needs to quickly identify the writer of the letter. The heading should include your street address; your city, state, and zip code; and the date. If you write to a person often, you may wish to omit your complete address from the heading. The use of either a block form or an indented form is equally acceptable in the heading of a personal letter.

Block form
1011 East 28th Street
Minneapolis, MN 55401
March 28, 1981

Indented form
1011 East 28th Street
    Minneapolis, MN 55401
        March 28, 1981

Do not use abbreviations in either the address or the date (except for the state abbreviation which the post office requests you use along with the zip code). Numbered street names should be spelled out if they are ten or less, but given in numerals if they are 11 or above (for example, *Fifth Avenue,* but *42nd Street*). Note that no punctuation appears at the end of a line.

2. *The salutation,* or greeting, is followed by a comma.

Dear David,   Dear Mom and Dad,   Dear Mrs. Smith,

It is placed at the left-hand margin of the letter, about four lines below the heading.

3. *The body* of the letter should begin two lines below the salutation. The body contains the message you wish to communicate to the reader. Paragraphs within the body of the letter may be set off in either one of two ways. The first line of each paragraph may be indented. In this case, the space between paragraphs should be the same as the space between lines within each paragraph. Or the first line of each paragraph may be aligned with the left-hand margin of the letter. In this case, extra space should be left between paragraphs.

4. *The complimentary close* should be placed two lines below the body of the letter and should be aligned with the heading. The complimentary close is followed by a comma.

Sincerely yours,   Your friend,   Love,

5. *The signature* is written below the complimentary close. It may be aligned with the first letter or the last letter of the complimentary close, or it may be centered below the close.

Sincerely yours,   Love,   Your friend,
Kevin   Kevin   Kevin

The envelope for a personal letter should follow the same style (block or indented) that was used in the heading of the letter. The writer's return address can be placed on the back flap or in the upper left-hand corner of the envelope. The name and address of the person to whom the letter has been written should be centered slightly below the middle of the envelope. Be sure to write out in full the name of the person to whom you are writing.

Now study the sample envelope on page 83 and the sample showing personal letter format on page 84. Both were prepared using block style. The numbers added to the letter correspond to the five parts of a personal letter just described.

Personal letter envelope

L. M. Jones
1174 Home Avenue
Oak Park, IL 60304

Mr. David Anderson
15 Nautilus Court
Pittsburg, CA 94521

Content of personal letters

The *content* is what makes up the body of a personal letter. It is what a letter is all about. Letters can center on one topic or on several. Some letters that concentrate on one topic are invitations, replies to invitations, thank-you notes, and sympathy notes. Samples of these and other kinds of personal letters are given in 5, "Model letters for selected occasions."

However, some personal letters may revolve around several different topics. Such personal letters are usually the long, newsletter kinds of communications you may write to close friends or family members.

Even though long personal letters may contain many separate topics, these kinds of letters should not become collections of unconnected notes. It is very difficult to maintain a reader's interest if he or she must continuously jump from one topic to another. And if a reader's interest is not held, you are not accomplishing your main purpose—communication.

Make sure each separate topic is fully developed, sprinkled with the kind of rich detail you think your reader would find interesting. Try to create transitions between topics. Transitions will help one topic flow smoothly and evenly into the next and will make your letter much easier to read.

Remember, the thoughts in your personal letters should be well-organized and clearly presented. Your letter should use transitions to move smoothly from one idea to another. Do not abruptly break into one idea with "Oh, I forgot to mention before when I was saying. . . ." Put all your thoughts about one item together in the same paragraph.

Personal letter format

1. 1174 Home Avenue
   Oak Park, IL 60304
   June 5, 1981

2. Dear David,

3. How surprised I was to receive your letter. I know you must be busy unpacking at home and settling in at your new job. The company that you work for has a division in Illinois. One of Joe's best friends is a sales manager for them.

   You asked when we could come out for a visit. Well, we don't have any vacation time left this year. Perhaps next February we could fly out and stay a week. Would you be able to take time from work then?

   We are all happy for you and would enjoy visiting you in California.

4. Love,
5. Linda

The people to whom you write personal letters are probably the people who are closest and most important to you. Show that you truly care about them and value their friendship by taking time to plan and then write thoughtful, legible letters.

Business letters

You may have looked at the title of this section and thought, "Well, this is not for me. I don't work at a job that requires me to write letters." On the other hand, you may have thought, "I write many business letters every day. I don't need any advice on how such letters should be written."

Well, both attitudes should be reconsidered. The person whose job requires the writing of many business letters should always be searching for ways to make those letters clearer. And the person who believes that he or she never deals with business letters is in for a surprise.

Everyone both sends and receives business letters—not just business people. Business letters are sent from one company or organization to another, from companies and organizations to individuals, and from individuals to companies and organizations. You probably receive, either at work or at home, several business letters every week. Letters asking you to subscribe to magazines or apologizing for not properly crediting your checking account are some examples of business letters you receive at home.

You have many occasions to write business letters yourself. You might wish to cancel a subscription, to apply for a job, to complain about faulty merchandise, or to request a copy of a doctor's bill. All of these are examples of business letters. Whenever you write a business letter, you should follow the established format.

A business letter always has six parts: (1) the heading, (2) the inside address, (3) the salutation, (4) the body, (5) the complimentary close, and (6) the signature. An explanation of these parts follows:

Format for business letters

1. *The heading* is placed in the upper right-hand corner of your letter. It includes your street address; your city, state, and zip code; and the date. The heading should be arranged in block form. The block form is preferred because it is easier to set up and has cleaner lines.

   Block form

   210 Park Boulevard
   Glen Ellyn, IL 60305
   April 12, 1981

Do not use abbreviations in either the address or the date (except for the state abbreviation that is used with the zip code). Numbered street names should be spelled out if they are ten or less, but given in numerals if they are 11 or above (for example, write *First Street,* but *12th Avenue*).

If you are using stationary with a printed letterhead, add the date two or three lines below it. The date may be placed flush with the right-hand margin or flush with the left-hand margin.

2. *The inside address* is placed four lines below the heading and flush with the left-hand margin. The inside address consists of the recipient's name and title; the name of the department or office, if any; the name of the company; the street address; and the city, state, and zip code.

When you write to an individual in a company or organization, use the person's personal, professional, or business title. For example, write *Ms. Jane Smith, President* or *Dr. James Bentley, Registrar.* If the person's business title is long, place it on the second line. Use the same form—block—for the inside address as you did for the heading. If your letter is short, you may add extra space between the heading and the inside address.

Block form

Mrs. Ellen Smith
Editorial Vice-President
Mathematics Department
Read-It Publishing Company
120 East Adams Street
Chicago, IL 60635

3. *The salutation,* or greeting, is placed two lines below the inside address and is followed by a colon. When you write to an individual in a company, use the individual's name *(Dear Mr. Jones:).* If the person to whom you are writing has a professional title *(Doctor, Professor),* it should be used *(Dear Professor Smith:).* When you are addressing a woman, use the title *(Ms., Mrs.,* or *Miss)* that she prefers. When you write to a company or to an individual whose name you do not know, use *Gentlemen:, Dear Sir:,* or *Madam:.* If you do not know if the person reading the letter will be a man or a woman, you could use *Dear Sir or Madam:* or *Ladies and Gentlemen:* as a salutation.

4. *The body* of the letter begins two lines below the salutation. All the information that you wish to communicate to the recipient of your letter is placed in the body. It is recommended that block style be used throughout the body of a business letter. The body should be single-spaced; double-space between paragraphs.

5. *The complimentary close* is begun two lines below the body of the letter. You may align the complimentary close either with the left-hand margin or with the heading. Only the first word in the complimentary close is capitalized. The complimentary close is followed by a comma. Here are some suitable complimentary closes for a business letter arranged from the most formal to the least formal: *Respectfully yours, Yours truly, Very truly yours, Yours very truly, Yours very sincerely, Sincerely yours,* and *Cordially yours,*.

6. *The signature* is handwritten below the complimentary close. Your name should be typed below your signature. Usually, your typed name appears four lines below the complimentary close, with your signature written between them.

7. If you *enclose* something with your letter—a check, a bill, or an article—you should call attention to it by writing the word *Enclosure* or *Enclosures*. This notation should be placed two lines below your typed name, flush with the left-hand margin.

8. If you are sending a *carbon copy* of your letter to someone, that person's name should be mentioned after the abbreviation *cc:,* which stands for "carbon copy." This notation should be placed flush with the left-hand margin, two lines below your typed name, or two lines below the notation *Enclosure* if that has been used.

   The *envelope* for a business letter should follow the block style that you used in the heading and inside address of your letter. Place your full name and address in the upper left-hand corner. Center the recipient's full name and address slightly below the middle of the envelope. The recipient's name and address on the envelope should be the same as in the inside address.

   Look at the samples of a business letter and an envelope which show the proper format (pages 88–89). The numbers added to the letter correspond to the eight parts of a business letter just described.

The *content* is in the body of a business letter; it is the subject matter that you wish to communicate. Business letters often deal with only one topic. And such letters are usually classified according to the content, or subject matter, that they contain. A few of the different kinds of business letters are letters of inquiry, application, introduction, and recommendation; order letters; complaint letters; and sales letters. Samples of several kinds of business letters may be found in 5, "Model letters for selected occasions."

Content of business letters

Business letter format

1. 784 Chatham Place
   Elmhurst, IL   60126
   January 5, 1981

2. Ms. Pamela Marsh, Director
   Office of Admissions
   Marquette University
   1380 West Wisconsin Avenue
   Milwaukee, WI   53233

3. Dear Ms. Marsh:

4. Thank you for sending me the brochures and the application
   forms for the College of Journalism. I also appreciated
   your suggestion about writing to Dr. Jones. He has arranged
   for me to visit with some journalism professors and students
   in March.

   I have enclosed the application forms and the $20.00
   application fee.

   Would you please send me another brochure? My counselor
   would like one to show to other interested students.

   5. Sincerely yours,

   Joseph F. Wesley

   6. Joseph F. Wesley

7. Enclosures

8. cc: Dr. Albert Jones

Business letter envelope

```
Joseph F. Wesley
784 Chatham Place
Elmhurst, IL   60126



                    Ms. Pamela Marsh, Director
                    Office of Admissions
                    Marquette University
                    1380 West Wisconsin Avenue
                    Milwaukee, WI   53233
```

Your letters represent you. They should be brief, to the point, clear, and courteous. The message you wish to communicate must be the main, most obvious part of the letter. When your letter is received, you will not be present to explain what you really *meant* to say. You must state your message clearly in the letter. Much time and money will be wasted—by both you and the recipient—if other letters must be written to clarify the message of the first letter.

Your letters should be arranged in a logical, orderly manner. To do this you should gather all the facts you need *before* you write the letter. Know to whom you are writing, why you are writing, and what the order of importance is of your ideas.

For example, you see an advertisement in a magazine for a product that none of the stores in your town carry. You decide to write to the manufacturer to find out more about the product and where you can purchase it. In your letter, put first things first:

1. Tell where you saw the advertisement.
2. Tell why you need more information.
3. Ask for the information.

Your letters should be written in a straightforward, natural manner. Which of the following statements would you use in a letter?

1. The matter has been attended to by my office.
2. My office has taken care of some matters.
3. Mr. Jones, my assistant, has solved your problem.

If you chose the third statement, you chose a statement that shows a person *(Mr. Jones)* doing *(has solved)* a definite task *(your problem)*. The first statement is written in the passive voice and shows a thing *(office)* doing the action. In the second statement, a thing *(office)* is doing an indefinite task *(some matters)*. You should, therefore, use the active voice and show people doing the action in your letters. As much as possible, you should write your business letters to read as if you were present and speaking to the receiver.

There is no special language for business letters. You should avoid stiff, stilted, or stuffy words and phrases. Above all, avoid the use of clichés. The list at the right shows a few of the many clichés you should avoid in business letters. You would not use such clichés if you were talking to someone on the telephone or face-to-face; don't use them in your letters either.

Your letters should also be courteous. You are entering another person's home or office through your letter, so maintain a friendly tone. By choosing your words carefully, you can even express displeasure or register a complaint without making an enemy. If you want some positive action to result from your letter, avoid annoying the intended receiver.

Clichés to avoid in business letters

according to our records
answering yours of
anticipating your favor/order/reply
as per
as regards
beg to advise/assure
check to cover
duly noted
enclosed find
for your files
for your information
hereby advise
hoping your order
I have your letter of
I am [ending last sentence]
in due course
in reference to
in receipt of
kind order
kindly advise
looking forward to
may we suggest
of the above date
our records show
permit us to remind
please accept/find/note/rest assured
recent date
referring to yours of
regarding the matter
regret to advise/inform/state
take pleasure in
take the liberty of
thanking you in advance
trusting to have
under separate cover
valued favor/order
we are [ending last sentence]
we are pleased to advise/note
wish to advise/state
with reference to
your kind indulgence
your letter of recent date
your Mr., Mrs., Miss _____
your valued patronage

Filling in forms

Forms, forms, forms! In the course of your life, you will fill in many different kinds of forms. Look in your wallet. You probably have a driver's license, a social security card, insurance cards (health and auto), credit cards, a library card, and membership cards for various clubs and associations. Before you received any of these cards, you had to fill in a form. If you rent an apartment, own a home or a car, or have ordered anything from a catalog, you first had to fill in a form.

Even if you currently do not have a driver's license or any of the other cards mentioned here, or if you have not yet made a major purchase on credit, you probably will someday. So you should know something about filling in forms.

Forms ask questions, and you supply the answers. You should answer all questions completely and honestly. At the end of some forms—income tax forms, insurance forms, and employment applications—you are asked to sign your name to show that the information you have given is true. If, however, there are questions that do not apply to you or that are not appropriate to the circumstances, feel free to write "Does not apply" or to draw a line through the space that has been provided for your answer.

Be brief in your answers. Most forms do not leave much space for answers. You must answer, therefore, with carefully chosen words and phrases. On some forms—applications for employment or for admission to a school or college—you are asked questions such as, "What contributions could you make to this company?" or "What qualities do you have that would help you in the position you are seeking?" If a quarter of a page is allowed for your answer, write in complete, well thought-out sentences. Such questions are asked not only to find out your reasons for seeking a position, but also to determine how well you express your ideas, what kind of vocabulary you use, and if you observe standard rules of grammar.

Be neat. Put all check marks or x's neatly within the boxes, spaces, or parentheses that are provided. Write or type on the lines or in the spaces that are given. Your handwriting should be clear and legible. Use a pen that does not smudge or skip.

Forms have a purpose. Each kind of form is made with a definite purpose in mind. Order forms are used so that orders can be filled quickly, accurately, and uniformly. Income tax returns are arranged both so that you can fill them in logically and so that they can be checked quickly. Questionnaires, surveys, and census forms are organized in such a way that various kinds of information may be gathered from large groups of people and then processed quickly.

On the job—in the office, the store, or the factory—there are forms to be filled in. If your job involves traveling, there are itineraries and travel vouchers. In many jobs, you might be asked to keep a checklist of the work you have done. If you are a supervisor, you have to fill in forms to evaluate the work of others.

There are many more kinds of forms than have been discussed here. But space does not permit complete coverage of every kind of form you might encounter. In fact, entire books have been written that do nothing but give advice about completing various kinds of forms.

However, you should be able to deal effectively with most forms if you keep in mind a few simple guidelines.

1. Read all the directions before you begin.
2. Make sure you understand the directions. If you do not understand, seek help.
3. Read each question thoroughly before you attempt to answer.
4. Answer each question briefly, honestly, and in a straightforward manner.
5. If you are handwriting your responses, do so neatly and legibly.
6. Check all of your responses before you hand in or send in the form.
7. If possible, retain a copy of the completed form for your personal records.

The sample forms in this section show some of the kinds of forms you might be asked to complete. Study these examples as guidelines that could help you to deal more effectively with forms.

Form requesting service on an appliance

INFORMATION FOR SERVICE CENTER

THIS IS NOT A GUARANTEE CARD

IMPORTANT - When service is needed, fill in this form. Send
form along with appliance to the nearest Service Center.

Product name _____

Model no. _____

Serial number or series _____

Your name _____

Your address _____

City and state _____

From whom purchased _____

City and state _____

Date purchased _____

Remarks _____

_____

_____

Post card requesting information on social security earnings

YOUR SOCIAL SECURITY EARNINGS RECORD

For a *free* statement of earnings credited to your social security record, complete other side of this card. Use card for only *one* person.

All covered wages and self-employment income are reported under your *name* and social security *number.* So show your name and number *exactly* as on your card. If you ever used another name or number, show this too.

Be sure to put a stamp on this card or it won't be delivered. You can mail the card in a stamped envelope if you wish.

If you have a separate question about social security, or want to discuss your statement when you get it, the people at any social security office will be glad to help you.

Form SSA-7004 PC (1-79)
(Prior Editions May Be Used Until Supply Is Exhausted)

POSTAGE REQUIRED

SOCIAL SECURITY ADMINISTRATION
P. O. BOX 57
BALTIMORE, MARYLAND 21203

(Please read instructions on back before completing)
REQUEST FOR SOCIAL SECURITY STATEMENT OF EARNINGS

Your social security number

Date of Birth

Month	Day	Year

Print Name and Address in ink or use typewriter

Please send a statement of my social security earnings to:

Name _____

Number & Street _____

City & State _____ Zip Code _____

Sign Your Name Here _____
(Do Not Print)

I am the individual to whom the record pertains. I understand that if I knowingly and willingly request or receive a record about an individual under false pretenses I would be guilty of a Federal crime and could be fined up to $5,000.

If you ever used a name (such as a maiden name) on a social security card different from the one above, please print name here:

_____

Magazine survey form

Please fill in this survey so that we can determine who our readers are. By doing this, you will assist us in publishing a magazine that suits your interests.

In each of the four lists, put a check next to the item(s) that apply to you.

Field of work

____ 1. Agriculture
____ 2. Business
____ 3. Education
____ 4. Finance
____ 5. Government
____ 6. Health care
____ 7. Industry
____ 8. Journalism
____ 9. Law
____ 10. Manufacturing
____ 11. Medicine
____ 12. Sales
____ 13. Social services
____ 14. Other _____

Position

____ 1. Administrator
____ 2. Clerk
____ 3. Editor
____ 4. Engineer
____ 5. Farmer
____ 6. Field representative
____ 7. Janitor
____ 8. Manager
____ 9. Mechanic
____ 10. Secretary
____ 11. Teacher
____ 12. Technician
____ 13. Writer
____ 14. Other _____

Age

____ 1. 18-25
____ 2. 26-30
____ 3. 31-40
____ 4. 41-65
____ 5. over 65

Hobbies

____ 1. Collecting
____ 2. Cooking
____ 3. Crafts
____ 4. Fitness
____ 5. Music
____ 6. Photography
____ 7. Sports
____ 8. Travel
____ 9. Other _____

Employment application form

EMPLOYMENT APPLICATION

PERSONAL   Date: _____

Name: _____ Citizen of U.S. ☐   Other _____

Address: _____

How long have you lived there? _____ Phone Number: _____
                                                                                    Area

Last Previous Address: _____ How long did you live there? _____

Date of Birth: * _____ Can you furnish proof of age if necessary? _____

Social Security Number: _____ Number of Dependents: _____

What hobbies or activities do you participate in or pursue? _____

_____

Position(s) Applying for: _____

Check Preference(s): Full-time _____ Temporary _____ Part-time _____ Summer _____

What transportation would you use? _____

Estimated Travel Time: _____ Date Available to Start Work: _____

Do you have any relatives or friends who are or have worked for this company? _____ _____
                                                                                          Yes   No

Their Names: _____

How or by whom were you referred to this company? _____

*"The Age Discrimination in Employment Act of 1967 prohibits discrimination on the basis of age with respect to individuals who are at least 40 but less than 70 years of age."

HEALTH DATA

Height _____ Weight _____ Vision _____ Hearing _____ Are you presently under doctor's care? _____

Date of Last Physical Examination: _____ Status of Health _____

Any Health Problems or Physical Defects? _____

List any serious illness, operations, accidents, or nervous disorders you may have had in the last five years: _____

_____

_____

In emergency notify _____ Relationship _____

Address _____ Phone Number _____

EDUCATIONAL BACKGROUND

Are you attending school now? _____ Course _____

Number of Nights _____ When will you finish? _____

	Name	City and State	No. Years	Date Left	Grad?	Course/ Major
High School						
College/ University						
Graduate School						
Other						

CLERICAL SKILLS: MACHINE SKILLS:

Typing Speed _____   Dictaphone _____

Shorthand Speed _____   Mimeo _____

Filing _____   Adding Machine _____

Other _____   Other Machines: _____

BUSINESS EXPERIENCE

LIST MOST RECENT EMPLOYERS FIRST. *(May we contact your present employer if presently employed?)*

1. *Name of Firm:* _____ *Employed from* _____ *to* _____

    Address: _____ *Telephone Number* _____

    Job Title and Duties: _____

    _____

    Supervisor's Name _____ *Starting Salary* _____ *Final* _____

    Reasons for Leaving: _____

2. *Name of Firm:* _____ *Employed from* _____ *to* _____

    Address: _____ *Telephone Number* _____

    Job Title and Duties: _____

    _____

    Supervisor's Name _____ *Starting Salary* _____ *Final* _____

    Reason for Leaving _____

3. *Name of Firm:* _____ *Employed from* _____ *to* _____

    Address: _____ *Telephone Number* _____

    Job Title and Duties: _____

    _____

    Supervisor's Name _____ *Starting Salary* _____ *Final* _____

    Reasons for Leaving: _____

4. *Name of Firm:* _____ *Employed from* _____ *to* _____

    Address: _____ *Telephone Number* _____

    Job Title and Duties: _____

    Supervisor's Name _____ *Starting Salary* _____ *Final* _____

    Reasons for Leaving _____

It is understood that any hiring agreement is dependent upon the truthfulness of the information herein contained.

_____
                                                                Signature of applicant

Business reports and memorandums

Writing and reading reports and memorandums are often considered necessary evils in the business world. They are necessary, but they need not be evils. Poorly written, hard-to-read reports and memorandums are often the result of either one or a combination of the following problems:

1. The subject is unfamiliar to you and you do not know how to obtain necessary facts that would clarify the communication.
2. You do not fully understand the subject.
3. You are not able to communicate your meaning clearly because you are unsure of the purpose or audience.
4. You are not able to organize your information clearly because you are unsure of the form—report or memorandum—your communication should follow.
5. Your reader has not been given enough background information to understand the subject.
6. The form selected—report or memorandum—might not be suitable for the length of the communication.

Business reports and memorandums can be effectively written, however, when you, the business writer, understand their purpose, audience, form, and content.

Purpose of business reports

All business reports should have one *general* purpose: *to present information in an orderly, objective manner.* Your reports should be based on facts not opinions; they should show a fair and true picture of whatever situation you are attempting to deal with. The purpose of your reports is to communicate a message to your reader; therefore, do not bury your message under ambiguous words and phrases.

Each business report also has a *specific* purpose. Some reports—progress reports and annual reports—merely *state facts.* Progress reports tell how far along a project is. Annual reports show the stockholders how well or how poorly an organization has performed during the year. Other reports *explain* or *interpret* the facts. For example, a report might be written primarily to explain a new method which could be used to make motors. Besides telling what the method is and how it works, such a report might also explain how the company could use this new method to make production more efficient.

The most complex types of reports are those that *analyze* a subject. For example, your company is considering building a plant in Brazil. You have been asked to study the situation in Brazil to find out whether or not building a plant there would be a good idea. Your report should analyze several elements, such as the political and economic conditions in Brazil, and the availability of raw materials and skilled workers. When your analysis is completed, you should be able to make your recommendations: to build or not to build.

The purpose of your report will usually determine whether the report should be informal or formal. *Informal reports* usually deal with the smaller parts of large projects. A monthly progress report would be an example of an informal report. An informal report could be contained in a letter or memorandum.

Formal reports are usually long; they may be many pages long, even book length. Such reports are sometimes published. However, this does not mean that any less care should go into the creation of a short, informal report. A large part of the way in which an organization views you may depend on how well you are able to communicate. So careful planning and execution should be your goal at all times. And careful planning begins with establishing a format that is logical and easy to follow.

The format of short, informal business reports may vary considerably, depending on the purpose of the report. The various sections of a short report should have headings. These headings may be placed on a separate line at the left-hand margin and underlined; or they may simply be underlined at the beginnings of paragraphs. Headings help you organize the information and help your reader understand the information. Organizations often have their own standard formats for reports that are frequently written, such as sales reports, progress or status reports, budget reports, and production reports. The first time you are asked to do a particular kind of report, ask if there is a standard format. Whether or not the format is standard, you might look at previously written reports, if possible, to get ideas for setting up your report. If you have to set up your own format, use brief, clear headings that will help you put your information in a logical order.

Format of informal business reports

There are six main parts to most long, formal business reports: (1) the introduction, (2) the summary, (3) the body, (4) the conclusions, (5) the recommendations, and (6) the appendix. Most companies have their own established structure for formal business reports. Some structures place the conclusions and recommendations before the body of the report; others put the summary before the introduction. There are, however, specific kinds of information that make up each part of a long, formal report.

Format of formal business reports

1. *The introduction* presents a clear statement of the problem or problems that will be covered in the report. It gives the purpose and aim of the report and tells why the report was compiled. The methods used to gather and analyze the facts are often described in the introduction.

2. *The summary* is a brief overview of the main points of the report. The results, conclusions, and your recommendations should be emphasized in the summary. Executives and managers sometimes receive only the summaries of reports. They want to know what should be done to solve problems; they do not want to be bothered with the details. The summary is sometimes called a *synopsis* or an *abstract*.

3. *The body* of the report presents the facts, explains what, if any, action was undertaken, and analyzes the results. The body of a report could be contained in one or two paragraphs, or it could involve many pages.

4. *The conclusions* tell what the results of the study mean. The conclusions are always based on the facts that were presented in the body of the report.

5. The *recommendations* are suggestions for what should be done to solve the problem or to clarify the situation that prompted creation of the report. The recommendation may be that action be taken or changes be made, or the recommendation might be that nothing should be done, or that additional study of the subject is required before a decision can be made.

6. *The appendix* is further information for the reader. Maps, charts, graphs, and tables that would break into the text of a report are usually placed in the appendix. If the report is lengthy, an index might be included in the appendix. A bibliography could also be added to an appendix.

Extremely long reports sometimes include one or more additional parts. These additional parts might be—

1. *A title page* which gives (a) the title of the report, (b) the name of the person or company who authorized the report, (c) the author's name, and (d) the date the report was submitted.

2. *A table of contents* which lists the major sections of the report and the page numbers on which each section is located.

3. *A letter of authorization* written by the person who authorized the report.

4. *A letter of transmittal* from the person who wrote the report to the person or persons who will receive the report.

Appearance of formal reports. Each part of a report has a heading—*Introduction, Conclusion, Appendix.* If the report is long, the heading should be centered at the top of the page on which the section begins. If the report is short, the heading can be placed at the left-hand margin and underlined. You may use the terms *Introduction, Summary, Conclusion, Recommendations,* and *Appendix* for headings. But you should devise a descriptive term or title for the heading of the body.

Maps, charts, graphs, and tables that are referred to in the report may be placed within the text if they are necessary to understanding the main points of the report. If these items just provide additional information, they should be placed in the appendix.

Use numbers or letters—(1), (2), (a), (b)—to set off items in a list. Such listed items are much easier to read.

Readability is also improved if you leave adequate white space in your report. Double-space the text of a long report, and single-space that of a short report. Leave additional space between the text and lists or between the text and illustrations.

Content of business reports

The content of a business report is what the report is all about. Whether you are writing a brief status report or a long analysis of a problem, the final judgment of a report's accuracy and effectiveness is based upon the report's content.

The facts. Facts are the foundation upon which you build your report. You must know where to find the facts and how to interpret them. You must decide which facts to emphasize and which ones to omit.

One central idea. Your report centers on one specific problem or idea. All your facts, results, conclusions, and recommendations must relate to this one central idea or problem. You want to keep the reader aware of the central idea. Do not introduce irrelevant material into your report, or get sidetracked by remotely related material.

Clear, concise writing. Your reports should be written in a straightforward, clear, and concise manner. Clear writing reflects clear thinking. Explain to the reader why you did or did not do certain things, and what procedures you used. Remember, the purpose of a report is to communicate information.

Unclear, ambiguous writing is what causes most business reports to fall apart. The writers are afraid to take responsibility. They hide behind ambiguous statements, use the passive voice, or show objects doing actions. Readers quickly lose interest in such vague writing.

Logical arrangement. The ideas in your report should fit together to create a clear, orderly picture of the problem. There are many different kinds of arrangements that you can use—chronological, spatial, simple to complex, or cause and effect. Before you start to write, make an outline. It will help you put your ideas in a logical arrangement.

Courteous tone. As is true for all forms of written communication, business reports should be courteous in tone. Do not assume that the reader has as much background in the subject as you have. You are the expert; you have done the research. Now you must write the report so that the readers can share, understand, and use the information you have gathered.

You should know exactly to whom the report will be sent— your immediate supervisor, the president of the company, all managers, the stockholders, or the plant's supervisors. When you know who your readers will be, you can choose appropriate language and reading level for your report. In general, the number of words containing more than three syllables should be kept low. Sentences should usually not be more than 25 words long. And the length of most paragraphs should be about 150 words.

Do not use business or technical jargon when it is not necessary. If you cannot explain in simple and clear language how a system or method works, you probably do not understand how it works yourself.

Many times reports are made to evaluate existing problems or situations. These problems and situations usually involve many people. Therefore, you should be diplomatic in your suggestions for making improvements.

Steps in preparing a report

Now that you know something about the format and content of business reports, you are ready to prepare a report. The following list suggests seven steps you should use in preparing a report:

1. Know the problem with which your report will deal, and set limits on the range of your study. Know who the readers of the report will be and to what use the report will be put.
2. Find out what already has been suggested or done to attempt to solve the problem.
3. Gather your facts from the files, from libraries, from laboratory experiments, or from interviews with people who are involved in the problem.

4. Make an outline that organizes your facts into logical groups of ideas. Arrange these groups of ideas into a logical sequence.
5. Write your report using the active voice, concrete nouns, and specific examples.
6. Have your report typed according to your organization's format.
7. Proofread your report, and ask an objective person to read and critique it *before* you submit the report.

Writing memorandums

Memorandums are used for communication within an organization whenever a written record of information or of a message is required. A memorandum can be sent from one department to another, from one person to another, or from a person to a department. Memorandums—memos—can be used for something as simple as notifying people about a department meeting, or as complex as reporting the results of a study to relocate the company.

Most companies have preprinted forms for memorandums. The forms usually have five parts.

1. *To:* (The name of the person to whom the message is sent. The names of several people, or of a department, could be listed here.)
2. *From:* (The name of the person or department who sent the message, sometimes followed by the initials of the person who authorized the message.)
3. *Date:*
4. *Subject:* (A brief phrase or a sentence that tells what the message is about.)
5. The rest of the page is for the message.

Sometimes other materials—letters, charts, pamphlets—are attached to a memo. In those cases, an *enclosure* or *attachment* line should be added toward the bottom of the memo sheet and all the attached materials should be listed.

The message in a memo is given briefly and concisely. Therefore, the writer must try a little harder to be accurate, clear, and complete. Do not repeat information that has already been given in another part of the memo. Read the first sample memo on page 106 and answer the following questions:

1. Is the title of the subject accurate?
2. Was anything repeated in the message that was already in a heading?
3. Was the memo complete?

Now look at the second version of the sample memo. Compare it with the first version. In what ways is the second version better?

Sample memo—first version

```
TO:  All department heads

FROM:  E. B. Jones, Personnel Director

DATE:  June 10, 1981

SUBJECT:  Vacation schedules


The personnel department is putting together the vacation
schedule for the period July 1981 to June 1982.  Please have
your employees fill in the attached forms indicating their
first and second choices for vacations to be taken during
the period July 1981 to June 1982.
```

Sample memo—improved version

```
TO:  All department heads

FROM:  E. B. Jones, Director of Personnel

DATE:  June 10, 1981

SUBJECT:  Vacation schedules for
          July 1, 1981 through June 30, 1982


Please distribute one of the attached forms to each of your
employees.  Ask them to follow the directions carefully so
that you can return the forms by June 20, 1981.

We need everyone's cooperation.  Thank you for yours.


Employee vacation preference forms
```

Some words and phrases are used so often in business reports and memos that they have become clichés. Instead of using such business clichés, try to use simple, direct words and phrases.

Clichés to avoid in reports and memos

Instead of	Use
ahead of schedule	early
a large number of	many
almost never	seldom
a majority of	most
are of the opinion	believe, think
at the present time	now, today
comes into conflict	conflicts
costs the sum of	costs
created the possibility	made possible
due in large measure to	due largely to
endeavor	attempt, try
fabricate	build
for a period of a week	for a week
for the purpose of	for
give encouragement to	encourage
give rise to	cause
have need for	need
in all cases	always
in a most careful manner	carefully
inaugurate	begin
indigenous	native
initial	first
in the amount of	for
in the event that	if
in the near future	soon
make inquiry regarding	inquire
maximum	most
minimum	least
of a confidential nature	confidential
optimum	best
substantial portion	many, much
take into consideration	consider
to conduct an investigation of	to investigate
utilize	use

Résumés and cover letters

Writing a résumé and cover letter is the first step in finding a job. The *résumé* is a brief summary of your work experiences and achievements, your educational background, and your personal activities. Your résumé introduces you to a potential employer. The résumé should make a good impression so that a potential employer will respond by setting up an interview. A résumé does not get the job for you—but it might get you an interview.

A *cover letter* accompanies each résumé you send. In it, you tell why you sent the résumé, make reference to a skill or experience that especially qualifies you for the job you are interested in applying for, and politely ask for an interview. The cover letter should be brief and should not simply repeat information that is in the résumé, though it may emphasize or call attention to key portions of the résumé.

Who should write a résumé?

Anyone applying for a job should write and submit a résumé. Each person's résumé will stress different things. If you have just graduated from college, or from business or technical school, your résumé should emphasize your educational background, as well as any part-time or summer work that relates to the job you seek. You might also list specific courses you believe would help you perform more effectively in the job you are interested in getting.

If you are looking for a better job in the same field or want to enter a new field, you should stress your work experiences, achievements, and successes. If you are changing careers, you might have taken some courses or had some training which makes the change possible. List these items on your résumé.

If you are reentering the job market after several years of military service, homemaking, or retirement, you should write a résumé that highlights activities you have done that could be related to your career interests. For example, a lieutenant in the army seeking a managerial position might stress his or her leadership qualities and ability to handle routine office matters. Or a person who has been out of the job market because of homemaking and child-care duties might point out his or her successful running of a household or leadership in community affairs as demonstrating an ability to organize. Finally, a recently retired person seeking part-time employment in a related field might emphasize significant portions of his or her career history.

Whatever your background, whatever your training, whatever your career goals, a well-organized résumé is a must if you are applying for a job. Without a résumé you lessen your chances of reaching the people who will eventually make the decisions that could guide your career.

You have already been given some ideas as to what information to include in your résumé. Now let's divide the résumé into its separate parts and see just exactly what should be included in each part.

The heading. This is positioned at the top of the first page—either centered or at the left-hand margin. In the heading you include (1) your full name, (2) your street address, (3) your city, state, and zip code, and (4) your telephone number with area code. If you have a home address *and* a school address, include both.

Statement of objectives. Name the kind of position you are seeking. If you are considering a variety of related positions, list them all. That way you can send the same résumé to several different companies. And the potential employer can consider you for several different openings. The statement of objectives should be brief. Someone applying for a job on a newspaper might write:

<u>OBJECTIVES:</u>   Newswriting, reporting, advertising production

Education. If you have just graduated, this section should follow the statement of objectives. If you are currently employed, this section should follow *Experience*. Here you list in reverse chronological order the schools you have attended (last school attended is listed first). Include (1) the name of the school, (2) the number of years you attended or the dates, (3) the year you graduated, (4) if college, the degree you received, (5) your major and minor fields, and (6) your grade-point average—if it was *B* or better. If you are currently employed, you should also list any additional courses and training programs that you may have completed.

Experience. This portion of your résumé is your career history. Here you list the jobs or positions you have held—once again in reverse chronological order. For each company at which you were employed, list the following information:

1. The company's name, location, and a brief description of the product or service.
2. The title of your last position.
3. Your major responsibilities.
4. Your achievements in the position—such as projects completed, production records broken, earnings for the company increased.

Related activities. These include school, civic, and personal activities that might interest an employer. Membership in social clubs or organizations should not be mentioned unless you have held an office or served on an active committee. Some related activities that you could mention are—

1. Membership in academic, professional, or business organizations.
2. Involvement in student government or community affairs.
3. Interest in social functions related to work, such as organizing a company softball team or a retirement dinner.

Other factors. This section is not required for all résumés. Here you could state if you would be willing to travel or to relocate. You could also state when you would be available to begin a new job and whether or not your present employer could be contacted for a reference.

What *not* to include in a résumé

Some information should not be included in a résumé. These are matters that will be obvious to an employer during the interview, or that can be more fully explained and discussed during an interview.

1. *Salary.* By giving a salary range, you might price yourself out of a job. Salary is something that should be discussed in person. Other benefits such as a pension plan, medical insurance, vacation plan, company car, or bonus system might make a lower salary acceptable.
2. *Age.* Your age can usually be determined by the year you finished school or by the date of your first job. Your age should not matter to an employer; therefore, do not call attention to it.
3. *Marital status and children.* This information is usually not necessary and may be brought up naturally during an interview. If you have been out of the job market because of maternity leave, you should explain that in a résumé.
4. *Handicaps.* If you are looking for a position that you *honestly* believe you can handle, you do not have to mention a handicap in a résumé.

Remember: Only put things in a résumé that will emphasize your strong points, that will favorably impress a potential employer, and that will get an interview for you.

Format of a résumé

You should word your résumé in a concise, straightforward, and positive manner. You do not have to use complete sentences, but be sure that your phrases are parallel in construction. Tell what *you* have accomplished, not what your *office* or *company* has achieved.

Explain what you are *willing* to do—travel, relocate, work overtime. You need not state, unless asked, what you will *not* do. If you do not want to travel, relocate, or work overtime, do not mention these things in your résumé. During the interview, you and the interviewer can discuss these matters.

There are many different formats you can use for a résumé. You should develop a format that you are comfortable with and that best shows your background and experiences. Here are a few things to keep in mind:

1. Your résumé should be typed and free of spelling and grammatical errors.
2. Leave sufficient space between sections of the résumé and between parts of a section so that the résumé can be read easily.
3. Use capital letters for handling titles, and use underlining to set off important parts of your résumé.
4. Have your résumé printed if you are sending out a great number of them.
5. Never send a carbon copy of your résumé. If you do not have printed résumés, send a freshly typed copy to each of your intended recipients.
6. Try to limit the length of your résumé to one or two pages.

Cover letters

A cover letter should be sent with each résumé. The cover letter may be the most important part of your entire package. Dozens and sometimes hundreds of résumés may be received by a personnel department every week. For the most part there is little to distinguish one résumé from another. All résumés are merely straightforward catalogs of a person's educational and employment history. Often résumés by themselves are given only brief attention.

This is where the cover letter takes on importance. Your cover letter should draw attention to your résumé. A concise and businesslike cover letter can make the difference between a résumé being glanced at and put aside, or a résumé being studied carefully and an interview arranged. Your résumé should describe what you are. Your cover letter should attempt to explain who you are.

There are three main kinds of cover letters. Each kind is related to a different, specific purpose.

Answer to a newspaper advertisement. Some newspaper advertisements are "blind" ads; that is, they do not include the name of the company or person who will receive the letter and résumé. You address these kinds of letters to a box number given in the advertisement.

Your inside address and salutation for a letter responding to a blind ad would look something like this:

Box 220
Chicago Tribune
435 North Michigan Avenue
Chicago, IL 60611

Gentlemen:

If a person's name, department name, or company name is given, address your letter accordingly. For example:

Mr. Robert Low	Personnel Department
XYZ Book Company	XYZ Book Company
2200 West Jackson	220 West Jackson
Chicago, IL 60621	Chicago, IL 60621
Dear Mr. Low:	Dear Sir or Madam:

Unsolicited letters. These letters are not sent in response to an advertisement. You send this kind of letter to a company that you are interested in and that you think might have a use for your talents.

You should address unsolicited letters by name and title to an individual, or at least to a department, that has the authority to hire you. Reference books such as *Dun & Bradstreet Million Dollar Directory* and *Moody's Industrial Manual* contain lists of the names, titles, and business addresses for many management-level people. Ask your librarian to help you find these books.

Letters to business associates. You might send letters and your résumé to business associates in your field or in related fields. In this kind of letter, you ask your business associates if they know of any openings in other companies, or if they can make any suggestions for your job search.

Format for cover letters

Each cover letter should contain the following three parts:

1. A paragraph that explains why you are sending the letter and résumé.
2. A paragraph or two briefly describing what qualifies you for the specific position. Even though you may be using the same résumé to apply for several different positions, you should not use the same cover letter with each application. Tailor each cover letter to fit a particular job.
3. A paragraph in which you politely request an interview.

Sample résumés and a sample cover letter follow. Refer to them and use them as *guides* as you develop your own cover letters and résumé.

Sample cover letter

123 Main Street
Wheaton, IL 60187
June 10, 1981

Box BX 305
Chicago Tribune
435 North Michigan Avenue
Chicago, IL 60611

Gentlemen:

Your June 8 advertisement in the <u>Chicago Tribune</u> described a
position for an editor of social studies textbooks and other
instructional materials. I do not plan to resume teaching
in the fall; therefore, I wish to be considered for this
position.

My background in history and in teaching social studies,
along with the various experiences that I have had in
editing and writing, convinces me that this is the kind of
interesting and challenging new career direction that I have
been searching for.

I have enclosed my résumé. I am available to interview for
the position at your convenience.

Sincerely yours,

Peter P. Mounds

Peter P. Mounds

Enclosure

Sample résumé

```
Peter P. Mounds
123 Main Street
Wheaton, IL  60187
312-691-5546


OBJECTIVES          Writer--educational materials
                    Editor--general materials


EXPERIENCE

September 1975-     John Adams Middle School, Winfield,
June 1981           Illinois.
                    Teacher.  Responsibilities included:
                    1. Preparing multilevel individual
                    learning packets for 6th, 7th, and 8th
                    grade social studies students.
                    2. Writing units for gifted 7th and 8th
                    grade reading students.

September 1969-     James Fowler Junior High School, Geneva,
June 1975           Illinois.
                    Teacher.  Responsibilities included:
                    1. Preparing units and lessons in
                    American history and U.S. government for
                    8th grade students.
                    2. Directed 8th grade students in
                    guidance and preparation for high school.

September 1967-     Northwestern University, Department of
May 1969            History, Evanston, Illinois.
                    1. Teaching four weekly history quiz
                    sections, correcting tests, and assigning
                    grades.
                    2. Aiding a professor in research, and
                    proofreading his papers and manuscripts.


EDUCATION

April-June 1978     University of Chicago, Extension
                    Division.
                    Completed course in manuscript editing.
```

Peter P. Mounds
Page 2

September 1967– May 1969	Northwestern University, Evanston, Illinois. M.A. in 1969. 3.8 GPA. Major: British history. Minors: American history and British literature.
September 1963– May 1967	Carleton College, Northfield, Minnesota. B.A. in 1967. 3.7 GPA. Major: History. Minors: Political science and secondary education.

RELATED ACTIVITIES

1970–present	Member of the Illinois Education Association.
	Member of the National Council for the Social Studies.
	Member of the Illinois Council for the Social Studies.
November 1979	Chaired committee that organized DuPage County regional meeting of the Illinois Council for the Social Studies.
April 1977	Participated in District 209 workshop on "Writing Proposals for Government-Funded Programs."
October 1976	Wrote "A Sample Suburban Middle School," which was published by District 209 as a workshop guide.
September 1963– May 1967	Editorial board member of Carleton College's literary magazine.

Sample résumé

Susan A. Fischer
783 Wagner Drive
Huntsville, TX   77340
713-886-3125

OBJECTIVE   Computer programmer

EDUCATION

September 1977–   Sam Houston State University, Huntsville,
June 1981   Texas.
                    B.S. in June, 1981.   3.2 GPA.   Major:
                    Computer science.
                    Significant courses: Introduction to
                    information systems design and management,
                    programming courses in FORTRAN and COBOL,
                    course in job control language.

EXPERIENCE

September 1980–   Sam Houston State University, Huntsville,
June 1981   Texas.
                    Part-time job as computer operator in
                    the university data center.

June–August 1980   Bergstrom Corporation, Huntsville, Texas.
                    Performing program maintenance on
                    personnel system.

ACTIVITIES

September 1980–   Served on Student-Faculty Committee for
June 1981   Academic Policies.

September 1979–   President of the Residence Hall Council.
June 1980

OTHER FACTORS   Available for employment July, 1981.
                    Willing to relocate.

Sample résumé

June, 1981

William C. Greene
1224 Lester Road
Franklin Park, IL 60131
312-633-4081

OBJECTIVES | To obtain a position as a medical
laboratory technician.
Also to obtain a B.S. degree in medical
laboratory technology.

EDUCATION

September 1979–
May 1981

Triton College, River Grove, Illinois.
Associate in Science degree in medical
laboratory technician, May, 1981.
Obtained clinical experience in
departments of clinical chemistry,
hematology, microbiology, blood banking,
and immunoserology at various area
hospitals as part of the degree program.

MILITARY EXPERIENCE

July 1976–
July 1979

Active duty in the United States Army.
Rank: Specialist 4.   Honorably discharged
July, 1979.
Served two years as a medic. Attended
92B Basic Medical Laboratory Technician
course (15 weeks) at Fort Sam Houston,
Texas, followed by 6 months on-the-job
training.

CERTIFICATION | Took NCA-CLT Examination in June, 1981;
results pending.
Will take ASCP Medical Laboratory
Technician Certification Examination in
August, 1981.

Use what you know

These activities have been designed to give you practice in using some of the suggestions and skills that were presented in this section. The answers to these activities can be found in the **Answer Key** that begins on page 270.

Match the audience to the message
Decide which person or group in column *B* should receive each kind of message described in column *A*. Match the letter in column *B* to the number in column *A*.

A	**B**
1. a newsy letter	a. librarians
2. an invitation to visit you	b. a lawn equipment
3. an annual report	manufacturer
4. a description of an old	c. stockholders
vase which you bought	d. your mother
5. a résumé	e. a close business associate
6. a complaint about a power	whose father died
mower	f. a friend who collects
7. a letter to sell encyclopedias	antiques
8. a sympathy letter	g. a personnel department
	h. a friend you want to see

Correcting form and content in a business letter
The writer of the following business letter intended that it be set up in block form. Each line of the letter has been numbered. Identify by line number any errors in form or content (such as format, wording, tone, order) and correct those errors on a separate piece of paper.

1. 281 N. Jackson
2. Milwaukee, WI
3. 6-10-81

4. Jack Jones
5. Consolidated Buyers
6. 2201 1st Street
7. New York City 20015

8. Dear Mr. Jones,

9. According to your last letter, I owe you $105.98 for a set
10. of lamps. Well, your bookkeeping department must keep
11. terrible records because I paid that bill two months ago.

12.   I am herewith notifying your company that I no longer care
13. to be a customer.

14. Enclosed find my cut up charge card.

15. Sincerely

Robert S Smith

16. Robert S. Smith

17.

Identifying the parts of a business report

A company is trying to determine whether or not it should provide more parking space for its employees. A committee has gathered information and drawn some conclusions about this problem. Now a report must be issued. But in which part of the report should each piece of information and each conclusion be placed? Organize a model report by matching each statement in column *A* with the part of a business report in which the statement should be placed. The parts of a business report are listed in column *B*.

A

1. All the facts point to the need for more employee parking space.
2. The members of this committee suggest that land north of the building be purchased for an employee parking lot.
3. More people are driving to work because there is no public transportation in this area.
4. A map showing the building and proposed site for the parking lot.
5. This report determines whether or not additional parking space is needed for employees. We conducted a poll among the employees and observed parking patterns for a week.
6. More parking space is needed for employees. The land directly north of the building should be purchased for a new parking lot.

B

a. introduction
b. summary
c. body
d. conclusions
e. recommendations
f. appendix

Writing a memorandum

Communicate the following information in memo form:

On January 1981, Mr. Roger F. Less decides to call a meeting of the sales managers. The meeting will be held on January 9, 1981, in the conference room at 10:30 A.M. Mr. Less wants the sales managers to bring their copies of the sales reports for the year 1980. The current sales training program will be evaluated in the light of the 1980 sales figures, and the possible need for a new training program will be discussed.

Constructing a résumé

Putting together an effective résumé requires thought and planning. This might be a good opportunity for you to practice writing a résumé. Develop a format that you can easily manage. Include the following kinds of information:

1. Your name, address, and telephone number.
2. A statement of objective or objectives.
3. Your career history.
4. Your educational background.
5. Related activities.
6. Other factors, if applicable.

5 Model letters for selected occasions

What do you do when you have a specific kind of letter to write—one to complain, or to make a request, or to send sympathy or congratulations? Do you wonder what to say and how to say it? Are you uncertain about how to start or end the letter? Do you grope for the right words and phrasing? Are you afraid that you will write more than is necessary, or forget something important? These are common problems for most people.

This section will help you solve some of these letter-writing problems. You will find samples of business and personal letters for various occasions and situations. You may use them as basic models for your own letters. This section explains the purpose of each type of letter. It gives advice for what to include and offers some suggestions for proper tone and wording.

How to use the model letters

The suggestions for writing various kinds of letters are divided
into two sections: business letters and personal letters. The
business letters are those that you would most likely write to
a company or institution. The personal letters included are the
kind that have one basic purpose—those that you write for
special occasions or circumstances. Long newsy, friendly letters
are not included, since the purpose and content of such letters
is purely a matter of individual choice.

First, take a quick look through the sections of business
letters and personal letters to become familiar with the types
of letters that are included. Then when you have a specific
letter to write—an inquiry, a complaint, or a thank-you—turn
to the suggestions for that kind of letter. Read about the
purpose of that type of letter. Read the suggestions for what
to include and how to word the letter.

Then find the model letter and read it. Notice how the tone
and ideas suit both the reader and the purpose of the letter.
(See "Plan before you write," pages 79–81.) Study the wording
and phrasing. What kinds of words were used? Did the letter
get straight to the point? Or did it build up slowly to the
main idea? How would you react to the letter if you received
it? Was the letter effective?

After you have studied the model, think about your own
letter. What is your specific purpose? What kind of person are
you addressing? What tone would be suitable for that reader
and the particular situation? Then look again at the
suggestions for what to include in the kind of letter you are
writing. Jot down those items you need to include for your
situation. Are there additional items you need to add to your
letter?

Once you have a list of what you need to say, you are
ready to begin writing. Use the model letter only as a guide or
a starting point—to get some ideas about the *kinds* of things
you might want to say. Do not copy the model letter. You
want your letter to suit *your* situation and to sound like *you*—
not like someone else.

Write in a natural manner. You already have your own
ways of wording things—your own writing style. Use words
and phrases that are part of your vocabulary. Adapt your
wording to the situation—choosing more formal language in
some cases, informal language in others. Organize your letter
in a logical order so it is easy to follow. And always be careful
to maintain an appropriate tone.

As you write more letters, you will learn to adapt your
writing style to different kinds of letter-writing situations.
And you will become more and more confident about writing
letters for both business and social occasions.

Kinds of business letters

Here are a few things to keep in mind when you write any business letter:

1. Try to type all of your business letters. Use business-sized paper (8½ x 11) and business-sized envelopes.
2. Use a proper business-letter format. Include all the necessary parts (heading, inside address, body, salutation, and closing) and place them properly on the page. (See pages 85–89 for proper format.)
3. Follow the rules for formal writing. Your language need not be overly stiff and formal. But you should avoid using slang or sounding too casual.
4. Be clear and precise. In business matters, it is especially important that there be no confusion or misunderstanding. Include all necessary information so your reader understands exactly what you want to communicate.
5. Make a carbon copy of each letter. Then you will have something to refer to when you receive a reply or if you need to write again.
6. Include a self-addressed, stamped envelope when you are requesting information from a company that is under no obligation to you. This is a courtesy, and it might also speed up the reply.

Order letters

The purpose of an order letter is to request a shipment of goods. You should include the following information in an order letter:

1. An exact description of the goods—name, size, color, style, model number, series.
2. The catalog number, if there is one.
3. The quantity you want.
4. The price.
5. The address to which the goods are to be shipped.
6. How you want the order shipped—express, freight, parcel post.
7. The method of payment—C.O.D., check, credit card, or money order.

An order letter should be brief, to the point, and courteous.

Order letter

346 Oak Street
Minneapolis, MN 55106
April 22, 1981

U.S. Committee for UNICEF
Greeting Cards
P.O. Box 5050
Grand Central Station
New York, NY   10161

Dear Sir or Madam:

Please send the following items to the above address:

```
  1 box, A Birthday Treat, #506BG @ $3.00               $3.00

  2 sets, World Card Game, #5060 @ $3.00                 6.00

  2 boxes, Spring Blossoms, Rose design, #52BR @ $3.00   6.00

  1 box, Spring Blossoms, Daisy print, #52BD @ $3.00     3.00
                                                       ───────

                                           Total   $18.00
```

Add the cost of postage and handling to send this order by
parcel post.

I would like these purchases charged to my Quick Charge
account, number 8888-523-0000, which expires November 1, 1983.

                              Sincerely yours,

                              Jane S. Paxton

                              Jane S. Paxton

Letters requesting information

The purpose of letters requesting information is to obtain a simple fact (such as a price) or to ask for a pamphlet, brochure, catalog, or form. These letters may be brief, because the information or material you are requesting is easy for the recipient to supply. You should do the following in a letter requesting information:

1. Identify yourself—for example, a student, a homeowner, an owner of a small business.
2. Tell exactly what you need.
3. Explain briefly why you need the information and how you intend to use it. (If your reasons are obvious, as in the model letter, you need not explain them.)
4. Express your appreciation.

Letters of inquiry

The purpose of letters of inquiry is to obtain detailed information. Because you are asking the recipient to spend some time researching and gathering information, a letter of inquiry is often longer and more detailed than a letter requesting a simple fact or a catalog. Letters of inquiry should be written in the following manner:

1. Identify yourself.
2. Explain why you are asking for the information and how you plan to use it.
3. Ask your questions. Be specific and thorough so that the recipient understands exactly what you need to know.
4. List and number your questions, if there are several.
5. If you need the information by a certain date, mention the date in the letter. But allow the recipient a reasonable amount of time to answer.
6. Express your appreciation.

Letters giving information

The purpose of this kind of letter is to provide information that someone else has requested. In a letter giving information you should—

1. Briefly identify yourself.
2. Give the information that was requested.

Letter requesting information

385 Creek Court
Middleton, OH 35011
May 19, 1981

Mr. George Duncan, Director
Office of Admissions
State University
Columbus, OH 35745

Dear Mr. Duncan:

I am a junior in high school and want to start college in
September 1982. I plan to major in business administration.

Would you please send me a copy of the university catalog,
information on financial aid and housing, and material about
your business administration program?

Thank you for your help.

Yours truly,

Margaret E. Rowe

Margaret E. Rowe

Letter of inquiry

632 Hanley Drive
Middleton, OH 35011
February 3, 1981

Director of Public Relations
Smith Electronics, Inc.
800 West Ridge Avenue
Cleveland, OH 35725

Dear Sir or Madam:

I am a junior at State University, majoring in business
administration. In the course Public Relations and
Business, I have been assigned to find out how businesses
create and maintain good will in the community.

Because your company is well known and respected in our
area, I am interested in knowing how your company has
established this relationship with the community. I would
appreciate information about the following:

1. Does a company representative participate in local high
   school or college career days?
2. Does the company participate in any other community
   programs or events?
3. Does your local advertising ever mention company
   activities that benefit the community?
4. Does your department provide public service information
   or news about company activities to local newspapers?

Please also let me know if it is acceptable to mention the
company by name in my report.

I know that providing this information will take some time.
I would, however, appreciate having it by February 20, so
that I can complete my assignment.

I appreciate whatever time and assistance you can give me in
this matter.

Yours truly,

Gordon Weatherspoon

Gordon Weatherspoon

Letter giving information

370 Willow Drive
River City, IL   60021
April 20, 1981

Mr. Michael Whitehead
Public Relations Department
Baxter Oil Company
240 South Michigan Avenue
Chicago, IL   60653

Dear Mr. Whitehead:

On April 18, 1981 you requested that I rate the service I
received on my car at the Baxter service station at 228 Main
Street, River City, Illinois.

Here is my rating of the service:

1. The appointment was set up easily and was kept on time.
2. The mechanics were courteous and efficient.
3. The cost seemed fair.
4. The repairs were completed to my satisfaction.

Sincerely yours,

Marjorie Kirk

Marjorie Kirk

Cover letters

The purpose of a cover letter is to introduce other material you are sending—such as forms, a check, or a package. A cover letter should—

1. Identify what is being sent.
2. Tell why it is being sent (unless the reason is obvious).
3. Tell whether the material is enclosed in the same envelope or is being sent in a separate package.

Complaint letters

The purpose of a complaint letter is to receive better service or to get a mistake corrected. Letters of complaint should be brief, calm, and courteous. Sarcasm, rudeness, and anger are never appropriate. If your letter shows that you are being reasonable, your complaint will more likely be taken as reasonable and legitimate.

The following information should be included in a letter of complaint regarding a product or service:

1. A detailed description of the product—model, serial number, part number.
2. The date of purchase, and whether or not it is still under warranty.
3. A copy of your purchase receipt, and copies of any receipts for service calls.
4. A brief explanation of the problem.

Claim letters

The purpose of claim letters is to receive payment for damages or losses. Include the following information in a claim letter:

1. Give your account number or policy number. This information is sometimes given in a *reference line*, which appears between the inside address and the salutation. (See the model letter.)
2. Describe the damage or loss: tell what happened, the date, the names of people involved, and the amount of loss or damage.
3. Include copies of bills, receipts, estimates, or other necessary documents.

Cover letter

385 Creek Court
Middleton, OH 35011
October 8, 1981

Mr. George Duncan, Director
Office of Admissions
State University
Columbus, OH 35745

Dear Mr. Duncan:

Thank you for sending me all the information I needed about
State University. I have now decided to apply for admission
to the university to begin in September 1982.

I have enclosed (1) my application form, (2) a check for my
application fee, and (3) my application for financial aid.

Please let me know if there is anything else I should send
to complete my application.

Yours truly,

Margaret E. Rowe

Margaret E. Rowe

Enclosures

Complaint letter

5800 Martin Drive
St. Louis, MO 63114
September 25, 1981

Mr. Jerome R. Drake, Manager
Service Department
Acme Music Company
711 South First Street
St. Louis, MO 63114

Dear Mr. Drake:

I purchased an Acme 3500 organ in January 1975. Until this
month, it performed beautifully. When I played it on
September 1, the repeat percussion key did not work. I
called your service department, and a repairman fixed the
repeat percussion key on September 7.

Yesterday (September 24) the repeat percussion key did not
work again. The terms of your 30-day warranty on parts and
service entitle me to have the repeat key replaced without
an additional charge for parts or labor.

When I called your service department yesterday, Judy Jones
told me that she could not find a copy of the service report
for the repairs done on September 7. She suggested that I
send you a copy of my receipt for the service call.

I have, therefore, enclosed a copy of my receipt and a copy
of my cancelled check for the work done on September 7.

Could you quickly take care of this problem for me?

Yours truly,

Edward L. Wright

Edward L. Wright

Enclosures

Claim letter

123 Main Street
Geneva, IL 60185
February 1, 1981

Mrs. Alice Owens
Claim Department
Safe Home Insurance Company
120 West Lake Street
Chicago, IL · 60642

Re: Policy number 7500-221-71

Dear Mrs. Owens:

On December 12, 1980, a water pipe burst in our bathroom.
The water damaged the wall and floor in the bathroom and the
wall and carpet in the adjoining bedroom.

Mr. George Johnson, the insurance adjuster for your company,
came to the house on December 13, 1980. He gave us an
estimate of $800.00 to repair the damage.

We have had the damage repaired, and the cost was $750.00.
I have enclosed a copy of Mr. Johnson's estimate and copies
of our receipts from the plumber, carpenter, and decorating
service.

Please send us a check for $750.00.

Sincerely yours,

Ellen James

Ellen James

Enclosures

**Letters
requesting action**

The purpose of a letter requesting action is obviously to get someone to do something. This kind of letter could be used to raise funds or to increase membership in an organization or to ask for participation in some activity. The letter requesting action should be written in the following way:

1. Make a brief introduction to get the reader on your side. You might suggest why the reader might want to do what you're asking. Or you could refer to something similar the person has done in the past.
2. State your request: tell *what* is wanted and *when* it is wanted.
3. Tell *how* the person can go about doing what you ask.
4. Express your appreciation.

Letters of refusal

The purpose of a letter of refusal is to say no in a polite and positive manner. A letter of refusal should contain the following:

1. A positive opening to soften the refusal.
2. Reasons for the refusal.
3. If you would have liked to say yes to the request but were simply unable to, you might offer to help in some other way or at some other time.

**Letters to the
editor**

A letter to the editor expresses your opinion about an issue or problem of public concern. It may express your agreement or disagreement with a statement made in the newspaper or magazine. Or it may point out a factual error made in the publication. Here are some things to keep in mind when writing a letter to the editor:

1. Know the facts of the issue, and state them clearly. This makes your point more convincing.
2. Especially if you are pointing out a factual error, state the source of your own information.
3. You might quote directly from their article to show exactly what statement you are responding to.
4. Be brief. A short letter is more likely to be published.
5. Your letter is also more likely to be published if the topic is of current interest.
6. It is all right to show some emotion, but try to back up your emotion with reasons. Never be rude or insulting, and offer any criticism in a constructive manner.
7. Always sign your letter. Newspapers and magazines will generally not publish letters that are unsigned.

Letter requesting action

2500 School Street
River City, IL 60021
March 14, 1981

Mr. James Gregory, President
Hilltop Manufacturing Company
280 Crest Road
River City, IL   60021

Dear Mr. Gregory:

You are a valued and respected member of River City's
business community. Your active participation in community
affairs has not gone unnoticed. And your generous
contributions to the Jones School P.T.A. have been greatly
appreciated.

Once again, the Jones School needs your help. Last year the
P.T.A. was able to buy an overhead projector for each
classroom. This year our goal is to raise enough money to
buy gymnastic equipment.

Would you please fill in the enclosed form and let us know
how much you can contribute? Use the enclosed self-
addressed, stamped envelope to return the form. We would
appreciate your response by March 28, 1981.

The many budding gymnasts at the Jones School are counting
on you.

Very truly yours,

Mark Anderson

Mark Anderson
President
Jones School P.T.A.

Enclosures

Letter of refusal

370 Willow Drive
River City, IL 60021
September 15, 1981

Mr. Mark Anderson, President
Jones School P.T.A.
2500 School Street
River City, IL 60021

Dear Mr. Anderson:

I always enjoyed serving on the fund-raising committee of
the Jones School P.T.A. The members were hard workers, and
we succeeded in raising funds for many worthwhile school
projects.

In July, I started working full time. Since I can no longer
attend the afternoon meetings, I will not be able to serve
on the committee this year.

I will be happy to help in some other way, such as running a
booth at the Weekend Winter Carnival. And I will continue
to attend the P.T.A. meetings that are held in the evening.

Sincerely yours,

Marjorie Kirk

Marjorie Kirk

Letter to the editor

123 Main Street
River City, IL   60021
May 15, 1981

To the Editor
River City Journal
200 River Road
River City, IL   60021

Dear Sir or Madam:

The information in "Sewage Rate Hike Imminent," May 14
<u>Journal</u>, filled me with outrage. Why should the sewage rate
be linked to water usage? Much of the water is used for
outdoor pools and for watering lawns. This water never goes
into the sewer system.

If the sewage system has not been properly maintained, the
utility company--not its customers--should pay for the
improvements. I think there should be public hearings on
this matter so that solutions--other than a rate increase--
can be presented.

Sincerely yours,

John P. Citizen

John P. Citizen

Kinds of personal letters

Personal letters and notes are usually written by hand; this is always proper, and in some cases preferable. While you may have formal invitations printed, handwriting them is equally proper. Some people choose to type their casual, newsy letters to friends. But thank-you notes and letters of condolence should always be handwritten, since the personal touch is very important when expressing your feelings of gratitude or sympathy.

Your personal letters and notes are just that—personal and very individual. What you say and how you say it depend a great deal on the situation and the person to whom you are writing. This section offers some general suggestions for the personal letters you would write for a few specific occasions. Begin with these suggestions, and then add to or modify them to suit the situation in which you are writing.

Formal invitations and replies

Whether written by hand or printed, a formal invitation for a wedding or party should follow a set form. All formal invitations should include the following information:

1. The names of the people extending the invitation.
2. The type of occasion: wedding, dinner, open house, anniversary party.
3. The date, time, and place of the event.
4. A request to respond. (*R.S.V.P.* is the abbreviation for the French phrase *répondez s'il vous plait,* which means "please respond.")

A formal invitation requires a formal reply. You should always reply immediately to an invitation so that the host and hostess know how many people to expect. Whether you are accepting the invitation or sending your regrets, you should follow a set format. A formal reply should include—

1. Your name(s).
2. Whether you accept or regret that you are unable to accept the invitation.
3. The names of the people extending the invitation.
4. The occasion and the date.

Formal wedding invitation

Mary and Henry Smith
invite you to witness
the marriage of their daughter
Jane Ellen

to

Robert Brown
on Saturday, the seventh of June
nineteen hundred and eighty-one
at three o'clock in the afternoon
Emmanuel Lutheran Church
Glen Ellyn, Illinois

and afterward at
The Glen Ellyn Manor
R.S.V.P.

Formal dinner invitation

Mr. and Mrs. Paul Kirk
request the pleasure of your company
at dinner
on Thursday, the twelfth of June
at eight o'clock
370 Willow Drive
River City, Illinois

R.S.V.P.

Formal reply—accepting

Mr. and Mrs. Robert White
accept with pleasure
the kind invitation of Mary and Henry Smith
to attend the wedding
of their daughter and Robert Brown
and the reception at the Glen Ellyn Manor
on Saturday, the seventh of June

Formal reply—regrets

> *Ms. Ellen Wright*
> *regrets*
> *that she will be unable to accept*
> *Mr. and Mrs. Paul Kirk's*
> *kind invitation to dinner*
> *for Thursday, the twelfth of June*

Informal invitations and replies

Informal invitations may be sent for parties, visits, dinners, and luncheons. They follow the same format that you use for personal letters (see pages 81–84). They should be handwritten and brief. You include the same basic information about the occasion, date, time, and place that you would in a formal invitation. But you need not follow a set form; simply state the information in sentences as you wish.

You should reply to an informal invitation just as quickly as you would to a formal invitation. An informal reply allows you to add your own comments, if you like, or to explain why you cannot accept an invitation.

Informal invitation

123 Main Street
Geneva, IL 60185
May 15, 1981

Dear Jane,

Your summer break from classes should be starting soon. Will you be able to visit us during the first week in June? If you can come, I would like to have a luncheon for you with some of the old gang on Saturday, June 7.

Let me know when you will be arriving so that I can meet your plane.

Love,
Ellen

Informal reply—accepting

280 West Layton Road
Minneapolis, MN 55106
May 19, 1981

Dear Ellen,

Yes, my summer break starts May 28, and I
would love to visit you the following week. Your
plans for lunch with the gang sound great.
It should be fun to find out what Mary
and Jill have been up to.

I have made reservations for Trans America's
flight 209 that arrives at O'Hare at 5:30 P.M.
on Tuesday, June 3. My return flight is on
Sunday, June 8, at 4:30 P.M.

I look forward to seeing you soon.

Love,
Jane

Informal invitation

123 Main Street
Geneva, IL 60185
May 23, 1981

Dear Jill,

Jane Hayes is staying with me June 3-8.
I thought it might be fun if we all got
together for lunch. Could you come to my
home in Geneva for lunch on Saturday,
June 7, at 1:00 P.M.?

Sincerely,
Ellen

Informal reply—regrets

6501 North Ridgewood
Chicago, IL 60622
May 28, 1981

Dear Ellen,

Thank you for the invitation to lunch! I will
not be able to make it, however, because my
family and I are leaving for Canada that
morning.

Tell Jane that I would have liked visiting
with her. Hope you all have a good time. I'll
call you when I get back from Canada, since
I'm eager to hear how everyone is doing.

Affectionately,
Jill

Thank-you notes   A thank-you note should always be sent to acknowledge wedding, shower, and baby gifts—and any other gifts that are sent through the mail. They should also be sent after a weekend or a longer stay at someone's home. Thank-yous should be written soon after you receive a gift or have returned home from your visit.

Letters of condolence   These letters are sent to comfort someone after the death of a spouse, parent, or child. They are, of course, one of the most difficult kinds of letters to write. What you say and how you say it may vary a great deal—depending on your own feelings and your relationship with the person to whom you are writing. Write these letters carefully, using your own judgment about what is appropriate for that person and the particular situation. Because they are so personal, letters of condolence should always be handwritten.

Letters of condolence should usually be brief and should not dwell on your own sorrow. If you think it's appropriate, you might mention some special remembrance you have about the person who died. If you are writing to someone you know well, you might offer your help in some way. Whatever you decide to say, always keep in mind the feelings of the person to whom you are writing.

School excuses   The purpose of an excuse for school is to let your child's teacher know why your child was late or absent. Send the note to the proper person at the school—teacher, nurse, or attendance clerk. Be sure to use your child's last name (especially if it is different from your own).

Letters of apology   A letter of apology might be sent when a matter of a serious nature has occurred between you and a friend or a neighbor. You should make a carbon copy of any letter in which you offer to pay for or replace damaged property.

Thank-you notes

280 Layton Road
Minneapolis, MN 55106
June 10, 1981

Dear Ellen,

You always plan such great activities for my visits. I really enjoyed antiquing in Geneva and shopping at Water Tower Place in Chicago. The lunch with Mary and Joan, of course, was the high point. It did not seem as if it had been five years since we had all been together.

The pleasant memories of our visit will last until next year when I hope you will be able to come to Minneapolis.

Love,
Jane

123 Main Street
Geneva, IL 60185
June 20, 1981

Dear Aunt Mary and Uncle Jim,

How did you know I needed a travel kit? Thank you for a very thoughtful and useful gift. It's big enough to hold all I need and still fit into my suitcase. I'll use it a lot during the next four years when I'm away at college.

Love,
John

Letter of condolence

123 Main Street
Geneva, IL 60185
August 8, 1981

Dear Jack,

Louise's death has saddened all of us. She was such a good friend to me and my family. I know that you must be taking great comfort in your three children. I will be glad to baby-sit with the children anytime or help you get the children ready for school next month.

Sincerely,
Ellen James

School excuse

850 South Maple Avenue
River City, IL 60021
May 9, 1981

Dear Mr. Martin,

Please excuse Mary Smith's absence from school on May 6-8. She had oral surgery and needed a few days to recover. Let her know what assignments she should make up.

Sincerely,
Janet Smith

Letter of apology

> 850 South Maple Avenue
> River City, IL 60021
> June 11, 1981

Dear Dorothy and Tom,

Joe and I are so sorry to hear about the damage that our dog Scruffy has done to your flower garden. We know how much work you have put into your garden and how much pride you take in it.

We have talked to Jack Binney at the River City Nursery about replacing the plants that were destroyed. Mr. Binney should call you in a day or two to find out what plants have to be replaced. The River City Nursery will deliver and plant the new flowers at our expense.

You will be glad to know that we are building a run for Scruffy between the house and the garage. It should be completed by next weekend.

> Sincerely,
> Joe and Janet Smith

Use what you know

These activities have been designed to help you improve your letter-writing skills.

A checklist for writing letters

Before you write your next letter—business or personal—go through the checklist that follows. You might also wish to review some of the information in 4, "Tips about everyday writing."

	Yes	No
1. Do you know exactly to whom you should address your letter?	_____	_____
2. Do you have a clear idea of the purpose of your letter?	_____	_____
3. Do you have all the information that will be necessary to convey your message?	_____	_____
4. Are you in the right mood to write the letter so that your letter will have an appropriate tone?	_____	_____
5. Do you know the correct format for your letter and its envelope?	_____	_____
6. Should you type your letter or write it by hand?	_____	_____

Analyzing letters

The best way to improve your letter-writing skills is to write letters. Another way to improve them is to study the letters you receive. Look at the business letters that you receive—such as those asking you to buy a product, to support an organization or cause, or to contribute to a charity. Also examine letters that provide information—such as explaining a new policy at the bank or a new village ordinance. Most of these letters have been written very carefully. Study these letters, and ask yourself the following questions:

1. Did the letter arouse my interest? How?
2. Did the letter present the information clearly?
3. Did the letter cause me to do anything? What?
4. What made the letter effective—the wording? the tone? the arrangement of ideas?

Remember what you appreciate in the business letters you receive and then use those techniques in your own letters.

Also reread some of the personal letters, notes, and invitations that you have received recently. Whose letters do you look forward to receiving? Why do you enjoy reading them? Once again, try to write the kinds of letters that you enjoy receiving.

6   Writing tips for school situations

Are you able to transfer your thoughts, ideas, and opinions onto paper in a clear, concise way? Do you know how to research and organize information for your reports and papers? Do you know how to prepare successfully for written tests? All of these skills are necessary for you to succeed in school.

This section reviews the basic procedures for effective writing. Then it shows how to apply these basic procedures to researching and writing a short report and a term paper. And it offers some guidelines for taking written tests.

Organizing for effective writing

In all kinds of schooling, at all levels, you are asked to complete many different kinds of writing assignments. Some writing assignments are based on your own ideas, opinions, experiences, and imagination—such as essays, themes, and stories. Other writing assignments are based on reading and research—such as book reports, short reports, and term papers.

No matter what kind of writing assignment you receive, you—the writer—must have a plan to achieve a finished piece of writing. In this section, you will be given some guidelines for organizing an effective piece of writing. These guidelines for choosing, analyzing, researching, and outlining a topic are necessary steps for most kinds of writing. Although some of the guidelines apply specifically to writing based on research, the suggestions given will help you to organize any kind of writing assignment more effectively.

For most writing assignments you are asked to choose a topic. Your instructor might give you a list from which to choose. Or you might be asked to choose a topic that relates to the material you are studying in class. Choosing a topic wisely is one of the more important steps in writing.

Choosing a topic

How then do you choose a topic? Your topic should be something that interests you, something that you want to know more about, or something that you know well and want to inform others about. If you're not interested in your topic, it will be difficult to make the topic interesting to your readers. Your best papers will come when you have a genuine interest in your topic and believe that it is important enough to learn more about or to inform others about.

Consider the time factor. When you are choosing your topic, you must also consider how much time you have before your paper is due. The amount of time will determine how much research you will be able to do. You might have two days to write a theme or an essay; two weeks to read a book and write a report on it. A short report of 300 to 500 words could have a three-week deadline. And you might have as much as a whole quarter or semester in which to prepare a term paper.

The topic you choose should be appropriate for the amount of time you have for reading, researching, and writing. If your time is short, don't choose a topic that is too broad or that is too complex to learn about in a short time. Save the broader topics, and topics you know nothing about, for longer assignments when you have more time for researching and writing.

Consider available materials. It is also important to know the kinds and amount of reference materials that are available on your topic. When you have decided on a general topic, go to the library and find out if there is enough information readily available for your research. The fastest way to do this is to check both the card catalog and the most recent issues of the *Readers' Guide to Periodical Literature.*

The card catalog contains cards for all the books that your library has. For each book, cards are entered under the subject, the title, and the author's name. All these cards are arranged alphabetically. If you were writing a paper about ecology, you would look in the card catalog under "Ecology." The sample cards from the card catalog show the kinds of information such cards contain. Look carefully at the subject card, since this is the kind of card you will look for first when seeking available material on your topic.

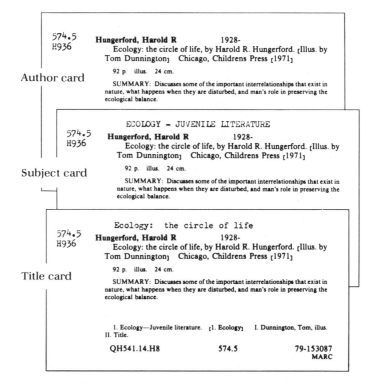

The *Readers' Guide* helps you find information about available articles in magazines and journals. It is arranged alphabetically by author, subject, and sometimes by title for plays and books. Look at the sample *Readers' Guide* entry to see the kinds of information such entries include.

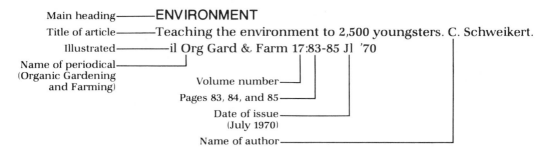

Main heading———————ENVIRONMENT
Title of article————————Teaching the environment to 2,500 youngsters. C. Schweikert.
Illustrated————————il Org Gard & Farm 17:83-85 Jl '70
Name of periodical
(Organic Gardening
and Farming)
Volume number
Pages 83, 84, and 85
Date of issue
(July 1970)
Name of author

When you have decided that there is enough material available in your area of general interest, it is then time to limit your topic. You must decide whether your topic is too broad or too narrow. Establishing suitable limits for your topic is a crucial step in organizing an effective paper. You should remember that you want to focus on one main idea or event. Any information that you use should be related to that one idea or event.

Limiting your topic

Let's look at some possible general topics and some ways to limit them. In an American history class you might be studying the Constitution; in biology, systems of the human body; and in English, the drama. You first might choose broad topics, such as "The Constitutional Convention," "The Circulatory System," or "Shakespeare's Comedies." After looking through the card catalog and the *Readers' Guide,* you would realize that these topics are too broad. If your topic is a main heading in these guides, your topic is probably too broad for one paper.

For a workable paper, those topics must be narrowed down. The following are examples of more limited topics:

Compromises Made in the Constitutional Convention
The Function of White Blood Cells
The Purpose of Disguise in *The Merchant of Venice*

These topics could be limited even further; you could, for example, write about only *one* of the compromises made in the Constitutional Convention. How much you limit your topic depends on the length of your paper. The shorter your paper, the more you need to limit your topic.

But in any length paper, the more specific your topic is, the better your paper will probably be. A mistake students frequently make is to choose a subject that is too large to cover thoroughly. A paper that presents detailed ideas on a smaller topic is almost always preferable to a paper that presents only general ideas on a larger topic. If you are unsure whether you have limited your topic appropriately, you might ask your instructor if the topic is narrow enough (or broad enough) for the paper assigned.

Now that you have chosen a topic, determined if you have enough time and materials available for your research, and limited your topic accordingly, you are ready for the next step.

Analyzing a topic

In this step of the writing process, you should do some background reading and make a preliminary outline. Your preliminary outline might simply be a list of ideas that you might include in your paper. Or your preliminary outline could be done in the form of a series of questions about your topic.

If you are doing background reading for a book report, look through the table of contents, read the preface or introduction, and find out something about the author. Then, ask yourself some questions and write them down. Leave enough space so that you can jot down answers or notes as you read. For a book report, you might start with questions like these: Who are the main characters? What are their relations to one another? What is the main plot or story that the author is telling? How does the setting influence the characters or the mood of the story? What message is the author getting across? Along with these general questions, jot down any other specific questions you might have about the book.

If you are doing a short report or term paper, you should do background reading to become generally familiar with the topic. Encyclopedia articles dealing with your topic would be good sources for background reading. Getting a general idea of what the topic is all about should help you decide what parts of the topic you will include in your paper—and what parts you'll leave out. After you've finished your background reading, ask yourself some questions that you hope to answer in your paper. If your topic is "Compromises Made in the Constitutional Convention," you might ask yourself questions like this: What were the compromises? Why were compromises necessary? Who were the leaders in the debates? How were the compromises reached? Use such questions to guide you in your research. You will probably be able to use these questions later when you prepare the actual outline of your paper.

Researching a topic

Research is a two-step process consisting of locating information and reading and taking notes.

Locating information. First, you must locate the sources for your research. You probably found some sources when you were deciding whether or not there are enough reference materials available on your topic. Now you must gather together all the books and articles that you think will aid you in researching your topic.

You should make a bibliography card for each source. (Look back to the section on preparing bibliographic entries in 2, "Rules of style," if you have forgotten what information to include on a bibliography card.) By making a complete bibliography card for each source at this point, you will avoid a lot of trouble when it is time to prepare the bibliography for your paper. A bibliography is required for most papers that require research.

Besides the card catalog and *Readers' Guide,* there are other places in which to find information. The *New York Times Index* and *Facts on File* are sources of information on current events. Materials that are hard to store on a shelf are found in the vertical file. The *vertical file* is a set of file cabinets in which pamphlets, pictures, and maps are filed alphabetically by subject. Other sources of information might be personal interviews and radio or television programs. No matter where you get your information, be sure to make a bibliography card for each source.

Reading and taking notes. Now that you have gathered your sources, you should begin reading and taking notes. The single-note system works best. In the *single-note system,* you write only one idea or quotation per note card. In that way, your note system remains flexible. You can rearrange your notes as you develop a logical order for your topic.

Your note cards should be different in size or color from your bibliography cards. By doing that, you can easily keep your two sets of information—bibliography and notes— separate.

What information should your note cards contain?

1. *A heading.* A heading briefly identifies the material on the note card. It should be placed at the top of the note card. The heading might be an idea listed in your preliminary outline (and might later become a main heading or a subheading in the actual outline) of your paper.
2. *The source.* Below the heading you should record the author's last name, a shortened form of the source's title, and the page number in the source where the material was found. This makes it possible to recheck your information quickly, if necessary. It also makes it easy for you to write your footnotes, if you quoted or paraphrased the author.
3. *The body of the note.* There is no one way to write a note. The note could be a few words, a summary, or a direct quotation. But your note should be written clearly and legibly, and it should be exact and complete. It's a good

idea to write the note in your own words. Don't copy word for word from your source, unless you want to use a direct quotation. Use direct quotations only if they are significant or if they support your position. Be sure to put quotation marks around any direct quotations so that you remember to give the author credit for the quote.

Look at the sample note card for a paper on the British parliament to see how a note card should be set up.

Sample note card

Heading ——————

Source ——————

Body of note ——————

> The power of the House of Lords
>
> Bagehot, *The English Constitution,* p. 141.
> Although the House of Lords was always respected, it never was as important as the House of Commons.

Outlining a topic   After you have finished taking notes but before you write the first draft, you should make an outline. An outline will help you organize your notes and thus make it easier for you to write the first draft. You will not be required to submit an outline with every writing assignment. But you should make at least a working outline for your own use—as a guide for writing your first draft.

Take the preliminary outline that you prepared and all your note cards. Lay them out on a large desk or table. Arrange the note cards according to the headings. Once you have your note cards arranged under the headings, then decide what topics belong together under main headings. Organize your cards under main headings and subheadings. If you are writing about the compromises made in the Constitutional Convention, for example, your notes might indicate that these should be your main headings:

The three-fifths compromise
Trade compromises
The Great Compromise

Now decide on a logical order in which to present your information. Put the main headings in order and number each one with a roman numeral.

  I. The Great Compromise
 II. The three-fifths compromise
III. Compromises about trade

Your note cards will also help you determine the subheadings for your outline. The subheadings go below the main headings and begin with a capital letter.

  I. The Great Compromise
     A. Created a Congress of two houses
     B. Pleased both large and small states

You may or may not have subheadings under the other main headings. But never have just one subheading under a main heading. If, for example, you had "No taxes on exports" as the only subheading under "Compromises about trade," you should change the main heading to read:

III. Compromise about trade

or:

III. Trade compromise: no taxes on exports

A topic outline. The kind of outline about which you have just been reading is called a *topic outline.* A topic outline is perhaps the easiest kind of outline to prepare. It consists of brief phrases or short clauses for all the headings. The first word of each main heading and subheading is capitalized. But periods are not used after the phrases and clauses.

All headings in a topic outline must have parallel construction. That is, all main headings must be similar in form. If you used parallel construction, the main headings for the outline on "Compromises Made in the Constitutional Convention" would look like this:

  I. The Great Compromise
 II. The three-fifths compromise
III. The trade compromises

All subheadings under one main heading must be similar in form, also.

  I. The Great Compromise
     A. Created a Congress made up of two houses
     B. Pleased both large and small states

A sentence outline. In a *sentence outline,* each heading is a complete sentence. This kind of outline takes more time to write, but it does have some advantages.

1. You are forced to state your thoughts clearly and completely.
2. You can usually transfer the sentences from your outline directly to your first draft.
3. You can use the main headings (and some subheadings) as topic sentences for the various parts of your paper.

Like the topic outline, the sentence outline is divided into main headings *(I, II, III)* and subheadings *(A, B, C).* The following is an example of a sentence outline. This outline is also divided into sub-subheadings *(1, 2, 3).*

WHY STUDENTS SHOULD HAVE A JOB AFTER SCHOOL

I. A job provides students with a way to earn money.
  A. Some students need extra money to pay for clothes, hobbies, and car expenses.
  B. Some students use their earnings for high school or college tuition.

II. A job gives students more responsibility.
  A. Students must budget their time for school, work, and leisure.
  B. Students learn to fulfill certain duties on the job.
    1. They must arrive at work on time.
    2. They must follow the directions of a supervisor.
    3. They must carry out certain procedures in doing their jobs.

III. A job after school helps students prepare themselves for a long-term job or career.
  A. By trying a variety of after-school jobs, students can discover what kind of work they like best.
  B. Through contact with adults at work, students find out what training or education is needed for certain jobs.

Outlining a theme or an essay. Up to this point, you have been given examples of outlining for a research-related paper. Outlining is also helpful before you write the first draft of a theme or an essay. It will help you sort out your thoughts and ideas so that you can arrange them in logical order. A good outline will make your final paper more interesting and easier to read. The following is an example of a topic outline for an essay.

WHY I LIKE SPORTS

I. A way to improve my health
   A. By exercising indoors
      1. Weight training
      2. Swimming
   B. By being outdoors in the fresh air
      1. Jogging
      2. Bicycling

II. A form of competition
   A. As an individual
      1. Tennis
      2. Golf
      3. Handball
   B. As a member of a team
      1. Softball
      2. Basketball
      3. Soccer

III. A way to relax
   A. Going to a sports event
   B. Watching a sports event on television

Writing a short report

During a school year, you will usually write several short reports for various courses you take. A short report presents ideas on one particular subject, based on research from one or more sources. Your job in a short report is to clearly present the information from the sources. You should write the report in your own words. And you should make the report interesting and informative for your reader.

A short report is usually between 300 and 500 words long and runs from 1½ to 3 typewritten pages. Your instructor will usually tell you how long the report should be. If you're to write a 400-word report, don't count the words as you are writing. Cover the topic thoroughly, and don't worry if you are a little over or under the 400 words. Your instructor is not going to count them. Do not, however, turn in a one-page or a twenty-page report when you were assigned 400 words.

If you have not read "Organizing for effective writing" (pages 153–161), you should do so now. That section gives you suggestions for choosing, analyzing, researching, and outlining a topic. After you have completed the steps explained in that section, you are ready to move on to the next steps described in this section. Here you will find out how to plan the actual writing of a short report. You have chosen a topic, done your

Planning a short report

research, taken useful notes, and written an outline. Now you are ready to plan the writing of your report.

Keep your reader in mind. The reader is usually your teacher. But sometimes reports are read aloud, or distributed to all members of the class, as the basis for class discussion. Decide how you will keep the reader's attention. Give clear, complete descriptions and brief summaries to help the reader understand your ideas.

You must convince the reader that the statements in your report are accurate. Be sure that you have enough facts to back up the main points in your outline.

Keep your purpose in mind. There are two kinds of short reports: summary reports and critical reports. Each has a different purpose. In a *summary report* you present the information you have found. You do not make any judgments about the information or give your opinions. Say, for example, that you have been assigned to write a summary report on the boycott of the 1980 summer Olympics. In such a report you could (1) tell what events led up to the boycott; (2) compare and contrast the views that various groups of people had about the boycott; or (3) explain why other countries joined the boycott.

In a *critical report,* you are called upon to evaluate what you have read. You take a position, make judgments, and justify your ideas. This time, for example, you have been assigned to write a critical report about the boycott of the Olympic games. You could (1) evaluate the effect the boycott had on foreign relations; (2) judge whether or not the boycott was an adequate or appropriate response; or (3) justify the boycott.

Your instructor will usually tell you to write either a summary report or a critical report. If the choice is left to you, the material itself might suggest which kind of report you might write. Material that lends itself to being listed or put into categories might be presented in a summary report. Material that you strongly agree with—or strongly disagree with—could be given in a critical report.

Write a thesis sentence. What does all the information you have gathered seem to say? What does it all relate to? In other words, what main idea has your research uncovered? Decide what your main idea is and summarize it. This statement of your main idea is your *thesis sentence.* It should be placed near the beginning of the report. It will help both you and your reader focus on the main thought and message of your report. As you write the report, make sure that everything in it relates to the thesis sentence.

Here are some examples of possible thesis sentences for a report about the Olympic boycott:

> The decision to boycott the 1980 Olympics in Moscow received a mixed reaction from the American people.
>
> The boycott of the 1980 Olympics changed the careers of many American athletes.
>
> Many Third World nations supported the boycott of the 1980 summer Olympics.

After you have written your thesis sentence, be sure you have enough facts to support the statement. You must use facts, examples, and details to convince your reader that your thesis sentence is true and accurate.

Check your outline. Now that you have written a thesis sentence, you should reread your outline. Your thesis sentence might indicate that you should emphasize some ideas and delete others. Perhaps you should organize your material differently. If that is the case, revise your outline. Remember: the outline is a writing tool. You don't have to stay with the original outline. Change it to meet the needs of your report. The following example shows how the title and outline for a report were changed.

The Olympic Boycott and United States Foreign Policy
  I. With the Soviet Union
 II. With its allies
III. With the Third World

The Olympic Boycott Affected Relations with the Soviet Union
  I. An end to detente
 II. A stall on the SALT treaty
III. A slowdown in trade

Writing the first draft

Put all your sources away; don't be tempted to look at them while you are writing. If you do, you might start to copy from them. Rely on your notes instead. Your report is supposed to show what you think, or what you have found, in your own words.

Now you are ready to write the first draft of your report. Put your outline in front of you, and keep your notes close by for reference. Use wide-lined paper; it will make revising easier. And leave wide margins so that you can make notes to yourself in the margins as you write.

Start writing! When writing the first draft, don't worry about mistakes in spelling, grammar, or sentence and paragraph structure. Put question marks or notes in the margins if you are unsure of a spelling or think you've made some other error. You will correct these errors in the revision stage.

In the first-draft stage, you want to get all your thoughts and ideas down on paper. Use your outline as a guide. Refer to your note cards when you need more examples to support a major point. Be sure to use footnotes if you use a direct quotation or someone else's opinion or idea. (See 2, "Rules of style," for advice on preparing footnotes.)

Put your thesis sentence in the first paragraph. Then get the reader on your side with convincing evidence and arguments. State your ideas clearly. Bring all the facts, examples, and details together. Define and describe your ideas. Make comparisons and contrasts between ideas when appropriate.

You want the reader on your side, but you don't want to write only what the reader wants to hear. Your job is to inform or to persuade your reader. Therefore, be straightforward and honest in your writing.

Revising the first draft

Try to plan the writing of your report so that you have a day between writing the first draft and revising it. The literal meaning of *revise* is "to look again." You should put some time and distance between the first draft and this second look. By doing that, you will see your writing with a fresh eye. It will be easier to see if you actually said what you meant to say—and if you said it clearly and correctly.

Mechanics of revising. When you revise your report, use a colored pencil or a different color of ink. Make your corrections right in the copy. If there are big corrections—a sentence that should be added—put them in the margin. Use an arrow to show where they belong in the report. That way, when you write your final copy, you won't forget these corrections and additions.

Reread your report. First, read the thesis sentence. Then go through your report and take out all the parts that do not relate to the thesis sentence. Circle those parts rather than crossing them out. You might be able to rephrase them so they fit with the thesis sentence. If an idea relates to the thesis sentence but doesn't seem to fit in its paragraph, see if it belongs in a different part of the report.

Emphasize major points. Be sure that you have emphasized the major points of your report. Treat each major point in a separate paragraph. Provide the facts and evidence to support your major points. You can't make statements without backing them up. The following statements could not stand alone in a report:

> The oil shortage is a myth.
> A draft during peacetime is illegal.
> The decision to boycott the 1980 summer Olympics unified the American people.

The first statement needs support from facts and figures. The second statement would require mentioning specific laws or the opinions of legal experts. And the third statement would have to be backed up by the results of public opinion polls and interviews.

Improve weak points. Clear up any parts of the report that seem unclear or that could be confusing to your reader. Here are a few suggestions for clearing up confusion:

1. Reword the sentence.
2. Rearrange the sentences in the paragraph if a different order would be clearer.
3. Give a more complete explanation by adding related details.

Add description to parts of the report that seem uninteresting but are important to your thesis. You don't want to lose your reader. The following paragraph isn't very exciting:

> Many people wrote to the President. Some of them felt that the United States should not send a team to the Olympics. Others believed that athletics and politics should not be mixed.

By adding some detail and descriptive phrasing, the paragraph takes on new life:

> Thousands of people flooded President Carter's office with letters. Many of the people strongly agreed with the President and said that the United States definitely should not participate in the 1980 summer Olympics. Another vocal group, however, strongly felt that the President and Congress had no business mixing politics with athletics.

Maintain coherence. *Cohere* means "to stick together." Make sure that the parts of your paragraph "stick together." The material in each paragraph should be related to one idea. The main point of the paragraph should be stated in the topic sentence. The topic sentence can be placed at the beginning or the end of the paragraph. But all the other sentences in the paragraph must relate to, develop, and support the topic sentence. If they don't, those sentences should be left out.

Also check to make sure that the paragraphs "stick" to each other. Are they presented in a logical order? Does one paragraph flow into the next? In other words, have you provided transition words to take your reader from one idea to the next? *Transition words* show the relationships or connections between ideas. Some common transition words are *therefore, thus, nevertheless, however, on the other hand, in contrast, first, second, next.*

And "stick" to the main subject. Don't get sidetracked by interesting but unrelated material. But keep in mind the material that sidetracked you; it could be used in another report.

Check for weakness in writing style. At this point of the revision process, you delete any unnecessary words or phrases—words and phrases that add clutter but not meaning to your report. Some words and phrases that you can eliminate are any unnecessary *who's, which's, that's* and phrases like *in order that, in order to,* and *want to be able to.*

Also correct any faults in sentence structure. Make sure every sentence is a complete sentence. If you have many short, choppy sentences, you can occasionally combine the ideas of two sentences into one sentence. If some sentences seem too long, you can break some of them into shorter sentences.

Check your word choices. Avoid repeating the same word or using words with the same root word. For example, "The information informed us . . ." should be changed to "The facts in the report informed us . . ." or "The information explained that . . ." And refer to the "Word finder thesaurus" for different words that express the same idea; this will help you use a variety of words in your writing.

Correct grammatical errors. You may have already corrected major grammatical errors as you were revising for ideas and writing style. After you have completed those other parts of the revision process, however, it's important to read through the report once more to catch the "little" mistakes. These are errors in spelling, punctuation, capitalization, and word usage. Keep a dictionary at your side. And refer to sections 1, 2, and 3 of this volume if you need to review any of the basic rules for writing.

Check your verb tenses and point of view. Generally you should stay primarily with one verb tense in a paper. Some reports are written primarily in the past tense, particularly when relating past events. But some are written primarily in the present tense. And use the correct verb sequence in relation to the main tense. For example:

> The members of the union *met* and *rejected* the contract. But they *said* that they *would consider* another offer.

Decide which *person* you are going to use: *I, you, he, she, it.* In some formal writing, *I* and *you* are avoided and the third person is used. For example:

> *This report* proves that . . . *(third person)*

rather than:

> *I* will prove in this report that . . . *(first person)*

or:

> *You* will understand that . . . *(second person)*

Some formal writing, however, uses *I* and *you.* You might check with your instructor to see what person is appropriate for your paper.

When you have decided which person you are going to use, don't change persons or point of view. Maintain the same point of view throughout the report.

Now you are ready to prepare the final copy of your report.

Preparing the final copy

Learn to type if you don't know how. Reports that are typed look neater and are easier to read than handwritten reports. And typing can take less time than writing by hand. Use high-quality typing paper, a clean typewriter, and a fresh ribbon.

If you have not learned how to type yet, write in your best handwriting. Use a good pen and wide-lined white paper.

Write or type the final copy from the revised first draft. Be sure to include all corrections and additions in the final copy. When your report is in its final form, read it once again. Check for any typing errors and neatly correct them. And look for any errors in spelling and punctuation.

Now submit your report!

Writing a term paper

The term paper, like the short report, is a research paper. But it differs from the short report in many ways. Term papers have broader topics and are longer than short reports. Many term papers are eight to fifteen pages in length, but some are even longer. The research for a term paper requires more sources than that for a short report. And term papers have more parts—a title page, an outline, footnotes, and a bibliography.

Term papers serve many purposes. Some students think that the only purpose a term paper has is to crowd into their leisure time. Researching and writing a term paper, however, has several positive purposes that are both immediate and long-range. First, it gives you a chance to explore in depth a topic that interests you. Second, it gives you practice developing research skills that you will need throughout your school years and in many careers and professions. Here are some of those research skills.

1. Using a library to find information. Learning how to use the card catalog, periodical indexes, and microfilm readers.
2. Selecting information and using it to answer questions.
3. Taking notes.
4. Analyzing information and putting it in your own words.
5. Organizing information so that it is understandable and useful.
6. Documenting the sources of your information.
7. Preparing footnotes and a bibliography.

Planning a term paper

If you have not read "Organizing for effective writing" (pages 153–161), you should do so now. That section presents suggestions for choosing, analyzing, researching, and outlining a topic. You should follow the steps explained in that section. This section offers some additional suggestions that apply to preparing a term paper.

Make a schedule. As soon as you receive an assignment to write a term paper, make a schedule. By making a schedule you will realize the amount of time and work needed to prepare a term paper. And you will see that you cannot put off starting your work until the week before the paper is due.

Mark the due date for the term paper on your calendar, and start counting backward from that date. This is one time you put last things first. Start by allowing time to type the final copy. Next figure out how much time you will need to revise the first draft. Third, decide how long it will take you to write the first draft. And allow time to organize your note cards and to construct a final outline. The amount of time left before you organize the note cards will be used to gather information and take notes.

Let's say, for example, that you have between 6 and 8 weeks to prepare a 10-page term paper. Since you need to attach a final outline and a bibliography, we'll build a schedule that allows for preparing about 12 full pages of material.

1. Allow at least an hour per page to type the final copy. This includes time for last minute corrections, proofreading each page after you have typed it, and placing footnotes correctly. That means 12 hours for typing the final copy. You will not do this in one 12-hour stretch. Type about 3 hours a day over 4 days.
2. Count on at least 2 hours per page to revise the first draft, or 24 total hours. If you work 3 hours each day, plan on taking 8 days for revising.
3. Give youself at least an hour to write each page of the first draft, or 12 total hours. This again should be written over 4 days.
4. Allow 1 day to organize your note cards and 1 day to construct the final outline.

This means you will spend 18 days—about three and a half school weeks—organizing, writing, revising, and typing your paper. You have the rest of the available time to do your research and take notes. And if you know you won't be able to work as many as 3 hours every day, you'll have to adjust your schedule accordingly.

Choose a topic. Your instructor will often let you choose your own topic for a term paper. Therefore, choose something that interests you—something you will enjoy learning more about. Pick a topic that you can easily find information about. But don't choose what is considered a traditional term paper topic. Topics such as "The Causes of the Civil War" or "How to Dissect a Frog" are no longer interesting because they have been done so frequently.

When you have chosen your topic, decide how you are going to present it. Try to take a fresh approach to your topic, view it from a new or different angle. For example, instead of simply telling what happened at the time of the Boston Tea Party, you could show how John Adams, Thomas Paine, and a recent historian viewed the Boston Tea Party.

Getting started. Ask yourself questions that you want to answer in your term paper. Write these questions down, and use them as the basis for a preliminary outline. The questions and outline should guide your reading.

At first, read widely to gain a broad background about your topic. You may not be able to use all the information in your paper, but you will be able to write a better paper. While you are doing this background reading, you should be adding to your preliminary outline, noting ideas you might decide to include in your paper. If you don't have time for background reading, limit your reading to your specific topic.

Sources of information. You will find most of the sources for your paper in the library—books, articles, and pamphlets. There are, however, additional useful sources of information. Depending on your topic, you might want to use some of these other sources.

1. *Personal interviews* allow you to get firsthand information from people. You can find out their opinions, ideas, or special knowledge about a topic. Before you interview anyone, prepare a set of questions to guide you during the interview.
2. *Questionnaires* and *surveys* give you a chance to ask a large number of people the same questions. These sources will help you determine general trends in opinion.
3. *Family records* are also good sources of information—records of births, marriages, deaths, and ownership of property. Bills, receipts, and check registers that cover a number of years could be used to show a family's buying trends or to illustrate how prices have increased. Other family sources are scrapbooks, photographs, home movies, a family Bible, and tape recordings.
4. *Government record offices* and *historical societies* are also good sources of information.

Compiling the final outline

The sample outlines shown in "Organizing for effective writing" were outlines that you would use as writing tools. The outline discussed here is the final outline you may be required to include with your term paper. The final outline contains the title of your paper, your thesis sentence, and the outline of your paper. You should use your rough, preliminary outline and your note cards to prepare the final outline.

Choosing a title. The title of your term paper should tell the reader exactly what the paper is about. You must carefully word the title so that it specifically and accurately reflects the topic of your paper. If your paper is about the battle of Vicksburg, don't title it "Battles of the Civil War" or even "The Battle of Vicksburg." Be specific. Here are some examples of more specific titles:

Military Strategies Used at the Battle of Vicksburg
The Effects of the Battle of Vicksburg on the South
The Battle of Vicksburg: Turning Point of the Civil War

The thesis sentence. The thesis sentence of your term paper is like the thesis sentence of a short report. In the thesis sentence, you state the main idea of your paper. You must write your thesis sentence carefully so that your reader has a clear understanding of the paper's main idea. Here is a thesis sentence for a paper about the battle of Vicksburg:

By cutting Arkansas, Louisiana, and Texas from the Confederacy and by reuniting the states of the Mississippi Valley, the victory at Vicksburg turned the Civil War in the Union's favor.

The outline. Three to five main headings (roman numerals) are usually enough for a term paper's outline. If you have more than five, check to see whether or not two or more headings are about the same idea. If they are, put the ideas together and write a new heading. Although you won't often use all these levels of subheadings in your outline, here is the correct form for subheadings:

   I.
      A.
          1.
             a.
                (1)
                   (a)

Remember that you should not have single subheadings. For every *A* you must have a *B;* for every *1,* a *2.*

   Here is an example of a final outline page. It is in the form that yours should be when you submit your term paper.

NATIONAL SERVICE: ALTERNATIVES TO THE DRAFT
IN PEACETIME

Outline

Thesis sentence: A program of national service that would enable all Americans to actively serve their country should be considered as an alternative to the military draft in peacetime.

  I. Purposes of national service
     A. Unite Americans in a common goal
     B. Create positive aspects of partiotism
     C. Give citizens opportunities to solve their country's
       problems

 II. Kinds of national service
     A. VISTA
     B. Peace Corps
     C. Conservation programs
     D. Research and development programs

III. Requirements of national service
     A. Two years of service
     B. No deferments

IV. Pay for national service
     A. Based on minimum wage
     B. Not taxed

Writing the first draft

Writing the first draft of a term paper is similar in many ways to writing the first draft of a short report. Keep your final outline and note cards in front of you. Your note cards should contain all the information you will need for your paper. They should have the quotations set off in quotation marks. The cards containing summaries of information should be written in your own words.

Put your thesis sentence in the first paragraph. Develop each heading and subheading of your outline to support the thesis sentence. You will usually need at least one or two paragraphs to present the information from each subheading *(A, B, C)*. Conclude your paper with a paragraph that sums up the main points and arguments.

Direct quotations. When you use a direct quotation, introduce the quotation and relate it to the idea that it is supporting. Be sure to provide a transition between the quotation and your own words. In that way, your paper will read smoothly. It won't lurch along from quotation to quotation.

Use direct quotations sparingly. Most of the paper should be in your own words. The quotations should emphasize, agree with, or support the points you are making.

If the quotation is less than four lines long, use quotation marks and keep it in the text of the paper. If it is longer than four lines, set off the quotation by indenting on both sides and single-spacing it like this:

Footnotes serve a variety of purposes. In addition to documenting sources, a footnote may also (1) explain a point more fully, (2) make an editorial comment, (3) add an interesting sidelight, (4) be a cross reference to another part of the report, or (5) offer a difference of opinion.[1]

[1] "How to Do Research," The World Book Encyclopedia, Vol. 22, p. 27.

Notice that quotation marks are usually not used with indented, single-spaced quotations. For the correct use of ellipses (. . .), single quotation marks (' '), and brackets ([ ]) with direct quotations, see "Punctuation: kinds and use," pages 33–42.

Footnotes. As the sample direct quotation stated, "Footnotes serve a variety of purposes." The main purpose—and usually the only purpose—for footnotes in your school papers is to document sources. To *document sources* is to give credit to the author whom you are quoting or whose ideas you have used. If you do not use quotation marks and footnotes where they are required, you are guilty of *plagiarism*. This means that you have stolen someone else's words or ideas and have passed them off as your own. If you are very careful when taking notes, you can avoid accidentally plagiarizing. Put quotation marks around those notes that will be used as direct quotations; write all other notes in your own words. In that way, you will avoid the problem of plagiarism.

When you write your first draft, keep a separate sheet on which to list the footnotes. Put the footnote number in the text of your paper. On the separate sheet, record the footnote number and the information about the source—author's name, source title, and page number. By recording this information now, it will be ready when you type the final copy. For more information about correct footnote form and some examples of footnotes, read "Preparing footnotes" on pages 47–49.

The bibliography. When you have finished writing the first draft, prepare the bibliography for your paper. The bibliography should list all the sources that you used and consulted during the preparation of your paper. By correctly preparing the bibliography at this point, you will only have to type it when you do the final copy of the paper. For the correct form for bibliographic entries, see "Preparing a bibliography," pages 49–51.

You follow the same basic procedures in revising the first draft of a term paper that you would for a short report (see pages 164–167). But you must check a few more things. Here are some additional tips for revising the first draft of a term paper:

Revising the first draft

1. Allow several days for revising.
2. Be sure your thesis sentence is in the first paragraph.
3. Check your footnotes. Are they in the correct order? Do the numbers in the text of your paper correspond with the numbers on the separate sheet? Do you have all the required information in each footnote?
4. Check the direct quotations in your paper against your note cards. Be sure the wording in your paper is accurate.
5. Check the bibliography. Is it alphabetized correctly? Do you have all the required information for each entry? Have you included all the sources that you used or consulted?

Term papers should always be typed. If you do not know how to type, pay someone to type it for you. Use high-quality paper, a clean typewriter, and a fresh black ribbon. Read each page after you have typed it. You can catch most of your

Preparing the final copy

typing errors in this way. And it is especially important to make sure you have not skipped any sentences or paragraphs *before* you type the next page.

Most instructors and schools have an established format for term papers. If yours does not, follow these suggestions for typing your paper:

1. Leave a margin of 1½ inches on the left, and margins of 1 inch on the right, the top, and the bottom of the paper. But start the outline page and the title on the first page 2 inches from the top.
2. Indent all paragraphs 5 spaces.
3. Double-space the text of your paper.
4. Single-space the outline, but double-space between the main sections.
5. Single-space each footnote and bibliographic entry; double-space between footnotes and between bibliographic entries.
6. Single-space and indent quotations that are set off from the text.

Find out if you should put your footnotes at the bottom of each page or on a separate page at the end of the paper. If you put them at the bottom of each page, be sure to leave enough space for them. All footnote numbers on a page must have a corresponding number and note at the bottom of that page.

Number the pages starting with the first page of the paper and ending with the last page of the bibliography. If you number the pages in the outline, use lower case roman numerals *(i, ii)*. Center the number at the bottom of the first page of the paper and the first page of the bibliography and outline. Center the number at the top of all the other pages. Do not put a number on the title page.

Assembling the final paper. Your final paper should be assembled in the following order:

1. The *title page* with the title of the paper, your name, the date, and sometimes the course title and the instructor's name.
2. The *outline,* which includes the title of the paper, the thesis sentence, and the final outline.
3. The *text* of the paper. The title of the paper is repeated in all capital letters on the first page of the text.
4. A page titled *NOTES* that lists the footnotes if you did not put them at the bottom of the pages.
5. A page titled *BIBLIOGRAPHY* that lists the bibliographic entries.

Reread your paper once more to check for typing errors and mistakes in spelling and punctuation. Check the accuracy of the information in your footnotes and bibliography. Now you can put your paper in a binder or in a manuscript-sized folder and submit it to your instructor.

Taking written examinations

The preparation for an examination starts during the first lecture and while you are doing the first assignment for a class. You and your instructor don't necessarily think of it as preparing for an examination—you call it learning. But then tests are the means by which learning is measured.

Preparing for tests

Preparing for examinations, like learning, is a continuous process. Look over your notes from previous lectures before the next lecture. Review the notes you took while reading before you read another chapter. Don't wait until the night before the examination to begin preparing for it.

Don't cram. Cramming is a poor technique for studying. A student cramming is like a glutton eating. Just as a glutton's body cannot *properly* absorb too much food in one sitting, a student's brain cannot properly absorb too many facts and ideas in one night. The glutton's overload of food turns to fat, and the student's overload of facts causes confusion.

If you start to study at the last minute, you will panic. You will be overwhelmed by the amount of material you have to learn. You will forget the facts you cram before a test as soon as the test is over. This happens because you did not have enough time to associate the overload of facts with your other knowledge and experiences.

Guidelines for study. Your instructors will usually tell you at least a few days in advance about an examination. And midterm and final exams are planned weeks in advance. Teachers will usually let you know what kind of test they are preparing—an objective test, or an essay test, or a combination. If your teacher has not told you, ask! Teachers don't want you to be unnecessarily nervous because you don't know what to expect. After you find out when the test will be given and what kind of test it will be, you can prepare for it. Here are some suggestions to help you prepare for an examination:

1. Organize your notes. You will have notes from lectures, discussions, and reading. Put all your notes about each topic in the same section of your notebook.

2. Read quickly through your notes to gain an overview of the material. Put a question mark in the margin next to facts and ideas that you do not understand.

3. Review the material you do not understand. See how it relates to facts or ideas that you *do* understand. Go back to your textbook to see if you can clarify an idea; or ask your instructor or another student.

4. Read the material aloud, and then recite to yourself those things you need to memorize.

5. Memorize facts, definitions, names, and dates for *objective* tests. Concentrate on theories, concepts, trends, movements, thoughts, and ideas for *essay* tests—but remember that you will also need to know facts to back up those theories and ideas.

6. Make a brief outline of important points. You can study parts of it whenever you have a few extra minutes. Each time you read the outline you should be able to fill in—from memory—more information about each point.

7. Construct questions that you think your teacher might ask. Some of these questions might appear on the actual examination.

8. Study with two or three other students who take good notes and prepare for class. Through discussion, you might clear up the facts or ideas that you do not understand.

9. Be confident of your ability to do well. If you have prepared for an examination and take the examination with a positive attitude, you will do well.

10. Get enough sleep the night before an exam, and have a nutritious breakfast the morning of an exam.

11. Come to the test prepared. Bring paper, several pens or sharp pencils, an eraser, and anything else your instructor wants you to have. Arrive early, get comfortable in your seat, and read your brief outline of important points once more.

12. Don't panic. While you are waiting to receive your test, try to remain calm. Don't be completely relaxed, however. A little nervousness, or an edge, is necessary to spur you on to do your best. Performers and athletes are always a bit nervous just before a performance or game.

Taking the test   Though good preparation is essential, there are also some things that you can do while taking the test. Here are a few points to keep in mind during a test:

1. *Identify yourself.* Put your name, date, and class or section number on the first page of the test, and put your name on all other pages.

2. *Follow the directions.* Read the directions for each part of the test, not once but twice. Be sure you understand what you are expected to do. If you do not, raise your hand and ask your instructor to explain it.

3. *Skim through the test.* See how long it is, how many parts it has, how many questions there are in each part, and how many points there are for each part.

4. *Set a time limit.* Decide how many minutes you will spend on each part of the test. For example, if an essay question is worth 25 points out of 100, you should spend 25 per cent or one fourth of the test time answering that question. Allow part of that time for rereading your essay answer.

5. *Read each question carefully.* Answer all the easy questions first. Put marks next to any answers you are unsure of so you can go back to them later. If you do not understand a question, try to rephrase it to see if that clears it up for you. If there is no penalty for wrong answers, or guessing, answer all the questions.

6. *Check your answers.* Go back to the questions you were unsure of. Change any answers that you think are wrong.

7. *Look for mechanical errors.* If your answers are letters (*T, F* or *a, b, c, d*) or numbers *(1, 2, 3, 4)*, be sure you have put down the choice you wanted and that the numbers and letters are written legibly. If your answers are on a separate sheet of paper, be sure each answer corresponds to the right question. On mechanically scored tests, be sure your answers are in the right boxes and that the boxes are neatly filled in. Erase any extra marks and notes that you have made on the test or answer sheet.

8. *Be sure that your name is on each page of the test.*

Different kinds of questions

Most of the tests that your teachers construct are a combination of different kinds of questions—multiple-choice, true or false, matching, fill in the blank, rearranging, and essay. Each kind of question is put in a separate part of the test and has its own set of directions. Each kind of question requires you to think in a different way. What follows is a description of these different kinds of questions and some suggestions for answering them.

Multiple-choice. The multiple-choice section of a test contains questions or incomplete statements followed by several choices. You are asked to choose the correct or the most correct answer. First, be sure you know what you are looking for. Next, eliminate the choices that are definitely wrong. Now based on your knowledge or experience choose the best answer.

Example: A written plan for a government is called
  a. a treaty
  b. an alliance
  c. a constitution
  d. a caucus
  e. a charter

First eliminate *d. a caucus* because that is a meeting; eliminate *b. an alliance* since that is an agreement between nations; and eliminate *a. a treaty* since that is also between nations. You are left with *c* and *e.* Now think a minute—charters are *granted* by governments. That leaves *c. a constitution* as the only correct answer.

True or false. These kinds of questions require you to decide if the statement given is *true* or *false.* Each statement must be true in every way before you can answer *true.* If any part of the statement is false, your answer must be *false.* Watch out for words like *always, never, no, every, all,* and *entirely* in true-or-false items. If these words are used and there is an exception to the statement, then the statement is false. And don't read extra information into true-or-false items.

Example: T F 1. Veins carry blood back to the heart.
         T F 2. The heart is made of muscle, nerves, and bone.

Matching. These questions usually consist of two columns or lists of items. You must match one item in one column with an item in the other column. First, match the items you are sure about. Mark out the choices as you use them. Study the remaining choices to complete the difficult matches.

Example: **Column A**   **Column B**
          _____1. California   a. corn
          _____2. Georgia   b. oranges
          _____3. Iowa   c. butter
          _____4. Wisconsin   d. peaches

Fill in the blank. These questions ask you to complete a statement with a word or phrase. You are asked to decide what word or phrase is missing by looking at how the rest of the statement is phrased.

Example: The best laid plans of _____ and men often go awry.

Rearranging information. These questions present a list of items that you are asked to put in order, such as in order of importance or in chronological order. Read the instructions carefully so that you know what you are supposed to do. Once again, start with the items that you know and work from there.

Example: Put the following events in chronological order:
Battle of Bunker Hill
French and Indian War
Boston Tea Party
Boston Massacre
Publication of *Common Sense*

Essay questions. Essay questions require you to answer in complete sentences or paragraphs. You are asked to provide information in a complete, concise, and organized manner. Here are some guidelines to help you improve your essay answers:

1. *Read each question carefully.* If you have more than one essay question, see whether or not any of the questions are related. That way you won't put information in one answer that would fit better in another answer.

2. *Understand the verb portion of the question*—the verb that tells you what *you* must do in your answer. Some essay question verbs and their meanings follow:

    analyze—break down into parts and show relationships
    compare—show how things are alike
    contrast—show how things are different
    evaluate—determine the importance, significance, or value
        of something
    explain—give reasons or causes for something, or tell how
        something works
    identify—describe or define something

    Be sure you do exactly what you are asked to do. If you are asked to *analyze,* don't simply *identify.*

3. *Organize your answers.* Make a brief outline of key points and ideas you want to include in your answer before you start writing. A well-organized answer will get a better grade.

4. *Be complete.* Include all the information that is necessary for a complete and clear answer. Try to back up ideas and theories with specific facts and reasons. But do not pad an answer with unrelated information. Teachers don't appreciate padding.

5. *Answer all questions.* If you don't have time to answer all the essays, at least write an outline of the main ideas you intended to cover. Your teacher might give you some

credit for an outline or a partial answer. If you only know some of the answer, at least say what you know.

6. *Write legibly.* Even though you are under the pressure of a time limit, write legibly. An instructor can't evaluate an answer that can't be read.

7. *Proofread.* When you have finished your essays, check them for correct grammar, punctuation, spelling, and sentence structure. In some classes, the correctness of your writing will be considered in your grade. But even when the quality of your writing is not officially part of the grade, your essays will be more understandable if you observe the standards for good writing.

Use what you know

These activities have been designed to help you practice some of the skills that were presented in this section. Answers to the activities can be found in the **Answer Key** that begins on page 270.

Practice in outlining

Imagine that you are writing a term paper about the contributions of Plato's thought to modern civilization. You have finished your research, you have a title, and you have written a thesis sentence. Now you must write your final outline. Suppose the items in the list that follows are the headings from your note cards. How would you rearrange them into an outline with main headings and subheadings?

THE CONTRIBUTIONS OF PLATO'S THOUGHT TO MODERN CIVILIZATION

Outline

Thesis sentence: Many of Plato's ideals and principles are still important in modern civilization.

Importance of the inquiring mind
Athletic contests
Loyalty
Principles of government
Scientific investigation
Importance of physical fitness
Public service
Personal cleanliness
Form
Philosophical theories
Standards of beauty
Democracy
Careful diet
Simplicity

The library as a research tool

Most of your research will begin in a library. Libraries contain many different kinds of resource materials, not just books. That is why many libraries today are called learning resource centers or community resource centers. Most people do not realize how many different kinds of materials their libraries have. Make a copy of the checklist that follows. Use it to find out what materials your school and community libraries have. And ask if you can check the materials out to use at home, or if you must use them in the library. You might also note whether or not they have especially good selections of material on topics that interest you.

	School library		Community library	
	Check out	*Use there*	*Check out*	*Use there*
Art works	_____	_____	_____	_____
Artifacts	_____	_____	_____	_____
Cameras	_____	_____	_____	_____
Documents	_____	_____	_____	_____
Films	_____	_____	_____	_____
Filmstrips	_____	_____	_____	_____
Historic prints	_____	_____	_____	_____
Interlibrary loan	_____	_____	_____	_____
Listening room	_____	_____	_____	_____
Local history collection	_____	_____	_____	_____
Magazines	_____	_____	_____	_____
Maps	_____	_____	_____	_____
Microfilm reader	_____	_____	_____	_____
Newspapers	_____	_____	_____	_____
Pamphlets	_____	_____	_____	_____
Posters	_____	_____	_____	_____
Projectors	_____	_____	_____	_____
Records	_____	_____	_____	_____
Study prints	_____	_____	_____	_____
Tape recorders	_____	_____	_____	_____
Tape recordings	_____	_____	_____	_____
Videotapes	_____	_____	_____	_____
Viewing room	_____	_____	_____	_____
Xerox machine	_____	_____	_____	_____

Other material and services _____

Keep a copy of this checklist in your notebook as a research aid.

7   Speaking before a group

Do you enjoy speaking to a group? Or do you panic when you are called upon to speak? No matter how you feel about public speaking, you will probably need to speak before a group at some time in your life. And it would help to learn more about effective speaking.

Even if you never give a formal speech to a large audience, most people speak before groups from time to time. You may need to give a report at a business meeting or a community meeting. You might be the head of a committee and need to lead the committee in group discussion. Or you might simply want to stand up for a minute to state your opinion to the PTA or the city council. Although this section primarily offers advice for giving a formal speech, the suggestions for planning what you will say and presenting your ideas effectively can also be applied in other kinds of speaking situations. Learning such techniques can help you gain confidence and poise whenever you speak.

This section explains what public speaking is and outlines the steps you should take to prepare a speech. It also describes the various formats for delivering a speech. And it suggests many techniques for presenting your ideas—and yourself—more effectively.

The elements of spoken communication

Communication. What is it? Simply stated, *communication* is successfully making your wants, needs, ideas, and feelings known to other people. You communicate with other people in three ways. In the first place, you use your body to communicate: you wave your hand, shake your head, shrug your shoulders, or stamp your feet. Making these gestures gets a message to another person: "hello," "yes," "I don't know," or "definitely not."

In the second place, you communicate through writing. You write letters to other people, notes to your family as reminders, and papers or reports for school or business. Through writing, you hope to convey a message to another person.

In the third place, you communicate by speaking. You communicate by speaking when you converse with your friends, answer questions in class, contribute ideas during a meeting, or talk to a large group. This last way of speaking— speaking before a large group—is called public speaking.

Public speaking is an attempt by a speaker to send a message to a listener. The message that the listener receives should be as close as possible to what the speaker had in mind. Successful public speaking thus occurs when what was in the mind of the speaker is accurately communicated to the listener. It is effective when the speaker gets the message to the listener.

What is public speaking?

In public speaking, you the speaker have one chance to get your message across. Your listeners cannot "rehear" or "relisten" to an idea that they did not understand. And most often, listeners do not interrupt to ask you to repeat a statement. That is why you must choose your words carefully, organize your thoughts logically, and make use of effective repetition. These and other skills of effective public speaking are what this section is all about.

There are six elements necessary for successful public speaking:

The six elements of public speaking

1. The speaker;
2. The speech, or message;
3. A channel, or method by which the message is sent;
4. An audience or group of listeners;
5. The effect of the speech;
6. The feedback—the reactions and response of the audience to both the speaker and the message.

Let's look more closely at each of these six elements.

The speaker. You are the speaker. To be a successful speaker, you must work hard at getting your message across. You must know how to put a speech together and how to present it. You cannot just stand up and talk, or ramble on and on about a topic.

Some people seem to have an easier time presenting public speeches than others do. They make it seem easier because they have worked hard preparing and practicing their speeches. Very few people are just naturally good public speakers. Most successful speakers have simply learned the techniques of planning and delivering a speech.

If you feel nervous about speaking before a group, you are not alone. Most people feel some degree of fear or hesitation about public speaking. Learning the techniques of public speaking can help lessen that fear. People are usually most nervous about doing things they haven't done before or don't know how to do. People feel more confident about things they do often and do well. The more you learn how to speak before a group, and the more experience you get at doing this, the more confident you will become.

And remember: A little nervousness is a natural reaction. Many professional actors and athletes talk about feeling some stage fright before a performance or a game. And some of these professionals think that a little stage fright can serve a *positive* purpose; it can give them an "edge" that spurs them on to perform well.

If you are afraid to speak before a group, you must push yourself into speaking situations. Volunteer to give the first book report, or to locate and present some information at the next committee meeting. The more times you speak before a group, the easier and more natural it will become.

The speech. The speech is the message you want the audience to receive. It must have a purpose—a reason why you are giving the speech. It must include accurate, relevant information. The wording should be easy to follow, direct, and natural. Do not use unnecessarily complicated sentences or unnecessarily difficult words. Your audience cannot look up words in a dictionary or reread a difficult sentence. If you need to use technical terms, be sure to define them carefully and give examples.

The channel. The channel is the means by which a message is sent. In public speaking, the most important channels for sending messages are your voice and your gestures. You might also use audio-visual aids as another channel for conveying your message. The effective use of your voice, gestures, and audio-visual aids is explained later in this section.

The audience. Your audience could be a large group assembled in an auditorium or in a banquet hall. Or it could be a small group—one class or a committee. The audience might be immediately receptive to your ideas, or it might have to be won over. Knowing who your audience will be is important when you are planning a speech.

The effect. Your speech will have an effect on your audience. It might persuade the listeners to do something—join a club or vote a certain way. The listeners might be entertained by the speech. Or they might be informed on a topic of interest to them. They might be reassured that their property taxes will not be increased, for example. When you are preparing a speech, you should keep in mind the effect you want it to have on the audience.

The feedback. You receive feedback from the audience throughout a speech. Feedback tells you if your message is getting across and how your speech is affecting the audience. There are silent responses—facial expressions, nods of agreement or approval, fidgeting, sleeping. And there are audible responses—laughter, applause, cheers, boos, or disinterested background conversation. Feedback lets you know if you should change the direction of your speech or emphasize other points.

Understanding how these six elements of spoken communication work together will help you present more effective speeches and avoid breakdowns in communication.

Six steps in preparation and practice

When you give a speech, you do not just get up and start talking. You must spend hours, days, or weeks preparing your material and practicing the delivery of your speech. If you have properly prepared a speech, you will be more confident about your ability to actually deliver it.

There are six basic steps in the preparation and practice of a speech. You should follow these steps whenever you are called upon to give a speech—a report to the class, a presentation at a meeting, or an address at a civic function. The six steps are—

1. Analyzing the audience.
2. Choosing a topic.
3. Determining the purpose.
4. Gathering materials.
5. Developing an outline.
6. Rehearsing the speech.

Analyzing the audience

A speech is intended for a specific audience, a specific group of people. If your speech is to convey a message to those people, you need to find out as much as you can about the audience.

In some cases, you will already know quite a bit about your audience. But if you don't, you might talk to someone who will be in the group or to the person who invited you to speak. If the group is an established organization, you could talk to members of the organization or do background reading on the organization's history and purposes.

Here are some things that you need to find out about your audience.

Size. Will you speak to a large group or to a small group of people? If the group is small, you can sometimes take a less formal approach. Perhaps you and the group will sit around a table. If the group is large, you will probably be farther away from the audience—on a stage or behind a podium.

Composition. Will the people in the group all have similar interests and backgrounds? Or will there be a mixture of people with different interests and backgrounds? If they have different backgrounds, try to figure out why they would all be present to hear your speech. Find some common ground that they all share. Then make your speech appeal to their common interests. In some cases, there might be different groups in the audience who are opposed to one another on some issue. In that case, try to show how your cause, plan, or program might benefit each group in some way.

Views and attitudes. Try to determine what the group's attitudes might be toward your topic. Will most of the audience be in favor of your views? opposed to your views? indifferent to your views? You will have to win over the opposition and create enthusiasm in the indifferent. You should also try to reinforce the attitudes of those who already agree with you.

Age and educational levels. You do not speak to children, adolescents, and adults in the same way. Different age groups often have different interests and different abilities to understand ideas. And they should be talked to in language that they understand. Don't talk down to adults or over the heads of children.

You must also consider the educational level of your audience and the amount of knowledge they already have on your topic. Imagine, for example, that you are preparing a speech on the reasons for inflation. The language and ideas in a speech to high school students would be different from that in a speech to a group of teachers. And that speech on inflation to teachers would be quite different from a speech to a group of accountants.

By knowing the audience, you can select a topic that will interest them. And you can decide how to approach that topic: choosing material that will maintain their attention and language that they will be likely to understand.

Choosing a topic for a speech is similar to choosing a topic for a paper. First, you must choose something that interests you or that you know something about. You must be excited enough about discussing your topic so that your audience will be eager to hear about it. Second, your topic must suit the occasion. You would not give the same kind of speech at a memorial service that you would at a fund-raising dinner. Both the topic and the tone of your speech must be appropriate for the situation.

Choosing a topic

Third, if your topic requires research, be sure that the necessary sources of information are available. And fourth, make sure that you can cover the topic adequately in the time allowed for your speech. If you would need an hour to discuss your topic, but you've been asked to speak for ten minutes, limit your topic. You might have to leave out some details; or better yet, choose one aspect of the topic and discuss that aspect in detail.

Every speech has one of three main purposes: *to inform, to persuade,* or *to entertain.* Before you prepare any speech, decide on a general purpose—on what effect you want the speech to have on your audience. Do you want the audience to gain knowledge about the topic? Do you want the listeners to do a definite thing after they have heard your speech? Or do you want them to simply enjoy listening to your speech?

Determining the purpose

Informative speeches present knowledge, or information, to the audience. For example, you might tell a garden club how to properly prepare the ground before planting roses; tell a group of office workers how to use new equipment; or tell a biology class about the habitat of some animal.

Persuasive speeches are designed to convince the listeners to change their thinking or to act in a particular way. Some examples of persuasive speeches are campaign speeches and speeches to raise money. Speeches that tell why you should change poor eating habits or conserve energy are also persuasive speeches.

Entertaining speeches give an audience pleasure. They are often humorous. Sometimes you can make a serious point by using humor. After-dinner speeches are often speeches to entertain.

A speech can, of course, contain two or more of these general purposes at the same time. For example, a persuasive speech usually also gives information—facts and figures that help prove your point. And you might entertain an audience—to get them on your side—in order to persuade them. Once again, you must know your audience and the occasion before you decide whether you will inform, persuade, or entertain them.

After you have determined the general purpose—to inform, persuade, or entertain—you must decide on your specific purpose or goal in the speech. For example, the general purpose of a speech might be to persuade a group to raise money to buy new band uniforms. Your specific purpose or goal might be to explain why new uniforms are needed. Depending on the group, you might meet your goal by emphasizing school pride or by describing the condition of the old uniforms.

Gathering materials

If your speech requires any information or knowledge you do not already have, you will need to do research. Here are three ways in which you can gather information:

1. *Observe the subject matter itself.* For example, if your talk is about how a machine works, you might watch someone using the machine or taking it apart.
2. *Talk to people who are informed about your topic.* If your subject is the problems of small businesses during a recession, local owners of small businesses would be good people to interview for information.
3. *Do research in the library.* You'll find information in the library on almost any speech topic. (For tips on library research, see pages 154–158.)

Developing an outline

Your speech must have a beginning, a middle, and an end. These parts are called the *introduction,* the *body,* and the *conclusion* of your speech. You prepare the outline of your speech around these three parts.

The outline for a speech is a guide. You use it to organize the ideas in your speech. And if you plan to give your speech from the outline, you use it when practicing your speech. The more you practice, the less you will need to refer to the outline when you actually deliver the speech.

The introduction. In the introduction of a speech, you usually introduce yourself, make a remark about the occasion, and tell what the speech is about. But you don't say, "My speech is about. . . ." The introduction should get the audience on your side by arousing their interest. You might attract the audience's attention with a quotation or a story that relates to your topic. Remember, if you lose your audience at the beginning of your speech, you'll have a hard time getting them back.

The body. The body of the speech contains the main points you want to make and the subpoints which explain and support your main ideas. You will usually have from one to five main points for most speeches. Be sure you have enough material to explain each point. Limit your subpoints to things that are especially interesting or convincing to your particular audience.

Determine the order of your main points. In speeches, you will often place your ideas in the order of their *importance*—making your most important point first so that the audience knows right away what it is. But there are other orders you might use to arrange your ideas. You might use *chronological* order when you want to relate a sequence of incidents or events that happened over a period of time. If you want to introduce your audience to a new idea, you could use *familiar to unfamiliar* order; you would begin with something the audience already knows that would help them understand the new or unfamiliar idea you want to get across to them. If your topic might be a little difficult to understand, you could order your ideas from *simple to complex*—starting with the easier points and leading up to the more difficult ones. Or you could use *concrete to abstract* order for explaining a theory or other more abstract thought; you would start with concrete facts or events that would convince the audience of the abstract idea or principle you want to prove.

You will also need to include some attention-holding devices in the body of your speech. There are many kinds of attention-holding devices you can use:

1. Relating stories and anecdotes.
2. Using quotations and literary allusions.
3. Asking the audience questions to catch their interest and get them involved.
4. Referring to everyday experiences the audience may have had.
5. Using humor.
6. Repeating key words and phrases.

Be sure to weave these attention-holding devices into the context of your speech. They should not stand out by themselves in a speech. Only use attention-holding devices that are clearly related to your topic—that will actually help you get your message across.

Decide how you will make transitions from point to point in your speech. Transitions are the sentences that link the ideas of a speech together. Transition sentences move your speech smoothly along to the conclusion. You don't want your audience to wonder what Point B has to do with Point A. Use a transition sentence that explains how Point A and Point B are related. Are two ideas or people similar to each other? or different from each other? Did one event cause another event to occur? You must provide transitions that will show your audience the relationships between the ideas you are expressing.

The conclusion. The conclusion is your last chance to make an impression on the audience. The kind of conclusion you use will depend on the purpose of your speech. If it is an informative speech, you could summarize your main ideas and restate your purpose in the speech. You could use a quotation from a famous person which summarizes your main idea in an interesting or unusual way. You might use a "big bang" ending for a persuasive speech. A startling statement or a statement that stirs the audience's emotions could spark your one last appeal for action. If the purpose of your speech is to entertain, you would probably try to leave the audience laughing.

Rehearsing the speech

Rehearsing a speech is a crucial step in your preparation. This is the step in which you improve and polish the speech. In some ways it is similar to the revising step when you are writing a letter or a paper. And like some writers, speakers often do not allow enough time for this important part of preparation. When you have your speech prepared, you should start rehearsing it—as many times as possible.

Begin practicing the speech using the outline or manuscript you have prepared. As you become more at ease with the information, you will naturally depend less on the outline or manuscript.

Rehearsing the speech will help you notice if the speech is working—or if it needs some revising. Is the wording right? Do any points need to be more fully explained? If points do not seem to follow each other well, rearrange them. Don't tie yourself to the original plan; if your rehearsal shows that a few changes could improve the speech, make those changes.

Next, practice your speech in front of a mirror so that you can watch your facial expressions, posture, and gestures. Try to say the speech at least once in the place where you will actually deliver the speech. That way you will know how large the room is, if there is a stage, podium, or microphone, and whether or not you will have to talk above outside noises.

Finally, ask someone to listen to your speech. Have the person tell you whether or not the speech is clear and understandable. Ask if the speech seems appropriate for the audience and the occasion. Also have the person point out if your gestures are effective and if your voice carries to the back of the room.

The way you rehearse will of course depend on the format you choose for delivering the speech. You will practice giving your speech in whatever way you decide to deliver it: reading from a manuscript; giving the speech from memory; speaking impromptu; or speaking from an outline. The following section explains these types of delivery and gives you some hints to help you choose what type of delivery might be best for you and the situation. Your rehearsal is a good time to become comfortable with the kind of delivery you have chosen—and to see if it is working well for you. If not, you might need to change your method of delivery to one that will work better for you.

If you follow these six steps for preparing a speech, you should be ready to deliver an effective and appropriate speech for any school, business, civic, or social occasion.

Kinds of delivery

How effectively you deliver a speech is every bit as important as what you have to say. This section offers suggestions for choosing a format for delivering your speech. Then the next section will present many specific techniques that you can use during the speech to help you get your message across to your audience.

There are four different formats for delivering a speech: (1) *speaking from a manuscript;* (2) *memorizing a speech;* (3) *speaking impromptu;* and (4) *extemporaneous speaking.* Each of these types of delivery has its own advantages and disadvantages. For every speech you make, you will need to decide which method of delivery best suits you, your audience, your topic, and the occasion.

Speaking from a manuscript

When you deliver a speech from a manuscript, you write out the complete speech and read it aloud to your audience. Many campaign speeches, official reports, and speeches given on radio or television are read from a manuscript.

This method of delivery has several advantages. You can explain your ideas in great detail and not forget anything in the actual speech. You can refer back to your speech later to recall exactly what you said. You don't have to worry about being misquoted because you can distribute exact copies of your speech to the audience or to the press. And if you are going to use audio-visual aids, you can mark on your manuscript exactly when you will use them. This kind of delivery also allows you to stay within your time limit. You can read through your speech ahead of time, note exactly how long it takes, and adjust the length of the speech to the time you have.

Speaking from a manuscript also has some disadvantages. Most people do not read aloud well; thus speaking from a manuscript tends to be stilted and unnatural. There is also the tendency to stumble, lose your place, or develop a monotone. When speaking from a manuscript, it is difficult to maintain eye contact with the audience. Some speakers help solve this problem by putting their speech on large file cards rather than on long sheets of paper. This helps remind them to look up at the audience at least at the end of each file card. They also have the manuscript typed and double-spaced for easier reading. Another disadvantage of this kind of delivery is that you are more tied to the manuscript. It is more difficult to adjust your language and ideas to suit your audience's reactions.

Although speaking from a manuscript may seem like the safest way to give a speech, it can actually be the most difficult to do. Most people become so involved in the manuscript that they lose sight of their audience. And keeping in contact with your audience—keeping them interested and involved—is essential for an effective speech.

Memorizing a speech

If you decide to memorize your speech, you must first write out the complete speech. Then you must memorize it word for word. You deliver the speech from memory; you don't use a manuscript, an outline, or notes.

This kind of delivery has more disadvantages than advantages. You might leave out an important part of the speech. Or even worse, you might forget what comes next and stand in front of your audience with nothing to say. Because you are concentrating on remembering the exact words of the speech, your way of speaking can become unnatural and stiff. And in a memorized speech, it is difficult to add remarks or to adjust the speech to the audience.

Speaking impromptu

An impromptu speech is given without extensive preparation—sometimes without any specific preparation at all. You can speak impromptu only if the subject is something about which you have general knowledge or well-formed opinions. However, impromptu speaking is not aimless rambling. Some examples of impromptu speaking would be extensive remarks in response to something said at a business meeting or at a village or city council meeting. Many speeches that legislators make are impromptu.

The advantage of impromptu speeches is that you are not tied to an outline or manuscript. Therefore, you can easily adjust the content and approach to suit your audience. Impromptu speeches also have disadvantages. Because they are not carefully laid out ahead of time, impromptu speeches often are unorganized and hard to follow. And it's easy to speak on and on about the issue without ever getting to the point.

Because of the many pitfalls in impromptu speaking, few people actually choose this kind of delivery when asked to give a formal speech. You will more often speak impromptu when attending business or community meetings. If you know before a meeting that you have something you want to say— or that someone may ask for your opinions—it never hurts to prepare your thinking. Think generally about what you might want to say on the issue. You could jot down your basic ideas, as well as any facts or figures that might be useful to you.

The most commonly used type of delivery is the extemporaneous speech. For this kind of speech, you gather your information, select important ideas, and organize them in a speech outline. Then you deliver the speech using the outline as a guide. In an extemporaneous speech, you know what ideas you'll include and what order you'll present them in. But you have not written down the exact words or sentences you will use.

Extemporaneous speaking

There are several advantages to extemporaneous speaking. First, your delivery is spontaneous. Your speech would be a little different each time you present it. You can easily add or delete material according to the reactions of your audience. An extemporaneous delivery also allows you to maintain eye contact with your audience because you are not always looking at a manuscript for your exact words. In these ways, an extemporaneous speech avoids many of the pitfalls of memorized speeches and speeches read from a manuscript.

Another advantage of extemporaneous speeches is that they are just as carefully prepared as written or memorized speeches. You must gather information, do research, and organize the material for an extemporaneous speech. And you set a clear purpose. Therefore, you avoid the disadvantages of impromptu speeches as well.

Finally, in an extemporaneous speech you always have your outline as a guide. If you forget what you want to say next, you can quickly refer to the outline. The outline solves one of the problems of memorized speeches.

The main disadvantage of extemporaneous speeches is that you could become too tied to your outline and ignore the reactions of the audience. The way to avoid being too tied to your outline is to rehearse your speech using the outline as your guide. The more you practice the speech, the less you will need to rely on your outline during your actual presentation. If you prepare your outline carefully and practice delivering your speech, an extemporaneous delivery style can create a well-balanced speech: a speech that is orderly and complete, and yet flexible.

When choosing one of these four styles of delivery, remember to consider which style best fits you, your audience, your material, and the occasion. If you have a poor memory, don't try to memorize your speeches. If your audience is composed of children or adolescents, don't read from a manuscript. If you are presenting a complicated report, don't try to speak impromptu.

Techniques of effective delivery

After you have prepared your speech and have decided on the type of delivery, you should work on the techniques for delivering your speech effectively. These techniques involve the ways you use your voice and your body as effective channels for your message. Here are some general suggestions to keep in mind, both when you practice your speech and during the actual delivery:

1. Look at your audience to gain its attention before you start to speak.
2. Make some introductory remarks to capture the audience's attention. Then begin your speech.
3. Move and speak in a natural manner. Talk as naturally as you do in conversation, but don't use slang or incomplete sentences.

The appropriate and effective use of your voice and your body will gain and maintain the audience's attention.

Your voice

The most important channel for your message, or speech, is your voice. Your voice carries your ideas to the audience. Your audience will judge your speech partly on the characteristics of your voice. Your vocal characteristics include *volume, pitch, speed, energy level, quality,* and *clarity of pronunciation.*

Volume. Volume refers to the loudness or softness of your voice. You can call attention to important ideas in your speech by changing the volume of your voice. You might speak more loudly to emphasize certain words or phrases. Or you might speak softly to make your audience listen more carefully to a point. Be sure to vary the volume of your voice; it helps to keep the audience's attention. Other factors that will determine the volume you use are (1) the size of the room in which you are speaking; (2) whether or not you have a microphone; and (3) whether or not there are noises you must talk above—such as construction noises next door or a plane flying overhead. Always speak loudly enough for the audience to hear you.

Pitch. Pitch is the highness or lowness of the sound or tone of your voice. Your voice has a natural pitch. And you automatically vary that pitch when you talk. If you are excited, your voice will have a higher pitch. If you are being somber and serious, you will use a lower pitch. Since this is how you naturally speak—and you usually want your speech to sound natural—be sure you vary your pitch in speeches. Don't tense up and speak in an unnatural monotone. In some cases, you can vary your pitch even more than you would in ordinary conversation for a dramatic effect. But be careful not to be too dramatic—or to be dramatic when its not appropriate. In most speeches, your voice should sound natural and relaxed.

Speed. Your voice also has a rate of speed. Some people talk fast and others speak slowly. During a speech, you can make important ideas stand out by speaking slowly. If an idea is not important, you can speak a little faster to get past it. Never speak so fast, however, that your audience cannot follow you. If you have a time limit, pace the speech to fit the time. Don't start speaking fast at the end of a speech just to get all the material across.

Energy level. Your voice's energy level tells the audience how bored or excited you are about your speech. If your voice is dry, boring, or flat, it will turn your audience off. They will not get your message. If your voice is energetic and full of enthusiasm, however, your audience will respond to your enthusiasm. A boring voice can make the most interesting material seem dull. On the other hand, a lively presentation can make a complex or serious subject appealing to an audience.

Quality. The quality is the general tone of your voice. It is what makes your voice distinct from other voices. Your voice may be pleasant, neutral, or unpleasant. If your voice has a thin, harsh, or nasal quality, you should practice to improve it. Most people are not very aware of how they sound to others.

One way to check the quality of your voice is to tape-record it. Listen to the tape and decide how you might improve the way you sound. Work on making your voice as pleasant to listen to as possible. An audience is sometimes more receptive to ideas if they are presented by a pleasant voice.

Clarity of pronunciation. You must pronounce all words in your speech clearly, distinctly, and correctly. If you mispronounce words, your audience may doubt your knowledge of the subject of your speech. Mispronunciation can also give the appearance of a lack of learning or refinement. Don't say *git* instead of *get;* or *jist* instead of *just;* or *pitcher* when you mean *picture.*

Speak clearly. Do not slur syllables or words together so that your audience cannot understand them. And don't muffle your voice or speak in undertones. The audience will wonder if you are speaking to them or to yourself. You should also avoid using "ah," "er," "like," and "you know." These words give the impression that you are unsure of yourself or are unsure of what you're saying.

Your manner and appearance

The way you look to an audience is as important as how you sound. In general your dress and appearance should be appropriate for the occasion, the audience, and the setting. Wear something that you are comfortable in and that you won't fuss or fidget with. Avoid wearing clothes or jewelry that will distract the audience from your speech. If you are neat and clean, you should not have to worry.

You should especially consider your mannerisms—how you use your body as you are speaking. Some mannerisms can be distracting and have a negative effect on the way you appear to an audience. But properly used mannerisms can actually aid you in getting your message across. Some techniques you can use are *eye contact, facial expressions, posture, movement,* and *gestures.*

Eye contact. Look at individual members of the audience as you speak. Establish eye contact with as many people and as many parts of the audience as you can. Eye contact shows the people in the audience that you are interested in communicating with each one of them. Don't look over the heads in the audience. Listeners will trust you more if you look them in the eyes when speaking to them. Good eye contact also helps you get feedback from the audience—to see their reactions. Then if necessary, you can make changes in your speech according to the reactions you're getting.

Facial expressions. Your facial expressions should be appropriate to the topic and the occasion. In general, you want to appear pleasant and look pleased to be speaking to your audience. Don't let your face tense up into a blank stare, or a frightened look. Allow your expressions to vary with what you are saying, just as you naturally would in a conversation.

Posture. You should stand up straight and yet be relaxed. Your arms loosely at your sides, feet slightly apart and one a little in front of the other, is usually a comfortable position. Don't be stiff, but don't slouch or slump; these positions will make your audience think that you are either afraid or bored. Your posture should show that you are alert, confident, and energetic.

Movement. Any movements you make during a speech should be related to the speech. Moving forward or sideways a step or two could catch the audience's attention when you are making an important point or moving on to a new idea. But don't pace aimlessly back and forth in front of your audience. And don't make quick moves, unless you want to emphasize a point very strongly. Your movements should keep your audience's attention, not startle them or distract them from what you're saying.

Gestures. Knowing how to appropriately and effectively use gestures is an important speaking technique. Gestures can be made with your hands, your arms, or your head. You can emphasize important points or show transitions through proper gestures. But try to make your gestures as natural as possible. Though dramatic gestures are sometimes effective, fist waving and podium pounding can be seen as overly dramatic or inappropriate to many occasions. Only use gestures that you are comfortable with. At first, don't force yourself to use gestures. As you give more speeches, you will naturally use gestures that are effective for you.

By practicing these various delivery techniques, you can make your speaking more effective and interesting. But remember to try out these techniques when you are rehearsing your speech. That will help you decide which techniques are best for you, your audience, and the occasion.

Using audio-visual aids

There are several reasons why you might consider using an audio-visual aid in a speech. Most people are not oriented to listening for long periods of time. That is, people can receive only a limited amount of information by ear. There is also a limited amount of time that people can keep their attention on any one thing. An audio-visual aid can add a measure of needed variety. It can give your audience something concrete—besides you—to focus on at some point during the speech.

In addition, some things are simply easier to understand if you can visualize them. A picture, a chart, or a model can often help make an idea clearer to an audience.

But don't use audio-visual aids just to use them. Aids may be appropriate to some topics but not to others. The variety an aid may add to a long speech may be unnecessary in a very short speech. Whatever you do, use audio-visual aids appropriately and wisely.

Here is a list of some audio-visual aids that you could use during a speech:

Chalkboard or blackboard
Charts, graphs, diagrams, and tables
Handouts of printed materials, such as statistics
Drawings, pictures, and photographs
Globes, maps, and models
Movie film and projector
Opaque projector
Records and tape recordings
Slides
Transparencies and overhead projector
Videotape

Use audio-visual aids effectively

The audio or visual aid is used to help your speech. It should not become a focal point of the speech. Aids are a channel for getting your message across; they should not distract from the message. Here are some suggestions for effectively using audio-visual aids:

1. Use an aid only if it will assist the purpose, message, or outcome of your speech. An aid should carry part of the message, not simply provide entertainment. For example, tape recordings would illustrate a speech about dialects spoken in different parts of the United States.
2. Make sure that the chalkboard, pictures, charts, or models can be seen by all members of the audience. Visuals should be large enough to see or read.
3. Avoid hand-held visuals. Mount pictures or charts on poster board and prop them on a table or on an easel. Floppy pictures are hard to look at.
4. Be sure well ahead of time that you can obtain any films and projectors that you will need. Check to see if electrical outlets are handy and if the room can be darkened for films or slides.

5. Practice using the equipment before you give the speech.
6. Have any projectors set up before you start your speech, and have maps, models, or pictures handy. Then you won't need to fumble with them while you are talking. If you think an aid will be distracting, keep it out of the audience's sight until you actually need it.
7. If you are giving the audience handouts of printed material, pass them around either before or after the speech. If you distribute them while you are talking, you could lose the audience's attention.

Use what you know

These activities are designed to help you use the speaking skills presented in this section.

Constructing a speaker's kit

As a speaker, your hardest tasks will be choosing topics and finding appropriate materials for your speeches. If you had a file of topics with assorted materials, your job would be much easier. Many people who are often called on to speak have a speaker's kit. They refer to their kit when they need a topic for a speech.

You too can construct a speaker's kit. First, make a list of general topics that you could speak about. These might be topics related to your profession or topics related to your hobbies or special interests. They could be topics such as art, education, parenting, government, community affairs, ecology, the energy crisis, health, hang gliding, chess, sports, stamp collecting—whatever topics you find interesting or know something about.

Next, prepare a file folder for each topic. Then collect articles, anecdotes, quotations, and human interest stories that would provide good material for speaking. You might find these articles in newspapers, Sunday supplements, and magazines. Put the articles and stories in the appropriate file folder.

Continually update your speaker's kit. Add new topics and material; discard material that is no longer current or of general interest. Now that you have an up-to-date speaker's kit, you should have no trouble finding material the next time you are called upon to speak.

Evaluating speeches

You probably hear speeches at least twice a week. They might not all be formal speeches from a podium. But you do hear speeches—long or short—on television or radio, at school or church, or during meetings or dinners. They could be presidential addresses, television editorials, lectures, sermons, or civic or social presentations. But they are all speeches. Some you enjoy; some you don't understand or care about. You might think to yourself, "Wow! That really got the point across." Or you might think, "Now, what was that all about?"

The next time you listen to a speech of any length, critique it. That is, criticize and evaluate it. Write up a form like the one on page 204 to help you evaluate the weak points and strong points of the speech and of the speaker. Studying the techniques of people who frequently speak in public can give you ideas for improving your own speaking skills.

Speech evaluation form

Speaker _____   Occasion _____
Topic _____   Date _____

	Excellent	Good	Fair	Poor
Topic appropriate to—				
Audience	____	____	____	____
Occasion	____	____	____	____
Time limit	____	____	____	____
Purpose of speech				
Clearly stated	____	____	____	____
Effect on audience	____	____	____	____
Organization of speech				
Introduction	____	____	____	____
Body	____	____	____	____
Conclusion	____	____	____	____
Use of stories, anecdotes, quotations, or humor	____	____	____	____
Voice of speaker				
Volume	____	____	____	____
Pitch	____	____	____	____
Speed	____	____	____	____
Pronunciation	____	____	____	____
Appearance of speaker				
Posture	____	____	____	____
Facial expressions	____	____	____	____
Eye contact	____	____	____	____
Gestures	____	____	____	____
Use of audio-visual aids	____	____	____	____

Other remarks: _____

_____

Face to face and over the phone

Do you enjoy talking with other people? Are you a good listener? Are you at ease during interviews? Do you make effective use of the telephone?

All of these things involve your use of speaking and listening skills. These communication skills may be among the most important you can develop. For, after all, these are the communication skills you use most regularly.

In this section you will be given suggestions that could help you to improve your speaking and listening skills. Some techniques for conducting yourself during an interview will also be presented. And you will be given some tips that could help you to make the best use of your telephone.

Having better conversations

What is conversation?

Many people think that good conversation, like the concise letter, is a dying art. If this is true, it is probably because some people do not understand what conversation is. Conversation is supposed to be a form of communication. It is an *exchange* of ideas, thoughts, opinions, or feelings—a *sharing* of those ideas between people. At least two people are necessary to have a conversation. And these people talk *with* each other, not *to* each other. The purpose of conversation is to exchange communication in the most direct and personal manner.

Perhaps good conversation is rare today because people are so often in a hurry for one reason or another. They have little time to think about what they really intend to say. And effective spoken communication takes thought to organize and time to develop.

Much of the talking you do is to give information or to get information. On some occasions, you might discuss your opinions and feelings about the information.

There are also many opportunities each day to have good conversations that are of a social nature—communication held for pleasure. You might have social conversations walking home from school with friends, riding to and from work in a car pool, having coffee with a neighbor, eating lunch with friends or fellow employees, or having dinner with your family.

But whatever the reason for communication, be it a simple exchange of information or an occasion for pleasurable relaxation, there is no guarantee that a conversation will turn out well. Because it involves direct communication between two or more people, there are so many factors involved that more times than we might wish, something goes wrong and communication does not take place. Here are a few "do's" and "don'ts" that can help increase your chances of having effective conversations.

Contribute to conversations, don't monopolize them. Good conversationalists are eager to learn from everyone. They know that conversations are a way to share ideas with other people; they don't impose their ideas on others. This means that you should give everyone a chance to talk. Don't use conversations only as forums to expound your own ideas.

Be a good listener. You should spend at least as much time listening as you do talking during a conversation. Give your complete attention to whomever is talking. Don't just wait for your next opportunity to talk; don't concentrate so strongly on what you are going to say next that you fail to understand what others are saying. Being a good listener is just as important, if not more important, as being an effective talker.

Be assertive, not aggressive. If you have something to say—something that may contribute to the conversation—by all means say it. But wait for a natural opening in the conversation. Don't cut someone else off or talk over them.

When you are talking with people you have just met, don't give advice or tell everything there is to know about yourself. People will doubt your sincerity and probably not give any weight to important things you may have to say.

Be modest, not reserved. It's fine to thoughtfully assess the content and direction of any conversation before you say something. That is, after all, part and parcel of well-developed listening skills. But don't act too reserved or withdrawn. When people try to draw you into a conversation, don't give one-word answers. Remember that all conversation, no matter what its purpose, involves sharing. It requires participation by everyone. People quickly tire of trying to converse with anyone who is not participating. If you do not wish to share in a conversation, you owe it to the other participants to wait for a natural break and then politely leave.

Don't be an authority. Don't take the position that you are always right and that everyone else is always wrong. This attitude is commonly held by many people. Yet any reasonable person should quickly realize that no one can possibly be right even most of the time, much less all of the time.

Keep in mind the fact that unless you are involved in a debate, you need not view your communication exchange as a confrontation. Give others a chance to agree, disagree, or expand on your thoughts and ideas. This also implies that you should avoid giving the impression that you have a simple answer to every problem. Problems are usually complex, not solved easily. You know that; so do others. People who tend to be too simplistic in attitude or opinion are seldom taken seriously by others.

Be constructive and positive. It's easy to be negative about virtually anything another person might say. But does such a position add anything to the communication that is supposedly being shared?

Obviously, if someone says something that is demonstrably false, you should point that out. However, this can usually be done without assuming an authoritarian tone or resorting to ridicule. If you must make what you feel is a legitimate criticism of a statement, do so. But concentrate on criticizing the *statement,* not the *person* who made it.

Don't be rude. Don't interrupt when someone else is speaking. Don't mumble under your breath. Don't take the words out of the speaker's mouth—let the speaker make the point.

Don't flatly contradict others. If you disagree, say so and explain why. But don't imply that the other person doesn't know what he or she is talking about. Good conversation may be spirited—even argumentative. But even when there is disagreement, you should show respect for other people and their opinions. When all persons in a conversation are shown respect, they participate more freely. And everyone must participate in order for sharing to occur in a conversation.

Don't abruptly change the subject. Wait for a natural pause in the conversation to introduce a new subject. And don't think you're being polite when you say, "Not to change the subject, but. . . ." Your use of such a statement merely shows that you understand fully well that you are about to force the conversation into a different direction, something the other participants may not be anxious to do.

Be prepared when there is a lull in the conversation. Some studies have been done about conversation, and the results show that conversations, whatever their content or effectiveness, run in 10–12 minute cycles. It is natural that there will be lulls, some shorter and some longer, in every conversation. For many people such pauses are long moments spent groping for something, anything, to say.

Try to be prepared for the inevitable lull. Sometimes all that is needed is a simple transition from one part of a topic to another. At other times, the lull may signify that a topic has been exhausted and a new topic is needed if the conversation is to continue. And, finally, an extended lull may well be a signal by all participants that the conversation has ended. But whatever its length or outcome, be ready to read each conversational lull for what it is, a sign that the conversation has reached a certain stage in its development.

Know how to tell good stories or jokes. If it is appropriate to the main intent of the conversation, the introduction of an anecdote or joke can help to relieve tension and, therefore, make communication more effective. Naturally, you should not use this technique if the subject of the conversation is weighty or serious. Introducing a joke while talking to your boss about a job-related problem would be both foolish and counterproductive. But in the right spot and at the right time, this can become an excellent technique for making a conversation more lively.

If you're going to use an anecdote or joke, know it well enough so that you can tell it without stumbling. Don't laugh while you're telling a story or before you get to the end of a joke. Don't use anecdotes and jokes as a way to monopolize a conversation. And vary your stories—don't tell the same ones over and over again to the same people.

Have a variety of subjects that you can talk about. Don't have one subject that you always talk about—that you always sneak into every conversation. Know enough about a lot of subjects so that you can talk with people who have different interests. You can gain knowledge by reading widely, listening, and observing.

Varying your subjects is particularly important when you are meeting someone for the first time. An excellent way to break the ice is to get that person to talk about himself or herself. Ask questions about such things as careers, interests, and hobbies. Encourage the other person to talk about his or her background. You may discover that the two of you have something in common. And you may learn some things you did not know.

Suit the conversation to the group. Some topics are not appropriate for general conversation. Among these topics are problems with your spouse or parents, the wonders of your children, and health matters. Politics and religion were once regarded as impolite topics for conversation; but today these subjects are the focal point of many animated conversations. It's perfectly fine to talk about controversial subjects as long as everyone's opinions are respected.

However, you should keep in mind the fact that a suitable topic of conversation for one person may well be considered offensive by another. Look for clues in what you know about the background and interests of a conversation's participants. These could help you to tailor at least your part of the conversation to the group with which you are dealing.

Look at all the people in a conversation. Don't focus your attention on an object—vase, lamp, or picture—while you are talking. And if the conversation has several participants, don't look at just one person while you talk. To hold everyone's attention, vary the direction of your gaze so that you look at each person while you are talking. Look at each person's face and into each person's eyes. By doing this, you help to hold the group together and you add a sense of unity that reinforces the feeling that all participants are sharing in the flow of communication.

Speak so that others can understand you. Speak loudly enough so that all participants can hear you. Use a pleasant tone of voice. Don't shout to be heard, and don't mumble.

Being a good listener

The forgotten art

Speaking or talking is just one part of the communication process; listening is the other. Without listeners, there would be no need for speakers. You spend much more time listening than you do speaking. At school you listen to lectures, to other students' reports, and to instructions. At work you listen during meetings, on the telephone, and to co-workers' suggestions. At home you listen to conversations, to the radio and television, and to records or tapes. At church you listen to sermons.

And yet listening is probably the most poorly understood and the least developed formally of the communication skills. It has only been during recent years that much attention has been given to listening skills in school. Listening was assumed to be a natural skill or ability that did not require practice. Yet the deeper various communication problems are studied, the more obvious it becomes that one basic cause is poorly developed listening skills. Conversation might be called a dying art, but listening has become the forgotten art.

Ways to improve listening

Listening is a communication skill, and like speaking and writing, it can be improved with practice. The suggestions which follow may help you improve your listening skills:

1. *Concentrate on listening.* Before you can listen well, you must learn to be more aware of what you hear. To increase your awareness, concentrate on listening. Be alert to all the sounds around you. Get out of the habit of "tuning out" and instead practice "tuning in" to the sounds around you. Listen for high-pitched sounds and faraway noises. Try to identify voices before you see the people. Listen to music; don't use it just for background effect.
2. *Be an eager listener.* Approach every lecture, speech, or conversation with an open mind. Be receptive to the ideas of others. Be responsive to the person who is speaking—

laugh, smile, frown, nod your head, or lean forward in your seat. Be able to feed back to people what they have said to you.

3. *Pay attention.* Concentrate on what the person who is talking is saying; tune out everything—sights, sounds, and your own thoughts—except the speaker's voice. Try repeating to yourself what was said. Don't let your mind wander.

4. *Listen for main ideas.* Don't sort out isolated words and phrases—listen for the conversation's main ideas. Ask yourself, "What is the speaker getting at?" If possible, ask questions that will help clarify what the other person is saying. Be sure you have really heard and understood what has been said.

5. *Look at the speaker's face.* Show that you are an attentive listener by looking the speaker directly in the eyes. This will be taken as a sign that you are interested in or care about what is being said.

6. *Converse in quiet places.* Don't try to carry on a formal conversation on a busy street corner or at a basketball game. You won't be able to hear the conversation, let alone listen to it. If you are trying to listen to a conversation, turn off the television set, radio, and stereo. Close the windows and doors to shut out noises that may distract you.

The list which follows contains some commonly experienced bad listening habits. Avoid developing these listening habits. Or try to correct them if you become aware that you have already developed them.

Correct bad listening habits

1. Don't "turn someone off" just because you don't like the way he or she looks or sounds. Tune out the distractions of the speaker's appearance or voice. Concentrate on what he or she has to say; listen for the ideas.

2. Don't stop listening just because the speech, lecture, or conversation sounds boring. Instead, concentrate and try to isolate bits of information that might be useful to you now or at some later date.

3. Don't stop listening just because the person who is speaking says something with which you disagree. In a conversation, ask some questions to clarify what was said. In a lecture, take extra notes about any remark you believe to be controversial, and try to question the speaker after the lecture. Always hear the speaker out— you might be convinced to change your mind.

4. Don't stop listening just because a topic is difficult to understand. Don't be quick to blame the speaker for not

giving a good explanation. The problem may well be your own poorly developed listening skills. Give your entire attention to what is being said. Try to take notes about especially difficult points. Your goal should be to learn enough about the topic to ask intelligent questions. In that way you may eventually understand what is being said.

Remember that listeners should always be courteous and tolerant—even when the people who are speaking may be poorly organized and uninteresting.

Making a good impression during interviews

Different kinds of interviews

Interviews usually have one of three purposes: to get information, to solve problems, or to make an evaluation. Some interviews, such as the employment interview, might combine two purposes. The intent of the employment interview is to both obtain information and make an evaluation.

There are many occasions on which you could be interviewed. If you are a new student at a school, a new family in the neighborhood, or a new employee, you might be interviewed for an article in the school paper, the community newspaper, or the company newsletter. These kinds of interviews ask for information in order to introduce you to other students, to other members of the community, or to co-workers.

If you are applying for an insurance policy or a loan, you might be interviewed. These interviews evaluate whether or not you would be a good risk for the policy or the loan. Whether you are in school or on the job, you will probably be interviewed periodically by your counselor or supervisor. These interviews are intended to help you recognize and solve any problems you may be having and perhaps evaluate your skills and abilities.

And finally there is the job, or employment, interview. At some point—and usually at several points—during your working life, you will be interviewed for a new job or a promotion. How you conduct yourself during the interview may well determine whether or not you get the job or promotion.

Since the employment interview is so important, this section gives specific suggestions about preparing yourself for and conducting yourself during such an interview. Many of the suggestions given here can also be applied to other kinds of interview situations.

Before you have an interview, you have usually sent in a résumé or filled in an application form. That you've been granted an interview means your résumé or application has shown that you have some qualifications that might suit you for the position. The interviewer now wants to find out what your thoughts and opinions are, how you get along with others, and how you act under stress (since an interview itself is a stressful situation).

Preparing for a job interview

As soon as an appointment is made with you for an interview, begin preparing for it. Here are some suggestions for things to do before an interview:

1. Write down the date, time, place of the interview, and the interviewer's name. Be sure you have the name of the interviewer spelled correctly and that you know how to pronounce it. Since most interviews are arranged over the phone, ask the person who is making the appointment to spell and slowly pronounce all names.
2. Look over a copy of your résumé. Mark the parts which you think the interviewer might want clarified or about which more information might be needed. Determine what this extra information could be and how you will present that information.
3. Try to think of questions the interviewer might ask about your goals, achievements, leisure activities, and personal life. Prepare clear, concise, and direct answers. (Some questions that are frequently asked during interviews are given at the end of this section.)
4. Find out as much as you can about the company or institution. What products or services does it deal in? Is it part of a larger corporation? Does it conduct business in foreign countries? You might try to get a copy of its latest annual report; study the organization's history, structure, goals, and current status.
5. Find out about the interviewer. Is the interviewer from the personnel department, or is he or she a department head or a vice-president? Does the interviewer have the authority to hire? Or does the interviewer merely screen applicants to see if they are qualified before sending them on to the person who will do the hiring?

After you have thoroughly prepared yourself, you should be ready for the actual interview.

Being interviewed doesn't guarantee that you will be offered a job. There are probably several other people being considered for the same position. During the interview, you must present yourself as the most desirable person for the job. Since each interviewer is an individual and is looking for different things

Conducting yourself during an interview

in the people he or she is interviewing, there is no formula for guaranteed success. However, the suggestions that follow could help you to avoid some of the more common pitfalls encountered during an interview.

1. *Dress appropriately.* Be neat, clean, and unrumpled. Choose simple, tasteful, and comfortable clothing. Don't be gaudy or wear flashy, noisy jewelry.

2. *Arrive on time.* Better yet be early. That will give you time to check your appearance and relax. Several moments spent thinking through what you intend to say can pay great dividends during the conduct of the interview.

3. *Be courteous.* Use the interviewer's name as soon as possible. Don't offer to shake hands until the interviewer does. Don't sit down until you are offered a chair. Don't smoke unless the interviewer asks you if you wish to smoke.

4. *Be confident but not overconfident.* Sit in a relaxed manner, but don't slouch or sprawl over the chair. Show that you have a sense of humor, but don't tell jokes or funny stories. You're not there to entertain the interviewer.

5. *Be in control of yourself at all times.* Don't show nervousness by playing with jewelry, fidgeting, or chewing gum. You will be nervous, and the interviewer knows this. Just don't show how nervous you are.

6. *Make a quick assessment of the interviewer.* Does he or she look tired, pleasant, stern, disciplined, or disorganized? This might determine *how* you will answer questions—where you will put emphasis.

7. *Look at the interviewer.* When you are being asked a question, listen carefully and wait until the interviewer stops talking before you give your answer.

8. *Think before you answer each question.* Give thoughtful, direct, and honest answers.

9. *Ask the interviewer questions.* This is your chance to find out about the position—what responsibilities are involved and how the position fits into the overall operation of the company.

10. *Don't ask about salary.* The interviewer will start to talk about salary as an indication that you are being seriously considered for the position. If you are asked how much you are presently making, turn the question to the interviewer. Courteously ask what the salary range for the position is. That way if you are presently earning a low salary, the interviewer cannot offer you less than the lowest amount in the salary range.

11. *Don't be upset by silence during an interview.* Sometimes an interviewer uses silence to test your composure. Just look

at the interviewer as if you expect another question. Wait for the interviewer to break the silence. Don't fidget or elaborate unnecessarily on your last answer during a silence.

Write down a brief review of the interview after you have left the office. Such a review will help you to prepare for other interviews, possibly with the same company, possibly with others. Include questions that were asked, answers that you or the interviewer gave, information about the position and the company, and your evaluation of the position and the company. Finally, you should write a thank-you note to the interviewer. Such a sign of common courtesy demonstrates an attitude that many organizations find very desirable in employees.

Questions frequently asked during interviews

1. What are your professional goals for the next five or ten years?
2. Do you prefer working with others or by yourself?
3. Can you accept criticism without getting upset?
4. Why would you like to work for this company?
5. How do you spend your time away from work?
6. What are your personal goals for the next five or ten years?
7. Why have you decided to leave your current position?
8. What extracurricular activities did you participate in while at school?

Using the telephone

You probably use the telephone every day. Phoning saves time, particularly when a quick response is required. Rather than writing letters, you telephone because it is both faster and more convenient than using the mail. You use the telephone to obtain information, to receive services, or to converse with friends. Yet few people understand that effective use of this means of communication requires both thought and planning. Unlike a letter which can be reread several times, a telephone communication must be clear the first time. A misunderstanding that requires additional communication defeats the entire purpose of using the telephone.

Suggestions for making the best use of the telephone follow. These suggestions apply to both personal and business calls.

When you make a call, follow this suggested procedure:

1. Keep the telephone book, your personal or business directory, and a list of frequently called numbers by the phone.

2. Know the number you are calling and dial it carefully.
3. Allow enough time for the other person to answer. The phone company suggests letting the phone ring 10 times for calls to homes. For business calls, 4 rings should be enough. If the phone has not been answered by then, no one is in the office.
4. Always speak clearly, loudly enough, and slowly enough so that you can be understood easily. Identify yourself as soon as the person answers. Say, "Hello, this is _____." Don't play guessing games on the phone.
5. Be ready to talk. Have any information or questions written down in front of you. If you can avoid it, don't leave the person hanging on the phone while you get more information.
6. Get your message across quickly. The other person probably has many other things to do.
7. If the person you are calling doesn't have time to talk or doesn't have the information you need, suggest a time that you can call back. Be sure to return the call on time.
8. Read the information in the front of your phone book about making long-distance calls.

When you receive a call, there are also certain things you should do.

1. Answer the phone as quickly as possible.
2. Identify yourself so that callers know they have reached the right number and person. And give a pleasant greeting: "Hello," "Good morning," or "Good afternoon."
3. Be a good listener. Find out the purpose of the call, and give the requested information. If it's a business call, try to avoid having to place the caller on hold. If it's a personal call, don't monopolize the conversation.
4. When the conversation is over, say good-bye and hang up quietly.

Use what you know

The following activity has been designed to help you improve your aural communication skills.

Check your listening skills

Good listening skills are needed to accurately receive the messages that are communicated by others. You must listen to carry on a conversation, to answer questions in an interview, and to talk on the telephone. Use this checklist to determine how you can improve your listening skills. Be honest in your answers. The point of the activity is to permit you to identify areas where improvement can help you to communicate with others more effectively.

	Yes	Needs improvement
1. My concentration is as good as it can be.	___	___
2. I am interested in what others have to say.	___	___
3. I let the speaker complete his or her thoughts before I make a judgment.	___	___
4. I am a responsive listener. I laugh, smile, or frown to show my reactions.	___	___
5. I look at people when they are talking.	___	___
6. I can tune out everything except the speaker's voice.	___	___
7. I listen for main ideas.	___	___
8. I carry on conversations in quiet places.	___	___

10,000 Commonly used words

How many times while writing have you come to the end of a line and discovered you had enough room to add part, but not all, of a word? When was the last time you stumbled over the spelling of a word, or wondered whether or not a compound word contains a hyphen? If you are like most people, these questions arise frequently when you are writing.

What follows is a quick reference list of 10,000 of the words most commonly encountered in everyday communication. These are the words you use at work or in school, hear on radio and television, and read in the newspaper. These are the words that very likely form the basis of your written vocabulary.

The list has been arranged in alphabetical order for ease of use. Commonly accepted syllable breaks have been indicated. Remember, however, that you cannot always divide a word at every syllable break shown. Once you find what the syllables in a word are, turn to the guidelines on pages 38–39 which tell when you should or should not divide a word at the end of a line. Spellings, syllable breaks, and hyphenation of words are all based upon those that appear in the highly respected and authoritative *The World Book Dictionary,* compiled under the direction of Clarence L. Barnhart.

A

a·ban·don
a·bate
ab·bey
ab·bre·vi·ate
ab·bre·vi·a·tion
ab·di·cate
ab·do·men
ab·dom·i·nal
ab·duct
a·bet
ab·hor
a·bide
a·bil·i·ty
ab·ject
a·ble
ab·nor·mal
a·board
a·bol·ish
ab·o·li·tion
a·bom·i·na·ble
a·bor·tion
a·bound
a·bout
a·bove
a·bridge
a·bridg·ment
a·broad
a·brupt
ab·scess
ab·sence
ab·sent
ab·so·lute
ab·solve
ab·sorb·ent
ab·sorp·tion
ab·stain
ab·sti·nence
ab·stract
ab·surd
a·bun·dance
a·bun·dant
a·buse
a·bys·mal
a·byss
ac·a·dem·ic
a·cad·e·my
ac·cel·er·ate
ac·cel·er·a·tor
ac·cent
ac·cept

ac·cept·a·ble
ac·cept·ance
ac·cess
ac·ces·so·ry
ac·ci·dent
ac·ci·den·tal
ac·com·mo·date
ac·com·mo·da·tion
ac·com·pa·ny
ac·com·plish
ac·cord
ac·cord·ance
ac·cord·ing·ly
ac·count
ac·count·a·bil·i·ty
ac·cred·i·ted
ac·cu·mu·late
ac·cu·mu·la·tion
ac·cur·ate
ac·curs·ed
ac·cu·sa·tion
ac·cuse
ac·cus·tom
ache
a·chieve
a·chieve·ment
ac·id
ac·knowl·edge
ac·knowl·edg·ment
a·corn
a·cous·tic
ac·quaint
ac·quaint·ance
ac·qui·esce
ac·quire
ac·qui·si·tion
ac·quit
ac·quit·tal
a·cre
a·cre·age
ac·ro·bat
a·cross
act
ac·tion
ac·tive
ac·tiv·i·ty
ac·tor
ac·tress
ac·tu·al
a·cute
ad
a·dapt

ad·ap·ta·tion
ad·dict·ed
ad·di·tion
ad·di·tive
ad·dress
ad·e·quate
ad·here
ad·he·sive
ad·ja·cent
ad·jec·tive
ad·join
ad·journ
ad·judge
ad·just
ad·min·is·ter
ad·min·is·tra·tion
ad·min·is·tra·tor
ad·mi·ra·ble
ad·mi·ral
ad·mi·ra·tion
ad·mire
ad·mis·sion
ad·mit
ad·mon·ish
ad·mo·ni·tion
ad·o·les·cent
a·dopt
a·dop·tion
a·dore
a·dorn
ad·ren·al·in
a·dult
a·dul·te·rate
a·dul·ter·y
ad·vance
ad·van·tage
ad·van·ta·geous
ad·ven·ture
ad·ven·tur·er
ad·ven·tur·ous
ad·verb
ad·ver·sar·y
ad·verse
ad·ver·si·ty
ad·ver·tise
ad·ver·tise·ment
ad·ver·tis·ing
ad·vice
ad·vis·a·ble
ad·vise
ad·vi·so·ry
ad·vo·cate

aer·i·al
aer·o·nau·tics
aer·o·sol
aes·thet·ic
af·fair
af·fect
af·fec·ta·tion
af·fec·tion
af·fec·tion·ate
af·fi·da·vit
af·firm
af·flict
af·flic·tion
af·flu·ence
af·flu·ent
af·ford
af·front
a·fire
a·float
a·foot
a·fraid
af·ter
af·ter·noon
af·ter·wards
a·gain
a·gainst
a·ged
a·gen·cy
a·gen·da
a·gent
ag·gra·vate
ag·gres·sion
ag·gres·sive
ag·ile
ag·i·tate
ag·i·ta·tion
a·go
ag·o·ny
a·gree
a·gree·a·ble
a·gree·ment
ag·ri·cul·tur·al
ag·ri·cul·ture
a·head
aid
ail
aim
air
air·con·di·tioned
air con·di·tion·ing
air·craft
air·line

air·mail
air·plane
air·port
air·tight
air·y
aisle
a·kin
a·larm
al·bum
al·co·hol
ale
a·lert
al·gae
al·ge·bra
a·li·as
al·i·bi
al·ien
al·ien·ate
a·light
a·like
a·live
al·lay
al·le·ga·tion
al·lege
al·le·giance
al·ler·gic
al·ler·gy
al·ley
al·li·ance
al·lied
al·li·ga·tor
al·lo·cate
al·low
al·low·ance
al·loy
all right
all-star
al·lure
al·lu·sion
al·ly
al·ma·nac
al·might·y
al·mond
al·most
alms
a·lone
a·long
a·long·side
a·loof
a·loud
al·pha·bet
al·read·y

al·so
al·tar
al·ter
al·ter·a·tion
al·ter·nate
al·ter·na·tive
al·though
al·ti·tude
al·to·geth·er
a·lu·mi·num
a·lum·ni
al·ways
am·a·teur
a·maze
am·bas·sa·dor
am·ber
am·big·u·ous
am·bi·tion
am·bu·lance
am·bush
a·mend
a·mend·ment
A·mer·i·can
a·mi·a·ble
a·mid
a·miss
am·mu·ni·tion
am·nes·ty
a·mong
a·mount
am·ple
am·pli·fi·er
am·pu·tate
a·muse
a·nal·y·sis
an·a·lyze
an·ar·chy
a·nat·o·my
an·ces·tor
an·chor
an·cient
an·ec·dote
a·ne·mi·a
a·ne·mic
an·es·thet·ic
a·new
an·gel
an·ger
an·gle
an·gri·ly
an·gry
an·guish

an·i·mal
an·i·mate
an·i·mos·i·ty
an·kle
an·nals
an·nex
an·ni·hi·late
an·ni·ver·sa·ry
an·no·tate
an·nounce
an·noy
an·nu·al
an·nul
a·noint
a·non·y·mous
an·oth·er
an·swer
ant
an·tag·o·nism
an·tag·o·nist
ant·arc·tic
an·te·ced·ent
an·ten·na
an·ti·bi·ot·ic
an·ti·bod·y
an·tic·i·pate
an·ti·dote
an·ti·freeze
an·ti·his·ta·mine
an·tique
an·tiq·ui·ty
an·ti-Se·mit·ic
an·ti·sep·tic
an·vil
anx·i·e·ty
anx·ious
an·y
an·y·bod·y
an·y·how
an·y·one
an·y·place
an·y·thing
an·y·time
an·y·way
an·y·where
a·part
a·part·ment
ape
a·pol·o·gize
a·pol·o·gy
a·pos·tle
ap·pall

ap·pall·ing
ap·par·el
ap·par·ent
ap·pa·ri·tion
ap·peal
ap·pear
ap·pease
ap·pen·dix
ap·pe·tite
ap·plaud
ap·plause
ap·ple
ap·pli·ance
ap·pli·cant
ap·pli·ca·tion
ap·plied
ap·ply
ap·point
ap·point·ment
ap·praise
ap·pre·ci·ate
ap·pre·ci·a·tion
ap·pre·hend
ap·pre·hen·sion
ap·pren·tice
ap·proach
ap·pro·pri·ate
ap·pro·pri·a·tion
ap·prov·al
ap·prove
ap·prox·i·mate
a·pri·cot
a·pron
apt
ap·ti·tude
a·quar·i·um
a·quat·ic
ar·bi·trar·y
ar·bi·tra·tion
arch
ar·chae·ol·o·gy
arch·bish·op
ar·chi·tect
ar·chi·tec·ture
ar·chives
arch·way
arc·tic
ar·dent
are
ar·e·a
a·re·na
ar·gue

ar·gu·ment
ar·id
a·rise
a·ris·to·crat·ic
a·rith·me·tic
ark
arm
ar·ma·ment
arm·ful
arm·hole
ar·mi·stice
ar·mor
ar·mored
ar·my
a·ro·ma
a·round
a·rouse
ar·raign
ar·range
ar·range·ment
ar·ray
ar·rears
ar·rest
ar·riv·al
ar·rive
ar·ro·gant
ar·row
ar·se·nal
ar·son
art
ar·te·ri·al
ar·ter·y
art·ful
ar·thri·tis
ar·ti·cle
ar·ti·fi·cial
ar·til·ler·y
ar·ti·san
art·ist
ar·tis·tic
art·less
as·bes·tos
as·cend
as·cent
as·cer·tain
ash
a·shamed
ash·es
a·shore
a·side
ask
a·sleep

as·par·a·gus
as·pect
as·phalt
as·phyx·i·ate
as·pi·ra·tion
as·pire
as·pir·in
ass
as·sail
as·sail·ant
as·sas·si·nate
as·sas·si·na·tion
as·sault
as·sem·ble
as·sem·bly
as·sent
as·sert
as·ser·tion
as·sess
as·sess·ment
as·set
as·sign
as·sign·ment
as·sim·i·late
as·sist
as·sist·ant
as·so·ci·ate
as·so·ci·a·tion
as·sort·ment
as·sume
as·sump·tion
as·sur·ance
as·sure
as·ter
as·ter·isk
as·ton·ish
as·ton·ish·ment
as·tound
a·stray
as·trol·o·gy
as·tro·naut
as·tro·nom·i·cal
as·tron·o·my
as·tute
a·sun·der
a·sy·lum
a·sym·met·ric
ate
ath·lete
ath·let·ic
at·las
at·mos·phere

at·om
a·tom·ic
a·tone
at·tach
at·tach·ment
at·tack
at·tain
at·tempt
at·tend
at·ten·tion
at·ten·tive
at·test
at·tic
at·tire
at·ti·tude
at·tor·ney
at·tract
at·trac·tion
at·trib·ute
at·tri·tion
auc·tion
auc·tion·eer
au·da·cious
au·di·ble
au·di·ence
au·di·o·vis·u·al
au·dit
au·di·tion
au·di·to·ri·um
aug·ment
aunt
aus·pi·ces
aus·pi·cious
aus·tere
aus·ter·i·ty
au·then·tic
au·then·tic·i·ty
au·thor
au·thor·i·tar·i·an
au·thor·i·ty
au·thor·i·za·tion
au·thor·ize
au·to·bi·og·ra·phy
au·to·crat·ic
au·to·mat·ic
au·to·ma·tion
au·to·mo·bile
au·ton·o·mous
au·top·sy
au·tumn
aux·il·ia·ry
a·vail

a·vail·a·ble
av·a·lanche
av·ar·ice
a·venge
av·e·nue
av·er·age
a·ver·sion
a·vert
av·id
a·void
a·wait
a·wake
a·wak·en
a·ward
a·ware
a·way
awe
aw·ful
a·while
awk·ward
ax
ax·is
ax·le
aye

B

bab·ble
babe
ba·by
ba·by-sit
ba·by sit·ter
bach·e·lor
back
back·ache
back·bone
back·fire
back·gam·mon
back·ground
back·hand·ed
back·ward
ba·con
bac·ter·i·a
badge
baf·fle
bag·gage
bag·pipe
bail
bait
bake
bak·er

bal·ance
bal·co·ny
bald
balk
ball
bal·lad
bal·let
bal·lis·tic
bal·loon
bal·lot
ball·point
balm
bam·boo
ba·nan·a
band
band·age
ban·dit
bang
ban·ish
ban·jo
bank
bank·er
bank·rupt
bank·rupt·cy
ban·ner
ban·quet
bap·tism
Bap·tist
bap·tize
bar
bar·bar·i·an
bar·bar·ic
bar·ba·rous
bar·be·cue
bar·ber
bard
bare
bare·foot
bar·gain
barge
bark
bar·ley
barn
barn·yard
ba·rom·e·ter
bar·o·met·ric
bar·racks
bar·rel
bar·ren
bar·ri·cade
bar·ri·er
bar·ter

base
base·ball
base·ment
bash·ful
ba·sic
ba·sin
ba·sis
bask
bas·ket
bas·ket·ball
bas·tard
baste
batch
bath
bathe
bath·robe
bath·room
ba·ton
bat·tal·ion
bat·ter·y
bat·tle
bat·tle·field
bat·tle·ment
bat·tle·ship
bau·ble
bawl
bay
bay·o·net
ba·zaar
beach
bea·con
bead
beak
beam
bean
bear
bear·a·ble
beard
bear·er
bear·ing
beast
beat
beat·en
beau·ti·fi·ca·tion
beau·ti·ful
beau·ti·fy
beau·ty
bea·ver
be·came
be·cause
beck
beck·on

be·come
be·com·ing
bed·ding
bed·lam
bed·room
bed·spread
bed·stead
bed·time
bee
beech
beef
bee·hive
been
beer
beet
bee·tle
be·fore
be·fore·hand
be·friend
be·fud·dle
be·gan
be·get
beg·gar
be·gin
be·gin·ner
be·gin·ning
be·gone
be·got
be·gun
be·half
be·have
be·hav·ior
be·head
be·held
be·hind
be·hold
be·ing
be·lat·ed
belch
bel·fry
be·lie
be·lief
be·lieve
be·liev·er
be·lit·tle
bell
belle
bel·lig·er·ent
bel·low
bel·ly
be·long
be·lov·ed

be·low
belt
be·moan
bench
bend
be·neath
ben·e·dic·tion
ben·e·fac·tor
ben·e·fi·cial
ben·e·fi·ci·ar·y
ben·e·fit
be·nev·o·lence
be·nev·o·lent
be·nign
bent
be·queath
be·quest
be·reave
be·reft
be·ret
ber·ry
be·set
be·side
be·sides
be·siege
best
be·stow
be·tray
be·tray·al
be·trothed
bet·ter
be·tween
bev·er·age
be·wail
be·ware
be·wil·der
be·witch
be·yond
bi·an·nu·al
bi·as
Bi·ble
bib·li·cal
bib·li·og·ra·phy
bick·er
bi·cy·cle
bid·der
bide
bi·en·ni·al
bier
big·ger
big·gest
bilge

bill	bleak	bod·y·guard	boul·der
bil·liards	bleat	bog·gle	bounce
bil·lion	bled	boil	bound
bil·low	bleed	boil·er	bound·ar·y
bi·na·ry	blem·ish	bois·ter·ous	boun·ti·ful
bind	blend	bold	boun·ty
bind·er	bless	bo·lo·gna	bou·quet
bin·go	bless·ed	bol·ster	bour·bon
bi·noc·u·lars	bless·ing	bolt	bout
bi·o·chem·is·try	blew	bomb	bow
bi·og·ra·phy	blight	bom·bard	bow·el
bi·o·log·i·cal	blind	bomb·shell	bowl
bi·ol·o·gy	blink	bond	bowl·ing
birch	bliss	bond·age	box
bird	bliss·ful	bonds·man	box·er
bird·house	blis·ter	bone	boy
bird·ie	blithe	bon·fire	boy·cott
bird's·eye	bliz·zard	bon·net	boy·hood
birth	bloat	bo·nus	brace
birth·day	blond	book	brace·let
birth·place	blood	book·case	brack·et
birth rate	blood pres·sure	book·keep·er	brag
birth·right	blood·stream	book·keep·ing	braid
bis·cuit	blood·y	book·let	brain
bish·op	bloom	book·sell·er	brake
bi·son	blos·som	book·shelf	bran
bite	blot	book·shop	branch
bit·ter	blotch	book·store	brand
bi·zarre	blouse	boom	bran·dish
black	blow	boon	brand-new
black·ber·ry	blow·out	boost	bran·dy
black·bird	blow·torch	boot	brass
black·board	blub·ber	booth	brave
black·en	blue	boo·ty	brav·er·y
black eye	blue·ber·ry	bo·rax	brawl
black·list	blue·bird	bor·der	brawn
black·mail	blue·grass	bore	bra·zen
black mar·ket	blue jay	bore·dom	breach
black·out	blue·print	bor·ough	bread
black·smith	bluff	bor·row	breadth
blad·der	blun·der	bos·om	break
blade	blunt	boss	break·a·ble
blame	blur	boss·y	break·down
blanch	blush	bo·tan·i·cal	break·er
bland	blus·ter	bot·a·ny	break·fast
blank	boar	both	break·through
blan·ket	board	both·er	breast
blas·phe·my	board·er	bot·tle	breath
blast	boast	bot·tom	breathe
bla·tant	boat	bough	breath·less
blaze	bode	bought	bred
bleach	bod·y	bouil·lon	breech

breech·es
breed
breed·ing
breeze
breez·y
brev·i·ty
brew
bribe
brib·er·y
brick
brid·al
bride
bridge
bri·dle
brief
bri·gade
brig·a·dier
bright
bright·en
bril·liance
bril·liant
brim
brine
bring
brink
brisk
bris·tle
Brit·ain
Brit·ish
brit·tle
broad
broad·cast
broad·cloth
broad·en
broad·loom
broad-mind·ed
broad·side
broc·co·li
broil
broil·er
broke
bro·ken
bro·ker
bronze
brooch
brood
brook
broom
broth
broth·er
broth·er·hood
brought

brow
brown
brown·ie
browse
bruise
brush
bru·tal
brute
brut·ish
bub·ble
buck
buck·et
buck·le
buck·shot
buck·skin
buck·wheat
budge
budg·et
buff
buf·fa·lo
buff·er
buf·fet
bug·gy
build
build·er
build·ing
build-up
built
built-in
bulb
bulge
bulk
bull
bull·dog
bull·doz·er
bul·let
bul·le·tin
bull·fight·er
bul·lion
bul·ly
bul·wark
bump
bump·er
bump·y
bunch
bun·dle
bun·gle
bun·ion
bun·ny
bun·ting
buoy
buoy·ant

bur·den
bur·eau
bu·reauc·ra·cy
bur·glar
bur·i·al
bur·ied
bur·lap
bur·lesque
burn
burn·er
bur·nish
burr
burst
bur·y
bush
bush·el
bush·y
bus·i·ly
busi·ness
bust
bus·tle
bus·y
butch·er
butt
but·ter
but·ter·fly
but·ter·milk
but·ton
but·ton·hole
but·tress
buy
buy·er
buzz
by-pass
by-prod·uct
by·stand·er

C

cab·bage
cab·driv·er
cab·in
cab·i·net
ca·ble
cack·le
ca·fe
caf·e·te·ri·a
caf·feine
cage
cake
ca·lam·i·ty

cal·cu·late
cal·cu·la·tion
cal·cu·la·tor
cal·en·dar
calf
cal·i·ber
cal·i·co
call
call·er
cal·lous
calm
cal·o·rie
calves
came
cam·el
cam·er·a
cam·er·a·man
cam·ou·flage
camp
cam·paign
camp·er
ca·nal
ca·nar·y
can·cel
can·cel·la·tion
can·cer
can·cer·ous
can·did
can·di·da·cy
can·di·date
can·dle
can·dle·stick
can·dor
can·dy
cane
ca·nine
can·ker
canned
can·ni·bal
can·non
ca·noe
can·o·py
can't
can·yon
ca·pa·bil·i·ty
ca·pa·ble
ca·pac·i·ty
cape
ca·per
cap·i·tal
cap·i·tal·ism
cap·i·tal·ize

ca·pit·u·late
ca·price
ca·pri·cious
cap·size
cap·sule
cap·tain
cap·tion
cap·ti·vate
cap·tive
cap·tiv·i·ty
cap·ture
car
car·a·mel
car·at
car·a·van
car·bo·hy·drate
car·bon
car·bun·cle
car·bu·re·tor
car·cass
card
card·board
car·di·gan
car·di·nal
care
ca·reer
care·ful
care·less
ca·ress
car·go
car·i·ca·ture
car·ies
car·nal
car·ni·val
car·niv·o·rous
car·ol
ca·rouse
car·pen·ter
car·pet
car·riage
car·ri·er
car·rot
car·ry
cart
car·tel
cart·er
car·ti·lage
car·tog·ra·phy
car·ton
car·toon
car·tridge
carve

case
cash
cash·ier
cash·mere
cas·ing
ca·si·no
cas·ket
cas·se·role
cast
cast·er
cast·ing
cas·tle
cas·tor
cas·u·al
cas·u·al·ty
cat·a·log
cat·a·lyst
cat·a·ract
ca·tas·tro·phe
catch
cat·e·chism
cat·e·gor·i·cal
cat·e·go·ry
ca·ter
cat·er·pil·lar
ca·the·dral
Cath·o·lic
cat·nip
cat·tle
cat·ty
caught
cau·li·flow·er
caulk
cause
caus·tic
cau·ter·ize
cau·tion
cau·tious
cav·a·lier
cav·al·ry
cave
cave-in
cav·ern
cease
cease·less
ce·dar
cede
ceil·ing
cel·e·brate
cel·e·bra·tion
ce·leb·ri·ty
cel·er·y

ce·les·tial
cell
cel·lar
cel·lo·phane
cel·lu·lar
cel·lu·lose
Cel·si·us
ce·ment
cem·e·ter·y
cen·sor
cen·sor·ship
cen·sure
cen·sus
cent
cen·ter
cen·ti·grade
cen·ti·me·ter
cen·ti·pede
cen·tral
cen·tral·i·za·tion
cen·tral·ize
cen·tur·y
ce·ram·ic
cer·e·al
ce·re·bral
cer·e·mo·ni·al
cer·e·mo·ny
cer·tain
cer·tain·ty
cer·tif·i·cate
cer·ti·fi·ca·tion
cer·ti·fied
cer·ti·fy
ces·sa·tion
chafe
chaff
chain
chair
chair·man
chair·per·son
chalk
chalk·board
chal·lenge
cham·ber
cham·ber·maid
cham·pagne
cham·pi·on
chance
chan·cel·lor
chan·de·lier
change
change·a·ble

chan·nel
chant
cha·os
cha·ot·ic
chap·el
chap·lain
chap·ter
char·ac·ter
char·ac·ter·is·tic
char·ac·ter·ize
cha·rade
char·coal
charge
charge·a·ble
cha·ris·ma
char·i·ta·ble
char·i·ty
charm
chart
char·ter
chase
chas·sis
chaste
chas·tise
chas·ti·ty
chat
chat·tel
chat·ter
chauf·feur
chau·vin·ism
cheap
cheat
check
check·book
check·ered
check·er
check·list
check·mate
check·point
check·up
cheek
cheer
cheer·ful
cheer·i·ness
cheer·y
cheese
chef
chem·i·cal
chem·is·try
cher·ish
cher·ry
chess

chest
chest·nut
chew
chew·y
chick
chick·en
chide
chief
chif·fon
child
child·birth
child·hood
child·ish
child·like
chil·dren
chill
chill·y
chime
chim·ney
chim·pan·zee
chin
chi·na
Chi·nese
chink
chip
chi·ro·prac·tor
chirp
chis·el
chiv·al·rous
chiv·al·ry
chlo·ride
chlo·rine
chlo·ro·phyll
choc·o·late
choice
choir
choke
cho·les·ter·ol
choose
chop
chop·per
cho·ral
chord
cho·re·og·ra·pher
cho·rus
chose
cho·sen
Christ
chris·ten
Chris·tian
Chris·ti·an·i·ty
Christ·mas

chro·mi·um
chro·mo·some
chron·ic
chron·i·cle
chron·o·log·i·cal
chry·san·the·mum
chuck
chuck·le
chum
church
church·go·er
church·yard
churn
chute
ci·der
ci·gar
cig·a·rette
cinch
cin·der
cin·e·ma
cin·na·mon
ci·pher
cir·cle
cir·cuit
cir·cu·lar
cir·cu·late
cir·cu·la·tion
cir·cu·la·to·ry
cir·cum·fer·ence
cir·cum·scribe
cir·cum·stance
cir·cum·stan·tial
cir·cus
ci·ta·tion
cite
cit·i·zen
cit·ric
cit·rus
cit·y
civ·ic
civ·il
ci·vil·ian
ci·vil·i·ty
civ·i·li·za·tion
civ·i·lize
clad
claim
clam
clam·mi·ness
clam·my
clam·or
clamp

clan
clan·des·tine
clang
clank
clap
clap·board
clar·i·fy
clar·i·ty
clash
clasp
class
clas·sic
clas·si·cal
clas·si·fi·ca·tion
clas·si·fied
clas·si·fy
class·mate
class·room
clat·ter
clause
claw
clay
clean
clean·er
cleanse
cleans·er
clear
clear·ance
cleav·age
cleave
clef
cleft
clem·en·cy
clench
cler·gy
cler·gy·man
clerk
clev·er
cli·ent
cli·en·tele
cliff
cli·mate
cli·mat·ic
cli·max
climb
clinch
cling
clin·i·cal
clink
clip
clip·board
clip·pers

clique
cloak
clock
clock·wise
clock·work
clod
clog
clois·ter
close
clos·et
cloth
clothe
clothes
cloth·ing
cloud
cloud·i·ness
cloud·y
clout
clove
clo·ver
clown
club
cluck
clue
clump
clum·si·ness
clum·sy
clung
clus·ter
clutch
clut·ter
coach
co·ag·u·late
co·a·li·tion
coarse
coast
coat
coax
co·balt
cob·bler
co·bra
cob·web
co·caine
cock
cock·pit
cock·tail
cock·y
co·coa
co·co·nut
co·coon
code
co·ed

co·ef·fi·cient
co·er·cion
co·ex·ist·ence
cof·fee
cof·fee·pot
cof·fin
co·gent
co·gnac
co·her·ence
co·her·ent
co·he·sive
coil
coin
co·in·cide
co·in·ci·dence
co·in·ci·den·tal
coke
cold
cole·slaw
col·ic
col·lab·o·rate
col·lage
col·lapse
col·laps·i·ble
col·lar
col·lat·er·al
col·lect
col·lec·tion
col·lec·tive
col·lec·tor
col·lege
col·lide
col·lie
col·li·sion
co·logne
co·lon
colo·nel
co·lo·ni·al
col·o·nist
col·o·ni·za·tion
col·o·nize
col·o·ny
col·or
co·los·sal
colt
col·umn
co·ma
comb
com·bat
com·bi·na·tion
com·bine
com·bus·ti·ble

com·bus·tion
come
co·me·di·an
com·e·dy
com·et
com·fort
com·fort·a·ble
com·fort·er
com·ic
com·ing
com·ma
com·mand
com·mand·er
com·mand·ment
com·mem·o·rate
com·mence
com·mend
com·men·sur·ate
com·ment
com·men·tar·y
com·men·ta·tor
com·merce
com·mer·cial
com·mis·sion
com·mis·sion·er
com·mit
com·mit·tee
com·mod·i·ty
com·mon
com·mon·place
com·mon·wealth
com·mo·tion
com·mu·nal
com·mune
com·mu·ni·cate
com·mu·ni·ca·tion
com·mun·ion
com·mu·nism
com·mu·ni·ty
com·mute
com·mut·er
com·pact
com·pan·ion
com·pa·ny
com·par·a·ble
com·par·a·tive
com·pare
com·par·i·son
com·part·ment
com·pass
com·pas·sion
com·pat·i·ble

com·pel
com·pen·sate
com·pen·sa·tion
com·pete
com·pe·tence
com·pe·tent
com·pe·ti·tion
com·pet·i·tive
com·pet·i·tor
com·pile
com·plain
com·plaint
com·ple·ment
com·plete
com·ple·tion
com·plex
com·plex·ion
com·pli·ance
com·pli·cate
com·pli·cat·ed
com·pli·ca·tion
com·pli·ment
com·pli·men·ta·ry
com·ply
com·po·nent
com·pose
com·pos·ite
com·po·si·tion
com·po·sure
com·pound
com·pre·hen·sion
com·pre·hen·sive
com·press
com·prise
com·pro·mise
comp·trol·ler
com·pul·sion
com·pul·so·ry
com·put·er
con·ceal
con·cede
con·ceit
con·ceiv·a·ble
con·ceive
con·cen·trate
con·cen·tra·tion
con·cept
con·cep·tion
con·cern
con·cerned
con·cern·ing
con·cert

con·ces·sion
con·cil·i·a·to·ry
con·cise
con·clude
con·clu·sion
con·cord
con·crete
con·cur
con·cur·rent
con·demn
con·dem·na·tion
con·den·sa·tion
con·dense
con·de·scend
con·di·tion
con·du·cive
con·duct
con·duc·tor
cone
con·fed·er·a·cy
con·fed·er·ate
con·fed·e·ra·tion
con·fer
con·fer·ence
con·fess
con·fes·sion
con·fide
con·fi·dence
con·fi·dent
con·fi·den·tial
con·fig·u·ra·tion
con·fine
con·firm
con·fir·ma·tion
con·fis·cate
con·flict
con·form
con·form·i·ty
con·found
con·front
con·fuse
con·fu·sion
con·gen·ial
con·gen·i·tal
con·ges·tion
con·grat·u·late
con·grat·u·la·tion
con·gre·gate
con·gre·ga·tion
con·gress
con·gres·sion·al
con·jec·ture

con·junc·tion
con·nect
con·nec·tion
con·quer
con·quer·or
con·quest
con·science
con·sci·en·tious
con·scious
con·se·crate
con·sec·u·tive
con·sen·sus
con·sent
con·se·quence
con·se·quent·ly
con·ser·va·tion
con·serv·a·tive
con·serv·a·to·ry
con·serve
con·sid·er
con·sid·er·a·ble
con·sid·er·a·tion
con·sign·ment
con·sist
con·sist·ent
con·sole
con·sol·i·date
con·so·nant
con·spic·u·ous
con·spir·a·cy
con·spire
con·stant
con·stel·la·tion
con·sti·pa·tion
con·stit·u·ent
con·sti·tute
con·sti·tu·tion
con·strain
con·straint
con·strict
con·struct
con·struc·tion
con·sul
con·su·late
con·sult
con·sul·ta·tion
con·sume
con·sum·er
con·sump·tion
con·tact
con·ta·gion
con·ta·gious

con·tain
con·tain·er
con·tam·i·nate
con·tam·i·na·tion
con·tem·plate
con·tem·pla·tion
con·tem·po·rar·y
con·tempt
con·tempt·i·ble
con·temp·tu·ous
con·tend
con·tent
con·ten·tion
con·test
con·test·ant
con·ti·nent
con·ti·nen·tal
con·tin·gent
con·tin·u·al
con·tin·u·a·tion
con·tin·ue
con·tin·u·ous
con·tract
con·trac·tion
con·trac·tor
con·tra·dict
con·tra·dic·tion
con·tra·ry
con·trast
con·trib·ute
con·tri·bu·tion
con·trive
con·trol
con·trol·ler
con·tro·ver·sial
con·tro·ver·sy
con·va·les·cence
con·vene
con·ven·ience
con·ven·ient
con·vent
con·ven·tion
con·verge
con·ver·sa·tion
con·verse
con·ver·sion
con·vert
con·vey
con·vey·or
con·vict
con·vic·tion
con·vince

con·vul·sion
cook
cook·ie
cook·out
cool
cool·er
co·op·e·rate
co·op·e·ra·tion
co·op·e·ra·tive
co·or·di·nate
co·or·di·na·tion
cope
cop·ing
cop·per
cop·y
cop·y·right
cor·al
cord
cor·dial
cor·du·roy
core
cork
corn
cor·ne·a
cor·ner
cor·ner·stone
cor·nice
corn·stalk
cor·ol·lar·y
cor·o·nar·y
cor·o·na·tion
cor·o·ner
cor·po·ral
cor·por·ate
cor·po·ra·tion
corps
corpse
cor·ral
cor·rect
cor·rec·tion
cor·re·late
cor·res·pond
cor·res·pond·ence
cor·res·pond·ent
cor·ri·dor
cor·rode
cor·ro·sion
cor·ru·gat·ed
cor·rupt
cor·rup·tion
cor·ti·sone
cos·met·ic

cos·mic
cost
cost·ly
cos·tume
cot·tage
cot·ton
couch
cough
could
coun·cil
coun·ci·lor
coun·sel
coun·se·lor
count
count·down
coun·te·nance
count·er
coun·ter·act
coun·ter·feit
coun·ter·part
coun·ter·sign
count·ess
count·less
coun·try
coun·try·man
coun·try·side
coun·ty
coup
cou·ple
cou·pon
cour·age
cou·ra·geous
cour·i·er
course
court
cour·te·ous
cour·te·sy
court·house
court-mar·tial
court·room
court·yard
cous·in
cove
cov·e·nant
cov·er
cov·er·age
cov·ert
cov·et·ous
cow·ard
cow·hide
coy
coy·ote

co·zy
crab
crack
crack·er
crack·le
cra·dle
craft
crafts·man
craft·y
crag
cram
cramp
cran·ber·ry
crane
crank
crash
crate
cra·ter
crave
crawl
cray·on
craze
cra·zy
creak
cream
cream·er·y
cream·y
crease
cre·ate
cre·a·tion
cre·a·tive
cre·a·tor
crea·ture
cre·den·tials
cred·it
cred·i·tor
cred·u·lous
creed
creek
creep
cre·mate
crepe
crept
cre·scen·do
cres·cent
crest
crev·ice
crew
crib
crick·et
cried
cries

crime
crim·i·nal
crimp
crim·son
cringe
crin·kle
crip·ple
cri·sis
crisp
criss·cross
cri·te·ri·on
crit·ic
crit·i·cal
crit·i·cism
crit·i·cize
croak
cro·chet
croc·o·dile
crook
crop
cross
cross·breed
cross-ex·am·ine
cross-eyed
cross-pur·pose
cross-ref·er·ence
cross·road
cross·sec·tion
cross·walk
cross·word
crotch
crouch
crow
crowd
crown
cru·cial
cru·ci·fy
crude
cruel
cru·el·ty
cruise
crumb
crum·ble
cru·sade
crush
crust
crutch
cry
crys·tal
crys·tal·lize
cube
cu·bic

cuck·oo
cu·cum·ber
cud·dle
cue
cuff
cui·sine
cu·li·nar·y
cul·mi·nate
cul·pa·ble
cul·prit
cult
cul·ti·vate
cul·ti·va·tion
cul·ti·va·tor
cul·tur·al
cul·ture
cum·ber·some
cu·mu·la·tive
cun·ning
cup·cake
cup·ful
cur·a·ble
cu·ra·tor
curb
cure
cur·few
cur·i·os·i·ty
cur·i·ous
curl
curl·y
cur·ren·cy
cur·rent
cur·ric·u·lum
curse
cur·sor·y
cur·tail
cur·tain
curve
cush·ion
cus·tard
cus·to·di·an
cus·to·dy
cus·tom
cus·tom·ar·y
cus·tom·er
cut·back
cute
cut·ler·y
cut·let
cut·off
cut·out
cut·ter

cy·cle
cy·clic
cy·clone
cyl·in·der
cym·bal
cyn·i·cal
cy·press

D

dab·ble
Da·cron
dag·ger
dai·ly
dain·ty
dair·y
dai·sy
dam·age
dame
damn
dam·na·tion
damp
damp·er
dance
danc·er
dan·de·li·on
dan·druff
dan·dy
dan·ger
dan·ger·ous
dan·gle
Dan·ish
dare
dar·ing
dark
dark·en
dar·ling
darn
dart
dash
da·ta
date
daub
daugh·ter
dawn
day
day·break
day·dream
day·light
day·time
daze

daz·zle
dea·con
dead
dead·en
dead·line
dead·lock
dead·ly
deaf
deaf·en
deal
deal·er
deal·ing
dean
dear
death
death·bed
de·ba·cle
de·base
de·bat·a·ble
de·bate
deb·it
de·bris
debt
debt·or
de·but
dec·ade
de·ca·dent
de·cal
de·cay
de·cease
de·ceit
de·ceive
de·cen·cy
de·cent
de·cep·tion
de·cide
de·cid·ed·ly
dec·i·mal
de·ci·sion
de·ci·sive
deck
dec·la·ra·tion
de·clare
de·cline
de·code
de·com·pose
de·com·pres·sion
dec·o·rate
dec·o·ra·tion
de·coy
de·crease
de·cree

ded·i·cate
ded·i·ca·tion
de·duct
de·duc·tion
deed
deem
deep
deep·en
deer
de·face
de·fault
de·feat
de·fect
de·fec·tive
de·fend
de·fend·ant
de·fense
de·fen·sive
de·fer
def·er·ence
de·fi·ance
de·fi·ant
de·fi·cien·cy
def·i·cit
de·file
de·fine
def·i·nite
def·i·ni·tion
de·fin·i·tive
de·form
de·formed
de·form·i·ty
de·fraud
de·funct
de·fy
de·gen·e·rate
deg·ra·da·tion
de·grade
de·gree
de·hy·drate
deign
de·i·ty
de·ject·ed
de·lay
del·e·gate
del·e·ga·tion
de·lib·er·ate
de·lib·e·ra·tion
del·i·ca·cy
del·i·cate
del·i·ca·tes·sen
de·li·cious

de·light
de·light·ful
de·lin·quent
de·lir·i·ous
de·liv·er
de·liv·er·y
del·ta
de·lude
de·lu·sion
de·mand
de·mean·or
de·ment·ed
de·moc·ra·cy
dem·o·crat
dem·o·crat·ic
de·mol·ish
dem·o·li·tion
de·mon
dem·on·strate
dem·on·stra·tion
de·mon·stra·tive
dem·on·stra·tor
de·mor·al·ize
de·mo·tion
de·ni·al
den·im
de·nom·i·na·tion
de·note
de·nounce
dense
den·si·ty
den·tal
den·tist
de·nun·ci·a·tion
de·ny
de·o·dor·ant
de·part
de·part·ment
de·par·ture
de·pend
de·pend·a·ble
de·pend·ence
de·pend·en·cy
de·pend·ent
de·plore
de·por·ta·tion
de·pose
de·pos·it
dep·o·si·tion
de·pot
de·pre·ci·a·tion
de·press

de·pres·sant
de·pres·sion
de·prive
depth
dep·u·ty
de·ranged
de·ride
de·ri·sion
der·i·va·tion
de·rive
de·rog·a·to·ry
de·scend
de·scend·ant
de·scent
de·scribe
de·scrip·tion
de·seg·re·gate
de·seg·re·ga·tion
des·ert
de·serve
de·sign
des·ig·nate
des·ig·na·tion
de·sir·a·ble
de·sire
desk
des·o·late
de·o·la·tion
de·spair
des·per·ate
des·per·a·tion
de·spise
de·spite
de·spond·ent
des·sert
des·ti·na·tion
des·tine
des·ti·ny
des·ti·tute
de·stroy
de·struc·tion
de·struc·tive
de·tach
de·tail
de·tain
de·tect
de·tec·tive
de·tec·tor
de·ten·tion
de·ter·gent
de·te·ri·o·rate
de·ter·mi·na·tion

de·ter·mine
de·ter·rent
de·test
de·test·a·ble
de·tour
de·tract
det·ri·men·tal
de·val·u·a·tion
de·val·ue
dev·as·tate
dev·as·ta·tion
de·vel·op
de·vel·op·ment
de·vi·a·tion
de·vice
dev·il
de·vi·ous
de·vise
de·vote
de·vo·tion
de·vour
de·vout
dew
dex·ter·i·ty
di·a·be·tes
di·ag·nose
di·ag·no·sis
di·ag·nos·tic
di·ag·o·nal
di·a·gram
di·al
di·a·lect
di·a·logue
di·am·e·ter
dia·mond
di·a·per
di·a·phragm
di·ar·rhe·a
di·a·ry
dice
dic·tate
dic·ta·tion
dic·ta·tor
dic·ta·to·ri·al
dic·tion·ar·y
die
die·sel
di·et
di·e·tet·ic
dif·fer
dif·fer·ence
dif·fer·ent

dif·fe·ren·tial
dif·fi·cult
dif·fi·cul·ty
dif·fuse
dif·fu·sion
di·gest
di·ges·tion
dig·ger
dig·it·al
dig·ni·fied
dig·ni·fy
dig·ni·tar·y
dig·ni·ty
di·gress
di·gres·sion
di·late
di·la·tion
di·lem·ma
dil·i·gence
dil·i·gent
di·lute
di·lu·tion
dime
di·men·sion
di·min·ish
di·min·u·tive
dim·ple
dine
din·er
din·ner
di·no·saur
di·o·cese
di·plo·ma
di·plo·ma·cy
dip·lo·mat
dire
di·rect
di·rec·tion
di·rec·tor
di·rec·to·ry
dirt
dirt·y
dis·a·bil·i·ty
dis·ad·van·tage
dis·a·gree
dis·a·gree·a·ble
dis·ap·pear
dis·ap·pear·ance
dis·ap·point
dis·ap·point·ment
dis·ap·prov·al
dis·ap·prove

dis·arm
dis·ar·ma·ment
dis·ar·ray
dis·as·ter
dis·as·trous
dis·burse·ment
disc
dis·card
dis·cern
dis·charge
dis·ci·pline
dis·claim
dis·close
dis·clo·sure
dis·com·fit
dis·com·fort
dis·con·nect
dis·con·tent·ed
dis·con·tin·ue
dis·cord
dis·cord·ant
dis·count
dis·cour·age
dis·course
dis·cour·te·ous
dis·cov·er
dis·cov·er·y
dis·cred·it
dis·creet
dis·cre·tion
dis·crim·i·nate
dis·crim·i·na·tion
dis·cuss
dis·cus·sion
dis·dain
dis·ease
dis·en·chant·ment
dis·en·gage
dis·fav·or
dis·fig·ure
dis·grace
dis·grace·ful
dis·guise
dis·gust
dish
di·shev·eled
dis·hon·est
dis·hon·or
dis·il·lu·sion
dis·in·fect
dis·in·fect·ant
dis·in·her·it

dis·in·te·grate
dis·in·te·gra·tion
dis·in·ter·est·ed
dis·joint·ed
disk
dis·like
dis·lo·cate
dis·mal
dis·man·tle
dis·may
dis·miss
dis·miss·al
dis·mount
dis·o·be·di·ence
dis·o·be·di·ent
dis·o·bey
dis·or·der
dis·or·der·ly
dis·or·gan·ize
dis·own
dis·patch·er
dis·pel
dis·pen·sa·tion
dis·pense
dis·perse
dis·place
dis·play
dis·please
dis·pleas·ure
dis·pos·al
dis·pose
dis·po·si·tion
dis·pro·por·tion·ate
dis·pute
dis·qual·i·fy
dis·qui·et
dis·re·gard
dis·rep·u·ta·ble
dis·re·spect
dis·rup·tion
dis·sat·is·fac·tion
dis·sat·is·fied
dis·sect
dis·sem·i·nate
dis·sen·sion
dis·sent
dis·ser·ta·tion
dis·serv·ice
dis·sim·i·lar
dis·si·pate
dis·so·lu·tion
dis·solve

dis·suade
dis·tance
dis·tant
dis·taste·ful
dis·till
dis·till·er·y
dis·tinct
dis·tinc·tion
dis·tin·guish
dis·tort
dis·tract
dis·trac·tion
dis·tress
dis·trib·ute
dis·tri·bu·tion
dis·trib·u·tor
dis·trict
dis·trust
dis·turb
dis·turb·ance
ditch
dive
di·verge
di·ver·gent
di·verse
di·ver·si·fy
di·ver·sion
di·ver·si·ty
di·vert
di·vide
div·i·dend
di·vid·er
di·vine
di·vin·i·ty
di·vi·sion
di·vi·sor
di·vorce
di·vulge
diz·zy
doc·ile
dock
doc·tor
doc·trine
doc·u·ment
doc·u·men·tar·y
dodge
do·er
does
dog·house
dog·ma
dog·mat·ic
doi·ly

doll
dol·lar
doll·house
doll·y
dol·phin
do·main
dome
do·mes·tic
dom·i·nant
dom·i·nate
dom·i·na·tion
dom·i·neer·ing
do·min·ion
dom·i·no
do·na·tion
done
don·key
do·nor
doom
door
door·bell
door·knob
door·man
door·step
door·way
dor·mant
dor·mi·to·ry
dose
dou·ble
dou·bly
doubt
doubt·ful
dough
dough·nut
dove
down
down·cast
down·fall
down·hill
down·pour
down·right
down·stairs
down·town
down·ward
down·y
doze
doz·en
drab
draft
drag
drain
drain·age

dra·ma
dra·mat·ic
dram·a·tize
drank
drape
dra·per·y
dras·tic
draw
draw·back
drawer
drawl
drawn
dread·ful
dream
drear·y
dredge
drench
dress
dress·er
dress·mak·er
drew
drib·ble
dried
drift
drift·wood
drill
drink
drip
drive
drive-in
driv·er
drive·way
driz·zle
drool
droop
drop
drop-out
drought
drove
drown
drow·si·ness
drow·sy
drudge
drudg·er·y
drug
drug·gist
drug·store
drum
drunk
drunk·ard
drunk·en
dry

dry-clean
dry clean·ing
dry·er
du·al
duch·ess
duck
duct
dude
due
du·el
du·et
dug·out
duke
dull
dumb
dumb·bell
dumb·wait·er
dum·found
dump
dunce
dun·ga·rees
dun·geon
du·plex
du·pli·cate
du·plic·i·ty
du·ra·ble
du·ra·tion
dur·ing
dusk
dusk·y
dust
dust·er
dust·y
du·ti·a·ble
du·ty
dwarf
dwell
dwell·ing
dwin·dle
dye
dye·ing
dy·ing
dy·nam·ic
dy·na·mite

E

each
ea·ger
ea·gle
ear

ear·ly
ear·mark
earn
ear·nest
earn·ings
earth
earth·en·ware
earth·ly
earth·quake
ease
eas·i·ly
east
east·ern
east·ward
eas·y
eat
eaves
ebb
eb·on·y
ec·cen·tric
ec·cle·si·as·ti·cal
ech·o
e·clipse
e·col·o·gy
e·co·nom·ic
e·co·nom·i·cal
e·con·o·mist
e·con·o·mize
e·con·o·my
ec·sta·sy
edge
edg·ing
ed·i·ble
e·di·tion
ed·i·tor
ed·u·cate
ed·u·ca·tion
ed·u·ca·tion·al
eel
ef·fect
ef·fec·tive
ef·fec·tu·al
ef·fer·ves·cent
ef·fi·cien·cy
ef·fi·cient
ef·fort
egg
egg·shell
e·go·tism
eight
eight·een
eight·eenth

eighth
eight·i·eth
eight·y
ei·ther
e·ject
e·jec·tion
e·lab·or·ate
e·lapse
e·las·tic
e·late
el·bow
eld·er
e·lect
e·lec·tion
e·lec·tive
e·lec·tor
e·lec·tric
e·lec·tri·cal
e·lec·tri·cian
e·lec·tric·i·ty
e·lec·tri·fy
e·lec·tron
e·lec·tron·ic
e·lec·tron·i·cal·ly
e·lec·tron·ics
el·e·gance
el·e·gant
el·e·ment
el·e·men·tar·y
el·e·phant
el·e·vate
el·e·va·tion
el·e·va·tor
e·lev·en
e·lev·enth
el·i·gi·ble
e·lim·i·nate
e·lite
elm
el·o·quence
el·o·quent
else
else·where
e·lude
e·lu·sive
e·man·ci·pa·tion
em·bar·go
em·bark
em·bar·rass
em·bas·sy
em·bat·tled
em·bel·lish

em·ber
em·blem
em·bod·y
em·boss
em·brace
em·broi·der
em·broi·der·y
em·bry·o
em·er·ald
e·merge
e·mer·gen·cy
em·i·grant
em·i·grate
em·i·gra·tion
em·i·nence
em·i·nent
e·mis·sion
e·mit
e·mo·tion
e·mo·tion·al
em·per·or
em·pha·sis
em·pha·size
em·phat·ic
em·pire
em·ploy
em·ploy·ee
em·ploy·er
em·ploy·ment
em·pow·er
emp·ti·ness
emp·ty
e·mul·sion
en·a·ble
en·act
e·nam·el
en·am·ored
en·camp
en·case
en·chant
en·close
en·clo·sure
en·core
en·coun·ter
en·cour·age
en·cum·ber
en·cy·clo·pe·di·a
en·dan·ger
en·dear
en·deav·or
en·dem·ic
en·do·crine

en·dorse
en·dow·ment
en·dur·ance
en·dure
en·e·my
en·er·get·ic
en·er·gy
en·fold
en·force
en·gage
en·gine
en·gi·neer
Eng·lish
en·grave
en·grav·ing
en·gross
en·hance
e·nig·ma
en·joy
en·large
en·light·en
en·list
en·mi·ty
en·no·ble
e·nor·mous
e·nough
en·rage
en·rich
en·roll
en·sem·ble
en·sign
en·slave
en·snare
en·sue
en·tail
en·tan·gle
en·ter
en·ter·prise
en·ter·pris·ing
en·ter·tain
en·thu·si·asm
en·thu·si·ast
en·thu·si·as·tic
en·tice
en·tire
en·ti·tle
en·ti·ty
en·trails
en·trance
en·treat
en·trust
en·try

e·nu·mer·ate
en·vel·op
en·ve·lope
en·vi·a·ble
en·vi·ous
en·vi·ron·ment
en·vis·age
en·vy
en·zyme
ep·ic
ep·i·dem·ic
E·pis·co·pal
ep·i·sode
ep·i·taph
e·pit·o·me
ep·och
e·qual
e·qual·i·ty
e·qua·tion
e·qua·tor
e·qui·lib·ri·um
e·quip
e·quip·ment
eq·ui·ta·ble
eq·ui·ty
e·quiv·a·lent
e·quiv·o·cal
er·a
e·rad·i·cate
e·rase
e·rect
e·rec·tion
e·rode
e·ro·sion
err
er·rand
er·rat·ic
er·ro·ne·ous
er·ror
e·rup·tion
es·ca·late
es·ca·la·tor
es·cape
es·chew
es·cort
es·crow
es·pi·o·nage
es·say
es·sence
es·sen·tial
es·tab·lish
es·tate

es·teem
es·ti·mate
es·ti·ma·tion
e·ter·nal
e·ter·ni·ty
e·the·re·al
eth·i·cal
eth·ics
eth·nic
eu·tha·na·sia
e·vac·u·ate
e·vac·u·a·tion
e·vade
e·val·u·ate
e·val·u·a·tion
e·van·gel·i·cal
e·vap·o·rate
e·va·sion
e·ven
eve·ning
e·vent
e·ven·tu·al·i·ty
e·ven·tu·al·ly
ev·er
ev·er·green
eve·ry
eve·ry·bod·y
eve·ry·day
eve·ry·one
eve·ry·thing
eve·ry·where
e·vic·tion
ev·i·dence
ev·i·dent
e·vil
ev·o·lu·tion
ex·act
ex·ag·ger·ate
ex·alt
ex·am·i·na·tion
ex·am·ine
ex·am·ple
ex·as·per·ate
ex·ca·vate
ex·ceed
ex·cel
ex·cel·lence
ex·cel·lent
ex·cept
ex·cep·tion
ex·cerpt
ex·cess

ex·ces·sive
ex·change
ex·cise
ex·cite
ex·cit·ing
ex·claim
ex·cla·ma·tion
ex·clude
ex·clu·sive
ex·cre·tion
ex·cur·sion
ex·cuse
ex·e·cute
ex·e·cu·tion
ex·ec·u·tive
ex·ec·u·tor
ex·empt
ex·emp·tion
ex·er·cise
ex·ert
ex·er·tion
ex·hale
ex·haust
ex·haus·tion
ex·haus·tive
ex·hib·it
ex·hi·bi·tion
ex·hil·a·rate
ex·hort
ex·ile
ex·ist
ex·ist·ence
ex·it
ex·or·bi·tant
ex·ot·ic
ex·pand
ex·panse
ex·pan·sion
ex·pan·sive
ex·pect
ex·pect·ant
ex·pec·ta·tion
ex·pe·di·tion
ex·pel
ex·pend
ex·pend·i·ture
ex·pense
ex·pen·sive
ex·pe·ri·ence
ex·per·i·ment
ex·per·i·men·tal
ex·pert

ex·pi·ra·tion
ex·pire
ex·plain
ex·pla·na·tion
ex·ploit
ex·ploi·ta·tion
ex·plo·ra·tion
ex·plore
ex·plor·er
ex·plo·sion
ex·plo·sive
ex·po·nent
ex·port
ex·pose
ex·po·sure
ex·press
ex·pres·sion
ex·pres·sive
ex·pro·pri·ate
ex·pul·sion
ex·qui·site
ex·tend
ex·ten·sion
ex·ten·sive
ex·tent
ex·te·ri·or
ex·ter·mi·nate
ex·ter·nal
ex·tinct
ex·tinc·tion
ex·tin·guish
ex·tort
ex·tor·tion
ex·tra
ex·tract
ex·trac·tion
ex·tra·ne·ous
ex·traor·di·nar·y
ex·trav·a·gance
ex·trav·a·gant
ex·treme
ex·trem·i·ty
ex·tro·vert
eye
eye·ball
eye·brow
eye·glass·es
eye·lash
eye·lid
eye·sight
eye·wit·ness

F

fa·ble
fab·ric
fab·ri·cate
fab·u·lous
face
fa·cial
fac·ile
fa·cil·i·ty
fact
fac·tion
fac·tor
fac·to·ry
fac·tu·al
fac·ul·ty
fade
fail
fail·ure
faint
fair
fair·way
fair·y
faith
faith·ful
faith·less
fake
fal·con
fall
fal·la·cy
fall·en
fal·li·ble
fall·out
fal·low
false
false·hood
fal·si·fi·ca·tion
fal·si·fy
fal·ter
fame
fa·mil·iar
fa·mil·iar·i·ty
fa·mil·iar·ize
fam·i·ly
fam·ine
fam·ish
fa·mous
fa·nat·ic
fan·ci·ful
fan·cy
fan·fare
fan·tas·tic

fan·ta·sy
farce
fare
fare·well
farm
farm·er
farm·house
farm·yard
far-off
far-reach·ing
far-sight·ed
far·ther
far·thest
fas·ci·nate
fas·cism
fash·ion
fast
fas·ten
fas·tid·i·ous
fa·tal
fate
fa·ther
fa·tigue
fau·cet
fault
fault·y
fa·vor
fa·vor·a·ble
fa·vor·ite
fawn
fear
fear·ful
fea·si·ble
feast
feat
feath·er
fea·ture
fed·er·al
fed·e·ra·tion
fee·ble
feed
feed·back
feed·er
feel
feel·ing
feet
feign
feint
fe·lic·i·tate
fe·line
fell
fel·low

fel·low·ship
fel·on
fel·o·ny
felt
fe·male
fem·i·nine
fence
fend·er
fer·ment
fern
fe·ro·cious
fer·ry
fer·tile
fer·til·i·ty
fer·ti·lize
fer·ti·liz·er
fer·vent
fer·vid
fer·vor
fes·ter
fes·ti·val
fes·tive
fete
fe·tish
fet·ter
fe·tus
feud
fe·ver
few
fi·as·co
fi·ber
fic·tion
fic·ti·tious
fid·dle
fi·del·i·ty
fidg·et
field
field trip
fiend
fiend·ish
fierce
fie·ry
fi·es·ta
fif·teen
fifth
fif·ti·eth
fif·ty
fight
fight·er
fig·ment
fig·ur·a·tive
fig·ure

fig·ure·head
fil·a·ment
file
fi·let
fil·i·bus·ter
fill
fill·er
fil·let
film
film·strip
fil·ter
filth
filth·y
fil·tra·tion
fi·nal
fi·na·le
fi·nal·ly
fi·nance
fi·nan·cial
fin·an·cier
find
fine
fin·ger
fin·ger·print
fin·ish
fi·nite
fire
fire·arm
fire en·gine
fire es·cape
fire·fly
fire·house
fire·man
fire·place
fire·proof
fire·side
fire·trap
fire·wood
fire·works
firm
fir·ma·ment
first
first aid
first-born
first class
first la·dy
fis·cal
fish
fish·er·man
fish·er·y
fish·hook
fis·sion

fis·sure
fist
five
fix·ture
fiz·zle
flag
flag·pole
fla·grant
flair
flake
flam·boy·ant
flame
flam·ma·ble
flank
flan·nel
flap
flare
flash
flash·back
flash·bulb
flash·light
flask
flat
flat·ten
flat·ter
flat·ter·y
flaunt
fla·vor
flaw
flax
flea
flee
fleece
fleet
flesh
flesh·y
flew
flex·i·ble
flick·er
fli·er
flight
flim·sy
fling
flint
flint·y
flip
flip·pant
flirt
float
flock
flood
flood·light

flood·wa·ter
floor
floor·ing
flop
flo·ral
flor·id
flo·rist
flounce
floun·der
flour
flour·ish
flout
flow
flow·er
flow·er·y
flown
flu
fluc·tu·ate
flu·ent
flu·id
flung
flu·o·res·cent
fluor·i·date
flu·o·ride
flur·ry
flush
flute
flut·ter
fly
foam
foam rub·ber
fo·cus
fod·der
fog·gy
foil
fold
fold·er
fo·li·age
folk
folk·lore
folk song
fol·low
fol·low·er
fol·ly
fond
food
fool
fool·ish
fool·proof
foot
foot·ball
foot·hill

foot·lights
foot·print
foot·step
foot·stool
for
for·age
for·bade
for·bear
for·bear·ance
for·bid
for·bid·den
force
for·ci·ble
ford
fore·arm
fore·cast
fore·clo·sure
fore·fa·ther
fore·front
fore·gone
fore·hand
fore·head
for·eign
for·eign·er
fore·man
fore·most
fore·run·ner
fore·see
fore·shad·ow
fore·sight
for·est
for·est·ry
fore·tell
fore·thought
for·ev·er
fore·warn
fore·word
for·feit
for·ger·y
for·get
for·give
for·go
for·gone
fork
for·lorn
form
for·mal
for·ma·tion
for·mer
for·mi·da·ble
for·mu·la
for·sake

fort
forth
forth·com·ing
forth·right
for·ti·eth
for·ti·fi·ca·tion
for·ti·fy
fort·night
for·tress
for·tu·nate
for·tune
for·ty
fo·rum
for·ward
fos·sil
fos·ter
fought
foul
found
foun·da·tion
foun·der
found·ry
foun·tain
four
four·teen
fourth
fowl
foy·er
frac·tion
frac·ture
frag·ment
fra·grance
fra·grant
frail
frame
frame-up
frame·work
fran·chise
frank
frank·furt·er
fran·tic
fra·ter·nal
fra·ter·ni·ty
fraud
fraud·u·lent
fraught
fray
freak
freck·le
free
free·dom
freeze

freez·er
freight
fren·zy
fre·quen·cy
fre·quent
fresh
fresh·man
fresh·wa·ter
fret
fri·ar
fric·tion
fried
friend
friend·ship
fright
fright·en
fright·ful
frig·id
frisk·y
friv·o·lous
frock
frog
frog·man
frol·ic
front
fron·tier
frost
froth   .
frown
froze
fro·zen
fru·gal
fruit
fruit·ful
fru·i·tion
frus·trate
fry
fudge
fu·el
fu·gi·tive
ful·fill
full·back
ful·ly
fum·ble
fume
func·tion
fund
fun·da·men·tal
fu·ner·al
fun·gus
fun·nel
fun·ny

fur
fu·ri·ous
fur·nace
fur·nish
fur·ni·ture
fur·or
fur·ry
fur·ther
fur·ther·more
fu·ry
fuse
fu·sion
fuss
fu·tile
fu·til·i·ty
fu·ture

G

gadg·et
gage
gai·e·ty
gai·ly
gain
gal·ax·y
gale
gall
gal·lant
gal·lant·ry
gal·ler·y
gal·ley
gal·lon
gal·lop
gal·lows
gal·va·nize
gam·ble
game
gam·ma glob·u·lin
gam·ut
gang
gang·plank
gan·grene
gang·ster
gang·way
ga·rage
garb
gar·bage
gar·den
gar·gle
gar·land
gar·lic

gar·ment
gar·ner
gar·nish
gar·nish·ee
gar·ret
gar·ri·son
gar·ter
gas·e·ous
gash
gas·ket
gas·o·line
gasp
gas·tric
gate
gate·way
gath·er
gaud·y
gauge
gaunt
gaunt·let
gauze
gave
gav·el
gay
gaze
gear
gear·shift
geese
gel·a·tin
gen·der
gene
ge·ne·al·o·gy
gen·er·al
gen·er·al·i·za·tion
gen·er·al·ize
gen·er·ate
gen·er·a·tion
gen·e·ra·tor
gen·er·os·i·ty
gen·er·ous
ge·net·ic
gen·ial
gen·ius
gen·tle
gen·tle·man
gen·tle·wom·an
gen·tly
gen·u·ine
ge·o·graph·i·cal
ge·og·ra·phy
ge·o·log·i·cal
ge·ol·o·gy

ge·o·met·ric
ge·om·e·try
ge·o·phys·i·cal
ge·o·phys·ics
ger·i·at·rics
germ
ger·mane
ger·mi·nate
ger·mi·na·tion
ges·ta·tion
ges·tic·u·late
ges·ture
get-to·geth·er
gey·ser
ghast·ly
ghet·to
ghost
gi·ant
gib·ber·ish
gid·dy
gift
gi·gan·tic
gig·gle
gill
gim·mick
gin·ger
gin·ger·bread
ging·ham
gi·raffe
gird
gir·dle
girl
giv·en
giv·er
gla·cial
gla·cier
glad·den
glade
glam·or·ous
glam·our
glance
gland
glan·du·lar
glare
glar·ing
glass
glass·y
glau·co·ma
glaze
gleam
glean
glee

glide
glid·er
glim·mer
glimpse
glis·ten
glit·ter
glob·al
globe
glob·ule
gloom
glo·ri·fy
glo·ri·ous
glo·ry
gloss
glove
glow
glu·cose
glue
glut·ton
glyc·er·in
gnash
gnat
gnaw
goad
goal
goal·keep·er
goat
gob·ble
go-be·tween
gob·let
gob·lin
god·dess
god·fa·ther
god·like
god·ly
god·moth·er
god·par·ent
god·send
goes
go·ing
goi·ter
gold·en
gold·en·rod
gold-filled
gold·fish
golf
gone
gong
good-by
good·li·ness
good-look·ing
good-na·tured

good-sized
good will
goose
gore
gorge
gor·geous
go·ril·la
gor·y
gos·pel
gos·sip
got·ten
gouge
gourd
gour·met
gov·ern
gov·ern·ment
gov·er·nor
gown
grab
grace
grace·ful
gra·cious
grade
gra·di·ent
grad·u·al
grad·u·ate
grad·u·a·tion
graft
grain
gram
gram·mar
gram·mat·i·cal
gran·a·ry
grand
grand·child
grand·daugh·ter
gran·deur
grand·fa·ther
gran·di·ose
grand·moth·er
grand·par·ent
grand·son
grand·stand
gran·ite
grant
gran·u·lar
gran·u·late
grape
grape·fruit
grape·vine
graph
graph·ic

graph·ite
grap·ple
grasp
grass
grass·hop·per
grass roots
grate
grate·ful
grat·i·fi·ca·tion
grat·i·fy
grat·i·tude
grave
grav·el
grav·i·tate
grav·i·ta·tion
grav·i·ty
gra·vy
gray
graze
grease
great
greed
greed·i·ness
greed·y
green
green·house
green·ness
greet
gre·gar·i·ous
gre·nade
grew
grey
grey·hound
grid
grid·dle
grief
griev·ance
grieve
griev·ous
grill
grille
grim
grime
grim·y
grin
grind
grind·stone
grip
gripe
grit
groan
gro·cer

gro·cer·y
grog·gy
groin
groom
groove
grope
gross
gro·tesque
grouch
ground
ground·work
group
grove
grow
growl
grown
growth
grub
grudge
gru·el
gru·el·ing
grue·some
grum·ble
grunt
guar·an·tee
guar·an·tor
guar·an·ty
guard
guard·i·an
guer·ril·la
guess
guess·work
guest
guest·house
guid·ance
guide
guide·book
guide·post
guild
guile
guilt
guilt·y
guin·ea
gui·tar
gulf
gull
gul·ly
gulp
gum·drop
gun·fire
gun·pow·der
gun·shot

gun·smith
gur·gle
gush
gust
gut·ter
gym
gym·nas·tics
gyp·sy

H

hab·it
hab·it·a·ble
hab·i·ta·tion
ha·bit·u·al
hack
had·dock
hag·gard
hag·gle
hail
hail·stone
hair
hair·cut
hair·dress·er
hair·pin
hair's-breadth
hair·split·ting
hair·y
hale
half
half·back
half·way
hal·i·but
hall
hall·mark
Hal·low·een
hal·lu·ci·na·tion
hall·way
halt
hal·ter
halve
ham·burg·er
ham·let
ham·mer
ham·mock
ham·per
hand·bag
hand·ball
hand·book
hand·cuff
hand·ful

hand·i·cap
hand·i·work
hand·ker·chief
han·dle
hand·made
hand·out
hand·rail
hand·shake
hand·some
hand·writ·ing
hand·y
hand·y·man
hang
hang·ar
hang·er
hang·nail
hang·out
hang·o·ver
hap·haz·ard
hap·less
hap·pen
hap·pi·ly
hap·pi·ness
hap·py
ha·rangue
har·ass
har·bor
hard
hard·en
hard-head·ed
hard-heart·ed
hard·ly
hard·ship
hard·top
hard·ware
hard·wood
har·dy
hare
harm
harm·ful
harm·less
har·mo·ni·ous
har·mo·nize
har·mo·ny
har·ness
harp
har·poon
har·row
har·ry
harsh
har·vest
hash·ish

haste
has·ten
hast·i·ly
hast·y
hatch
hatch·et
hate
hate·ful
ha·tred
haugh·ty
haul
haunch
haunt
haunt·ed
have
ha·ven
hav·oc
hawk
haw·thorn
hay
hay fe·ver
hay·stack
hay·wire
haz·ard
haz·ard·ous
haze
ha·zel
ha·zy
head
head·ache
head·first
head·light
head·line
head·long
head-on
head·phone
head·quar·ters
head·stone
head·strong
head·wait·er
head·way
heal
health
health·ful
health·y
heap
hear
heard
hear·ing aid
hear·say
hearse
heart

heart·beat
heart·bro·ken
heart·felt
hearth
heart·i·ly
heart·y
heat
heat·er
heath
hea·then
heath·er
heave
heav·en
heav·en·ly
heav·i·ly
heav·i·ness
heav·y·weight
hec·tare
hec·tic
hedge
hedge·hog
heed
heed·less
heel
height
hei·nous
heir
heir·loom
held
hel·i·cop·ter
hel·i·port
he·li·um
hell·ish
hel·lo
helm
hel·met
helms·man
help
help·er
help·ful
help·less
hem·i·sphere
hem·lock
he·mo·glo·bin
hem·or·rhage
hemp
hence
hence·forth
her·ald
herb
herd
herds·man

here
here·af·ter
here·by
he·red·i·tar·y
he·red·i·ty
here·in
her·e·sy
her·e·tic
here·to·fore
here·with
her·it·age
her·met·i·cal·ly
her·mit
her·ni·a
he·ro
he·ro·ic
her·o·in
her·o·ine
her·o·ism
her·ring
hes·i·tate
hes·i·ta·tion
het·er·o·ge·ne·ous
hew
hi·ber·nate
hic·cup
hick·o·ry
hid·den
hide
hid·e·ous
hide·out
hi·er·ar·chy
hi·er·o·glyph·ics
high
high fi·del·i·ty
high·lands
high·light
high-mind·ed
high-pitched
high-pow·ered
high-pres·sure
high school
high·way
hi·jack
hike
hi·lar·i·ous
hill·bil·ly
hill·side
hill·top
hill·y
hilt
hind

hin·der
hin·drance
hinge
hint
hire
hiss
his·to·ri·an
his·tor·ic
his·tor·i·cal
his·tor·y
hit-and-run
hitch
hitch·hike
hith·er
hith·er·to
hive
hoard
hoarse
hoar·y
hoax
hob·ble
hob·by
hock·ey
hoe
hoist
hold
hold·er
hole
hol·i·day
ho·li·ness
hol·low
hol·ly
hol·o·caust
ho·ly
hom·age
home
home·less
home·ly
home·made
home run
home·sick
home·ward
home·work
hom·i·cide
ho·mo·ge·ne·ous
ho·mog·e·nize
hon·est
hon·es·ty
hon·ey
hon·ey·comb
hon·ey·moon
hon·or

hon·or·a·ble
hon·or·ar·y
hood
hood·lum
hoof
hook
hook·up
hoop
hoot
hope
hope·ful
hope·less
hop·per
horde
ho·ri·zon
ho·ri·zon·tal
hor·mone
horn
hor·net
ho·ro·scope
hor·ri·ble
hor·rid
hor·ri·fy
hor·ror
horse
horse·back
horse·hair
horse·man
horse·play
horse·pow·er
horse·shoe
hor·ti·cul·ture
hose
ho·sier·y
hos·pi·ta·ble
hos·pi·tal
hos·pi·tal·i·ty
hos·pi·tal·ize
host
hos·tage
hos·tel
host·ess
hos·tile
hos·til·i·ty
ho·tel
hot-head·ed
hot·house
hound
hour
hour·ly
house
house·boat

house·break·ing
house·bro·ken
house·fly
house·hold
house·keep·er
house·maid
house·top
house·wife
house·work
hov·el
hov·er
how·ev·er
howl
hub·cap
hud·dle
hue
huff
huge
hulk
hull
hu·man
hu·mane
hu·man·i·tar·i·an
hu·man·i·ty
hum·ble
hum·bug
hu·mid
hu·mid·i·ty
hu·mil·i·ate
hu·mil·i·a·tion
hu·mil·i·ty
hu·mor
hu·mor·ous
hunch
hun·dred
hun·dredth
hung
hun·ger
hun·gry
hunt
hunt·er
hur·dle
hurl
hur·ri·cane
hur·ried
hur·ry
hurt
hurt·ful
hus·band
hush
husk·y
hus·tle

hy·brid
hy·drant
hy·drau·lic
hy·dro·car·bon
hy·dro·e·lec·tric
hy·dro·foil
hy·dro·gen
hy·dro·pho·bi·a
hy·e·na
hy·gi·en·ic
hy·gien·ist
hymn
hy·per·bo·le
hy·per·sen·si·tive
hy·per·ten·sion
hy·phen
hy·phen·a·tion
hyp·no·sis
hyp·not·ic
hyp·no·tize
hy·po·chon·dri·ac
hy·poc·ri·sy
hyp·o·crite
hy·po·der·mic
hy·poth·e·sis
hy·po·thet·i·cal
hys·te·ri·a
hys·ter·i·cal

I

ice
ice·berg
ice·break·er
ice cream
ice skate
i·ci·cle
i·cy
i·de·a
i·de·al
i·den·ti·cal
i·den·ti·fi·ca·tion
i·den·ti·fy
i·de·o·log·i·cal
i·de·ol·o·gy
id·i·o·cy
id·i·om
id·i·ot
i·dle
i·dol
i·dol·a·try

i·dol·ize
ig·nite
ig·ni·tion
ig·no·min·i·ous
ig·no·rance
ig·no·rant
ig·nore
il·le·gal
il·le·git·i·mate
ill-fat·ed
il·lic·it
il·lit·er·a·cy
il·lit·er·ate
ill·ness
il·lu·mi·nate
il·lu·sion
il·lus·trate
il·lus·tra·tion
im·age
i·mag·i·na·ble
i·mag·i·na·tion
i·mag·i·na·tive
i·mag·ine
im·be·cile
im·i·tate
im·i·ta·tion
im·ma·te·ri·al
im·ma·ture
im·ma·tu·ri·ty
im·meas·ur·a·ble
im·me·di·ate
im·mense
im·merse
im·mi·grant
im·mi·grate
im·mi·gra·tion
im·mi·nent
im·mo·bi·lize
im·mo·ral
im·mor·tal
im·mov·a·ble
im·mune
im·mu·ni·ty
im·mu·ni·za·tion
im·mu·ta·ble
im·pair
im·pan·el
im·part
im·par·tial
im·pass·a·ble
im·pa·tience
im·pa·tient

im·peach
im·pede
im·pel
im·pend·ing
im·pen·e·tra·ble
im·per·a·tive
im·per·cep·ti·ble
im·per·fect
im·per·fec·tion
im·pe·ri·al
im·per·il
im·pe·ri·ous
im·per·me·a·ble
im·per·son·al
im·per·son·ate
im·per·ti·nence
im·per·ti·nent
im·pet·u·ous
im·pe·tus
im·pla·ca·ble
im·plant
im·ple·ment
im·pli·cate
im·pli·ca·tion
im·plic·it
im·plore
im·ply
im·po·lite
im·port
im·por·tance
im·por·tant
im·por·ta·tion
im·port·er
im·pose
im·po·si·tion
im·pos·si·ble
im·pos·tor
im·po·tent
im·pound
im·pov·er·ish
im·prac·ti·cal
im·preg·na·ble
im·press
im·pres·sion
im·pres·sive
im·print
im·pris·on
im·prob·a·ble
im·prop·er
im·prove
im·pro·vise
im·pru·dent

im·pu·dent
im·pugn
im·pulse
im·pul·sive
im·pu·ni·ty
im·pure
in·a·bil·i·ty
in·ac·ces·si·ble
in·ac·cur·ate
in·ac·tive
in·ad·e·quate
in·ad·mis·si·ble
in·ad·vert·ent
in·al·ien·a·ble
in·ap·pli·ca·ble
in·ap·pro·pri·ate
in·ar·tic·u·late
in·as·much
in·at·ten·tion
in·au·di·ble
in·au·gur·al
in·au·gu·rate
in·bred
in·cal·cu·la·ble
in·ca·pa·ble
in·ca·pac·i·tate
in·cen·di·ar·y
in·cense
in·ces·sant
in·ci·dence
in·ci·dent
in·ci·den·tal·ly
in·cin·er·a·tor
in·ci·sion
in·cite
in·cli·na·tion
in·cline
in·clude
in·clu·sion
in·clu·sive
in·co·her·ent
in·come
in·com·par·a·ble
in·com·pat·i·ble
in·com·pe·tent
in·com·plete
in·com·pre·hen·si·ble
in·con·ceiv·a·ble
in·con·clu·sive
in·con·gru·ous
in·con·se·quen·tial
in·con·sid·er·ate

in·con·sist·ent
in·con·spic·u·ous
in·con·ven·ience
in·con·ven·ient
in·cor·po·rate
in·cor·rect
in·cor·ri·gi·ble
in·cor·rupt·i·ble
in·crease
in·cred·i·ble
in·cred·u·lous
in·cre·ment
in·cu·ba·tor
in·cum·bent
in·cur
in·cur·a·ble
in·de·cent
in·de·ci·sive
in·deed
in·def·i·nite
in·del·i·ble
in·dem·ni·fy
in·dem·ni·ty
in·dent
in·de·pend·ence
in·de·pend·ent
in·de·struct·i·ble
in·dex
in·di·cate
in·di·ca·tion
in·dic·a·tive
in·di·ca·tor
in·dict·ment
in·dif·fer·ence
in·dif·fer·ent
in·dig·e·nous
in·di·ges·tion
in·dig·nant
in·dig·ni·ty
in·di·rect
in·dis·cre·tion
in·dis·crim·i·nate
in·dis·pen·sa·ble
in·dis·put·a·ble
in·dis·tinct
in·di·vid·u·al
in·di·vis·i·ble
in·do·lence
in·do·lent
in·doors
in·duce
in·duce·ment

in·duct
in·duc·tive
in·dulge
in·dul·gence
in·dus·tri·al
in·dus·tri·al·ize
in·dus·tri·ous
in·dus·try
in·ef·fec·tive
in·ef·fi·cient
in·el·i·gi·ble
in·e·qual·i·ty
in·eq·ui·ta·ble
in·er·tia
in·es·cap·a·ble
in·es·ti·ma·ble
in·ev·i·ta·ble
in·ex·haust·i·ble
in·ex·o·ra·ble
in·ex·pen·sive
in·ex·pe·ri·enced
in·ex·pli·ca·ble
in·fal·li·ble
in·fa·mous
in·fa·my
in·fan·cy
in·fant
in·fan·try
in·fect
in·fec·tion
in·fec·tious
in·fer
in·fe·ri·or
in·fer·nal
in·fest
in·fi·del·i·ty
in·fil·trate
in·fi·nite
in·fin·i·ty
in·firm
in·fir·ma·ry
in·flame
in·flam·ma·ble
in·flam·ma·tion
in·flate
in·fla·tion
in·flex·i·ble
in·flict
in·flu·ence
in·flu·en·tial
in·form
in·for·mal

in·for·ma·tion
in·fringe
in·fur·i·ate
in·fu·sion
in·gen·ious
in·ge·nu·i·ty
in·grained
in·grat·i·tude
in·gre·di·ent
in·hab·it
in·hab·it·ant
in·hale
in·her·ent
in·her·it
in·her·it·ance
in·hi·bi·tion
in·hos·pi·ta·ble
in·hu·man
in·im·i·cal
in·iq·ui·ty
i·ni·tial
i·ni·ti·ate
i·ni·ti·a·tive
in·jec·tion
in·junc·tion
in·jure
in·ju·ri·ous
in·jur·y
in·jus·tice
ink
in·laid
in·land
in·lay
in·let
in·mate
inn
in·ner
in·ning
in·no·cence
in·no·cent
in·noc·u·ous
in·no·va·tion
in·nu·en·do
in·nu·mer·a·ble
in·oc·u·la·tion
in·of·fen·sive
in·or·gan·ic
in·quest
in·quire
in·quir·y
in·quis·i·tive
in·sane

in·san·i·ty
in·sa·tia·ble
in·scribe
in·scrip·tion
in·sect
in·se·cure
in·sen·si·ble
in·sen·si·tive
in·sep·a·ra·ble
in·sert
in·ser·tion
in·side
in·sight
in·sig·ni·a
in·sig·nif·i·cant
in·sin·u·ate
in·sist
in·sist·ent
in·sole
in·so·lence
in·so·lent
in·sol·u·ble
in·som·ni·a
in·spec·tion
in·spec·tor
in·spi·ra·tion
in·spire
in·stall
in·stal·la·tion
in·stall·ment
in·stance
in·stant
in·stan·ta·ne·ous
in·stead
in·sti·gate
in·still
in·stinct
in·sti·tute
in·sti·tu·tion
in·struct
in·struc·tion
in·struc·tor
in·stru·ment
in·suf·fer·a·ble
in·suf·fi·cient
in·su·late
in·su·la·tion
in·su·lin
in·sult
in·sur·ance
in·sure
in·sur·gent

in·sur·mount·a·ble
in·sur·rec·tion
in·tan·gi·ble
in·te·gral
in·te·grate
in·te·gra·tion
in·teg·ri·ty
in·tel·lect
in·tel·lec·tu·al
in·tel·li·gence
in·tel·li·gent
in·tend
in·tense
in·ten·si·fy
in·ten·si·ty
in·tent
in·ten·tion
in·ter
in·ter·cede
in·ter·cept
in·ter·change
in·ter·com
in·ter·course
in·ter·est
in·ter·fere
in·ter·fer·ence
in·ter·im
in·te·ri·or
in·ter·ject
in·ter·lock
in·ter·lude
in·ter·me·di·ate
in·ter·mis·sion
in·ter·mit·tent
in·ter·nal
in·ter·na·tion·al
in·ter·pret
in·ter·pre·ta·tion
in·ter·pret·er
in·ter·ro·gate
in·ter·rupt
in·ter·rup·tion
in·ter·sec·tion
in·ter·state
in·ter·val
in·ter·vene
in·ter·view
in·tes·ti·nal
in·tes·tine
in·ti·mate
in·tim·i·date
in·tol·er·a·ble

in·tol·er·ance
in·to·na·tion
in·tox·i·cate
in·tra·ve·nous
in·tri·cate
in·trigue
in·trin·sic
in·tro·duce
in·tro·duc·tion
in·trude
in·tru·sion
in·tu·i·tion
in·un·date
in·vade
in·va·lid
in·val·u·a·ble
in·var·i·a·ble
in·va·sion
in·vent
in·ven·tion
in·ven·tor
in·ven·to·ry
in·vert
in·vest
in·ves·ti·gate
in·ves·ti·ga·tion
in·vest·ment
in·vet·er·ate
in·vig·or·ate
in·vin·ci·ble
in·vis·i·ble
in·vi·ta·tion
in·vite
in·voice
in·vol·un·tar·y
in·volve
in·ward
i·on
ire
i·ris
irk·some
i·ron
i·ron·ic
i·ro·ny
ir·ra·tion·al
ir·ref·u·ta·ble
ir·reg·u·lar
ir·rel·e·vant
ir·rep·a·ra·ble
ir·re·place·a·ble
ir·re·proach·a·ble
ir·re·sist·i·ble

ir·re·spon·si·ble
ir·re·vers·i·ble
ir·rev·o·ca·ble
ir·ri·gate
ir·ri·ga·tion
ir·ri·ta·ble
ir·ri·tate
is·land
isle
i·so·late
i·so·la·tion
is·sue
i·tal·ic
itch
i·tem
i·tem·ize
i·tin·er·ar·y
it·self
i·vor·y
i·vy

J

jack
jack·al
jack·et
jack·knife
jack·pot
jade
jail
jail·er
jam
jan·i·tor
jar·gon
jaun·dice
jaun·ty
jay·walk
jazz
jeal·ous
jeal·ous·y
jeep
jeer
jel·ly
jeop·ard·y
jerk
jer·sey
jest
jew·el
jew·el·er
jew·el·ry
jig·saw

jin·gle
jinx
jock·ey
joc·u·lar
jog·ger
join
join·er
joint
joke
jol·ly
jolt
jos·tle
jour·nal
jour·nal·ist
jour·ney
jo·vi·al
joy·ful
joy·ous
ju·bi·lant
ju·bi·lee
judge
judg·ment
ju·di·cial
ju·di·ci·ar·y
ju·di·cious
jug·gle
juice
juic·y
jum·ble
jump
junc·tion
jun·gle
jun·ior
ju·ni·per
ju·ris·dic·tion
ju·ror
ju·ry
just
jus·tice
jus·ti·fi·a·ble
jus·ti·fi·ca·tion
jus·ti·fy
ju·ve·nile
jux·ta·po·si·tion

K

ka·lei·do·scope
kan·ga·roo
ka·pok
kar·at

ka·ra·te
kay·ak
keel
keen
keep
keep·er
ken·nel
kept
ker·nel
ker·o·sene
ketch·up
ket·tle
key·board
key·hole
key·note
kick
kick·back
kick·off
kid·nap
kid·ney
ki·lo
kil·o·gram
kil·o·li·ter
kil·o·me·ter
kil·o·ton
kil·o·watt
ki·mo·no
kind
kin·der·gar·ten
kin·dle
kind·ly
kind·ness
kin·dred
king
king·dom
kins·man
ki·osk
kiss
kitch·en
kite
kit·ten
knack
knave
knead
knee
kneel
knell
knelt
knew
knife
knight
knit

knives
knob
knock
knock·out
knoll
knot
know
knowl·edge
knowl·edge·a·ble
known
knuck·le
ko·sher

L

la·bel
la·bor
lab·o·ra·to·ry
la·bor·er
la·bo·ri·ous
lace
lac·er·a·tion
lack
lac·quer
lad·der
lad·en
la·dle
la·dy
laid
lain
lake
lamb
lame
la·ment
lamp
lance
land
land·lord
land·mark
land·scape
lane
lan·guage
lan·o·lin
lan·tern
lapse
lar·ce·ny
lard
large
large-scale
lark
lar·va

las·civ·i·ous
la·ser
lash
last
latch
late
la·tent
lathe
lath·er
lat·i·tude
lat·ter
laugh
laugh·ter
launch
laun·der
laun·dry
lau·rel
la·va
lav·a·to·ry
lav·ish
law
law-a·bid·ing
law·ful
lawn
lawn mow·er
law·suit
law·yer
lax·a·tive
lay
lay·er
lay·man
lay·off
lay·out
la·zy
lead
lead·er·ship
leaf
leaf·let
leaf·y
league
leak
lean
leap
learn
lease
least
leath·er
leave
leaves
lec·ture
lec·tur·er
led

ledge
ledg·er
leek
leer
lee·way
left
left-hand·ed
left·o·ver
leg·a·cy
le·gal
le·gal·ize
leg·end
leg·end·ar·y
leg·i·ble
le·gion
leg·is·late
leg·is·la·tion
leg·is·la·tive
leg·is·la·tor
leg·is·la·ture
le·git·i·mate
lei·sure
lem·on
lem·on·ade
lend
length
length·en
len·ient
lens
lent
leop·ard
less
less·en
less·er
les·son
lest
le·thal
let·ter
let·tuce
leu·ke·mi·a
lev·el
lev·er
lev·er·age
lev·y
lewd
li·a·bil·i·ty
li·a·ble
li·ar
li·bel
lib·er·al
lib·er·ate
lib·er·ty

li·brar·i·an
li·brar·y
li·cense
lick
lie
lieu·ten·ant
life
life·guard
life·like
life·long
life-size
life·time
lift
lig·a·ment
light
light·en
light-head·ed
light·house
light·ning
light·weight
like
like·ly
lik·en
like·ness
like·wise
li·lac
lil·y
limb
lim·bo
lime
lim·it
lim·i·ta·tion
lim·ou·sine
limp
line
lin·e·ar
line·man
lin·en
line-up
lin·ger
lin·guis·tics
lin·i·ment
lin·ing
link
li·no·le·um
lin·seed
lint
li·on
li·on·ess
lip·stick
liq·ue·fy
liq·uid

liq·ui·date
liq·uor
lisp
list
lis·ten
lis·ten·er
list·less
li·ter
lit·er·a·cy
lit·er·al
lit·er·ar·y
lit·er·ate
lit·er·a·ture
lit·i·ga·tion
lit·ter
lit·tle
lit·ur·gy
live
live·li·hood
live·ly
liv·er
live·stock
liv·id
liv·ing
liz·ard
lla·ma
load
loaf
loan
loaves
lob·by
lob·by·ist
lob·ster
lo·cal
lo·cal·i·ty
lo·cal·ly
lo·cate
lo·ca·tion
lock
lock·er
lo·cust
lodge
lodg·ing
loft
loft·y
log·a·rithm
log·ic
log·i·cal
loin
loi·ter
lone
lone·li·ness

lone·ly
lone·some
lon·gi·tude
long-range
long·shore·man
look·out
loom
loop
loose
loos·en
lord
lore
lose
los·er
loss
lost
lo·tion
lot·ter·y
loud
lounge
louse
lov·a·ble
love
love·li·ness
love·ly
lov·er
low·er
low·li·ness
low·ly
loy·al
loy·al·ty
lu·bri·cant
lu·bri·cate
lu·bri·ca·tor
lu·cid
luck
luck·y
lu·cra·tive
lu·di·crous
luke·warm
lull
lum·ber
lu·mi·nous
lump
lu·nar
lu·na·tic
lunch
lunch·eon
lung
lunge
lure
lurk

lust
lus·ter
lust·y
lux·u·ri·ous
lux·ur·y
ly·ing
lymph
lym·phat·ic
lynx
lyr·ic

M

ma·chine
ma·chin·er·y
ma·chin·ist
mad·den
made
made-up
mad·man
mad·ness
mad·ras
mag·a·zine
mag·ic
mag·i·cal
ma·gi·cian
mag·is·trate
mag·net
mag·net·ic
mag·net·ize
mag·nif·i·cence
mag·nif·i·cent
mag·ni·fy
mag·ni·tude
ma·hog·a·ny
maid
maid·en
mail
mail·box
mail or·der
maim
main
main·land
main·stay
main·stream
main·tain
main·te·nance
ma·jes·tic
maj·es·ty
ma·jor
ma·jor·i·ty

make-be·lieve
mak·er
make·shift
make·up
mal·ad·just·ed
mal·a·dy
male
mal·func·tion
mal·ice
ma·li·cious
ma·lig·nant
mal·le·a·ble
mal·let
mal·nu·tri·tion
mal·prac·tice
malt
mam·mal
mam·moth
man·age
man·age·ment
man·ag·er
man·a·ge·ri·al
man·date
man·da·to·ry
mane
ma·neu·ver
man·ger
man·gle
man·hole
ma·ni·a
man·i·cure
man·i·fest
man·i·fes·ta·tion
man·i·fold
ma·nip·u·late
man·kind
man·ner
man·or
man·pow·er
man·sion
man·u·al
man·u·fac·ture
man·u·fac·tur·er
ma·nure
man·u·script
ma·ple
mar
mar·ble
march
mare
mar·gin
mar·gin·al

mar·i·jua·na
ma·rine
mar·i·ner
mar·i·tal
mar·i·time
mark
mar·ket
mar·ket·a·ble
mark·up
mar·ma·lade
ma·roon
mar·riage
mar·ried
mar·row
mar·ry
marsh
mar·shal
marsh·mal·low
mart
mar·tial
mar·tyr
mar·vel
mar·vel·ous
mas·cu·line
mash
mask
ma·son
ma·son·ry
mas·quer·ade
mass
mas·sa·cre
mas·sage
mas·sive
mast
mas·ter
mas·ter·piece
mas·ter·y
match
match·book
mate
ma·te·ri·al
ma·te·ri·al·ize
ma·ter·nal
ma·ter·ni·ty
math·e·mat·i·cal
math·e·mat·ics
mat·ri·mo·ny
ma·trix
ma·tron
mat·ter
mat·tress
mat·u·ra·tion

ma·ture
ma·tu·ri·ty
maul
max·i·mum
may·be
may·on·naise
may·or
maze
mead·ow
mea·ger
meal
meal·y
mean
me·an·der
meant
mean·time
mean·while
mea·sles
meas·ur·a·ble
meas·ure
meas·ure·ment
meat
me·chan·ic
me·chan·i·cal
mech·a·nism
mech·a·nize
med·al
med·dle
me·di·a
me·di·an
me·di·ate
me·di·a·tor
med·ic
med·i·cal
Med·i·care
med·i·cate
me·dic·i·nal
med·i·cine
me·di·e·val
me·di·o·cre
med·i·tate
med·i·ta·tion
me·di·um
med·ley
meek
meet
mel·an·chol·y
mel·low
me·lo·di·ous
mel·o·dra·ma
mel·o·dy
mel·on

melt
mem·ber
mem·ber·ship
mem·brane
mem·oir
mem·o·ra·ble
mem·o·ran·dum
me·mo·ri·al
mem·o·rize
mem·or·y
men·ace
me·nag·er·ie
mend
me·ni·al
men·tal
men·tal·i·ty
men·tion
men·u
mer·chan·dise
mer·chant
mer·ci·ful
mer·ci·less
mer·cu·ry
mer·cy
mere
merge
merg·er
me·ringue
mer·it
mer·i·to·ri·ous
mer·ri·ment
mer·ry
mesh
mess
mes·sage
mes·sen·ger
me·tab·o·lism
met·al
me·tal·lic
met·al·lur·gy
met·a·mor·pho·sis
met·a·phys·ics
me·te·or
me·te·or·o·log·i·cal
me·te·or·ol·o·gy
me·ter
meth·od
me·thod·i·cal
me·tic·u·lous
met·ric
me·trop·o·lis
met·ro·pol·i·tan

mice
mi·cro·bi·ol·o·gy
mi·cro·film
mi·crom·e·ter
mi·cro·or·gan·ism
mi·cro·scope
mi·cro·wave
mid·day
mid·dle
mid·dle-class
mid·dle·man
midg·et
mid·land
mid·night
mid·way
mid·wife
mid·win·ter
mid·year
might
might·y
mi·grant
mi·grate
mi·gra·tion
mild
mil·dew
mile
mile·age
mil·i·tant
mil·i·ta·rist
mil·i·tar·y
mil·li·tia
milk
milk·man
milk shake
milk·y
mill
mil·len·ni·um
mill·er
mil·li·gram
mil·li·li·ter
mil·li·ner·y
mil·lion
mil·lion·aire
mime
mim·ic
mince
mind
mind·less
mine
min·er
min·er·al
min·er·a·log·i·cal

min·er·al·o·gy
min·gle
min·i·a·ture
min·i·mal
min·i·mum
min·is·ter
min·is·try
min·now
mi·nor
mi·nor·i·ty
min·strel
mint
mi·nus
min·ute
mir·a·cle
mi·rac·u·lous
mi·rage
mir·ror
mis·ap·pre·hen·sion
mis·ap·pro·pri·a·tion
mis·be·have
mis·cal·cu·late
mis·car·riage
mis·cel·la·ne·ous
mis·chance
mis·chief
mis·chie·vous
mis·con·cep·tion
mis·de·mean·or
mi·ser
mis·er·a·ble
mis·er·y
mis·fire
mis·fit
mis·for·tune
mis·giv·ing
mis·guid·ed
mis·hap
mis·in·ter·pret
mis·lead
mis·led
mis·place
mis·pro·nounce
miss
mis·sile
mis·sion
mis·sion·ar·y
mis·spell
mist
mis·take
mis·tak·en
mis·tress

mis·tri·al
mis·trust
mist·y
mis·un·der·stand
mis·un·der·stood
mis·use
mit·i·gate
mitt
mit·ten
mix
mix·er
mix·ture
moan
mo·bile
mo·bil·i·ty
mo·bi·lize
moc·ca·sin
mock
mock·er·y
mode
mod·el
mod·er·ate
mod·er·a·tion
mod·ern
mod·ern·ize
mod·est
mod·es·ty
mod·i·fi·ca·tion
mod·i·fy
mod·u·late
moist
moist·en
mois·ture
mo·lar
mo·las·ses
mold
mold·ing
mold·y
mole
mo·lec·u·lar
mol·e·cule
mo·lest
mol·ten
mo·ment
mo·men·tar·y
mo·men·tum
mon·arch
mon·ar·chy
mon·as·ter·y
mon·e·tar·y
mon·ey
mon·grel

mon·i·tor
monk
mon·key
mon·o·gram
mon·o·logue
mo·nop·o·lize
mo·nop·o·ly
mo·not·o·nous
mon·ster
mon·strous
month
mon·u·ment
mon·u·men·tal
mood
moon
moon·light
moon·shine
moose
mope
mor·al
mo·rale
mo·ral·i·ty
mor·al·ize
mor·bid
more·o·ver
morgue
morn·ing
mo·ron
mor·phine
mor·sel
mor·tal
mor·tal·i·ty
mor·tar
mort·gage
mor·ti·fy
mor·tu·ar·y
mo·sa·ic
mos·qui·to
moss
mo·tel
moth
moth·er
mo·tif
mo·tion
mo·ti·vate
mo·tive
mot·ley
mo·tor
mo·tor·cy·cle
mo·tor·ist
mo·tor·man
mot·tle

mot·to
mound
mount
moun·tain
moun·tain·eer
moun·tain·ous
mourn
mourn·er
mourn·ful
mouse
mouth
mouth·ful
mov·a·ble
move
move·ment
mov·er
mov·ie
mov·ing
mow
mow·er
mud·dle
mud·dy
muff
muf·fin
muf·fle
muf·fler
mug·ger
mule
mul·ti·col·ored
mul·ti·lat·er·al
mul·ti·ple
mul·ti·pli·ca·tion
mul·ti·plic·i·ty
mul·ti·pli·er
mul·ti·ply
mul·ti·tude
mum·ble
munch
mu·nic·i·pal
mu·ni·tions
mu·ral
mur·der
mur·der·er
mur·der·ous
murk·y
mur·mur
mus·cle
mus·cu·lar
muse
mu·se·um
mush
mush·room

mu·sic
mu·si·cal
mu·si·cian
mu·si·col·o·gy
musk
mus·ket
musk·rat
mus·lin
mus·tache
mus·tard
mus·ter
mu·ta·tion
mute
mu·ti·late
mu·ti·ny
mut·ter
mu·tu·al
muz·zle
myr·i·ad
mys·te·ri·ous
mys·ter·y
mys·ti·cal
mys·ti·cism
myth
myth·i·cal
my·thol·o·gy

N

nail
na·ive
na·ked
name·less
name·ly
nap·kin
nar·cot·ic
nar·rate
nar·ra·tive
nar·row
nar·row-mind·ed
na·sal
nas·ty
na·tion
na·tion·al
na·tion·al·i·ty
na·tion·al·ize
na·tive
na·tiv·i·ty
nat·u·ral
nat·u·ral·ize
na·ture

naugh·ty
nau·sea
nau·seous
nau·ti·cal
na·val
nave
na·vel
nav·i·ga·ble
nav·i·gate
nav·i·ga·tion
nav·i·ga·tor
na·vy
near·by
neat
nec·es·sar·y
ne·ces·si·ty
neck·lace
neck·line
nec·tar
need
nee·dle
nee·dle·point
need·y
ne·gate
neg·a·tive
neg·lect
neg·li·gence
neg·li·gent
neg·li·gi·ble
ne·go·tia·ble
ne·go·ti·ate
ne·go·ti·a·tion
Ne·gro
neigh·bor
neigh·bor·hood
nei·ther
ne·on
neph·ew
nerve
nerv·ous
nest
nes·tle
neth·er
net·work
neu·rol·o·gy
neu·ro·sis
neu·rot·ic
neu·ter
neu·tral
neu·tral·i·ty
neu·tral·ize
neu·tron

nev·er
nev·er·the·less
new·born
new·com·er
news
news·cast
news·let·ter
news·pa·per
news·print
news·reel
news·stand
next
nib·ble
nice
nick
nick·el
nick·name
nic·o·tine
niece
night
night·cap
night·fall
night·gown
night·ly
night·mare
night school
night·time
nim·ble
nine
nine·teen
nine·teenth
nine·ti·eth
nine·ty
ninth
nip·ple
ni·tro·gen
ni·tro·glyc·er·in
no·bil·i·ty
no·ble
no·bly
no·bod·y
noc·tur·nal
noise
nois·y
no·mad
no·men·cla·ture
nom·i·nal
nom·i·nate
nom·i·na·tion
nom·i·nee
non·ag·gres·sion
non·com·mis·sioned

non·com·mit·tal
non·con·form·ist
none
non·en·ti·ty
non·ex·ist·ent
non·par·ti·san
non·prof·it
non·res·i·dent
non·sec·tar·i·an
non·sense
non·stop
non·vi·o·lent
noon
noon·day
noon·time
nor
nor·mal
nor·mal·ize
north
north·east
north·east·ern
north·ern
north·ern·most
north·ward
north·west
north·west·ern
nose
nos·tal·gia
nos·tril
no·ta·ble
no·ta·rize
no·tar·y public
no·ta·tion
notch
note
note·book
note·wor·thy
noth·ing
no·tice
no·tice·a·ble
no·ti·fi·ca·tion
no·ti·fy
no·tion
no·to·ri·e·ty
no·to·ri·ous
not·with·stand·ing
noun
nour·ish
no·va
nov·el
nov·el·ty
nov·ice

now·a·days
no·where
nox·ious
noz·zle
nu·cle·ar
nu·cle·us
nude
nug·get
nui·sance
nul·li·fi·ca·tion
nul·li·fy
numb
num·ber
nu·mer·al
nu·mer·i·cal
nu·mer·ous
nup·tial
nurse
nurs·er·y
nur·ture
nut·meg
nu·tri·ent
nu·tri·tion
nu·tri·tious
nut·shell
nut·ty
nuz·zle

O

oak
oar
o·a·sis
oat
oath
o·be·di·ence
o·be·di·ent
o·bese
o·bey
o·bit·u·ar·y
ob·ject
ob·jec·tion
ob·jec·tive
ob·li·ga·tion
o·blige
ob·lique
ob·lit·er·ate
ob·liv·i·on
ob·nox·ious
ob·scene
ob·scen·i·ty

ob·scure
ob·scu·ri·ty
ob·se·qui·ous
ob·serv·ance
ob·serv·ant
ob·ser·va·tion
ob·serv·a·to·ry
ob·serve
ob·sess
ob·ses·sion
ob·so·les·cence
ob·so·les·cent
ob·so·lete
ob·sta·cle
ob·ste·tri·cian
ob·stet·rics
ob·sti·na·cy
ob·sti·nate
ob·struct
ob·struc·tion
ob·tain
ob·tain·a·ble
ob·tru·sive
ob·tuse
ob·vi·ous
oc·ca·sion
oc·ca·sion·al
oc·cult
oc·cu·pant
oc·cu·pa·tion
oc·cu·py
oc·cur
oc·cur·rence
o·cean
o'clock
oc·tave
odd
ode
o·di·ous
o·dom·e·ter
o·dor
off·beat
of·fend
of·fend·er
of·fense
of·fen·sive
of·fer
off·hand
of·fice
of·fi·cer
of·fi·cial
of·fi·ci·ate

of·fi·cious
off·set
off·shoot
off·shore
off·spring
off-the-rec·ord
of·ten
o·gre
oil
oil·y
oint·ment
old-fash·ioned
ol·ive
om·e·let
o·men
om·i·nous
o·mis·sion
o·mit
om·nip·o·tent
once
on·com·ing
one·self
one-sid·ed
on·go·ing
on·ion
on·look·er
on·ly
on·rush
on·set
on·shore
on·slaught
on·ward
ooze
o·paque
o·pen
o·pen·ing
o·pen-mind·ed
op·er·a
op·er·ate
op·er·a·tion
op·er·a·tor
oph·thal·mol·o·gy
o·pin·ion
o·pin·ion·at·ed
o·pi·um
o·pos·sum
op·po·nent
op·por·tun·ist
op·por·tu·ni·ty
op·pose
op·po·site
op·po·si·tion

op·press
op·pres·sive
op·tic
op·ti·cal
op·ti·cian
op·ti·mism
op·ti·mis·tic
op·tion
op·tom·e·trist
op·u·lence
o·ra·cle
o·ral
or·ange
o·ra·tion
or·a·tor
or·a·to·ry
or·bit
or·chard
or·ches·tra
or·chid
or·dain
or·deal
or·der
or·di·nance
or·di·nar·i·ly
or·di·nar·y
ord·nance
ore
or·gan
or·gan·ic
or·gan·ism
or·gan·i·za·tion
or·gan·ize
o·ri·ent
O·ri·en·tal
o·ri·en·ta·tion
o·ri·gin
o·rig·i·nal
o·rig·i·nate
o·rig·i·na·tor
or·na·ment
or·nate
or·phan
or·tho·don·tia
or·tho·dox
or·tho·dox·y
or·tho·pe·dics
os·cil·late
os·mo·sis
os·si·fy
os·ten·si·bly
os·ten·ta·tious

os·tra·cize
os·trich
oth·er·wise
ought
ounce
our·self
our·selves
oust
out·break
out·cast
out·come
out·cry
out·dis·tance
out·doors
out·er
out·fit
out·go·ing
out·grow
out·ing
out·land·ish
out·law
out·let
out·line
out·live
out·look
out·ly·ing
out·num·ber
out-of-date
out·post
out·put
out·ra·geous
out·right
out·run
out·side
out·skirts
out·spo·ken
out·stand·ing
out·strip
out·ward
out·wit
o·val
o·va·ry
o·va·tion
ov·en
o·ver·alls
o·ver·bear·ing
o·ver·board
o·ver·cast
o·ver·coat
o·ver·come
o·ver·flow
o·ver·grown

o·ver·head
o·ver·heard
o·ver·land
o·ver·lap
o·ver·load
o·ver·look
o·ver·night
o·ver·pass
o·ver·pow·er
o·ver·rule
o·ver·run
o·ver·seas
o·ver·se·er
o·ver·shad·ow
o·ver·shoe
o·ver·sight
o·ver·step
o·vert
o·ver·take
o·ver·throw
o·ver·time
o·ver·tone
o·ver·ture
o·ver·turn
o·ver·weight
o·ver·whelm
o·ver·work
owe
owl
own·er
own·er·ship
ox
ox·y·gen
oys·ter
o·zone

P

pace
pa·cif·ic
pac·i·fy
pack
pack·age
pack·er
pact
pad·dle
pad·lock
pa·gan
page
pag·eant
paid

pail
pain
paint
paint·er
pair
pa·ja·mas
pal·ace
pal·at·a·ble
pal·ate
pa·la·tial
pale
pal·ette
palm
pal·pa·ble
pal·pi·tate
pal·sy
pal·try
pam·per
pam·phlet
pan·a·ce·a
pan·cake
pane
pan·el
pan·el·ing
pang
pan·ic
pan·ick·y
pan·o·ply
pan·o·ram·a
pan·sy
pant
pan·to·mime
pan·try
pants
pa·pal
pa·per
pa·per·back
par·a·ble
par·a·chute
pa·rade
par·a·dise
par·a·dox
par·af·fin
par·a·graph
par·al·lel
pa·ral·y·sis
par·a·lyze
par·a·mount
par·a·phrase
par·a·site
par·a·troop·er
par·cel

parch
par·don
pare
par·ent
pa·ren·tal
pa·ren·the·sis
par·ish
par·ish·ion·er
par·i·ty
park
par·ley
par·lia·ment
par·lia·men·ta·ry
par·lor
pa·ro·chi·al
par·o·dy
pa·role
par·ry
pars·ley
part
par·take
par·tial
par·ti·al·i·ty
par·tic·i·pate
par·ti·cle
par·tic·u·lar
par·ti·san
par·ti·tion
part·ner·ship
part-time
par·ty
pass
pas·sage
pas·sage·way
pas·sen·ger
pas·sion
pas·sion·ate
pas·sive
pass·port
past
paste
pas·tel
pas·teur·ize
pas·time
pas·tor·al
pas·try
pas·ture
patch
pat·ent
pa·ter·nal
path
pa·thet·ic

path·way
pa·tience
pa·tient
pat·i·o
pa·tri·arch
pa·tri·ot
pa·tri·ot·ic
pa·trol
pa·trol·man
pa·tron
pa·tron·age
pa·tron·ize
pat·tern
pat·ty
pause
pave·ment
pa·vil·ion
paw
pawn
pay
pay·a·ble
pay·ment
pay·roll
pea
peace
peace·ful
peach
pea·cock
peak
pea·nut
pear
pearl
peas·ant
peb·ble
pe·can
peck
pe·cul·iar
pe·cu·li·ar·i·ty
ped·al
pe·dan·tic
ped·ant·ry
ped·dle
ped·dler
ped·es·tal
pe·des·tri·an
pe·di·a·tri·cian
ped·i·gree
peek
peel
peep
peer
pee·vish

pel·i·can
pel·let
pelt
pel·vic
pe·nal·ize
pen·al·ty
pen·ance
pen·cil
pend·ing
pen·du·lum
pen·e·tra·ble
pen·e·trate
pen·e·trat·ing
pen·guin
pen·i·cil·lin
pe·nin·su·la
pen·i·tent
pen·i·ten·tia·ry
pen·knife
pen·nant
pen·ni·less
pen·ny
pen·sion
pen·ta·gon
peo·ple
pep·per
per·cale
per·ceive
per cent
per·cent·age
per·cep·ti·ble
per·cep·tion
perch
per·co·late
per·cus·sion
pe·ren·ni·al
per·fect
per·fec·tion
per·fo·rate
per·form
per·form·ance
per·fume
per·haps
per·il
per·il·ous
pe·rim·e·ter
pe·ri·od
pe·ri·od·i·cal
pe·riph·er·al
per·ish
per·jure
per·ju·ry

per·ma·nent
per·me·a·ble
per·me·ate
per·mis·sion
per·mit
per·ni·cious
per·pe·trate
per·pe·tra·tor
per·pet·u·al
per·pet·u·ate
per·pe·tu·i·ty
per·plex
per·plex·i·ty
per·se·cute
per·se·cu·tion
per·se·cu·tor
per·se·ver·ance
per·se·vere
per·sist
per·sist·ence
per·sist·ent
per·son
per·son·a·ble
per·son·al
per·son·al·i·ty
per·son·i·fy
per·spec·tive
per·spi·ra·tion
per·suade
per·sua·sion
per·sua·sive
per·tain
per·ti·nence
per·ti·nent
pe·ruse
per·vade
per·verse
per·ver·sion
per·vert
pes·si·mism
pes·si·mis·tic
pet·al
pe·ti·tion
pe·tro·le·um
pet·ty
pet·u·lant
pew·ter
phan·tom
phar·ma·ceu·ti·cal
phar·ma·cist
phase
pheas·ant

phe·nom·e·nal

phe·nom·e·non

phi·lan·throp·ic

phil·lan·thro·pist

phil·har·mon·ic

phi·los·o·pher

phil·o·soph·i·cal

phi·los·o·phy

phlegm

pho·bi·a

phoe·nix

phone

pho·net·ic

pho·no·graph

phos·phate

phos·phor·ous

phos·phor·us

pho·to

pho·to·graph

pho·tog·ra·pher

pho·to·graph·ic

phrase

phys·i·cal

phy·si·cian

phys·i·cist

phys·ics

phys·i·ol·o·gy

pi·an·ist

pi·an·o

pick

pick·er

pick·et

pick·le

pic·nic

pic·ture

pic·tur·esque

pie

piece

piece·meal

pier

pierce

pi·e·ty

pi·geon

pig·gy

pig·ment

pike

pile

pil·fer

pil·grim

pil·grim·age

pill

pil·lage

pil·lar

pil·low

pi·lot

pi·lot light

pim·ple

pin·cers

pinch

pine

pine·ap·ple

pink

pin·na·cle

pin·point

pint

pi·o·neer

pi·ous

pipe

pipe·line

pip·er

pique

pi·ra·cy

pi·rate

pis·tol

pis·ton

pitch

pitch·er

pit·fall

pith

pit·i·a·ble

pit·i·ful

pit·i·less

pit·y

piv·ot

piz·za

pla·ca·ble

pla·cate

place

plac·id

plague

plaid

plain

plan

plane

plan·et

plank

plant

plan·ta·tion

plant·er

plas·ma

plas·ter

plas·tic

plate

pla·teau

plat·form

plat·i·num

plat·i·tude

pla·toon

plat·ter

plau·si·ble

play

play·er

play·ful

play·ground

play·mate

play-off

plea

plead

pleas·ant

pleas·ant·ry

please

pleas·ure

pleat

pledge

ple·na·ry

plen·ti·ful

plen·ty

pli·a·ble

pli·ant

pli·ers

plight

plod

plot

plow

plow·share

pluck

plug

plum

plum·age

plumb·er

plume

plum·met

plump

plun·der

plunge

plur·al

plu·ral·i·ty

plus

plush

plu·to·ni·um

ply

ply·wood

pneu·mat·ic

pneu·mo·nia

pock·et

pock·et·book

po·em

po·et

po·et·ic

po·et·ry

point

point-blank

poise

poi·son

poi·son·ous

poke

pok·er

po·lar

po·lar·i·ty

pole

po·lem·ic

po·lice

po·lice·man

po·lice·wom·an

pol·i·cy

po·li·o

pol·ish

po·lite

pol·i·tic

po·lit·i·cal

pol·i·ti·cian

pol·i·tics

pol·ka

poll

pol·len

pol·li·nate

pol·lute

pol·lu·tion

po·lo

po·lyg·a·my

pol·yp

pomp

pom·pous

pond

pon·der

pon·tiff

po·ny

poo·dle

pool

poor

pope

pop·lar

pop·lin

pop·py

pop·u·lace

pop·u·lar

pop·u·lar·i·ty

pop·u·lar·i·za·tion

pop·u·la·tion
pop·u·lous
por·ce·lain
porch
pore
pork
po·rous
por·poise
por·ridge
port
port·a·ble
por·tend
por·tent
por·ten·tous
por·ter
port·hole
por·tion
por·trait
por·tray
pose
po·si·tion
pos·i·tive
pos·sess
pos·ses·sion
pos·ses·sive
pos·ses·sor
pos·si·bil·i·ty
pos·si·ble
pos·si·bly
pos·sum
post
post·age
post·al
post card
pos·te·ri·or
pos·ter·i·ty
post·man
post·mark
post·mas·ter
post of·fice
post·pone
post·script
pos·tu·late
pos·ture
po·tas·si·um
po·ta·to
po·ten·cy
po·tent
po·ten·tate
po·ten·tial
po·ten·ti·al·i·ty
pot·hole

po·tion
pot·pour·ri
pot·ter
pouch
poul·try
pounce
pound
pour
pov·er·ty
pow·der
pow·er
pow·er·ful
prac·ti·cal
prac·ti·cal·i·ty
prac·tice
prac·ti·tion·er
prag·mat·ic
prai·rie
praise
prank
pray
prayer
preach
preach·er
pre·am·ble
pre·car·i·ous
pre·cau·tion
pre·cede
prec·e·dent
pre·cept
pre·cinct
pre·cious
pre·cip·i·tate
pre·cip·i·ta·tion
pre·cise
pre·ci·sion
pre·co·cious
pred·a·to·ry
pred·e·ces·sor
pre·de·ter·mine
pre·dic·a·ment
pred·i·cate
pre·dict
pre·dic·tion
pre·di·lec·tion
pre·dis·po·si·tion
pre·dom·i·nant
pre·dom·i·nate
pre·em·i·nent
pre·empt
pre·fab·ri·cate
pref·ace

pre·fer
pref·er·ence
pref·e·ren·tial
pre·fix
preg·nan·cy
preg·nant
pre·his·to·ric
prej·u·dice
prel·ate
pre·lim·i·nar·y
prel·ude
pre·ma·ture
pre·med·i·tate
pre·mier
prem·ise
pre·mi·um
pre·paid
prep·a·ra·tion
pre·par·a·to·ry
pre·pare
pre·pon·der·ance
prep·o·si·tion
pre·pos·sess·ing
pre·pos·ter·ous
pre·req·ui·site
pre·rog·a·tive
Pres·by·te·ri·an
pre·school
pre·sci·ence
pre·scribe
pre·scrip·tion
pres·ence
pres·ent
pre·sent·a·ble
pres·en·ta·tion
pres·er·va·tion
pre·serv·a·tive
pre·serve
pre·serv·er
pre·side
pres·i·den·cy
pres·i·dent
pres·i·den·tial
press
pres·sure
pres·sur·ize
pres·tige
pre·sume
pre·sump·tion
pre·sump·tu·ous
pre·tend
pre·tense

pre·ten·sion
pre·ten·tious
pre·text
pret·ty
pre·vail
prev·a·lent
pre·vent
pre·ven·tion
pre·view
pre·vi·ous
prey
price
prick
prick·le
pride
priest
pri·ma·ry
pri·mate
prime
prim·er
prim·i·tive
prim·rose
prince
prin·cess
prin·ci·pal
prin·ci·pal·i·ty
prin·ci·pal·ly
prin·ci·ple
print
print·er
pri·or
pri·or·i·ty
prism
pris·on
pris·on·er
pri·va·cy
pri·vate
priv·i·lege
prize
prob·a·bil·i·ty
prob·a·ble
pro·ba·tion
probe
prob·lem
pro·ce·dure
pro·ceed
proc·ess
pro·ces·sion
proc·es·sor
pro·claim
proc·la·ma·tion
pro·cure

prod·i·gal
pro·di·gious
prod·i·gy
pro·duce
prod·uct
pro·duc·tion
pro·fane
pro·fess
pro·fes·sion
pro·fes·sion·al
pro·fes·sor
pro·fi·cient
pro·file
prof·it
prof·it·a·ble
pro·found
pro·fuse
pro·gram
prog·ress
pro·gres·sive
pro·hib·it
pro·hi·bi·tion
pro·hib·i·tive
proj·ect
pro·jec·tion
pro·lif·ic
pro·logue
pro·long
prom·e·nade
prom·i·nence
prom·i·nent
prom·ise
prom·is·so·ry
prom·on·to·ry
pro·mote
pro·mo·tion
prompt
prone
pro·noun
pro·nounce
pro·nun·ci·a·tion
proof
prop
prop·a·gan·da
prop·a·gate
pro·pen·si·ty
prop·er
prop·er·ty
proph·e·cy
proph·e·sy
proph·et
pro·phet·ic

pro·pi·tious
pro·por·tion
pro·pos·al
pro·pose
prop·o·si·tion
pro·pri·e·tor
pro·pri·e·ty
pro·pul·sion
pro·sa·ic
prose
pros·e·cute
pros·e·cu·tion
pros·e·cu·tor
pros·pect
pro·spec·tive
pros·per
pros·per·i·ty
pros·per·ous
pros·the·sis
pros·ti·tute
pros·trate
pro·tect
pro·tec·tion
pro·tec·tive
pro·tec·tor
pro·test
Prot·es·tant
pro·ton
pro·to·type
pro·trude
pro·tru·sion
proud
prove
prov·erb
pro·vide
prov·i·dence
prov·ince
pro·vin·cial
pro·vi·sion
prov·o·ca·tion
pro·voke
prow·ess
prowl
prox·im·i·ty
prox·y
prude
pru·dence
pru·dent
prune
pry
psalm
pseu·do

psy·chi·at·ric
psy·chi·a·trist
psy·chi·a·try
psy·chic
psy·cho·a·nal·y·sis
psy·cho·an·a·lyst
psy·cho·log·i·cal·ly
psy·chol·o·gist
psy·chol·o·gy
psy·cho·sis
psy·cho·ther·a·py
psy·chot·ic
pu·ber·ty
pub·lic
pub·li·ca·tion
pub·lic·i·ty
pub·lish
pub·lish·er
pud·ding
pud·dle
puff
pulp
pul·pit
pul·sate
pulse
pul·ver·ize
pump
pump·kin
punch
punc·tu·al
punc·tu·ate
punc·tu·a·tion
pun·gent
pun·ish
pun·ish·ment
pu·ny
pu·pil
pup·pet
pup·py
pur·chase
pur·chas·er
pure
purge
pur·i·fi·ca·tion
pu·ri·fy
pu·ri·ty
pur·ple
pur·port
pur·pose
purse
pur·su·ant
pur·sue

pur·su·er
pur·suit
pus
push
pu·trid
put·ty
puz·zle
pyr·a·mid
py·thon

Q

quack
quake
qual·i·fi·ca·tion
qual·i·fied
qual·i·fy
qual·i·ta·tive
qual·i·ty
qualm
quan·ti·ta·tive
quan·ti·ty
quar·an·tine
quar·rel
quar·ry
quart
quar·ter
quar·ter·back
quar·tet
quartz
queen
queer
que·ry
quest
ques·tion
ques·tion·naire
quib·ble
quick
quick·en
qui·et
quilt
qui·nine
quin·tet
quirk
quit
quite
quiv·er
quiz
quo·rum
quo·ta
quo·ta·tion

quote
quo·tient

R

rab·bi
rab·bit
rab·id
ra·bies
rac·coon
race
rac·er
rac·ism
rack
rack·et
ra·dar
ra·di·al
ra·di·ant
ra·di·ate
ra·di·a·tion
ra·di·a·tor
rad·i·cal
ra·di·o
ra·di·o·ac·tive
ra·di·o·ac·tiv·i·ty
ra·di·ol·o·gy
ra·di·um
ra·di·us
raf·fle
raft
rage
rag·ged
rag·time
raid
rail
rail·road
rain
rain·bow
rain·coat
rain·fall
rain·storm
rain·y
raise
rai·sin
rake
ral·ly
ram·ble
ram·i·fi·ca·tion
ram·page
ramp·ant
ranch

ran·cid
ran·cor
ran·dom
rang
range
rang·er
rank
ran·sack
ran·som
rap
rape
rap·id
rap·port
rapt
rap·ture
rare
rar·i·ty
ras·cal
rash
rasp·ber·ry
rate
rath·er
rat·i·fy
ra·ti·o
ra·tion
ra·tion·al
rat·tle
rav·age
rave
rav·el
ra·ven
rav·en·ous
rav·ish
ray·on
ra·zor
reach
re·act
re·ac·tion
re·ac·tor
read
read·i·ly
read·i·ness
re·ad·just·ment
read·y
re·al
re·al·ism
re·al·is·tic
re·al·i·ty
re·al·ize
re·al·ly
realm
reap

re·ap·pear
rear
re·ar·range
rea·son
rea·son·a·ble
re·as·sem·ble
re·as·sure
reb·el
re·bel·lion
re·bel·lious
re·bound
re·buff
re·build
re·buke
re·call
re·cap·ture
re·cede
re·ceipt
re·ceive
re·ceiv·er
re·cent
re·cep·ta·cle
re·cep·tion
re·cess
re·ces·sion
rec·i·pe
re·cip·i·ent
re·cip·ro·cal
re·cip·ro·cate
re·cit·al
rec·i·ta·tion
re·cite
reck·less
re·claim
re·cline
rec·og·ni·tion
re·cog·ni·zance
rec·og·nize
rec·ol·lect
rec·om·mend
rec·om·men·da·tion
rec·om·pense
rec·on·cile
rec·on·cil·i·a·tion
re·con·sid·er
re·cord
re·cord·er
re·count
re·course
re·cov·er
re·cov·er·y
rec·re·a·tion

re·crim·i·na·tion
re·cruit
rec·tan·gle
rec·tan·gu·lar
rec·ti·fy
rec·tor
re·cu·per·ate
re·cur
re·cur·rence
re·deem
re·demp·tion
re·dou·ble
re·dress
re·duce
re·duc·i·ble
re·duc·tion
re·dun·dant
reed
reef
reek
reel
re·e·lect
re·e·lec·tion
re·en·ter
re·en·try
re·es·tab·lish
re·fer
ref·e·ree
ref·er·ence
ref·er·en·dum
re·fill
re·fine
re·fine·ment
re·fin·er·y
re·flect
re·flec·tion
re·flex
re·form
ref·or·ma·tion
re·fract
re·frain
re·fresh·er
re·fresh·ment
re·frig·er·a·tor
ref·uge
ref·u·gee
re·fund
re·fus·al
re·fuse
re·fute
re·gain
re·gard

re·gard·ing
re·gard·less
re·gen·er·ate
re·gent
re·gime
reg·i·men
reg·i·ment
re·gion
reg·is·ter
reg·is·tra·tion
re·gres·sion
re·gret
re·gret·ta·ble
reg·u·lar
reg·u·late
reg·u·la·tion
reg·u·la·tor
reg·u·la·to·ry
re·ha·bil·i·tate
re·hash
re·hears·al
re·hearse
reign
re·im·burse
re·in·force
re·in·state
re·it·er·ate
re·ject
re·joice
re·ju·ve·nate
re·lapse
re·late
re·la·tion
rel·a·tive
rel·a·tiv·i·ty
re·lax
re·lay
re·lease
re·lent
rel·e·van·cy
re·li·a·bil·i·ty
re·li·a·ble
re·li·ance
rel·ic
re·lief
re·lieve
re·li·gion
re·li·gious
re·lin·quish
rel·ish
re·luc·tance
re·luc·tant

re·ly
re·main
re·main·der
re·mark
re·mark·a·ble
re·me·di·al
rem·e·dy
re·mem·ber
re·mem·brance
re·mind
re·mind·er
rem·i·nis·cent
re·mis·sion
re·mit
re·mit·tance
rem·nant
re·morse
re·mote
re·mov·al
re·move
re·mov·er
re·mu·ner·ate
ren·der
re·new
re·new·a·ble
re·new·al
re·nounce
ren·o·vate
rent
rent·al
re·nun·ci·a·tion
re·o·pen
re·or·gan·ize
re·pair
re·pair·man
rep·a·ra·tion
re·past
re·pay
re·peal
re·peat
re·pel
re·pel·lent
re·pent
re·pent·ance
re·per·cus·sion
rep·er·toire
rep·e·ti·tion
rep·e·ti·tious
re·place
re·plen·ish
rep·li·ca
re·ply

re·port
re·pose
rep·re·hen·si·ble
rep·re·sent
rep·re·sen·ta·tion
rep·re·sent·a·tive
re·press
re·pres·sion
re·prieve
rep·ri·mand
re·proach
re·pro·duce
re·pro·duc·tion
rep·tile
re·pub·lic
re·pub·li·can
re·pu·di·ate
re·pug·nant
re·pulse
re·pul·sive
rep·u·ta·ble
rep·u·ta·tion
re·quest
re·quire
re·quire·ment
req·ui·site
req·ui·si·tion
re·scind
res·cue
re·search
re·sem·blance
re·sem·ble
re·sent
re·sent·ment
res·er·va·tion
re·serve
res·er·voir
re·side
res·i·dence
res·i·dent
re·sid·u·al
res·i·due
re·sign
res·ig·na·tion
re·sil·i·ent
res·in
re·sist
re·sist·ance
res·o·lu·tion
re·solve
re·sort
re·sound

re·source
re·spect
re·spect·a·ble
re·spect·ful
re·spec·tive
res·pi·ra·tion
res·pi·ra·tor
res·pite
re·spond
re·sponse
re·spon·si·bil·i·ty
re·spon·si·ble
rest
res·tau·rant
rest·ful
res·ti·tu·tion
rest·less
res·to·ra·tion
re·store
re·strain
re·straint
re·strict
re·stric·tion
rest room
re·sult
re·sume
re·sump·tion
re·sus·ci·ta·tor
re·tail
re·tain
re·tain·er
re·tal·i·ate
re·tard·ed
re·ten·tion
ret·i·cent
ret·i·na
re·tire
re·tire·ment
re·tort
re·touch
re·trace
re·tract
re·tread
re·treat
ret·ri·bu·tion
re·trieve
ret·ro·ac·tive
ret·ro·gres·sion
ret·ro·spect
re·turn
re·un·ion
re·u·nite

re·veal
rev·el
rev·e·la·tion
re·venge
rev·e·nue
re·vere
rev·er·ence
Rev·er·end
rev·er·ent
re·verse
re·vers·i·ble
re·vert
re·view
re·viv·al
re·vive
re·volt
rev·o·lu·tion
rev·o·lu·tion·ar·y
rev·o·lu·tion·ize
re·volve
re·volv·er
re·vue
re·vul·sion
re·ward
rhap·so·dy
rhet·o·ric
rheu·ma·tism
rhi·noc·er·os
rhyme
rhythm
rhyth·mi·cal
rib·bon
rice
rich
rich·es
rid
rid·den
rid·dle
ride
rid·er
ridge
rid·i·cule
ri·dic·u·lous
ri·fle
rift
right
right·eous
right-hand
rig·id
rig·or
rig·or·ous
rind

ring
ring·er
rinse
ri·ot
ri·ot·ous
ripe
rip·en
rip·ple
rise
ris·en
risk
rit·u·al
ri·val
riv·er
riv·er·side
riv·et
roach
road
road·block
road map
road·side
road·way
roam
roar
roast
rob·ber
rob·ber·y
robe
rob·in
ro·bot
ro·bust
rock
rock·er
rock·et
rock·y
rode
ro·dent
role
roll
roll·er
ro·mance
ro·man·tic
ro·man·ti·cize
romp
roof
roof·ing
room
room·y
roost
roost·er
root
rope

ro·sa·ry
rose
ro·sette
ros·y
ro·ta·ry
ro·tate
ro·tor
rot·ten
ro·tun·da
rough
round
round·up
rouse
route
rou·tine
rove
row
row·dy
roy·al
roy·al·ty
rub·ber
rub·bish
rub·ble
ru·by
rud·der
rude
ru·di·men·ta·ry
ruf·fle
rug·ged
ru·in
ru·in·ous
rule
rul·er
rum·ble
rum·mage
ru·mor
rump
run·a·way
run·down
rung
run·ner
run·off
run·way
rup·ture
ru·ral
ruse
rush
rust
rus·tic
rus·tler
rust·y
ruth·less

S

Sab·bath
sa·ber
sab·o·tage
sac·cha·rin
sa·chet
sack
sac·ra·ment
sa·cred
sac·ri·fice
sad·den
sad·dle
sa·dist
safe
safe·guard
safe·keep·ing
safe·ty
sage
sail
sail·boat
sail·or
saint
sake
sal·ad
sal·a·ry
sale
sales·clerk
sales·man
sa·li·ent
sa·line
sa·li·va
sal·ly
salm·on
sa·loon
salt
salt·wa·ter
sal·u·tar·y
sal·u·ta·tion
sa·lute
sal·vage
sal·va·tion
sam·ple
sanc·ti·fy
sanc·tion
sanc·ti·ty
sanc·tu·ar·y
sand
san·dal
sand·blast
sand·box
sand·pa·per

sand·stone
sand·wich
sane
sang
san·i·tar·y
san·i·ta·tion
san·i·ty
sank
sap·phire
sar·casm
sar·cas·tic
sar·dine
sash
Sa·tan
sa·teen
sat·el·lite
sa·ti·ate
sat·in
sat·ire
sat·i·rize
sat·is·fac·tion
sat·is·fac·to·ry
sat·is·fy
sat·u·rate
sat·u·ra·tion
sauce
sauce·pan
sau·cer
sau·cy
sauer·kraut
sau·sage
sav·age
save
sav·er
sav·ior
sa·vor·y
saw·dust
saw·mill
sax·o·phone
scab
scaf·fold
scald
scale
scal·lop
scalp
scal·y
scam·per
scan
scan·dal
scant
scant·y
scape·goat

scar
scarce
scar·ci·ty
scare
scare·crow
scarf
scar·let
scat·ter
scav·en·ger
scene
scen·er·y
sce·nic
scent
scep·ter
sched·ule
scheme
schism
schol·ar
schol·ar·ship
scho·las·tic
school
school·book
school·chil·dren
school·room
school·teach·er
school·work
school year
sci·ence
sci·en·tif·ic
sci·en·tist
scis·sors
scoff
scold
scoop
scope
scorch
score
score·board
scorn
scor·pi·on
scoun·drel
scour
scourge
scout
scowl
scram·ble
scrap
scrape
scrap·er
scratch
scrawl
scream

screech
screen
screw
screw·driv·er
scrib·ble
script
Scrip·ture
scroll
scrub
scru·ple
scru·pu·lous
scru·ti·nize
scru·ti·ny
scuf·fle
sculp·tor
sculp·ture
scum
scur·ry
scut·tle
sea
sea·board
sea·coast
sea·far·ing
sea·food
sea gull
seal
seam
sea·man
seam·stress
se·ance
sea·port
sear
search
sea·shore
sea·sick
sea·side
sea·son
sea·son·a·ble
seat
sea·wa·ter
sea·wor·thy
se·cede
se·ces·sion
se·clude
se·clu·sion
sec·ond
sec·ond·ar·y
se·cre·cy
se·cret
sec·re·tar·i·al
sec·re·tar·y
se·crete

se·cre·tion
sect
sec·tion
sec·u·lar
se·cure
se·cur·i·ty
se·dan
se·date
sed·a·tive
sed·i·ment
se·di·tion
se·duce
se·duc·tive
see
seed
seek
seem
seem·ly
seen
seg·ment
seg·re·ga·tion
seis·mic
seize
sei·zure
sel·dom
se·lect
se·lec·tion
self
self-as·sur·ance
self-cen·tered
self-con·fi·dence
self-con·scious
self-de·fense
self-em·ployed
self-ev·i·dent
self-help
self-im·prove·ment
self-in·dul·gent
self·ish
self·less
self-pres·er·va·tion
self-re·li·ant
self-right·eous
self-sac·ri·fice
self-sat·is·fied
self-serv·ice
self-suf·fi·cient
self-wind·ing
sell
sell·er
selves
sem·blance

se·mes·ter	sev·en	shelf	show·down
sem·i·au·to·mat·ic	sev·en·teen	shell	show·er
sem·i·cir·cle	sev·enth	shel·lac	show-off
sem·i·cir·cu·lar	sev·en·ti·eth	shell·fish	show·room
sem·i·con·duc·tor	sev·en·ty	shel·ter	shrank
sem·i·fi·nal	sev·er	shelve	shred
sem·i·nar	sev·er·al	shep·herd	shrewd
sem·i·nar·y	sev·er·ance	sher·bet	shriek
sen·ate	se·vere	sher·iff	shrill
sen·a·tor	se·ver·i·ty	sher·ry	shrimp
send	sew	shield	shrine
se·nile	sew·age	shift	shrink
sen·ior	sew·er	shil·ling	shriv·el
sen·sa·tion	sex	shim·mer	shroud
sen·sa·tion·al	sex·ton	shin	shrub
sense	sex·u·al	shine	shrug
sen·si·bil·i·ty	shab·by	shin·gle	shrunk
sen·si·ble	shack	shin·y	shud·der
sen·si·tive	shack·le	ship	shuf·fle
sen·su·al	shade	ship·build·er	shun
sen·su·ous	shad·ow	ship·load	shunt
sent	shad·y	ship·ment	shut
sen·tence	shaft	ship·wreck	shut·ter
sen·ti·ment	shag·gy	ship·yard	shut·tle
sen·ti·nel	shake	shirt	shy
sen·try	shak·er	shiv·er	sick
sep·a·rate	shake-up	shock	sick·en
sep·a·ra·tion	shak·y	shod	sick·le
se·quel	shale	shod·dy	sick·ly
se·quence	shal·low	shoe	side
se·ques·ter	sham	shoe·lace	side·board
ser·e·nade	shame	shoe·string	side·burns
se·rene	sham·poo	shoot	side·line
ser·geant	shape	shop	side·long
se·ri·al	share	shop·keep·er	side·swipe
se·ries	share·hold·er	shop·lift·er	side·track
se·ri·ous	shark	shore	side·walk
ser·mon	sharp	shorn	side·ways
ser·pent	sharp·en	short	siege
se·rum	shat·ter	short·age	sieve
serv·ant	shave	short·com·ing	sift
serve	shawl	short·en	sigh
serv·er	shear	short-sight·ed	sight
serv·ice	sheath	shot	sight·see·ing
serv·ice·a·ble	sheaves	shot·gun	sign
ser·vile	shed	should	sig·nal
ser·vi·tude	sheen	shoul·der	sig·na·ture
ses·a·me	sheep	shout	sig·net
ses·sion	sheep·ish	shove	sig·nif·i·cant
set·tle	sheep·skin	shov·el	sig·ni·fy
set·tle·ment	sheer	show	si·lence
set·tler	sheet	show·case	si·lent

silk	ski	slip·per	snort
silk·en	skies	slip·per·y	snout
sill	skill	slit	snow
sil·ly	skill·ful	sliv·er	snow·ball
si·lo	skim	slo·gan	snow·drift
sil·ver	skin	sloop	snow·fall
sil·ver·ware	skip	slop	snow·flake
sil·ver·y	skirt	slope	snow·man
sim·i·lar	skull	sloth	snow·plow
sim·i·lar·i·ty	skunk	slouch	snow·storm
sim·mer	sky	slow	snub
sim·ple	sky·line	sludge	snuff
sim·plic·i·ty	sky·scrap·er	slug	snug
sim·pli·fi·ca·tion	slab	slug·gish	snug·gle
sim·pli·fy	slack	slum·ber	soak
sim·ply	slack·en	slump	soap
sim·u·late	slain	sly	soar
sim·u·la·tion	slam	smack	so·ber
si·mul·ta·ne·ous	slan·der	small	soc·cer
since	slan·der·ous	smart	so·cia·ble
sin·cere	slang	smash	so·cial
sin·cer·i·ty	slant	smear	so·cial·ist
sing	slap	smell	so·ci·e·ty
sin·gle	slash	smelt·er	so·ci·ol·o·gy
sin·gle-hand·ed	slate	smile	sock
sin·gly	slaugh·ter	smirk	sock·et
sin·gu·lar	slave	smite	so·da
sin·is·ter	slav·er·y	smit·ten	so·di·um
sink	slav·ish	smock	so·fa
sin·ner	slay	smog	soft
si·nus	slea·zy	smoke	soft·ball
si·phon	sled	smok·er	soft·en
sir	sledge	smoke·stack	sog·gy
si·ren	sleek	smol·der	soil
sir·loin	sleep	smooth	sol·ace
sis·ter	sleep·y	smoth·er	so·lar
site	sleet	smudge	sold
sit-in	sleeve	smug	sol·der
sit·u·ate	sleigh	smug·gle	sol·dier
sit·u·a·tion	slen·der	snag	sole
six	slept	snail	sol·emn
six·teen	slew	snake	so·lem·ni·ty
sixth	slice	snap	so·lic·it
six·ti·eth	slick	snare	so·lic·i·tor
six·ty	slid	snarl	sol·id
siz·a·ble	slide	snatch	sol·i·dar·i·ty
size	slight	sneak	so·lid·i·fy
skate	slim	sneer	sol·i·tar·y
skel·e·ton	slime	sneeze	sol·i·tude
skep·tic	sling	sniff	so·lo
skep·ti·cal	slip	snore	sol·u·ble
sketch	slip·cov·er	snor·kel	so·lu·tion

solve	span·gle	spi·nal	square
sol·vent	span·iel	spin·dle	squash
som·ber	spank	spine	squat
some·bod·y	spare	spi·ral	squaw
some·how	spark	spire	squeak
some·one	spar·kle	spir·it	squeeze
some·place	spar·row	spir·i·tu·al	squire
some·thing	sparse	spit	squirm
some·time	spasm	spite	squir·rel
some·what	spas·mod·ic	splash	squirt
some·where	spas·tic	splash·down	stab
son	spat	spleen	sta·bil·i·ty
so·nar	spa·tial	splen·did	sta·ble
so·na·ta	spawn	splen·dor	stack
song	speak	splice	staff
son·ic	speak·er	splin·ter	stag
son·net	spear	split	stage
soot	spe·cial	spoil	stag·ger
soothe	spe·cial·ist	spoke	stag·nant
so·phis·ti·cat·ed	spe·cial·ize	spo·ken	staid
so·phis·ti·ca·tion	spe·cial·ty	sponge	stain
soph·o·more	spe·cies	spon·sor	stair
so·po·rif·ic	spe·cif·ic	spon·ta·ne·ous	stair·case
so·pran·o	spec·i·fi·ca·tion	spool	stair·way
sor·cer·er	spec·i·fy	spoon	stake
sor·cer·y	spec·i·men	spo·rad·ic	stale
sor·did	speck	sport	stale·mate
sore	speck·le	spot	stalk
sor·row	spec·ta·cle	spouse	stall
sor·ry	spec·tac·u·lar	spout	stam·mer
sort	spec·ta·tor	sprain	stamp
sought	spec·ter	sprawl	stam·pede
soul	spec·trum	spray	stand
sound	spec·u·late	spread	stand·ard
sound·proof	spec·u·la·tion	sprig	stand·ard·ize
soup	sped	spright·ly	stand-by
sour	speech	spring	stand·point
source	speed	sprin·kle	stan·za
south	speed·om·e·ter	sprint	sta·ple
south·east	speed·y	sprout	star
south·ern	spell	spruce	starch
south·ward	spend	sprung	stare
sou·ve·nir	spent	spry	stark
sov·er·eign·ty	sphere	spun	star·ry
so·vi·et	spher·i·cal	spur	start
sow	spice	spu·ri·ous	star·tle
soy·bean	spic·y	spurn	star·va·tion
space	spi·der	sput·ter	starve
spa·cious	spike	spy	state
spade	spill	squad	state·ly
spa·ghet·ti	spin	squal·id	state·ment
span	spin·ach	squan·der	states·man

states·man·ship	stim·u·late	straw·ber·ry	stu·pid
stat·ic	stim·u·lus	stray	stu·pid·i·ty
sta·tion	sting	streak	stu·por
sta·tion·ar·y	stink	stream	stur·dy
sta·tion·er·y	sti·pend	street	sty
sta·tis·tic	stip·u·la·tion	strength	style
sta·tis·ti·cal·ly	stir	stren·u·ous	styl·ish
stat·is·ti·cian	stir·rup	stress	styl·ize
stat·ue	stitch	stretch	sub·con·scious
stat·ure	stock	strew	sub·di·vide
sta·tus	stock·bro·ker	strewn	sub·due
stat·ute	stock·hold·er	strick·en	sub·ject
staunch	stock·ing	strict	sub·jec·tion
stay	stock·pile	stric·ture	sub·ju·gate
stead·fast	stock·room	stride	sub·let
stead·i·ly	sto·ic	stri·dent	sub·li·ma·tion
stead·y	stole	strife	sub·lime
steak	sto·len	strike	sub·merge
steal	stom·ach	string	sub·mis·sion
stealth	stone	strin·gent	sub·mis·sive
stealth·y	ston·y	strip	sub·mit
steam	stood	stripe	sub·or·di·nate
steam·er	stool	strive	sub·poe·na
steam·ship	stoop	strode	sub·scribe
steel	stop	stroke	sub·scrip·tion
steel·work·er	stop·o·ver	stroll	sub·se·quent
steep	stop·watch	strong	sub·ser·vi·ent
stee·ple	stor·age	strong·hold	sub·side
steer	store	strove	sub·sid·i·ar·y
stem	store·house	struck	sub·si·dize
stench	store·room	struc·tur·al	sub·sist
sten·cil	stork	struc·ture	sub·sist·ence
ste·nog·ra·pher	storm	strug·gle	sub·stance
step	sto·ry	strung	sub·stan·tial
step·fa·ther	stout	strut	sub·stan·ti·ate
step·moth·er	stove	stub·ble	sub·sti·tute
ster·e·o	strad·dle	stub·born	sub·sti·tu·tion
ster·e·o·phon·ic	straight	stuc·co	sub·tle
ster·e·o·type	straight·a·way	stuck	sub·tract
ster·ile	straight·en	stud	sub·urb
ster·i·lize	straight·for·ward	stu·dent	sub·ur·ban
ster·ling	strain	stud·ied	sub·ver·sive
stern	strain·er	stu·di·o	sub·vert
stew	strait	stu·di·ous	sub·way
stew·ard	strand	stud·y	suc·ceed
stick	strange	stuff	suc·cess
stiff	stran·ger	stum·ble	suc·cess·ful
stiff·en	stran·gle	stump	suc·ces·sion
sti·fle	strap	stung	suc·ces·sive
stig·ma	stra·te·gic	stunt	suc·ces·sor
still	strat·e·gy	stu·pe·fy	suc·cinct
stilt·ed	straw	stu·pen·dous	suc·cumb

suck
suck·le
suc·tion
sud·den
sue
suf·fer
suf·fice
suf·fi·cien·cy
suf·fi·cient
suf·fo·cate
suf·frage
sug·ar
sug·gest
sug·ges·tion
su·i·cide
suit
suit·a·ble
suite
suit·or
sul·fur
sulk·y
sul·len
sul·ly
sul·try
sum·ma·rize
sum·ma·ry
sum·ma·tion
sum·mer
sum·mit
sum·mon
sump·tu·ous
sun·beam
sun·burn
sun·down
sun·dry
sun·flow·er
sung
sun·glass·es
sunk
sun·light
sun·ny
sun·rise
sun·set
sun·shine
sun·spot
sun·tan
su·per·a·bun·dant
su·perb
su·per·fi·cial
su·per·flu·ous
su·per·high·way
su·per·in·tend·ent

su·pe·ri·or
su·pe·ri·or·i·ty
su·per·la·tive
su·per·mar·ket
su·per·nat·u·ral
su·per·sede
su·per·son·ic
su·per·sti·tion
su·per·struc·ture
su·per·vi·sion
su·per·vi·sor
sup·per
sup·plant
sup·ple
sup·ple·ment
sup·ple·men·ta·ry
sup·pli·ca·tion
sup·pli·er
sup·ply
sup·port
sup·pose
sup·po·si·tion
sup·press
su·prem·a·cy
su·preme
sur·charge
sure
sur·e·ty
surf
sur·face
surge
sur·geon
sur·ger·y
sur·ly
sur·mount
sur·name
sur·pass
sur·plus
sur·prise
sur·ren·der
sur·round
sur·veil·lance
sur·vey
sur·vey·or
sur·viv·al
sur·vive
sur·vi·vor
sus·cep·ti·ble
sus·pect
sus·pend
sus·pense
sus·pen·sion

sus·pi·cion
sus·pi·cious
sus·tain
su·ture
swal·low
swam
swamp
swan
swarm
swarth·y
sway
swear
sweat
sweat·er
sweep
sweep·er
sweet
sweet·en
sweet·heart
swell
swept
swerve
swift
swim
swim·mer
swin·dle
swine
swing
swirl
switch
swiv·el
swol·len
swoop
sword
sworn
swung
syl·la·ble
sym·bol
sym·bol·ize
sym·met·ri·cal
sym·me·try
sym·pa·thet·ic
sym·pa·thize
sym·pa·thy
sym·phon·ic
sym·pho·ny
sym·po·si·um
symp·tom
syn·a·gogue
syn·chro·nize
syn·di·cate
syn·o·nym

syn·op·sis
syn·the·sis
syn·thet·ic
sy·ringe
syr·up
sys·tem

T

tab·er·nac·le
ta·ble
ta·ble·cloth
ta·ble·spoon
ta·ble·spoon·ful
tab·let
ta·ble·ware
tab·loid
ta·boo
tab·u·lar
tab·u·late
tac·it
tack
tack·le
tact
tac·ti·cal
tac·tics
taf·fe·ta
tail
tail·gate
tai·lor
taint
take-off
take-o·ver
tale
tal·ent
talk
tall
tal·ly
tame
tan·gent
tan·gi·ble
tan·gle
tank
tan·ta·lize
tape
ta·per
tap·es·try
tar
tar·dy
tare
tar·get

tar·iff
tar·nish
tar·ry
tart
tar·tan
tar·tar
task
tas·sel
taste
tat·ter
tat·too
taught
taunt
tav·ern
taw·ny
tax
tax·a·tion
tax·i
tax·i·cab
tax·pay·er
tea
teach
teach·er
team
team·ster
team·work
tea·pot
tear
tease
tea·spoon
tech·ni·cal
tech·nique
tech·nol·o·gy
te·di·ous
tee
teem
teen–age
teeth
tel·e·cast
tel·e·gram
tel·e·graph
tel·e·phone
tel·e·scope
tel·e·type
tel·e·vise
tel·e·vi·sion
tell·er
tem·per
tem·per·a·ment
tem·per·ate
tem·per·a·ture
tem·pest

tem·ple
tem·po·rar·y
tempt
temp·ta·tion
te·na·cious
ten·ant
tend
ten·den·cy
ten·der
ten·don
ten·e·ment
ten·fold
ten·nis
ten·or
tense
ten·sion
tent
ten·ta·cle
ten·ta·tive
tenth
ten·u·ous
ten·ure
term
ter·mi·nal
ter·mi·nate
ter·mi·nol·o·gy
ter·race
ter·rain
ter·res·tri·al
ter·ri·ble
ter·ri·er
ter·rif·ic
ter·ri·fy
ter·ri·to·ri·al
ter·ri·to·ry
ter·ror
ter·ror·ism
ter·ror·ist
ter·ror·ize
test
tes·ta·ment
tes·ti·fy
tes·ti·mo·ny
text
text·book
tex·tile
tex·ture
than
thank
thank·ful
thanks·giv·ing
thatch

thaw
the·a·ter
the·at·ri·cal
theft
their
theme
them·selves
then
the·o·lo·gian
the·ol·o·gy
the·o·ret·i·cal
the·or·y
ther·a·pist
ther·a·py
there
there·af·ter
there·by
there·for
there·fore
there·up·on
there·with
ther·mom·e·ter
ther·mo·nu·cle·ar
ther·mo·stat
these
thick
thief
thieves
thigh
thin
thing
think
third
thirst
thirst·y
thir·teen
thir·ti·eth
thir·ty
tho·rax
thorn
thor·ough
thor·ough·fare
though
thought
thou·sand
thrall
thrash
thread
threat
three
thresh
thresh·old

threw
thrift
thrift·y
thrill
thrive
throat
throb
throm·bo·sis
throne
throng
throt·tle
through
through·out
throw
thrust
thru·way
thumb
thumb·nail
thumb·tack
thump
thun·der
thun·der·bolt
thun·der·ous
thun·der·storm
thus
thwart
thy·roid
tick
tick·et
tick·le
tide
ti·dings
ti·dy
tie
ti·ger
tight
tight·rope
tile
till
tilt
tim·ber
time
time·ly
tim·er
time·ta·ble
tim·id
tinc·ture
tin·der
tinge
tin·gle
tink·er
tin·kle

tin·sel
tint
ti·ny
tip·toe
tire
tire·some
tis·sue
tithe
tit·il·late
ti·tle
tit·u·lar
to
toad
toad·stool
toast
to·bac·co
to·bog·gan
to·day
toe
to·geth·er
toil
toi·let
to·ken
told
tol·er·a·ble
tol·er·ance
tol·er·ant
tol·e·rate
toll
to·ma·to
tomb
tomb·stone
to·mor·row
ton
tone
tongs
tongue
ton·ic
to·night
ton·nage
ton·sil
too
took
tool
toot
tooth
tooth·ache
tooth·brush
tooth·paste
top-heav·y
top·ic
top·i·cal

top-notch
to·pog·ra·phy
top·ple
torch
tore
tor·ment
torn
tor·na·do
tor·pe·do
tor·pid
torque
tor·rent
tor·sion
tor·toise
tor·tu·ous
tor·ture
toss
to·tal
to·tal·i·tar·i·an
tot·ter
touch
touch·down
tough
tour
tour·ist
tour·na·ment
tour·ni·quet
tow
to·ward
tow·el
tow·er
town
town·ship
towns·peo·ple
tox·ic
tox·ic·i·ty
tox·in
toy
trace
trac·er
track
tract
trac·ta·ble
trac·tion
trac·tor
trade-in
trade·mark
trad·er
tra·di·tion
traf·fic
trag·e·dy
trag·ic

trail
train
trait
trai·tor
tra·jec·to·ry
tramp
tram·ple
trance
tran·quil
tran·quil·iz·er
tran·quil·li·ty
trans·ac·tion
trans·at·lan·tic
tran·scend·ent
tran·scribe
tran·script
trans·fer
trans·fer·a·ble
trans·form
trans·fu·sion
trans·gress
trans·gres·sion
tran·sient
tran·sis·tor
tran·si·tion
trans·late
trans·la·tion
trans·mis·sion
trans·mit
trans·mit·ter
trans·par·ent
trans·plant
trans·port
trans·pose
trap
trash
trau·ma
trau·mat·ic
trav·ail
trav·el
trav·el·er
trav·erse
trawl·er
tray
treach·er·ous
treach·er·y
tread
trea·son
treas·ure
treas·ur·er
treas·ur·y
treat

treat·ment
trea·ty
tre·ble
tree
trem·ble
tre·men·dous
trem·or
trench
trend
tres·pass
tri·al
tri·an·gle
tribe
tri·bu·nal
trib·u·tar·y
trib·ute
trick
trick·le
tri·dent
tried
tri·fle
trig·ger
trig·o·nom·e·try
trill
tril·lion
tril·o·gy
trim
trin·i·ty
trip
tri·ple
trip·li·cate
tri·umph
tri·um·phal
tri·um·phant
triv·i·al
troll
troop
tro·phy
trop·ic
trop·i·cal
trot
trou·ble
trou·ble·some
trou·sers
trout
tru·ant
truce
truck
truc·u·lent
trudge
true
tru·ly

trump
trum·pet
trun·dle
trunk
truss
trust
trus·tee
trust·wor·thy
trust·y
truth
try
T-shirt
tube
tu·ber·cu·lo·sis
tuck
tuft
tu·i·tion
tu·lip
tum·ble
tu·mor
tu·mult
tu·mul·tu·ous
tu·na fish
tune
tun·er
tung·sten
tu·nic
tun·nel
tur·ban
tur·bine
tur·bu·lent
turf
tur·key
tur·moil
turn
tur·nip
turn·out
turn·o·ver
turn·pike
tur·pen·tine
tur·ret
tur·tle
tu·tor
tweed
twelfth
twelve
twen·ti·eth
twen·ty
twice
twig
twi·light
twill

twin
twine
twin·kle
twist
twitch
twit·ter
two
two·fold
type
type·writ·er
ty·phoid fe·ver
typ·i·cal
typ·ist
ty·ran·ni·cal
tyr·an·ny
ty·rant

U

ug·ly
ul·cer
ul·te·ri·or
ul·ti·mate
ul·tra·vi·o·let
um·brel·la
um·pire
un·a·ble
un·ac·com·pa·nied
un·ac·cus·tomed
u·nan·i·mous
un·armed
un·a·void·a·ble
un·a·ware
un·bal·anced
un·bear·a·ble
un·be·com·ing
un·be·liev·a·ble
un·bleached
un·born
un·bound
un·break·a·ble
un·bro·ken
un·can·ny
un·cer·tain
un·cer·tain·ty
un·changed
un·checked
un·civ·i·lized
un·cle
un·clean
un·com·fort·a·ble

un·com·mon
un·com·mu·ni·ca·tive
un·con·quer·a·ble
un·con·scious
un·con·sti·tu·tion·al
un·con·trol·la·ble
un·con·ven·tion·al
un·couth
un·cov·er
un·daunt·ed
un·de·cid·ed
un·de·ni·a·ble
un·der·arm
un·der·cov·er
un·der·cur·rent
un·der·de·vel·oped
un·der·es·ti·mate
un·der·foot
un·der·go
un·der·grad·u·ate
un·der·ground
un·der·hand·ed
un·der·line
un·der·mine
un·der·neath
un·der·pants
un·der·priv·i·leged
un·der·sell
un·der·shirt
un·der·stand
un·der·stood
un·der·take
un·der·tone
un·der·wa·ter
un·der·wear
un·der·writ·er
un·de·sir·a·ble
un·dis·ci·plined
un·dis·put·ed
un·dis·turbed
un·do
un·done
un·doubt·ed·ly
un·dress
un·due
un·dy·ing
un·eas·y
un·em·ployed
un·e·qualed
un·e·quiv·o·cal
un·err·ing
un·e·ven

un·ex·pect·ed
un·fair
un·fa·vor·a·ble
un·feel·ing
un·fin·ished
un·fit
un·fold
un·for·get·ta·ble
un·for·tu·nate
un·found·ed
un·friend·ly
un·furn·ished
un·god·ly
un·gra·cious
un·grate·ful
un·guard·ed
un·hap·py
un·health·y
un·hinge
un·ho·ly
un·hurt
u·ni·fi·ca·tion
u·ni·fied
u·ni·form
u·ni·form·i·ty
u·ni·lat·er·al
un·in·jured
un·in·tel·li·gi·ble
un·in·ter·est·ed
un·ion
u·nique
u·ni·son
u·nit
u·nite
u·ni·ty
u·ni·ver·sal
u·ni·verse
u·ni·ver·si·ty
un·just
un·kempt
un·kind
un·known
un·law·ful
un·less
un·like·ly
un·load
un·lock
un·luck·y
un·mis·tak·a·ble
un·mit·i·gat·ed
un·moved
un·nat·u·ral

un·nec·es·sar·y
un·oc·cu·pied
un·paid
un·par·al·leled
un·pleas·ant
un·prec·e·dent·ed
un·pre·dict·a·ble
un·prof·it·a·ble
un·qual·i·fied
un·ques·tion·a·bly
un·rav·el
un·rea·son·a·ble
un·re·lent·ing
un·re·served
un·re·strained
un·ri·valed
un·rul·y
un·safe
un·scru·pu·lous
un·sea·son·a·ble
un·seen
un·self·ish
un·set·tled
un·shak·en
un·sight·ly
un·skilled
un·sound
un·speak·a·ble
un·sta·ble
un·stead·y
un·suc·cess·ful
un·suit·a·ble
un·sus·pect·ed
un·think·ing
un·ti·dy
un·til
un·time·ly
un·to
un·told
un·touched
un·tried
un·true
un·used
un·u·su·al
un·veil
un·war·y
un·wel·come
un·will·ing
un·wise
un·wor·thy
un·yield·ing
up·braid

up·date
up·hold
up·hol·ster·y
up·keep
up·land
up·lift
up·per
up·per·most
up·right
up·ris·ing
up·roar
up·root
up·stairs
up·ward
ur·ban
urge
ur·gent
urn
us·a·ble
us·age
use
use·ful
use·less
ush·er
u·su·al
u·sur·y
u·ten·sil
u·ter·us
u·til·i·ty
u·ti·lize
ut·most
ut·ter

V

va·can·cy
va·cant
va·cate
va·ca·tion
vac·ci·nate
vac·cine
vac·u·um
va·grant
vague
vain
vale
val·en·tine
val·et
val·iant
val·id
va·lid·i·ty

val·ley
val·or
val·u·a·ble
val·u·a·tion
val·ue
valve
van·dal·ism
va·nil·la
van·ish
van·i·ty
van·quish
van·tage
va·por
va·por·ize
var·i·a·ble
var·i·a·tion
var·i·e·gat·ed
va·ri·e·ty
var·i·ous
var·nish
var·y
vase
vas·sal
vast
vault
vaunt
veal
vec·tor
veer
veg·e·ta·ble
veg·e·ta·tion
ve·he·ment
ve·hi·cle
veil
vein
ve·loc·i·ty
vel·vet
ve·neer
ven·er·a·ble
ve·ne·re·al
venge·ance
ven·om
ven·om·ous
vent
ven·ti·late
ven·ti·la·tion
ven·ture
ve·rac·i·ty
verb
ver·bal
ver·ba·tim
ver·bi·age

ver·dict
verge
ver·i·fi·ca·tion
ver·i·fy
ver·nac·u·lar
ver·nal
ver·sa·tile
verse
ver·sion
ver·sus
ver·te·brate
ver·ti·cal
ver·y
ves·sel
vest
ves·tige
vet·er·an
vet·er·i·nar·i·an
ve·to
vex·a·tion
vi·a
vi·a·ble
vi·al
vi·brate
vi·bra·tion
vi·car·i·ous
vice
vi·cin·i·ty
vi·cious
vic·tim
vic·tor
vic·to·ri·ous
vic·to·ry
vid·e·o·tape
view
view·point
vig·i·lance
vig·i·lant
vig·or·ous
vile
vil·lage
vil·lag·er
vil·lain
vin·di·cate
vin·dic·tive
vine
vin·e·gar
vine·yard
vin·tage
vi·nyl
vi·o·la·tion
vi·o·lence

vi·o·lent
vi·o·let
vi·o·lin
vi·per
vir·gin
vi·ril·i·ty
vir·tu·al
vir·tue
vir·tu·ous
vir·u·lent
vi·rus
vi·sa
vise
vis·i·bil·i·ty
vis·i·ble
vi·sion
vi·sion·ar·y
vis·it
vis·i·tor
vi·sor
vis·u·al
vi·tal
vi·ta·min
vi·va·cious
viv·id
vo·cab·u·lar·y
vo·cal
vo·ca·tion·al
vo·cif·er·ous
voice
void
vol·a·tile
vol·ca·no
vol·ley
volt
vol·ume
vo·lu·mi·nous
vol·un·tar·y
vol·un·teer
vo·lup·tu·ous
vom·it
vote
vot·er
vouch
vouch·er
vow
vow·el
voy·age
vul·gar
vul·ner·a·ble
vul·ture

W

wade
wa·fer
waf·fle
wage
wa·ger
wag·on
wail
waist
wait
wait·er
waiv·er
wake
walk
wall
wal·let
wal·low
wall·pa·per
wal·nut
wan
wand
wan·der
wane
wan·ton
ward
ward·en
ward·robe
ware
ware·house
war·fare
war·head
warm
warmth
warm-up
warn
warp
war·path
war·rant
war·ran·ty
war·ri·or
war·ship
wart
war·time
war·y
wash
wash·cloth
wash·er
wash·room
wasp
waste
waste·bas·ket

waste·land
waste·pa·per
watch
watch·dog
watch·man
watch·word
wa·ter
wa·ter-col·or
wa·ter·fall
wa·ter·front
wa·ter line
wa·ter main
wa·ter·mel·on
wa·ter·proof
wa·ter·shed
wa·ter-ski
watt
wave
wave·length
wa·ver
wax pa·per
way
way·lay
way·side
way·ward
weak
weak·ling
wealth
wean
weap·on
wear
wea·ri·ness
wea·ri·some
wea·ry
wea·sel
weath·er
weath·er·proof
weave
weav·er
wed·ding
wedge
wed·lock
weed
week
week·day
week·end
weep
weigh
weight
weird
wel·come
weld

wel·fare
well-be·ing
well-de·vel·oped
well-in·formed
well-known
well-pre·served
well-to-do
welt
wept
west
west·ern
whale
wharf
wharves
what·ev·er
wheat
wheel
wheel·chair
whelp
whence
when·ev·er
where·as
where·by
where·fore
where·up·on
wher·ev·er
wheth·er
which·ev·er
while
whim
whim·si·cal
whim·sy
whine
whip
whirl
whirl·pool
whirl·wind
whisk
whis·per
whis·tle
whit
white
white-col·lar
whit·en
white·wash
whiz
who·ev·er
whole
whole·heart·ed
whole·sale
whole·some
whole-wheat

whol·ly
whore
whose
wick
wick·ed
wide
wid·en
wide·spread
wid·ow
width
wield
wife
wig·gle
wild
wild·cat
wil·der·ness
wild·fire
will·ful
will·ing
wil·low
wilt
wil·y
wince
wind
wind·fall
wind·mill
win·dow
wind·pipe
wind·shield
wind-up
wind·y
wine
wing
wing·spread
wink
win·ner
win·now
win·ter
win·try
wipe
wire
wire·tap·ping
wis·dom
wise
wise·crack
wish
wisp
witch
witch·craft
with·draw
with·drew
with·hold

with·in
with·out
with·stand
wit·ness
wit·ty
wiz·ard
wob·ble
woe
wolf
wolves
wom·an
womb
wom·en
won
won·der
won·der·ful
wood
wood·chuck
wood·en
wood·land
wood·man
wood·peck·er
wood·shed
wood·wind
wood·work
wood·y
woof
wool
wool·en
wool·ly
word
wore
work
work·book
work·day
work·er
work·man
work·out
work·shop
world
world·ly
world·wide
worm
worn
wor·ry
worse
wor·ship
worst
worth
wor·thi·ness
worth·less
worth·while

wor·thy
would
wound
wove
wo·ven
wran·gle
wrap
wrap·per
wrath
wreak
wreck
wren
wrench
wrest
wres·tle
wretch·ed
wring
wrin·kle
wrist
writ
write
writ·er
write-up
writ·ten
wrong
wrong·do·er
wrote

X

X·ray (ray)

Y

yacht
yard
yard goods
yard·stick
yarn
yawn
year
year·book
yearn
yeast
yel·low
yelp
yeo·man
yes·ter·day
yield
yo·ga

yo·gurt
yoke
yolk
yon·der
young
young·ster
your
yours
youth
youth·ful
yo·yo

Z

zeal
zeal·ous
ze·bra
ze·nith
ze·ro
zest
zig·zag
zinc
Zip Code
zip·per
zir·con
zo·di·ac
zone
zo·o·log·i·cal
zo·ol·o·gy
zoom

Answer key

Each section in this "Guide to writing and speaking" concludes with an activity section called "Use what you know." The activities have been designed to help you reinforce your understanding of the ideas, skills, and procedures presented in each section. Some of these activities suggest methods that you can use to improve skills in various areas of communication. Many of those skill-building activities require no specific answers. But other activities take the form of self-check exercises to check your understanding of specific writing and speaking principles. These exercises ask for specific answers to specific questions. Answers to those activities follow.

1 Knowing the basics   *Pages 25–27*

Spelling words correctly

1. armies
2. Larrys
3. bushes
4. classes
5. boxes
6. crutches
7. radios
8. tomatoes
9. mothers-in-law
10. teaspoonfuls
11. wolves
12. staffs
13. outrageous
14. manageable
15. endurable
16. panicky
17. trying
18. already
19. fulfill
20. immortal
21. misspell
22. illiterate

Identifying parts of speech

1. interjection, noun, verb, verb
2. adjective, noun, adverb, conjunction, verb
3. conjunction, pronoun, preposition, adjective, verb, adverb
4. preposition, adjective, noun, preposition, verb, preposition, adjective
5. pronoun, verb, adjective
6. interjection, adjective, verb, pronoun
7. adverb, adverb, adjective

Analyzing parts of a sentence

1. in the lobby—adverb phrase; before the concert—adverb phrase
2. Puffing and hissing—adjective phrase
3. waiting in line—adjective phrase
4. Finding the right home—noun phrase
5. subordinate clause
6. main clause
7. subordinate clause
8. main clause
9. who lived next door—adjective clause; because their house was too small—adverb clause
10. What I want—noun clause
11. who is a serious student—adjective clause
12. If you write the report on Sunday—adverb clause
13. sentence
14. fragment
15. fragment
16. sentence

Writing effective sentences

No specific answers are required for this activity.

2   Rules of style   *Pages 52–53*

Reviewing capitalization and italics

1. Last, Bill, Mary, Joe, I, Wisconsin, Minnesota
2. We, Sunday, August
3. Vega, Wisconsin Dells
4. I, Lipton
5. That, Indian, Standing Rock
6. Arriving, Minneapolis, Aunt Alice
7. Then, Minneapolis Institute of Arts, Rembrandt's, *Lucretia,* Tudor-style

8. Since, Guthrie Theater, *Hamlet*
9. After, Burnsville High School, Gull Lake
10. We, U.S. Route, Little Falls, Minnesota, Charles Lindbergh, *Spirit of St. Louis*
11. Finally
12. Mary, Joe, Minnesota, Mike
13. And, Bill, I
14. Mother, Dad
15. The, Grandma, Grandpa

Reviewing punctuation

1. "Go sky diving? Never! I'd rather live to be a hundred than live dangerously today," said John.
2. I got up at 5:20 this morning, finished reading James A. Michener's book *Hawaii,* and went to work.
3. There are several ways to have a green yard: spread grass seed, roll sod, or lay Astro Turf.
4. Strolling up Main Street, we found a lovely restaurant, a gift shop, and a grocery store; but on turning the corner, we saw an ugly factory.
5. Are we going to the park? Why, of course, we are. First, put on your jacket.
6. Jan Smith, Ph.D., is married to Dr. Robert Jones, a surgeon at St. James Hospital.
7. In 1978 (or was it 1979?) we had over 100 inches of snow.
8. David Rockefeller, Nelson's brother, runs the Chase Manhattan Bank.

Using proper forms of address

Mayor Redford
Senator Woodson
Mrs./Miss/Ms. Brown
Father O'Leary
Bishop Smithfield

Writing footnotes and bibliographic entries

Your footnotes and bibliographic entries should follow the standard forms presented on pages 47–51.

3   Commonly misused words, phrases, and constructions   *Pages 76–77*

Recognizing correct word use

1. sitting, beside
2. into, rose
3. accepted, try to, expected
4. somewhat, lend
5. were enthusiastic, creditable
6. formally, respectfully
7. An, different from, a
8. principal, irritated, is that, badly

Correcting misspelled words

1. battalion
2. familiar
3. sacrilegious
4. seizure
5. itinerary
6. privilege
7. vacillate
8. questionnaire
9. souvenir
10. allege
11. copyrighted
12. protocol
13. supersede
14. appearance
15. ecstasy

Correcting misused constructions

1. Subject-verb agreement—test *shows,* dyes *cause*
2. Pronoun agreement—Each girl received *her* diploma.
3. Confusing pronoun reference—We had to repair the car before putting it in the garage.
4. Shift in point of view—I went to the window, and *I* could feel the wind blowing.
5. Run-on sentence—The children toured the museum. They learned many new things. *OR* The children toured the museum; they learned many new things. *OR* The children toured the museum, and they learned many new things. *OR* When the children toured the museum, they learned many new things.
6. Sentence fragment—When the plane landed in the storm, the passengers disembarked.
7. Dangling modifier—While driving on Eighth Street, *I* was in an accident. *OR* While *I was* driving on Eighth Street, an accident occurred.

Avoiding clichés

These clichés should have been eliminated:

wrapped up the deal
in the bag
lain back in the weeds
jumped at the opportunity
doomed to disappointment
after all is said and done
each and every one
shot down
left up a creek
none the worse for wear
chalked the whole thing up to experience
greener pastures

4   Tips about everyday writing   *Pages 118–121*

Match the audience to the message

1. d   5. g
2. h   6. b
3. c   7. a
4. f   8. e

Correcting form and content in a business letter

1. *N.* should be *North.*
2. No zip code.
3. June 10, 1981
4. *Mr.* Jack Jones
5. No error.
6. *First* Street
7. New York, NY 20015
8. Dear Mr. Jones*:*
9. *Your last letter says that I owe. . . .*
10. Discourteous tone.
11. No error.
12. Do not indent. And change to *I no longer care to be your customer.*
13. No error.
14. *I have enclosed.*
15. Sincerely,
16. No error.
17. Add enclosure line for charge card *(Enclosure).*

Identifying the parts of a business report

1. d
2. e
3. c
4. f
5. a
6. b

Writing a memorandum

To: All sales managers
From: Roger F. Less
Date: January 5, 1981
Subject: Sales managers meeting

A meeting of all sales managers will be held January 9, 1981, at 10:30 A.M. in the conference room. Please bring your copies of the sales reports for the year 1980. We will evaluate the current sales training program in the light of the 1980 sales figures. Please be ready to present your suggestions, thoughts, and opinions about the possible need for a new training program.

Constructing a résumé

No specific answers are required for this activity.

5   Model letters for selected occasions   *Pages 150–151*

A checklist for writing letters

No specific answers are required for this activity. Be sure that you can answer *yes* to the questions before you start to write.

Analyzing letters that you have received

No specific answers are required for this activity.

6   Writing tips for school situations   *Pages 181–183*

Practice in outlining

The following is a possible arrangement of the items as headings and subheadings in an outline.

 I. Principles of government
    A. Democracy
    B. Public service
    C. Loyalty
 II. Importance of the inquiring mind
    A. Scientific investigation
    B. Philosophical theories
III. Standards of beauty
    A. Form
    B. Simplicity
IV. Importance of physical fitness
    A. Personal cleanliness
    B. Careful diet
    C. Athletic contests

The library as a research tool

No specific answers are required for this activity.

7   Speaking before a group   *Pages 202–204*

Constructing a speaker's kit

No specific answers are required for this activity.

Evaluating speeches

No specific answers are required for this activity.

8   Face to face and over the phone   *Page 217*

Check your listening habits

No specific answers are required for this activity.

Index to Part 1

Part **2**

A word user's treasury of useful quotations

Introduction

"A word user's treasury of useful quotations" is a storehouse of words and ideas that you can use to stimulate your thinking, enliven your writing, and spark your conversations. It gathers together over 1500 thoughtful, lively quotations expressing the wit and wisdom of thinking men and women over the ages. The quotations include varying ideas and opinions on a wide range of subjects of concern to us all. These subjects range from our experiences in everyday living (such as friendship, marriage, children, education, work) to our philosophical, social, and political concerns (such as belief, virtue, justice, progress, peace). The quotations vary from the humorous and light-hearted to the serious and profound. And they reflect the thinking of men and women from ancient times to the present—from important historical figures to present-day leaders in government, business, science, the arts.

Whether you want to find an old, familiar saying or wish to find a new, fresh way of expressing an idea, the "Treasury of useful quotations" can help you find it. The quotations are organized into 121 different subject categories; these subjects are arranged in alphabetical order. Within each category, the quotations appear in chronological order—beginning with proverbs and the ideas of ancient thinkers and leading up to comments by people of our own time.

To help you better use and locate the quotations, the "Treasury of useful quotations" provides three additional sources of information. "Notes about the authors" briefly identifies the notable men and women quoted in the treasury. You may gain further insight into what a quotation says by knowing something about the person who said it. The "Index of authors and other sources" will help you find quotations from a given person or other source. And the "Index of opening words" lists in alphabetical order the beginning phrases of all quotations in the treasury. When you are seeking a quotation that you know, or one that you only partially remember, the "Index of opening words" can help you find it.

When you need a quotation on a given subject, try to look in several related or similar subject categories. If, for example, you were seeking quotations about "Heroes," you could also look under "Ability," "Bravery," "Character," "Courage," "Strength," "Success," and "Valor." Other times you might look in opposite categories, such as "Hope" and "Despair" or "Hate" and "Love."

There are many ways that you can use "A treasury of useful quotations" to enrich your word power. Including carefully chosen quotations can add interest and impact to your writing, speeches, and conversations. In the introduction to a speech or a paper, you can use a quote that raises a question about your topic or that states your main idea in a concise or clever or unusual way. You can even begin with a quote you disagree with and go on to explain your own point of view. A quote can create a powerful conclusion to a speech or paper, or can simply be used to add variety or emphasis or humor.

Whenever you use quotations in writing and speaking, be sure that they are appropriate—that the subjects, the words, and the tone of the quotations are ones that your audience will understand and appreciate. And check the "Notes about the authors" to be sure that the author is appropriate. A quotation will carry more weight if the person who said it is one that the audience respects and admires. You might briefly identify the person in your paper or speech. Knowing whether that person was a writer, scientist, senator, minister, or artist— and knowing when and where that person lived—can make a quotation more meaningful for both you and your audience.

Even if you don't actually include a quotation in a speech or a paper, you can use the treasury to stimulate your thinking on a subject. And don't forget to browse through the "Treasury of useful quotations" for the pure enjoyment of it. Reading the words and ideas of persons who express them well can enrich your own use of words—and your ability to express your ideas effectively in writing and speaking.

Ability

Behind an able man there are always other able men.

Chinese proverb

Everyone must row with the oars he has.

English proverb

They are able because they think they are able.

Virgil

It is a great ability to be able to conceal one's ability.

François de La Rochefoucauld

To make a fortune some assistance from fate is essential. Ability alone is insufficient.

Ihara Saikaku

The winds and waves are always on the side of the ablest navigators.

Edward Gibbon

A man must not deny his manifest abilities, for that is to evade his obligations.

Robert Louis Stevenson

Intelligence is quickness to apprehend as distinct from ability, which is capacity to act wisely on the thing apprehended.

Alfred North Whitehead

It is always pleasant to be urged to do something on the ground that one can do it well.

George Santayana

In a world as empirical as ours, a youngster who does not know what he is good *at* will not be sure what he is good *for*.

Edgar Z. Friedenberg

Adversity

In the day of prosperity be joyful, but in the day of adversity consider.

Ecclesiastes 7 : 14

Fire is the test of gold; adversity, of strong men.

Lucius Annaeus Seneca

In every kind of adversity, the bitterest part of a man's affliction is to remember that he once was happy.

Manlius Severinus Boethius

Prosperity getteth friends, but adversity trieth them.

Nicholas Ling

The virtue of prosperity is temperance; the virtue of adversity is fortitude, which in morals is the more heroical virtue.

Francis Bacon

Misery acquaints a man with strange bedfellows.

William Shakespeare

In the adversity of our best friends we often find something that is not wholly displeasing to us.

François de La Rochefoucauld

Adversity makes a man wise, not rich.

John Ray

Adversity is the state in which a man most easily becomes acquainted with himself, being especially free from admirers then.

Samuel Johnson

Adversity not only draws people together but brings forth that beautiful inward friendship, just as the cold winter forms ice-figures on the window-panes which the warmth of the sun effaces.

Søren Kierkegaard

By trying, we can easily learn to endure adversity. Another man's, I mean.

Mark Twain

When you are down and out, something always turns up—and it is usually the noses of your friends.

Orson Welles

Ambition

He who would leap high must take a long run.

Danish proverb

What shall it profit a man, if he shall gain the whole world, and lose his own soul?

Mark 8 : 36

Ambition drove many men to become false; to have one thought locked in the breast, another ready on the tongue.

Sallust

A man's worth is no greater than the worth of his ambitions.

Marcus Aurelius

Nothing arouses ambition so much in the heart as the trumpet-clang of another's fame.

Baltasar Gracián

A slave has but one master; an ambitious man has as many masters as there are people who may be useful in bettering his position.

Jean de la Bruyère

Ambition often puts men upon doing the meanest offices: so climbing is performed in the same posture with creeping.

Jonathan Swift

Ambition and suspicion always go together.

Georg Christoph Lichtenberg

Ambition is the last refuge of the failure.

Oscar Wilde

Keep away from people who try to belittle your ambitions. Small people always do that, but the really great make you feel that you, too, can become great.

Mark Twain

All sins have their origin in a sense of inferiority, otherwise called ambition.

Cesare Pavese

He who does not hope to win has already lost.

José Joaquín Olmedo

An ambitious man can never know peace.

J. Krishnamurti

Anger

Let not the sun go down upon your wrath.

Ephesians 4 : 26

He that is slow to anger is better than the mighty: and he that ruleth his spirit than he that taketh a city.

Proverbs 16 : 32

When you are angry say nothing and do nothing until you have recited the alphabet.

Ascribed to Athenodorus Cananites

Two things a man should never be angry at: what he can help, and what he cannot help.

Thomas Fuller

Anger is never without a reason, but seldom with a good one.

Benjamin Franklin

Nothing on earth consumes a man more quickly than the passion of resentment.

Friedrich Nietzsche

When angry, count four; when very angry, swear.

Mark Twain

Many people lose their tempers merely from seeing you keep yours.

Frank Moore Colby

The world needs anger. The world often continues to allow evil because it isn't angry enough.

Bede Jarrett

So we have had the second American revolution, and our very anger said a new "Yes" to life.

Betty Friedan

Apathy

Shame on the soul, to falter on the road of life while the body still perseveres.

Marcus Aurelius

Nothing is more conducive to peace of mind than not having any opinion at all.

Georg Christoph Lichtenberg

Most of us have no real loves and no real hatreds. Blessed is love, less blessed is hatred, but thrice accursed is that indifference which is neither one nor the other.

Mark Rutherford

By far the most dangerous foe we have to fight is *apathy*—indifference from whatever cause, not from a lack of knowledge, but from carelessness, from absorption in other pursuits, from a contempt bred of self-satisfaction.

Sir William Osler

It's extraordinary how we go through life with eyes half shut, with dull ears, with dormant thoughts. Perhaps it's just as well; and it may be that it is this very dullness that makes life to the incalculable majority so supportable and so welcome.

Joseph Conrad

Science may have found a cure for most evils; but it has found no remedy for the worst of them all—the apathy of human beings.

Helen Keller

Emotion is the chief source of all becoming-conscious. There can be no transforming of darkness into light and of apathy into movement without emotion.

Carl Gustav Jung

The death of democracy is not likely to be an assassination from ambush. It will be a slow extinction from apathy, indifference, and undernourishment.

Robert Maynard Hutchins

In the nineteenth century the problem was that God is dead; in the twentieth century the problem is that man is dead.

Erich Fromm

The fact that each individual sees apathy in his fellows perpetuates the common reluctance to organize for changes.

The Port Huron Statement of the Students for a Democratic Society

Art

Art is simply a right method of doing things. The test of the artist does not lie in the will with which he goes to work, but in the excellence of the work he produces.

Saint Thomas Aquinas

Nature seldom gives us the very best; for that we must have recourse to art.

Baltasar Gracián

If your work of art is good, if it is true, it will find its echo and make its place— in six months, in six years, or after you are gone. What is the difference?

Gustave Flaubert

When art is understood by everybody it will cease to be art.

Arsène Houssaye

Art is a human activity consisting in this, that one man consciously, by means of certain external signs, hands on to others feelings he has lived through, and that other people are infected by these feelings, and also experience them.

Leo Tolstoy

Without art, the crudeness of reality would make the world unbearable.

George Bernard Shaw

Without tradition, art is a flock of sheep without a shepherd. Without innovation, it is a corpse.

Sir Winston Churchill

The aim of every artist is to arrest motion, which is life, by artificial means and hold it fixed so that a hundred years later, when a stranger looks at it, it moves again since it is life.

William Faulkner

Art does not reproduce the visible; rather, it makes visible.

Paul Klee

We must never forget that art is not a form of propaganda; it is a form of truth.

John Fitzgerald Kennedy

Man is apt to be more moved by the art of his own period, not because it is more perfect, but because it is organically related to him.

   Ilya Ehrenburg

The artist is only given to sense more keenly than others the harmony of the world and all the beauty and savagery of the human contribution to it—and to communicate this poignantly to people.

   Alexander Solzhenitsyn

New art opens new worlds for our recognition and nourishment.

   Marshall McLuhan

Authority

The man whose authority is recent is always stern.

   Aeschylus

Authority without wisdom is like a heavy ax without an edge, fitter to bruise than polish.

   Anne Bradstreet

Lawful and settled authority is very seldom resisted when it is well employed.

   Samuel Johnson

All authority belongs to the people.

   Thomas Jefferson

Every great advance in natural knowledge has involved the absolute rejection of authority.

   Thomas Henry Huxley

There's very few men that can bear authority if they haven't been born with the shoulders for it. If you gave a man a nose who never had one, he would be blowing it all day.

   John Oliver Hobbes

I don't like authority, at least I don't like other people's authority.

   Arthur Christopher Benson

Most men, after a little freedom, have preferred authority with the consoling assurances and the economy of effort which it brings.

   Walter Lippmann

When you are saying something which doesn't mean much, you must say it with a great deal of authority.

   Virgil Thomson

Authority has every reason to fear the skeptic, for authority can rarely survive in the face of doubt.

   Robert Lindner

You can delegate authority, but you can never delegate responsibility for delegating a task to someone else. If you picked the right man, fine, but if you picked the wrong man, the responsibility is yours—not his.

   Richard E. Krafve

Beauty

All orators are dumb where beauty pleadeth.

   William Shakespeare

Ask a toad what is beauty . . . ; he will answer that it is a female with two great round eyes coming out of her little head, a large flat mouth, a yellow belly and a brown back.

   Voltaire

Whenever, at a party, I have been in the mood to study fools, I have always looked for a great beauty: they always gather round her like flies around a fruit-stall.

   Johann Paul Friedrich Richter

A thing of beauty is a joy for ever: Its loveliness increases; it will never Pass into nothingness. . . .

   John Keats

Beauty is truth, truth beauty,—that is all Ye know on earth, and all ye need to know.

   John Keats

Beauty is its own excuse for being.
Ralph Waldo Emerson

Remember that the most beautiful things in the world are the most useless: peacocks and lilies, for instance.
John Ruskin

The saying that beauty is but skin deep is but a skin deep saying.
John Ruskin

Beauty is in the eye of the beholder.
Margaret Wolfe Hungerford

Outstanding beauty, like outstanding gifts of any kind, tends to get in the way of normal emotional development, and thus of that particular success in life which we call happiness.
Milton R. Sapirstein

When I am working on a problem, I never think about beauty. I think only of how to solve the problem. But when I have finished, if the solution is not beautiful, I know it is wrong.
Buckminster Fuller

Belief

All things are possible to one who believes.
Saint Bernard of Clairvaux

Believe things, rather than man.
Benjamin Whichcote

To believe with certainty we must begin with doubting.
Stanislas I, King of Poland

Loving is half of believing.
Victor Hugo

A man lives by believing something; not by debating and arguing about many things.
Thomas Carlyle

Believe only half of what you see and nothing that you hear.
Dinah Mulock Craik

All ages of belief have been great; all of unbelief have been mean.
Ralph Waldo Emerson

Believe that life *is* worth living, and your belief will help create the fact.
William James

We ought to struggle earnestly to increase our beliefs. Every addition to them is an extension of life, both in breadth and depth.
Mark Rutherford

He who is swift to believe is swift to forget.
Abraham Joshua Heschel

Bravery

Without a sign, his sword the brave man
draws,
And asks no omen but his country's
cause.
Homer

It is easy to be brave from a safe distance.
Aesop

Fortune favors the brave.
Terence

Only the brave enjoy noble and glorious deaths.
Dionysius of Halicarnassus

None but the brave deserves the fair.
John Dryden

Some have been thought brave because they were afraid to run away.
Thomas Fuller

That man is not truly brave who is afraid either to seem to be, or to be, when it suits him, a coward.
Edgar Allan Poe

Bravery never goes out of fashion.
William Makepeace Thackeray

If you knew how cowardly your enemy is, you would slap him. Bravery is knowledge of the cowardice in the enemy.

Edgar Watson Howe

Bravery is the capacity to perform properly even when scared half to death.

General Omar Nelson Bradley

Business

Live together like brothers and do business like strangers.

Arabic proverb

Boldness in business is the first, second, and third thing.

Thomas Fuller

Few people do business well who do nothing else.

Lord Chesterfield

Here's the rule for bargains: "Do other men, for they would do you." That's the true business precept.

Charles Dickens

The gambling known as business looks with austere disfavor upon the business known as gambling.

Ambrose Bierce

Business underlies everything in our national life, including our spiritual life. Witness the fact that in the Lord's Prayer, the first petition is for daily bread. No one can worship God or love his neighbor on an empty stomach.

Woodrow Wilson

The business of America is business.

Calvin Coolidge

If you can build a business up big enough, it's respectable.

Will Rogers

Career

Blessed is he who has found his work; let him ask no other blessedness.

Thomas Carlyle

Every calling is great when greatly pursued.

Oliver Wendell Holmes, Jr.

The vocation of every man and woman is to serve other people.

Leo Tolstoy

A man with a career can have no time to waste upon his wife and friends; he has to devote it wholly to his enemies.

John Oliver Hobbes

Women have one great advantage over men. It is commonly thought that if they marry they have done enough, and need career no further. If a man marries, on the other hand, public opinion is all against him if he takes this view.

Rose Macaulay

The test of a vocation is the love of the drudgery it involves.

Logan Pearsall Smith

Whenever it is in any way possible, every boy and girl should choose as his life work some occupation which he should like to do anyhow, even if he did not need the money.

William Lyon Phelps

People don't choose their careers: they are engulfed by them.

John Dos Passos

The price one pays for pursuing any profession, or calling, is an intimate knowledge of its ugly side.

James Baldwin

Chance

Enjoy yourself, drink, call the life you
  live today
your own, but only that, the rest belongs
  to chance.

Euripides

The race is not to the swift, nor the battle to the strong, neither yet bread to the wise, nor yet riches to men of understanding, nor yet favor to men of skill; but time and chance happeneth to them all.

Ecclesiastes 9 : 11

Chance makes a football of man's life.

Marcus Annaeus Seneca

Chance has something to say in everything, even how to write a good letter.

Baltasar Gracián

Although men flatter themselves with their great actions, they are not so often the result of a great design as of chance.

François de La Rochefoucauld

A wise man turns chance into good fortune.

Thomas Fuller

Every possession and every happiness is but lent by chance for an uncertain time, and may therefore be demanded back the next hour.

Arthur Schopenhauer

They, believe me, who await
No gifts from chance, have conquered fate.

Matthew Arnold

It seems all the average fellow needs to make him take a chance is a warning.

Kin Hubbard

We cannot bear to regard ourselves simply as playthings of blind chance; we cannot admit to feeling ourselves abandoned.

Ugo Betti

Success is a fickle jade. The clothes on her back may be put there by hard work, but her jewels are the gifts of chance.

Sir Charles Wheeler

Change

All is change; all yields its place and goes.

Euripides

Nothing is permanent but change.

Heraclitus

Such is the state of life that none are happy but by the anticipation of change. The change itself is nothing: when we have made it the next wish is to change again.

Samuel Johnson

Nothing in progression can rest on its original plan. We might as well think of rocking a grown man in the cradle of an infant.

Edmund Burke

The absurd man is he who never changes.

Auguste Barthélémy

An individual is more apt to change, perhaps, than all the world around him.

Daniel Webster

The old order changeth yielding place to
  new,
And God fulfills himself in many ways,
Lest one good custom should corrupt the
  world.

Alfred, Lord Tennyson

All changes, even the most longed for, have their melancholy; for what we leave behind us is a part of ourselves; we must die to one life before we can enter into another!

Anatole France

Great cultural changes begin in affectation and end in routine.

Jacques Barzun

We live in a moment of history where change is so speeded up that we begin to see the present only when it is already disappearing.

R. D. Laing

Change is the law of life. And those who look only to the past or the present are certain to miss the future.

John Fitzgerald Kennedy

Life is not a static thing. The only people who do not change their minds are incompetents in asylums, who can't, and those in cemeteries.

Everett McKinley Dirksen

To remain young one must change. The perpetual campus hero is not a young man but an old boy.

Alexander Chase

People can cry much easier than they can change.

James Baldwin

Character

A good character carries with it the highest power of causing a thing to be believed.

Aristotle

Mankind is made up of inconsistencies, and no man acts invariably up to his predominant character. The wisest man sometimes acts weakly, and the weakest sometimes wisely.

Lord Chesterfield

Character is much easier kept than recovered.

Thomas Paine

Genius is formed in quiet, character in the stream of human life.

Johann Wolfgang von Goethe

I begin to find that too good a character is inconvenient.

Sir Walter Scott

Character is higher than intellect. Thinking is the function. Living is the functionary.

Ralph Waldo Emerson

Character is like a tree and reputation like its shadow. The shadow is what we think of it; the tree is the real thing.

Abraham Lincoln

Character cannot be developed in ease and quiet. Only through experience of trial and suffering can the soul be strengthened, vision cleared, ambition inspired, and success achieved.

Helen Keller

A man's character never changes radically from youth to old age. What happens is that circumstances bring out characteristics which had not been obvious to the superficial observer.

Hesketh Pearson

Out of our beliefs are born deeds. Out of our deeds we form habits; out of our habits grow our character; and on our character we build our destination.

Henry Hancock

Character is something each one of us must build for himself, out of the laws of God and nature, the examples of others, and—most of all—out of the trials and errors of daily life. . . . Character is the final decision to reject whatever is demeaning to oneself or to others and with confidence and honesty to choose the right.

General Arthur G. Trudeau

Children

Children are the anchors that hold a mother to life.

Sophocles

If you wish to study men you must not neglect to mix with the society of children.

Jesse Torrey

There never was a child so lovely but his mother was glad to get him asleep.

Ralph Waldo Emerson

Children need models rather than critics.

Joseph Joubert

That energy which makes a child hard to manage is the energy which afterward makes him a manager of life.

Henry Ward Beecher

Children begin by loving their parents. After a time they judge them. Rarely, if ever, do they forgive them.

Oscar Wilde

Nature makes boys and girls lovely to look upon so they can be tolerated until they acquire some sense.

William Lyon Phelps

I have found the best way to give advice to your children is to find out what they want and then advise them to do it.

Harry S. Truman

Reasoning with a child is fine, if you can reach the child's reason without destroying your own.

John Mason Brown

Nature kindly warps our judgment about our children, especially when they are young, when it would be a fatal thing for them if we did not love them.

George Santayana

Juvenile appraisals of other juveniles make up in clarity what they lack in charity.

Edgar Z. Friedenberg

One of the most obvious facts about grownups to a child, is that they have forgotten what it is like to be a child.

Randall Jarrell

The greatest gift you can give your child is the freedom to actualize his unique potential self.

Fitzhugh Dodson

Children have never been very good at listening to their elders, but they have never failed to imitate them.

James Baldwin

We can only know as adults what we can only feel as children.

Leslie Fiedler

Your children need your presence more than your presents.

Jesse Jackson

What's done to children, they will do to society.

Karl Augustus Menninger

If men do not keep on speaking terms with children, they cease to be men, and become merely machines for eating and for earning money.

John Updike

Civilization

Civilization does not consist in the eschewing of garlic or the keeping clean of a man's fingernails. It may lead to such delicacies and probably will do so. But the man who thinks that civilization cannot exist without them imagines that the church cannot stand without the spire.

Anthony Trollope

A sufficient measure of civilization is the influence of good women.

Ralph Waldo Emerson

Civilization degrades the many to exalt the few.

Bronson Alcott

The purpose of all civilization is to convert man, a beast of prey, into a tame and civilized animal, a domestic animal.

Friedrich Nietzsche

Civilization is the lamb's skin in which barbarism masquerades.

Thomas Bailey Aldrich

Civilizations die from philosophical calm, irony, and the sense of fair play quite as surely as they die of debauchery.

Joseph Wood Krutch

You can't say civilization don't advance, . . . for in every war they kill you a new way.

Will Rogers

Civilization is a movement and not a condition, a voyage and not a harbor.

Arnold Toynbee

Civilization begins with order, grows with liberty, and dies with chaos.

Will Durant

The progress of civilization consists in ridding the world of sham and shoddy.

A. S. Neill

Conformity

We should know mankind better if we were not so anxious to resemble one another.

Johann Wolfgang von Goethe

The man who aims to speak as books enable, as synods use, as the fashion guides, and as interest commands, babbles. Let him hush.

Ralph Waldo Emerson

We are half ruined by conformity, but we should be wholly ruined without it.

Charles Dudley Warner

The community in which each man acts like his neighbor is not yet a civilized community.

A. H. Sayce

There is truth in the high opinion that in so far as a man conforms, he ceases to exist.

Max Eastman

Men are created different; they lose their social freedom and their individual autonomy in seeking to become like each other.

David Riesman

One of the saddest things about conformity is the ghastly sort of non-conformity it breeds: the noisy protesting, the aggressive rebelliousness, the rigid counterfetishism.

Louis Kronenberger

What is it about us, the public, and what is it about conformity itself that causes us all to require it of our neighbors and of our artists and then, with consummate fickleness, to forget those who fall into line and eternally celebrate those who do not?

Ben Shahn

In almost any society, I think, the quality of the non-conformists is likely to be just as good as and no better than that of the conformists.

Margaret Mead

We cannot expect that all nations will adopt like systems, for conformity is the jailer of freedom and the enemy of growth.

John Fitzgerald Kennedy

Success, recognition, and conformity are the bywords of the modern world where everyone seems to crave the anesthetizing security of being identified with the majority.

Martin Luther King, Jr.

Today's conformity is . . . the retreat from controversiality.

Herman Kahn

The faces of men, while sheep in credulity, are wolves for conformity.

Carl Van Doren

Conscience

A guilty conscience needs no accuser.

English proverb

When a man is content with the testimony of his own conscience, he does not care to shine with the light of another's praise.

Saint Bernard of Clairvaux

The glory of good men is in their conscience and not in the mouths of men.

Thomas a Kempis

A good conscience is a continual Christmas.

Benjamin Franklin

Conscience without judgment is superstition.

Benjamin Whichcote

In many walks of life, a conscience is a more expensive encumbrance than a wife or a carriage.

Thomas De Quincey

Conscience is, in most men, an anticipation of the opinion of others.

Henry Taylor

I desire so to conduct the affairs of this administration that if at the end, when I come to lay down the reins of power, I have lost every other friend on earth, I shall at least have one friend left, and that friend shall be down inside of me.

Abraham Lincoln

Conscience is the name which the orthodox give to their prejudices.

John Oliver Hobbes

Our conscience is not the vessel of eternal verities. It grows with our social life, and a new social condition means a radical change in conscience.

Walter Lippmann

Conscience is the guardian in the individual of the rules which the community has evolved for its own preservation.

W. Somerset Maugham

Conscience is the inner voice which warns us that someone may be looking.

H. L. Mencken

Conscience gets a lot of credit that belongs to cold feet.

Anonymous quote in *Ladies' Home Journal* (March, 1974)

Your conscience is what your mother told you before you were six years old.

Dr. G. Brock Chisholm

Conscience is the perfect interpreter of life.

Karl Barth

A lively and vivid conscience is also the only thing that enables man to resist the effects of the existential vacuum, namely conformism and totalitarianism.

Viktor Frankl

Courage

This is courage in a man:
to bear unflinchingly what heaven sends.

Euripides

No one can answer for his courage when he has never been in danger.

François de La Rochefoucauld

True courage is to do without witnesses everything that one is capable of doing before the world.

François de La Rochefoucauld

Without justice, courage is weak.

Benjamin Franklin

A great part of courage is the courage of having done the thing before.

Ralph Waldo Emerson

Courage is resistance to fear, mastery of fear—not absence of fear. Except a creature be part coward it is not a compliment to say it is brave.

Mark Twain

People with courage and character always seem sinister to the rest.

Hermann Hesse

There is plenty of courage among us for the abstract but not for the concrete.

Helen Keller

Courage is fear that has said its prayers.

Karle Baker

Until the day of his death, no man can be sure of his courage.

Jean Anouilh

You gain strength, courage, and confidence by every experience in which you really stop to look fear in the face. You are able to say to yourself, "I lived through this horror. I can take the next thing that comes along."

Eleanor Roosevelt

Criticism

The blow of a whip raises a welt, but a blow of the tongue crushes bones.

Apocrypha, Ecclesiasticus 28 : 17

They have a right to censure that have a heart to help.

William Penn

If a man is often the subject of conversation he soon becomes the subject of criticism.

Immanuel Kant

Criticism strips the tree of both caterpillars and blossoms.

Johann Paul Friedrich Richter

Criticism should not be querulous and wasting, all knife and root-puller, but guiding, instructive, inspiring, a south wind, not an east wind.

Ralph Waldo Emerson

It is much easier to be critical than to be correct.

Benjamin Disraeli

No man can tell another his faults so as to benefit him, unless he loves him.

Henry Ward Beecher

I like criticism, but it must be my way.

Mark Twain

The critic creates nothing, he only points out. But his pointing may show you powers that were indeed always there, and that were even effective, but that, once afresh seen, suggest to active passion a thousand devices whereby the world is revolutionized.

Josiah Royce

To criticise is to neither praise or denounce, but to *get nearer your subject.*

John Butler Yeats

Criticism itself is much criticized,— which logically establishes its title.

William Crary Brownell

It is salutary to train oneself to be no more affected by censure than by praise.

W. Somerset Maugham

When a man tells you what people are saying about you, tell him what people are saying about him; that will immediately take his mind off your troubles.

Edgar Watson Howe

I have never found, in a long experience of politics, that criticism is ever inhibited by ignorance.

Harold Macmillan

To criticize one's country is to do it a service and pay it a compliment. It is a service because it may spur the country to do better than it is doing; it is a compliment because it evidences belief that the country can do better than it is doing.

William Faulkner

A critic is a man who knows the way but can't drive the car.

Kenneth Tynan

Death

To die with glory, if one has to die at all, is still, I think, pain for the dier.

Euripides

Any man's death diminishes me, because I am involved in mankind; and therefore never send to know for whom the bell tolls; it tolls for thee.

John Donne

Old men go to death; death comes to young men.

George Herbert

He who fears death dies every time he thinks of it.

Stanislas I, King of Poland

Let us endeavour so to live that when we come to die even the undertaker will be sorry.

Mark Twain

A man's dying is more the survivors' affair than his own.

Thomas Mann

Death is the supreme festival on the road to freedom.

Dietrich Bonhoeffer

Man imagines that it is death he fears; but what he fears is the unforeseen, the explosion. What man fears is himself, not death.

Antoine de Saint-Exupéry

If even dying is to be made a social function, then, please, grant me the favor of sneaking out on tiptoe without disturbing the party.

Dag Hammarskjöld

Do not seek death. Death will find you. But seek the road which makes death a fulfillment.

Dag Hammarskjöld

It is impossible to experience one's death objectively and still carry a happy tune.

Woody Allen

I've come to look upon death the same way I look upon root-canal work. Everyone else seems to get through it all right, so it couldn't be too difficult for me.

Joseph Heller

You can't learn to die as though it were a skill. People die in the way they have lived. Death becomes the expression of everything you are, and you can bring to it only what you have brought to your life.

Michael Roemer

There is nothing like death. Everything that approaches it is metaphor.

Flora Johnson

Death is simply a shedding of the physical body, like the butterfly coming out of a cocoon. It is a transition into a higher state of consciousness, where you continue to perceive, to understand, to laugh, to be able to grow, and the only thing you lose is something that you don't need anymore . . . your physical body. It's like putting away your winter coat when spring comes.

Elisabeth Kübler-Ross

It's a blessing to die for a cause, because you can so easily die for nothing.

Andrew Young

Defense

A man without a stick will be bitten even by sheep.

Hindu proverb

Isn't the best defense always a good attack?

Ovid

To be prepared for war is one of the most effectual means of preserving peace.

George Washington

Be as beneficent as the sun or the sea, but if your rights as a rational being are trenched on, die on the first inch of your territory.

Ralph Waldo Emerson

The nation that cannot resist aggression is constantly exposed to it. Its foreign policy is of necessity weak and its negotiations are conducted with disadvantage because it is not in condition to enforce the terms dictated by its sense of right and justice.

Grover Cleveland

No nation ever had an army large enough to guarantee it against attack in time of peace or insure it victory in time of war.

Calvin Coolidge

The core of our defense is the faith we have in the institutions we defend.

Franklin Delano Roosevelt

There is only one defense—a defense compounded of eternal vigilance, sound policies, and high courage.

John Foster Dulles

It is an unfortunate fact that we can secure peace only by preparing for war.

John Fitzgerald Kennedy

The guns and the bombs, the rockets and the warships, are all symbols of human failure. They are necessary symbols. They protect what we cherish. But they are witness to human folly.

Lyndon Baines Johnson

Democracy

Democracy arose from men thinking
that if they are equal in any respect they
are equal in all respects.

Aristotle

If liberty and equality, as is thought by
some, are chiefly to be found in
democracy, they will be best attained
when all persons alike share in the
government to the utmost.

Aristotle

Every government degenerates when
trusted to the rulers of the people alone.
The people themselves therefore are its
only safe depositories.

Thomas Jefferson

A perfect democracy is the most
shameless thing in the world.

Edmund Burke

A democracy can be distinguished, if its
citizens are distinguishable; if each has
an area of choice in which he really
chooses. To keep that area of choice as
large as possible is the real function of
freedom.

G. K. Chesterton

I believe in democracy because it
releases the energies of every human
being.

Woodrow Wilson

It would be folly to argue that the
people cannot make political mistakes.
They can and do make grave mistakes.
They know it, they pay the penalty, but
compared with the mistakes which have
been made by every kind of autocracy
they are unimportant.

Calvin Coolidge

All the ills of democracy can be cured
by more democracy.

Alfred E. Smith

One of the evils of democracy is, you
have to put up with the man you elect
whether you want him or not.

Will Rogers

Democracy means government by
discussion but it is only effective if you
can stop people talking.

Clement Attlee

Democracy demands reciprocity.

Zulfikar Ali Bhutto

Democracy depends on information
circulating freely in society.

Katharine Graham

Desire

The desire for imaginary benefits often
involves the loss of present blessings.

Aesop

We desire most what we ought not to
have.

Publilius Syrus

It is very much easier to extinguish a
first desire than to satisfy those which
follow it.

François de La Rochefoucauld

If you desire many things, many things
will seem but a few.

Benjamin Franklin

The fewer the desires, the more peace.

Thomas Wilson

A strong passion for any object will
ensure success, for the desire of the end
will point out the means.

William Hazlitt

There are two tragedies in life. One is
not to get your heart's desire. The other
is to get it.

George Bernard Shaw

We do not succeed in changing things
according to our desire, but gradually
our desire changes.

Marcel Proust

We are less dissatisfied when we lack
many things than when we seem to lack
but one thing.

Eric Hoffer

Often, the thing we pursue most passionately is but a substitute for the one thing we really want and cannot have.

  Eric Hoffer

Despair

Despair doubles our strength.

  John Ray

Despair exaggerates not only our misery but also our weakness.

  Marquis de Vauvenargues

The mass of men lead lives of quiet desperation. What is called resignation is confirmed desperation.

  Henry David Thoreau

People who are in despair always make a mistake when they hang themselves; the next day often brings the unknown.

  Henri Frédéric Amiel

Despair lames most people, but it wakes others fully up.

  William James

What's the good being hopeless, so long as one has a hobnailed boot to kick with?

  D. H. Lawrence

I can't tell if a straw ever saved a drowning man, but I know that a mere glance is enough to make despair pause. For in truth we who are creatures of impulse are not creatures of despair.

  Joseph Conrad

You may not know it, but at the far end of despair, there is a white clearing where one is almost happy.

  Jean Anouilh

Despair is the price one pays for setting oneself an impossible aim.

  Graham Greene

To eat bread without hope is still slowly to starve to death.

  Pearl S. Buck

I once counselled a man in despair to do what I myself did in similar circumstances: to live for short terms. Come, I said to myself at that time, at any rate you can bear it for a quarter of an hour!

  Theodor Haecker

We can destroy ourselves by cynicism and disillusion, just as effectively as by bombs.

  Kenneth Clark

Discord

He who incites to strife is worse than he who takes part in it.

  Aesop

Opposition brings concord. Out of discord comes the fairest harmony.

  Heraclitus

Discord gives a relish for concord.

  Publilius Syrus

No discord should arise between friends, but if it does, then our care should be that the friendships appear to have been burned out rather than to have been stamped out.

  Cicero

If a house be divided against itself, that house cannot stand.

  Mark 3 : 25

Medicine, to produce health, must know disease; music, to produce harmony, must know discord.

  Plutarch

Fortune can give no greater advantage than discord among the enemy.

  Tacitus

Discords make the sweetest airs,
And curses are a sort of prayers.

  Samuel Butler

Harmony would lose its attractiveness if it did not have a background of discord.

  Tehyi Hsieh

The ultimate measure of a man is not where he stands in moments of comfort and convenience, but where he stands at times of challenge and controversy.

Martin Luther King, Jr.

Education

The direction in which education starts a man, will determine his future life.

Plato

Children should be led into the right paths, not by severity, but by persuasion.

Menander

'Tis education forms the common mind; Just as the twig is bent the tree's inclined.

Alexander Pope

Education makes a people easy to lead but difficult to drive; easy to govern, but impossible to enslave.

Lord Henry Peter Brougham

What is really important in education is not that the child learns this and that, but that the mind is matured, that energy is aroused.

Søren Kierkegaard

If we succeed in giving the love of learning, the learning itself is sure to follow.

Sir John Lubbock

Children have to be educated, but they have also to be left to educate themselves.

Ernest Dimnet

In the traditional method, the child must say something that he has merely learned. There is all the difference in the world between having something to say and having to say something.

John Dewey

All education is a continuous dialogue—questions and answers that pursue every problem to the horizon. That is the essence of academic freedom.

William O. Douglas

The test and use of man's education is that he finds pleasure in the exercise of his mind.

Jacques Barzun

Much education today is monumentally ineffective. All too often we are giving young people cut flowers when we should be teaching them to grow their own plants.

John W. Gardner

Emotion

Seeing's believing, but feeling is God's own truth.

Irish proverb

Trust not to thy feeling, for whatever it be now, it will quickly be changed into another thing.

Thomas a Kempis

To give vent now and then to his feelings, whether of pleasure or discontent, is a great ease to a man's heart.

Francesco Guicciardini

Men, as well as women, are much oftener led by their hearts than by their understandings.

Lord Chesterfield

No emotion, any more than a wave, can long retain its own individual form.

Henry Ward Beecher

The advantage of the emotions is that they lead us astray.

Oscar Wilde

The secret of remaining young is never to have an emotion that is unbecoming.

Oscar Wilde

The important thing is being capable of emotions, but to experience only *one's own* would be a sorry limitation.

André Gide

We think we can have our emotions for nothing. We cannot. Even the finest and the most self-sacrificing emotions have to be paid for. Strangely enough, that is what makes them fine. . . . As soon as we have to pay for an emotion we shall know its quality and be better for such knowledge.

Oscar Wilde

Cherish your emotions and never undervalue them.

Robert Henri

It is true that if we abandon ourselves unreservedly to our emotional impulses, we often render ourselves incapable of doing any work.

André Maurois

In a full heart there is room for everything, and in any empty heart there is room for nothing.

Antonio Porchia

Equality

Before God and the bus driver we are all equal.

German proverb

The only stable state is the one in which all men are equal before the law.

Aristotle

We hold these truths to be self-evident, that all men are created equal, that they are endowed by their Creator with certain unalienable Rights, that among these are Life, Liberty and the pursuit of Happiness.

Thomas Jefferson

The puniest infant that comes wailing into the world in the squalidest room of the most miserable tenement-house becomes at that moment seized of an equal right with the millionaires. And it is robbed if the right is denied.

Henry George

There is no merit in equality, unless it be equality with the best.

John Lancaster Spalding

He who treats as equals those who are far below him in strength really makes them a gift of the quality of human beings, of which fate has deprived them. . . .

Simone Weil

Inside the polling booth every American man and woman stands as the equal of every other American man and woman. There they have no superiors. There they have no masters save their own minds and consciences.

Franklin Delano Roosevelt

The Lord so constituted everybody that no matter what color you are you require the same amount of nourishment.

Will Rogers

We clamor for equality chiefly in matters in which we ourselves cannot hope to obtain excellence.

Eric Hoffer

To live anywhere in the world today and be against equality because of race or color, is like living in Alaska and being against snow.

William Faulkner

Faith

It is by believing in roses that one brings them to bloom.

French proverb

Faith is to believe what you do not yet see; the reward for this faith is to see what you believe.

Saint Augustine

Faith is kept alive in us, and gathers strength, more from practise than from speculations.

Joseph Addison

Faith is like love: it cannot be forced.

Arthur Schopenhauer

We must have infinite faith in each other. If we have not, we must never let it leak out that we have not.

Henry David Thoreau

Let us have faith that right makes might; and in that faith let us dare to do our duty as we understand it.

Abraham Lincoln

Faith is the force of my life.

Leo Tolstoy

Religious faith, indeed, relates to that which is above us, but it must arise from that which is within us.

Josiah Royce

Faith is believing what you know ain't so.

Mark Twain

Faith may be defined briefly as an illogical belief in the occurrence of the improbable.

H. L. Mencken

It is faith and not reason which impels men to action. . . . Intelligence is content to point out the road but never drives us along it.

Alexis Carrel

Faith is the state of being ultimately concerned.

Paul Tillich

Faith is that quality or power by which the things desired become the things possessed.

Kathryn Kuhlman

Father

An angry father is most cruel toward himself.

Publilius Syrus

A father is very miserable who has no other hold on his children's affection than the need they have of his assistance, if that can be called affection.

Michel Eyquem de Montaigne

It is a wise father that knows his own child.

William Shakespeare

There must always be a struggle between a father and son, while one aims at power and the other at independence.

Samuel Johnson

If you've never seen a real, fully developed look of disgust, just tell your son how you conducted yourself when you were a boy.

Kin Hubbard

I could not point to any need in childhood as strong as that for a father's protection.

Sigmund Freud

You hear it said that fathers want their sons to be what they feel they cannot themselves be, but I tell you it also works the other way. A boy wants something very special from his father.

Sherwood Anderson

My daddy doesn't work, he just goes to the office; but sometimes he does errands on the way home.

Anonymous quote in *Ladies Home Journal* (November, 1946)

The fundamental defect of fathers is that they want their children to be a credit to them.

Bertrand Russell

You don't have to deserve your mother's love. You have to deserve your father's. He's more particular.

Robert Frost

To be sure, working—that is, earning a living—is one aspect of fathering. It's one means that the father has of extending protection to his family. But it's *just* one. If he concentrates on this to the exclusion of other aspects, it becomes not a form of fathering, but an escape.

Myron Brenton

The night you were born, I ceased being my father's boy and became my son's father. That night I began a new life.
  Henry Gregor Felsen

Fault

If the best man's faults were written on his forehead, it would make him pull his hat over his eyes.
  Gaelic proverb

The business of finding fault is very easy, and that of doing better very difficult.
  Saint Francis de Sales

Happy people rarely correct their faults.
  François de La Rochefoucauld

We forget our faults easily when they are known to ourselves alone.
  François de La Rochefoucauld

A benevolent man should allow a few faults in himself, to keep his friends in countenance.
  Benjamin Franklin

People will allow their faults to be shown them; they will let themselves be punished for them; they will patiently endure many things because of them; they only become impatient when they have to lay them aside.
  Johann Wolfgang von Goethe

The greatest of faults, I should say, is to be conscious of none.
  Thomas Carlyle

People who have no faults are terrible; there is no way of taking advantage of them.
  Anatole France

It is in our faults and failings, not in our virtues, that we touch one another and find sympathy.
  Jerome K. Jerome

None of us can stand other people having the same faults as ourselves.
  Oscar Wilde

There is only one way of getting rid of one's faults and that is to acquire the habits contradictory to them.
  Ernest Dimnet

Until I accept my faults I will most certainly doubt my virtues.
  Hugh Prather

There are only two kinds of perfectly faultless men—the dead and the deadly.
  Helen Rowland

Fear

He who fears something gives it power over him.
  Moorish proverb

Fear is stronger than arms.
  Aeschylus

Just as courage imperils life, fear protects it.
  Leonardo da Vinci

No passion so effectually robs the mind of all its powers of acting and reasoning as fear.
  Edmund Burke

The wise man in the storm prays God, not for safety from danger, but for deliverance from fear. It is the storm within which endangers him, not the storm without.
  Ralph Waldo Emerson

A good scare is worth more to a man than good advice.
  Edgar Watson Howe

Fear is never a good counselor and victory over fear is the first spiritual duty of man.
  Nicolas Berdyaev

Fears are educated into us, and can, if we wish, be educated out.
  Karl Augustus Menninger

The only thing we have to fear is fear itself—nameless, unreasoning, unjustified terror which paralyzes needed efforts to convert retreat into advance.
  Franklin Delano Roosevelt

Fear comes from uncertainty. When we are absolutely certain, whether of our worth or worthlessness, we are almost impervious to fear. Thus a feeling of utter unworthiness can be a source of courage.

Eric Hoffer

When men are ruled by fear, they strive to prevent the very changes that will abate it.

Alan Paton

Perhaps the most important thing we can undertake toward the reduction of fear is to make it easier for people to accept themselves; to like themselves.

Bonaro Overstreet

Freedom

Better starve free than be a fat slave.

Aesop

It is a worthy thing to fight for one's freedom; it is another sight finer to fight for another man's.

Mark Twain

To know how to free oneself is nothing; the arduous thing is to know what to do with one's freedom.

André Gide

It is better to die on your feet than to live on your knees.

Dolores Ibarruri

The moment the slave resolves that he will no longer be a slave, his fetters fall. He frees himself and shows the way to others. Freedom and slavery are mental states.

Mohandas K. Gandhi

"Freedom from fear" could be said to sum up the whole philosophy of human rights.

Dag Hammarskjöld

Freedom is not something that anybody can be given; freedom is something people take and people are as free as they want to be.

James Baldwin

The first principle of a free society is an untrammeled flow of words in an open forum.

Adlai E. Stevenson

There can be no real freedom without the freedom to fail.

Eric Hoffer

The basic test of freedom is perhaps less in what we are free to do than in what we are free not to do.

Eric Hoffer

Freedom is whole and cannot be allowed by degrees.

Maurice Girodias

You can't separate peace from freedom because no one can be at peace unless he has his freedom.

Malcolm X

There comes a point when too much freedom, particularly freedom to choose from an almost unlimited set of alternatives, becomes incapacitating and paralyzing.

Seymour L. Halleck

The most precious freedom secured to the individual by our Constitution is the privacy of his mind, the freedom of his thought and the sanctity of his conscience.

Sam J. Ervin, Jr.

Friendship

Friendship is equality.

Pythagoras

Friendship is a single soul dwelling in two bodies.

Aristotle

Forsake not an old friend, for a new one does not compare with him.

Apocrypha, Ecclesiasticus 9 : 10

Friendship adds a brighter radiance to prosperity and lightens the burden of adversity by dividing and sharing it.

Cicero

Friendships renewed demand more care than those which have never been broken.

François de La Rochefoucauld

There can be no friendship where there is no freedom. Friendship loves a free air, and will not be fenced up in straight and narrow enclosures.

William Penn

Friendship is a strong and habitual inclination in two persons to promote the good and happiness of one another.

Eustace Budgell

Friendship's the wine of life.

Edward Young

True friendship is a plant of slow growth, and must undergo and withstand the shocks of adversity before it is entitled to the appelation.

George Washington

The firmest friendships have been formed in mutual adversity, as iron is most strongly united by the fiercest flame.

Charles Caleb Colton

Friendship often ends in love; but love, in friendship—never.

Charles Caleb Colton

It is one of the blessings of old friends that you can afford to be stupid with them.

Ralph Waldo Emerson

The only way to have a friend is to be one.

Ralph Waldo Emerson

Friendship is like money, easier made than kept.

Samuel Butler

Any time friends have to be careful of what they say to friends, friendship is taking on another dimension.

Duke Ellington

In life you throw a ball. You hope it will reach a wall and bounce back so you can throw it again. You hope your friends will provide that wall.

Pablo Picasso

Future

If a man takes no thought about what is distant, he will find sorrow near at hand.

Confucius

The future
you shall know when it has become;
before then, forget it.

Aeschylus

Let us not go over the old ground, let us rather prepare for what is to come.

Cicero

He that fears not the future may enjoy the present.

Thomas Fuller

I like the dreams of the future better than the history of the past.

Thomas Jefferson

The best thing about the future is that it comes only one day at a time.

Abraham Lincoln

Future, n. That period of time in which our affairs prosper, our friends are true and our happiness is assured.

Ambrose Bierce

The trouble with our times is that the future is not what it used to be.

Paul Valéry

My interest is in the future because I am going to spend the rest of my life there.

Charles Kettering

A preoccupation with the future not only prevents us from seeing the present as it is but often prompts us to rearrange the past.

Eric Hoffer

The most prevalent opinion among our so confused contemporaries seems to be that tomorrow will be wonderful—that is unless it is indescribably terrible, or unless indeed there just isn't any.
Joseph Wood Krutch

The future is like heaven—everyone exalts it but no one wants to go there now.
James Baldwin

Yesterday is not ours to recover, but tomorrow is ours to win or to lose.
Lyndon Baines Johnson

The most effective way to ensure the value of the future is to confront the present courageously and constructively.
Rollo May

You can destroy your now by worrying about tomorrow.
Janis Joplin

As one went to Europe to see the living past, so one must visit Southern California to observe the future.
Alison Lurie

Every society faces not merely a succession of probable futures, but an array of possible futures, and a conflict over preferable futures.
Alvin Toffler

Future shock is the dizzying disorientation brought on by the premature arrival of the future.
Alvin Toffler

Genius

There is no great genius without some touch of madness.
Lucius Annaeus Seneca

Time, place, and action may with pains
be wrought,
But genius must be born, and never can
be taught.
John Dryden

When a true genius appears in the world, you may know him by this sign, that the dunces are all in confederacy against him.
Jonathan Swift

Genius is patience.
Comte de Buffon

Genius always finds itself a century too early.
Ralph Waldo Emerson

To do easily what is difficult for others is the mark of talent. To do what is impossible for talent is the mark of genius.
Henri Frédéric Amiel

Genius is mainly an affair of energy.
Matthew Arnold

Genius is one per cent inspiration and ninety-nine per cent perspiration.
Thomas Alva Edison

Geniuses are the luckiest of mortals because what they must do is the same as what they most want to do.
W. H. Auden

A genius is one who can do anything except make a living.
Joey Adams

Talent is what you possess; genius is what possesses you.
Malcolm Cowley

God

God is love; and he that dwelleth in love dwelleth in God, and God in him.
I John 4 : 16

If God be for us, who can be against us?
Romans 8 : 31

It is the heart which experiences God, and not the reason.
Blaise Pascal

Let us weigh the gain and the loss, in wagering that God is. Consider these alternatives: if you win, you win all; if you lose, you lose nothing. Do not hesitate, then, to wager that He is.

Blaise Pascal

God's perfections are marvellous but not lovable.

Immanuel Kant

God will forgive me; it is His trade.

Heinrich Heine

But I always think that the best way to know God is to love many things.

Vincent Van Gogh

We should find God in what we do know, not in what we don't; not in outstanding problems, but in those we have already solved.

Dietrich Bonhoeffer

Every man thinks God is on his side. The rich and powerful know He is.

Jean Anouilh

God is what man finds that is divine in himself. God is the best way man can behave in the ordinary occasions of life, and the farthest point to which man can stretch himself.

Max Lerner

God does not die on the day when we cease to believe in a personal deity.

Dag Hammarskjöld

Respectable society believed in God in order to avoid having to speak about him.

Jean-Paul Sartre

The word of the Lord falls with the force of a snowflake.

William Sloane Coffin

Why is it when we talk to God, we're said to be praying—but when God talks to us, we're schizophrenic?

Lily Tomlin

Goodness

It is easy to perform a good action, but not easy to acquire a settled habit of performing such actions.

Aristotle

Goodness and greatness go not always together.

John Clarke

Do good by stealth, and blush to find it fame.

Alexander Pope

Goodness that preaches undoes itself.

Ralph Waldo Emerson

Good men are not those who now and then do a good act, but men who join one good act to another.

Henry Ward Beecher

Be good, and you will be lonesome.

Mark Twain

To be good is noble; but to show others how to be good is nobler and no trouble.

Mark Twain

An act of goodness, the least act of true goodness, is indeed the best proof of the existence of God.

Jacques Maritain

On the whole, human beings want to be good, but not too good, and not quite all the time.

George Orwell

A man is only as good as what he loves.

Saul Bellow

Good people are good because they've come to wisdom through failure.

William Saroyan

A good man isn't good for everything.

John W. Gardner

Grief

There is no greater grief than, in misery, to recall happier times.

Dante Alighieri

Every one can master a grief but he that has it.

William Shakespeare

Grief is a species of idleness.

Samuel Johnson

Grief is itself a medicine.

William Cowper

Grief drives men into habits of serious reflection, sharpens the understanding and softens the heart.

John Adams

It is better to drink of deep griefs than to taste shallow pleasures.

William Hazlitt

Man sheds grief as his skin sheds rain.

Ralph Waldo Emerson

Grief even in a child hates the light and shrinks from human eyes.

Thomas De Quincey

The only cure for grief is action.

George Henry Lewes

Happiness is beneficial for the body, but it is grief that develops the powers of the mind.

Marcel Proust

Melancholy and remorse form the deep leaden keel which enables us to sail into the wind of reality.

Cyril Connolly

Grief can't be shared. Everyone carries it alone, his own burden, his own way.

Anne Morrow Lindbergh

Habits

Habit is a sort of second nature.

Cicero

Habit is overcome by habit.

Thomas a Kempis

An old dog can't alter his way of barking.

Thomas Fuller

The chains of habit are too weak to be felt until they are too strong to be broken.

Samuel Johnson

Habit with him was all the test of truth;
"It must be right: I've done it from my youth."

George Crabbe

Habit is habit, and not to be flung out of the window by any man, but coaxed downstairs a step at a time.

Mark Twain

Habit is stronger than reason.

George Santayana

For the ordinary business of life an ounce of habit is worth a pound of intellect.

Thomas B. Reed

The unfortunate thing about this world is that good habits are so much easier to give up than bad ones.

W. Somerset Maugham

Laws are never as effective as habits.

Adlai E. Stevenson

Wise living consists perhaps less in acquiring good habits than in acquiring as few habits as possible.

Eric Hoffer

Happiness

Happiness depends upon ourselves.

Aristotle

He that keepeth the law, happy is he.

Proverbs 29 : 18

He that is of a merry heart hath a continual feast.

Proverbs 17 : 22

The happy man is not he who seems thus to others, but who seems thus to himself.

Publilius Syrus

No man is happy unless he believes he is.

Publilius Syrus

If thou art sound in stomach, side, and feet, the riches of a king will add nothing to thy happiness.

> Horace

Oh, how bitter a thing it is to look into happiness through another man's eyes!

> William Shakespeare

We are more interested in making others believe we are happy than in trying to be happy ourselves.

> François de La Rochefoucauld

No man is happy but by comparison.

> Thomas Shadwell

Happiness, n. An agreeable sensation arising from contemplating the misery of another.

> Ambrose Bierce

When we are not rich enough to be able to purchase happiness, we must not approach too near and gaze on it in shop windows.

> Tristan Bernard

When one door of happiness closes, another opens; but often we look so long at the closed door that we do not see the one which has been opened for us.

> Helen Keller

The search for happiness is one of the chief sources of unhappiness.

> Eric Hoffer

The bird of paradise alights only upon the hand that does not grasp.

> John Berry

Happiness is having a scratch for every itch.

> Ogden Nash

Much happiness is overlooked because it doesn't cost anything.

> Author unknown

Harmony

The hidden harmony is better than the obvious.

> Heraclitus

Beauty of style and harmony and grace and good rhythm depend on simplicity.

> Plato

Harmony makes small things grow; lack of it makes great things decay.

> Sallust

Medicine, to produce health, must know disease; music, to produce harmony, must know discord.

> Plutarch

And when Love speaks, the voice of all the gods
Makes heaven drowsy with the harmony.
Never durst poet touch a pen to write
Until his ink were temper'd with Love's sighs.

> William Shakespeare

The tongues of dying men
Enforce attention like deep harmony.

> William Shakespeare

By harmony our souls are swayed;
By harmony the world was made.

> George Granville

This lesson teaching, which our souls may strike,
That harmonies may be in things unlike.

> Charles Lamb

How much finer things are in composition than alone.

> Ralph Waldo Emerson

Harmony would lose its attractiveness if it did not have a background of discord.

> Tehyi Hsieh

It is indeed from the experience of beauty and happiness, from the occasional harmony between our nature and our environment, that we draw our conception of the divine life.

> George Santayana

The external harmony and progress of the entire human race is founded on the internal harmony and progress of every individual.

Maharishi Mahesh Yogi

Hate

He that hateth his brother is in darkness, and walketh in the darkness, and knoweth not whither he goeth, because that darkness hath blinded his eyes.

I John 2 : 11

Hatreds are the cinders of affection.

Sir Walter Raleigh

When our hatred is too keen it places us beneath those we hate.

François de La Rochefoucauld

Men hate more steadily than they love.

Samuel Johnson

Hatred is by far the longest pleasure;
Men love in haste, but they detest at leisure.

Lord Byron

Pity is a thing often avowed, seldom felt; hatred is a thing often felt, seldom avowed.

Charles Caleb Colton

Hatred is the coward's revenge for being intimidated.

George Bernard Shaw

If you hate a person, you hate something in him that is a part of yourself. What isn't part of ourselves doesn't disturb us.

Hermann Hesse

The human heart as modern civilization has made it is more prone to hatred than to friendship. And it is prone to hatred because it is dissatisfied.

Bertrand Russell

Hate is the consequence of fear; we fear something before we hate it; a child who fears noises becomes a man who hates noise.

Cyril Connolly

To wrong those we hate is to add fuel to our hatred. Conversely, to treat an enemy with magnanimity is to blunt our hatred for him.

Eric Hoffer

Passionate hatred can give meaning and purpose to an empty life.

Eric Hoffer

The price of hating other human beings is loving oneself less.

Eldridge Cleaver

Hero

A hero is one who knows how to hang on one minute longer.

Norwegian proverb

Barren countries produce the most heroes.

Ascribed to Menander

Who is the noblest hero? The man who conquers his senses.

Bhartrihari

No man is a hero to his valet.

Ascribed to Madame Cornuel

See the conquering hero comes!
Sound the trumpet, beat the drums!

Thomas Morell

A light supper, a good night's sleep, and a fine morning have sometimes made a hero of the same man who, by an indigestion, a restless night, and rainy morning would have proved a coward.

Lord Chesterfield

Worship of a hero is transcendent admiration of a great man.

Thomas Carlyle

It will never make any difference to a hero what the laws are. His greatness will shine and accomplish itself unto the end, whether they second him or not.

Ralph Waldo Emerson

Each man is a hero and an oracle to somebody.

Ralph Waldo Emerson

What a hero one can be without moving a finger!

Henry David Thoreau

The political or spiritual hero will always be the one who, when others crumbled, stood firm till a new order built itself around him; who showed a way out and beyond where others could only see written "no thoroughfare."

William James

It is not heroes that make history, but history that makes heroes. It is not heroes who create a people, but the people who create heroes and move history forward.

Attributed to Joseph Stalin

The ordinary man is involved in action, the hero acts. An immense difference.

Henry Miller

As you get older it is harder to have heroes, but it is sort of necessary.

Ernest Hemingway

The opportunities for heroism are limited in this kind of world: the most people can do is sometimes not to be as weak as they've been at other times.

Angus Wilson

History

History repeats itself.

English proverb

Not to know what happened before one was born is always to be a child.

Cicero

It is the true office of history to represent the events themselves, together with the counsels, and to leave the observations and conclusions thereupon to the liberty and faculty of every man's judgment.

Francis Bacon

History can be well written only in a free country.

Voltaire

A morsel of genuine history is a thing so rare as to be always valuable.

Thomas Jefferson

The only history worth reading is that written at the time of which it treats, the history of what was done and seen, heard out of the mouths of the men who did and saw.

John Ruskin

History is a record of the gradual negation of man's original bestiality by the evolution of his humanity.

Mikhail Bakunin

History, n.   An account mostly false, of events mostly unimportant, which are brought about by rulers mostly knaves, and soldiers mostly fools.

Ambrose Bierce

We can chart our future clearly and wisely only when we know the path which has led to the present.

Adlai E. Stevenson II

That men do not learn very much from the lessons of history is the most important of all the lessons that history has to teach.

Aldous Huxley

More history's made by secret handshakes than by battles, bills, and proclamations.

John Barth

You don't change the course of history by turning the faces of portraits to the wall.

Jawaharlal Nehru

History never looks like history when you are living through it. It always looks confusing and messy, and it always feels uncomfortable.

John W. Gardner

Honesty

Honesty is for the most part less profitable than dishonesty.

Plato

In an honest man there is always something of a child.

Martial

An honest man's word is as good as his bond.

Miguel de Cervantes

A show of a certain amount of honesty is in any profession or business the surest way of growing rich.

Jean de La Bruyère

Honest men fear neither the light nor the dark.

Thomas Fuller

An honest man's the noblest work of God.

Alexander Pope

Honesty is the first chapter of the book of wisdom.

Thomas Jefferson

The surest way to remain poor is to be an honest man.

Napoleon I

To make your children capable of honesty is the beginning of education.

John Ruskin

We must make the world honest before we can honestly say to our children that honesty is the best policy.

George Bernard Shaw

Hope

Hope deferred maketh the heart sick.

Proverbs 13 : 12

As wisdom without courage is futile, even so faith without hope is nothing worth; for hope endures and overcomes misfortune and evil.

Martin Luther

True hope is swift, and flies with
    swallow's wings;
Kings it makes gods, and meaner
    creatures kings.

William Shakespeare

Hope is the poor man's bread.

George Herbert

Hope, deceitful as it is, serves at least to lead us to the end of our lives by an agreeable route.

François de La Rochefoucauld

Never give out while there is hope; but hope not beyond reason, for that shows more desire than judgment.

William Penn

Great hopes make great men.

Thomas Fuller

If it were not for hopes, the heart would break.

Thomas Fuller

If Winter comes, can Spring be far
    behind?

Percy Bysshe Shelley

Hope is the parent of faith.

C. A. Bartol

There is nothing so well known as that we should not expect something for nothing—but we all do and call it Hope.

Edgar Watson Howe

Hope is a risk that must be run.

Georges Bernanos

Humility

The fruits of humility are love and peace.

Hebrew proverb

The higher we are placed, the more we should be humble.

>Cicero

Plenty of people want to be pious, but no one yearns to be humble.

>François de La Rochefoucauld

Humility is a virtue all preach, none practice, and yet everybody is content to hear.

>John Selden

To be humble to superiors is duty, to equals courtesy, to inferiors nobleness.

>Benjamin Franklin

Humility is the first of the virtues—for other people.

>Oliver Wendell Holmes, Sr.

Never be haughty to the humble; never be humble to the haughty.

>Jefferson Davis

We come nearest to the great when we are great in humility.

>Rabindranath Tagore

Humility is not renunciation of pride but the substitution of one pride for another.

>Eric Hoffer

Humility is just as much the opposite of self-abasement as it is of self-exaltation.

>Dag Hammarskjöld

Don't be humble, you're not that great.

>Golda Meir

Ignorance

Not to know is bad; not to wish to know is worse.

>Nigerian proverb

If the blind lead the blind, both shall fall into the ditch.

>Matthew 15 : 14

He who would be cured of ignorance must confess it.

>Michel Eyquem de Montaigne

It is often the greatest wisdom to be ignorant.

>Baltasar Gracián

He that knows least commonly presumes most.

>Thomas Fuller

. . . where ignorance is bliss
'Tis folly to be wise.

>Thomas Gray

A seeming ignorance is often a most necessary part of worldly knowledge.

>Lord Chesterfield

Ignorance is preferable to error; and he is less remote from the truth who believes nothing than he who believes what is wrong.

>Thomas Jefferson

To be conscious that you are ignorant is a great step to knowledge.

>Benjamin Disraeli

How exactly proportioned to a man's ignorance of the subject is the noise he makes about it at a public meeting.

>Sir Arthur Helps

Everybody is ignorant, only on different subjects.

>Will Rogers

Far more crucial than what we know or do not know is what we do not want to know.

>Eric Hoffer

If ignorance paid dividends most Americans could make a fortune out of what they don't know about economics.

>Luther Hodges

Indifference

What makes men indifferent to their wives is that they can see them when they please.

>Ovid

Nothing is more conducive to peace of mind than not having any opinion at all.

>Georg Christoph Lichtenberg

There's no love lost between us.
  Oliver Goldsmith

Most of us have no real loves and no real hatreds. Blessed is love, less blessed is hatred, but thrice accursed is that indifference which is neither one nor the other.
  Mark Rutherford

The worst sin towards our fellow creatures is not to hate them, but to be indifferent to them: that's the essence of inhumanity.
  George Bernard Shaw

By far the most dangerous foe we have to fight is *apathy*—indifference from whatever cause, not from a lack of knowledge, but from carelessness, from absorption in other pursuits, from a contempt bred of self-satisfaction.
  Sir William Osler

The death of democracy is not likely to be an assassination from ambush. It will be a slow extinction from apathy, indifference, and undernourishment.
  Robert Maynard Hutchins

To know the good is to react against the bad. Indifference is the mark of deprivation.
  Marya Mannes

Many a deep secret that cannot be pried out by curiosity can be drawn out by indifference.
  Sydney J. Harris

The price of eternal vigilance is indifference.
  Marshall McLuhan

To try may be to die, but not to care is never to be born.
  William Redfield

The accomplice to the crime of corruption is frequently our own indifference.
  Bess Myerson

Individual

When two do the same thing it is never quite the same thing.
  Publilius Syrus

We fancy men are individuals; so are pumpkins; but every pumpkin in the field goes through every point of pumpkin history.
  Ralph Waldo Emerson

If a man does not keep pace with his companions, perhaps it is because he hears a different drummer. Let him step to the music he hears, however measured or far away.
  Henry David Thoreau

A people, it appears, may be progressive for a certain length of time, and then stop. When does it stop? When it ceases to possess individuality.
  John Stuart Mill

That cause is strong which has not a multitude, but one strong man behind it.
  James Russell Lowell

Any power must be the enemy of mankind which enslaves the individual by terror and force, whether it arises under a Fascist or Communist flag. All that is valuable in human society depends upon the opportunity for development accorded to the individual.
  Albert Einstein

Men are born equal but they are also born different.
  Erich Fromm

The best things and best people rise out of their separateness; I'm against a homogenized society because I want the cream to rise.
  Robert Frost

Individualism is rather like innocence; there must be something unconscious about it.
  Louis Kronenberger

The man who walks alone is soon trailed by the F.B.I.
  Wright Morris

Inequality

It is the nature of things to be unequal.
One is worth twice, or five times, or ten,
or a hundred, or a thousand, or ten
thousand times as much as another. To
think of them as equal is to upset the
whole scheme of things. Who would
make shoes if big ones were of the same
price as small ones?

　Mencius

Though all men were made of one
metal, yet they were not cast all in the
same mold.

　Thomas Fuller

We are all Adam's children, but silk
makes the difference.

　Thomas Fuller

Wherever there is great property, there
is great inequality . . . for one very rich
man, there must be at least five hundred
poor.

　Adam Smith

Oh, there are moments for us here,
　when seeing
Life's inequalities, and woe, and care,
The burdens laid upon our mortal being
Seem heavier than the human heart can
　bear.

　Willis G. Clark

Whatever may be the general endeavor
of a community to render its members
equal and alike, the personal pride of
individuals will always seek to rise
above the line, and to form somewhere
an inequality to their own advantage.

　Alexis de Tocqueville

Men are made by nature unequal. It is
vain, therefore, to treat them as if they
were equal.

　James Anthony Froude

True education makes for inequality; the
inequality of individuality, the
inequality of success; the glorious
inequality of talent, of genius; for
inequality, not mediocrity, individual

superiority, not standardization, is the
measure of the progress of the world.

　Felix E. Schelling

All animals are equal, but some animals
are more equal than others.

　George Orwell

Let us be very clear on this matter: if we
condemn people to inequality in our
society we also condemn them to
inequality in our economy.

　Lyndon Baines Johnson

Influence

He who goes with wolves learns to
howl.

　Spanish proverb

The rotten apple spoils his companions.

　Benjamin Franklin

The best effect of fine persons is felt
after we have left their presence.

　Ralph Waldo Emerson

Every life is a profession of faith, and
exercises a silent but inevitable
influence.

　Henri Frédéric Amiel

A teacher affects eternity; he can never
tell where his influence stops.

　Henry Brooks Adams

Influence is neither good nor bad in an
absolute manner, but only in relation to
the one who experiences it.

　André Gide

One of the things a man has to learn to
fight most bitterly is the influence of
those who love him.

　Sherwood Anderson

However brief may be the intercourse
we have with a man, we always come
away with it somewhat modified; we
find we are a little greater than we were
before, or a little less great, better or
worse, exalted or diminished.

　Georges Duhamel

Human beings are not influenced by anything to which they are not naturally disposed.

Hesketh Pearson

No writer or teacher or artist can escape the responsibility of influencing others, whether he intends to or not, whether he is conscious of it or not.

Arthur Koestler

Influence is like a savings account. The less you use it, the more you've got.

Andrew Young

Inspiration

No man was ever great without some portion of divine inspiration.

Cicero

Holy rapture . . . from the seeds of the divine mind sown in man.

Ovid

There is something in our minds like sunshine and the weather, which is not under our control. When I write, the best things come to me from I know not where.

Georg Christoph Lichtenberg

We cannot carry on inspiration and make it consecutive. One day there is no electricity in the air, and the next the world bristles with sparks like a cat's back.

Ralph Waldo Emerson

There is no inspiration in the ideals of plenty and stability.

John Lancaster Spalding

Genius is one per cent inspiration and ninety-nine per cent perspiration.

Thomas Alva Edison

Just as appetite comes by eating, so work brings inspiration, if inspiration is not discernible at the beginning.

Igor Stravinsky

My sole inspiration is a telephone call from a producer.

Cole Porter

Inspiration is a farce that poets have invented to give themselves importance.

Jean Anouilh

Inspiration could be called inhaling the memory of an act never experienced.

Ned Rorem

Integrity

Integrity is better than charity. The gods approve of the depth and not of the tumult of the soul.

Socrates

The just man walketh in his integrity.

Proverbs 20 : 7

He that is faithful in that which is least is faithful also in much; and he that is unjust in the least is unjust also in much.

Luke 16 : 10

Integrity is praised, and starves.

Juvenal

This above all: to thine own self be true, And it must follow, as the night the day, Thou canst not then be false to any man.

William Shakespeare

Integrity without knowledge is weak and useless, and knowledge without integrity is dangerous and dreadful.

Samuel Johnson

Nothing so completely baffles one who is full of trick and duplicity himself, than straightforward and simple integrity in another.

Charles Caleb Colton

A little integrity is better than any career.

Ralph Waldo Emerson

It is better to be hated for what you are than loved for what you are not.

André Gide

To be individually righteous is the first of all duties, come what may to one's self, to one's country, to society, and to civilization itself.

Joseph Wood Krutch

Justice

There is a point beyond which even justice becomes unjust.

Sophocles

All virtue is summed up in dealing justly.

Aristotle

There is no such thing as justice in the abstract; it is merely a compact between men.

Epicurus

Justice is the crowning glory of the virtues.

Cicero

The aim of justice is to give everyone his due.

Cicero

If you study the history and records of the world you must admit that the source of justice was the fear of injustice.

Horace

Justice is the end of government.

Daniel Defoe

Rigid justice is the greatest injustice.

Thomas Fuller

Justice is truth in action.

Joseph Joubert

It is impossible to be just if one is not generous.

Joseph Roux

There is no such thing as justice—in or out of court.

Clarence Darrow

Justice is like a train that's nearly always late.

Yevgeny Yevtushenko

Justice delayed is democracy denied.

Robert Francis Kennedy

To have true justice we must have equal harassment under the law.

Paul Krassner

The answer to the revolutionaries is to behave with justice.

I. F. Stone

Let lawmakers, judges and lawyers think less of the law and more of justice.

Phillip Berrigan

Knowledge

When you know a thing, to hold that you know it, and when you do not know it, to admit that you do not—this is true knowledge.

Confucius

The fear of the Lord is the beginning of knowledge.

Proverbs 1 : 7

He that increaseth knowledge increaseth sorrow.

Ecclesiastes 1 : 18

Nature has given to us the seeds of knowledge, but not knowledge itself.

Lucius Annaeus Seneca

All wish to know, but none want to pay the price.

Juvenal

Whoever acquires knowledge and does not practise it resembles him who ploughs his land and leaves it unsown.

Saadi

Knowledge is power.

Francis Bacon

It is much better to know something about everything than to know everything about one thing.

Blaise Pascal

A little learning is a dangerous thing;
Drink deep, or taste not the Pierian spring:
There shallow draughts intoxicate the brain,
And drinking largely sobers us again.

Alexander Pope

Knowledge is a comfortable and necessary retreat and shelter for us in an advanced age; and if we do not plant it while young, it will give us no shade when we grow old.

Lord Chesterfield

If a little knowledge is dangerous, where is the man who has so much as to be out of danger?

Thomas Henry Huxley

In order that knowledge be properly digested, it must have been swallowed with a good appetite.

Anatole France

Better know nothing than half-know many things.

Friedrich Nietzsche

The greater our knowledge increases, the greater our ignorance unfolds.

John Fitzgerald Kennedy

Law

The law is good, if a man use it lawfully.

I Timothy 1 : 8

The law is reason free from passion.

Aristotle

Good men need no laws, and bad men are not made better by them.

Ascribed to Demonax of Cyprus

The purpose of law is to prevent the strong always having their way.

Ovid

The law is not the same at morning and at night.

George Herbert

The law, being made, is but words and paper without the hands and swords of men.

James Harrington

Law can discover sin, but not remove.

John Milton

Wherever law ends, tyranny begins.

John Locke

Law is but a heathen word for power.

Daniel Defoe

The more laws, the more offenders.

Thomas Fuller

Laws too gentle are seldom obeyed; too severe, seldom executed.

Benjamin Franklin

Ignorance of the law is no excuse in any country. If it were, the laws would lose their effect, because it can be always pretended.

Thomas Jefferson

Anyone who takes it upon himself, on his private authority, to break a bad law, thereby authorizes everyone else to break the good ones.

Denis Diderot

If there were no bad people there would be no good lawyers.

Charles Dickens

Those who are too lazy and comfortable to think for themselves and be their own judges obey the laws. Others sense their own laws within them.

Hermann Hesse

There's no better way of exercising the imagination than the study of law. No poet ever interpreted nature as freely as a lawyer interprets truth.

Jean Giraudoux

Nobody has a more sacred obligation to obey the law than those who make the law.

Jean Anouilh

There are not enough jails, not enough policemen, not enough courts to enforce a law not supported by the people.

Hubert H. Humphrey

I . . . have been guided by a simple principle, the principle that the law must deal fairly with every man. For me, this is the oldest principle of democracy. It is this simple but great principle which enables man to live justly and in decency in a free society.

Peter Rodino

Law is the indispensable attribute of an ordered society.

Elliot Richardson

The law protects everybody who can afford to hire a good lawyer.

Author unknown

Liberty

No favor produces less permanent gratitude than the gift of liberty, especially among people who are ready to make a bad use of it.

Livy

Liberty plucks justice by the nose.

William Shakespeare

Liberty is the power that we have over ourselves.

Hugo Grotius

They that can give up essential liberty to obtain a little temporary safety deserve neither liberty nor safety.

Benjamin Franklin

Liberty is obedience to the law which one has laid down for oneself.

Jean Jacques Rousseau

Is life so dear or peace so sweet as to be purchased at the price of chains and slavery? Forbid it, Almighty God! I know not what course others may take, but as for me, give me liberty, or give me death.

Patrick Henry

The tree of liberty must be refreshed from time to time with the blood of patriots and tyrants. It is its natural manure.

Thomas Jefferson

Liberty is not a means to a higher political end. It is itself the highest political end.

Lord Acton

Liberty means responsibility. That is why most men dread it.

George Bernard Shaw

Liberty don't work as good in practice as it does in Speech.

Will Rogers

I am a lover of my own liberty and so I would do nothing to restrict yours.

Mohandas K. Gandhi

Life

Life is a theatre in which the worst people often have the best seats.

Ascribed to Aristonymus

Life is long to the miserable, but short to the happy.

Publilius Syrus

Life is short, but its ills make it seem long.

Publilius Syrus

The art of living is more like wrestling than dancing.

Marcus Aurelius

Life is as tedious as a twice-told tale,
Vexing the dull ear of a drowsy man.

William Shakespeare

Out, out, brief candle!
Life's but a walking shadow, a poor
    player
That struts and frets his hour upon the
    stage,
And then is heard no more; it is a tale
Told by an idiot, full of sound and fury,
Signifying nothing.

William Shakespeare

We are born crying, live complaining, and die disappointed.

Thomas Fuller

Short as life is, some find it long enough to outlive their characters, their constitutions and their estates.

Charles Caleb Colton

To most of us the real life is the life we do not lead.

Oscar Wilde

Life is one long process of getting tired.
Samuel Butler

Life is a long lesson in humility.
Sir James Matthew Barrie

Life is too short for men to take it
seriously.
George Bernard Shaw

The basic fact about human existence is
not that it is a tragedy, but that it is a
bore. It is not so much a war as an
endless standing in line.
H. L. Mencken

Life is a wonderful thing to talk about,
or to read about in history books—but it
is terrible when one has to live it.
Jean Anouilh

Life is like a B-picture script. It is that
corny. If I had my life story offered to
me to film, I'd turn it down.
Kirk Douglas

Man pines to live but cannot endure the
days of his life.
Edward Dahlberg

Life is like an onion: you peel it off one
layer at a time, and sometimes you
weep.
Carl Sandburg

Life is a gamble, at terrible odds—if it
was a bet you wouldn't take it.
Tom Stoppard

Life is an unanswered question, but let's
believe in the dignity and importance of
the question.
Tennessee Williams

The purpose of life is the expansion of
happiness.
Maharishi Mahesh Yogi

Life is like going through a girl's room; a
rambling mess as far as you can see.
Laurie Faure, age 12

Love

Try to reason about love, and you will
lose your reason.
French proverb

It is impossible to love and be wise.
Francis Bacon

We perceive when love begins and when
it declines by our embarrassment when
alone together.
Jean de La Bruyère

The first sigh of love is the last of
wisdom.
Antoine Bret

Love is the whole history of a woman's
life; it is only an episode in man's.
Madame de Staël

The magic of first love is our ignorance
that it can never end.
Benjamin Disraeli

Men always want to be a woman's first
love—women like to be a man's last
romance.
Oscar Wilde

Love is simple to understand if you
haven't got a mind soft and full of
holes. It's a crutch, that's all, and there
isn't a one of us doesn't need a crutch.
Norman Mailer

In love the paradox occurs that two
beings become one and yet remain two.
Erich Fromm

Love is the child of freedom, never that
of domination.
Erich Fromm

There is hardly any activity, any
enterprise, which is started with such
tremendous hopes and expectations, and
yet which fails so regularly, as love.
Erich Fromm

Love is an act of endless forgiveness, a
tender look which becomes a habit.
Peter Ustinov

Love is that condition in which the
happiness of another person is essential
to your own.
Robert A. Heinlein

Love dies only when growth stops.
Pearl S. Buck

People think love is an emotion. Love is good sense.

Ken Kesey

We receive love—from our children as well as others—not in proportion to our demands or sacrifices or needs, but roughly in proportion to our own capacity to love.

Rollo May

Man

Men should not care too much for good looks; neglect is becoming.

Ovid

Men, in general, are but great children.

Napoleon I

Show me the man you honor, and I will know what kind of a man you are, for it shows me what your ideal of manhood is, and what kind of a man you long to be.

Thomas Carlyle

A man who has no office to go to—I don't care who he is—is a trial of which you can have no conception.

George Bernard Shaw

Men don't understand, as a rule, that women like to get used to them by degrees.

John Oliver Hobbes

Male, n.   A member of the unconsidered, or negligible sex. The male of the human race is commonly known (to the female) as Mere Man. The genus has two varieties: good providers and bad providers.

Ambrose Bierce

Men build bridges and throw railroads across deserts, and yet they contend successfully that the job of sewing on a button is beyond them.

Heywood Broun

The great truth is that women actually like men, and men can never believe it.

Isabel Paterson

A man who has nothing to do with women is always incomplete.

Cyril Connolly

There's nothing so stubborn as a man when you want him to do something.

Jean Giraudoux

Manliness is not all swagger and swearing and mountain climbing. Manliness is also tenderness, gentleness, consideration.

Robert Anderson

I like a man who can cry. My father cried. My brother Rusty cries.

Jessamyn West

Men are more conventional than women and much slower to change their ideas.

Kathleen Norris

They say women talk too much. If you have worked in Congress you know that the filibuster was invented by men.

Clare Boothe Luce

A strong man doesn't have to be dominant toward a woman. He doesn't match his strength against a woman weak with love for him. He matches it against the world.

Marilyn Monroe

The male stereotype makes masculinity not just a fact of biology but something that must be proved and re-proved, a continual quest for an ever-receding Holy Grail.

Marc Feigen Fasteau

Marriage

There is nothing nobler or more admirable than when two people who see eye to eye keep house as man and wife, confounding their enemies and delighting their friends.

Homer

It is mind, not body, that makes marriage last.

Publilius Syrus

Keep thy eyes wide open before marriage, and half shut afterwards.

Benjamin Franklin

Men and women, in marrying, make a vow to love one another. Would it not be better for their happiness if they made a vow to please one another?

Stanislas I, King of Poland

If you marry, you will regret it; if you do not marry, you will also regret it.

Søren Kierkegaard

Marriage is the perfection which love aimed at, ignorant of what it sought.

Ralph Waldo Emerson

It doesn't much signify whom one marries, for one is sure to find next morning that it was someone else.

Samuel Rogers

Married and unmarried women waste a great deal of time in feeling sorry for each other.

Myrtle Reed

A good marriage is that in which each appoints the other guardian of his solitude.

Rainer Maria Rilke

Love seems the swiftest, but it is the slowest of all growths. No man or woman really knows what perfect love is until they have been married a quarter of a century.

Mark Twain

A man who marries a woman to educate her falls a victim to the same fallacy as the woman who marries a man to reform him.

Elbert Hubbard

It is really asking too much of a woman to expect her to bring up a husband and her children too.

Lilian Bell

The dread of loneliness is greater than the fear of bondage, so we get married.

Cyril Connolly

Before marriage, a man declares that he would lay down his life to serve you; after marriage, he won't even lay down his newspaper to talk to you.

Helen Rowland

The complaints which anyone voices against his mate indicate exactly the qualities which stimulated attraction before marriage.

Rudolf Dreikurs

In a successful marriage, there is no such thing as one's way. There is only the way of both, only the bumpy, dusty, difficult, but always mutual path.

Phyllis McGinley

Marriage is like a three-speed gearbox: affection, friendship, love. It is not advisable to crash your gears and go right through to love straightaway. You need to ease your way through. The basis of love is respect, and that needs to be learned from affection and friendship.

Peter Ustinov

A good marriage is one which allows for change and growth in the individuals and in the way they express their love.

Pearl S. Buck

The best of all possible marriages is a seesaw in which first one, then the other partner is dominant.

Dr. Joyce Brothers

All husbands are alike, but they have different faces so you can tell them apart.

Anonymous

We sleep in separate rooms, we have dinner apart, we take separate vacations—we're doing everything we can to keep our marriage together.

Rodney Dangerfield

Marrying a man is like buying something you've been admiring for a long time in a shop window. You may love it when you get home, but it doesn't always go with everything else in the house.

Jean Kerr

Marriage is a half step, a way to leave home without losing home.

Gail Sheehy

Marriage is an edifice that must be rebuilt every day.

André Maurois

A successful marriage is not a gift; it is an achievement.

Ann Landers

Mercy

In case of doubt it is best to lean to the side of mercy.

Legal maxim

The merciful man doeth good to his own soul.

Proverbs 11 : 17

It is impossible to imagine anything which better becomes a ruler than mercy.

Marcus Annaeus Seneca

Mercy passeth right.

Geoffrey Chaucer

The quality of mercy is not strained;
It droppeth as the gentle rain from
  heaven
Upon the place beneath. It is twice
  blessed—
It blesseth him that gives, and him that
  takes.

William Shakespeare

Less pleasure take brave minds in battles
  won,
Than in restoring such as are undone;
Tigers have courage, and the rugged bear,
But man alone can, whom he conquers,
  spare.

Edmund Waller

Cowards are cruel, but the brave
Love mercy and delight to save.

John Gay

Pour not water on a drowning mouse.

Thomas Fuller

Teach me to feel another's woe,
To hide the fault I see;
That mercy I to others show,
That mercy show to me.

Alexander Pope

We hand folks over to God's mercy, and show none ourselves.

George Eliot

Mind

The mind covers more ground than the heart but goes less far.

Chinese proverb

Rule your mind or it will rule you.

Horace

It is good to rub and polish your mind against the minds of others.

Michel Eyquem de Montaigne

The mind has great influence over the body, and maladies often have their origin there.

Molière

A feeble mind weakens the body.

Jean Jacques Rousseau

Minds differ still more than faces.

Voltaire

The mind is but a barren soil—a soil which is soon exhausted, and will produce no crop, or only one, unless it be continually fertilized and enriched with foreign matter.

Sir Joshua Reynolds

The direction of the mind is more important than its progress.

Joseph Joubert

Little minds are interested in the extraordinary; great minds in the commonplace.

Elbert Hubbard

Men are not prisoners of fate, but only prisoners of their own minds.

Franklin Delano Roosevelt

We should take care not to make the intellect our god; it has, of course, powerful muscles, but no personality.

Albert Einstein

The mind is the expression of the soul, which belongs to God and must be let alone by government.

Adlai E. Stevenson II

The grand thing about the human mind is that it can turn its own tables and see meaninglessness as ultimate meaning.

John Cage

Our minds are like crows. They pick up everything that glitters, no matter how uncomfortable our nets get with all that metal in them.

Thomas Merton

Many creatures have brains. Man alone has mind.

Buckminster Fuller

The way the human mind ordinarily works, in apparent contempt of the logicians, is *conclusion first, premises afterwards.*

Joseph Rickaby

Money

If rich people could hire other people to die for them, the poor could make a wonderful living.

Yiddish proverb

Money's the wise man's religion.

Euripides

The love of money is the root of all evil.

I Timothy 6 : 10

Money alone sets all the world in motion.

Publilius Syrus

The populace may hiss me, but when I go home and think of my money I applaud myself.

Horace

Money you know will hide many faults.

Miguel de Cervantes

No man will take counsel, but every man will take money; therefore money is better than counsel.

Jonathan Swift

Money makes not so many true friends as real enemies.

Thomas Fuller

If thou wouldst keep money, save money;
If thou wouldst reap money, sow money.

Thomas Fuller

He that is of opinion money will do everything may well be suspected of doing everything for money.

Benjamin Franklin

Money is a good servant but a bad master.

H. G. Bohn

He who has money has in his pocket those who have none.

Leo Tolstoy

I finally know what distinguishes man from the other beasts: financial worries.

Jules Renard

I'm opposed to millionaires, but it would be dangerous to offer me the position.

Mark Twain

Some men worship rank, some worship heroes, some worship power, some worship God, and over these ideals they dispute—but they all worship money.

Mark Twain

To learn the value of money, it is not necessary to know the nice things it can get for you, you have to have experienced the trouble of getting it.

Philippe Hériat

If you would know what the Lord God thinks of money, you have only to look at those to whom he gives it.

Maurice Baring

Money is not an aphrodisiac: the desire it may kindle in the female eye is more for the cash than the carrier.

Marya Mannes

There was a time when a fool and his money were soon parted, but now it happens to everybody.

Adlai E. Stevenson II

Money does not make you happy but it quiets the nerves.

Sean O'Casey

The man who damns money has obtained it dishonorably; the man who respects it has earned it.

Ayn Rand

The more money an American accumulates, the less interesting he becomes.

Gore Vidal

Morality

Be not too hasty to trust or to admire the teachers of morality: they discourse like angels, but they live like men.

Samuel Johnson

All sects differ, because they come from men; morality is everywhere the same, because it comes from God.

Voltaire

Whenever you are to do a thing, though it can never be known but to yourself, ask yourself how you would act were all the world looking at you, and act accordingly.

Thomas Jefferson

If only a tenth part of the morality that is in books existed in the heart!

Georg Christoph Lichtenberg

The great secret of morals is love.

Percy Bysshe Shelley

The foundation of morality is to have done, once and for all, with lying.

Thomas Henry Huxley

Morality is the best of all devices for leading mankind by the nose.

Friedrich Nietzsche

If your morals make you dreary, depend upon it, they are wrong.

Robert Louis Stevenson

Morality is a private and costly luxury.

Henry Brooks Adams

It is not best that we use our morals week days; it gets them out of repair for Sundays.

Mark Twain

What is moral is what you feel good after and what is immoral is what you feel bad after.

Ernest Hemingway

We must never delude ourselves into thinking that physical power is a substitute for moral power, which is the true sign of national greatness.

Adlai E. Stevenson II

The only immorality is to not do what one has to do when one has to do it.

Jean Anouilh

Morality is always higher than law and we cannot forget this ever.

Alexander Solzhenitsyn

I would define morality as enlightened self-interest. . . . That old Platonic ideal that there are certain pure moral forms just isn't where we are.

Andrew Young

Mother

In the eyes of its mother every beetle is a gazelle.

Moroccan proverb

Mother is the name for God in the lips and hearts of little children.

William Makepeace Thackeray

The mother's heart is the child's schoolroom.

Henry Ward Beecher

The hand that rocks the cradle
Is the hand that rules the world.
    W. R. Wallace

It is impossible for any woman to love her children twenty-four hours a day.
    Milton R. Sapirstein

We never make sport of religion, politics, race, or mothers. A mother never gets hit with a custard pie. Mothers-in-law—yes. But mothers—never.
    Mack Sennett

Some are kissing mothers and some are scolding mothers, but it is love just the same, and most mothers kiss and scold together.
    Pearl S. Buck

My mother was dead for five years before I knew that I loved her very much.
    Lillian Hellman

My mother was a wit, but never a sentimental one. Once, when somebody in our house stepped on our cat's paw, she turned to the cat and said sternly, "I *told* you not to go around barefoot."
    Zero Mostel

No matter how old a mother is she watches her middle-aged children for signs of improvement.
    Florida Scott-Maxwell

Nation

The ruin of a nation begins in the homes of its people.
    Ashanti proverb

Nothing is good for a nation but that which arises from its own core and its own general wants, without apish imitation of another.
    Johann Wolfgang von Goethe

A nation never falls but by suicide.
    Ralph Waldo Emerson

A nation may be said to consist of its territory, its people, and its laws. The territory is the only part which is of certain durability.
    Abraham Lincoln

Individualities may form communities, but it is institutions alone that can create a nation.
    Benjamin Disraeli

We can afford to exercise the self-restraint of a really great nation which realizes its own strength and scorns to misuse it.
    Woodrow Wilson

The driving force of a nation lies in its spiritual purpose, made effective by free, tolerant but unremitting national will.
    Franklin Delano Roosevelt

A nation can be no stronger abroad than she is at home. Only an America which practices what it preaches about equal rights and social justice will be respected by those whose choice affects our future.
    John Fitzgerald Kennedy

Men may be linked in friendship.
Nations are linked only by interests.
    Rolf Hochhuth

Nations, like individuals, have to limit their objectives, or take the consequences.
    James Reston

Nature

"Sail!" quoth the king; "Hold!" saith the wind.
    English proverb

Those things are better which are perfected by nature than those which are finished by art.
    Cicero

Nature is the art of God.
    Dante Alighieri

Let us permit nature to have her way: she understands her business better than we do.
    Michel Eyquem de Montaigne

Nature, to be commanded, must be obeyed.

Francis Bacon

Nature seldom gives us the very best; for that we must have recourse to art.

Baltasar Gracián

Nature has some perfections, to show that she is the image of God; and some defects, to show that she is only His image.

Blaise Pascal

Nature never quite goes along with us. She is sombre at weddings, sunny at funerals, and she frowns on ninety-nine out of a hundred picnics.

Alexander Smith

I do not believe that Nature has a heart; and I suspect that, like many another beauty, she has been credited with a heart because of her face.

Francis Thompson

Nature is entirely indifferent to any reform. She perpetuates a fault as persistently as a virtue.

Charles Dudley Warner

Forget not that the earth delights to feel your bare feet and the winds long to play with your hair.

Kahlil Gibran

When I realize how invigorating contact with the earth may sometimes be, I find myself wondering how humanity ever consented to come so far away from the jungle.

Ellen Glasgow

There is no forgiveness in nature.

Ugo Betti

Man masters nature not by force but by understanding.

Jacob Bronowski

The natural world is dynamic. From the expanding universe to the hair on a baby's head, nothing is the same from now to the next moment.

Helen Hoover

Man is wise and constantly in quest of more wisdom; but the ultimate wisdom, which deals with beginnings, remains locked in a seed. There it lies, the simplest fact of the universe and at the same time the one which calls forth faith rather than reason.

Hal Borland

Obedience

Learn to obey before you command.

Solon

Obedience is the mother of success, the wife of safety.

Aeschylus

He who yields a prudent obedience, exercises a partial control.

Publilius Syrus

He who obeys with modesty will be worthy some day of being allowed to command.

Cicero

The man who does something under orders is not unhappy; he is unhappy who does something against his will.

Marcus Annaeus Seneca

Let them obey that know not how to rule.

William Shakespeare

The height of ability in the least able consists in knowing how to submit to the good leadership of others.

François de La Rochefoucauld

Theirs not to make reply,
Theirs not to reason why,
Theirs but to do and die.

Alfred, Lord Tennyson

You cannot be a true man until you learn to obey.

Robert E. Lee

The man who obeys is nearly always better than the man who commands.

Ernest Renan

This free will business is a bit terrifying anyway. It's almost pleasanter to obey, and make the most of it.

Ugo Betti

Old Age

Old age has a great sense of calm and freedom. When the passions have relaxed their hold you have escaped, not from one master, but from many.

Plato

With the ancient is wisdom; and in length of days understanding.

Job 12 : 12

No one is so old that he does not think he could live another year.

Cicero

Old men like to give good advice in order to console themselves for not being any longer able to set bad examples.

François de La Rochefoucauld

We hope to grow old, and yet we dread old age.

Jean de La Bruyère

Old men and comets have been reverenced for the same reason: their long beards, and pretences to foretell events.

Jonathan Swift

Regrets are the natural property of grey hairs.

Charles Dickens

As we grow old, . . . the beauty steals inward.

Ralph Waldo Emerson

Grow old along with me!
The best is yet to be,
The last of life, for which the first was made.

Robert Browning

Before you contradict an old man, my fair friend, you should endeavour to understand him.

George Santayana

Old age has its pleasures, which, though different, are not less than the pleasures of youth.

W. Somerset Maugham

To me, old age is always fifteen years older than I am.

Bernard Baruch

Growing old is no more than a bad habit which a busy man has no time to form.

André Maurois

Old age is like everything else. To make a success of it, you've got to start young.

Fred Astaire

Old age isn't so bad when you consider the alternative.

Maurice Chevalier

Old age is like a plane flying through a storm. Once you're aboard, there's nothing you can do.

Golda Meir

You're never too old to become younger.

Mae West

Opinion

Every man values himself more than all the rest of men, but he always values others' opinion of himself more than his own.

Marcus Aurelius

Where there is much desire to learn, there of necessity will be much arguing, much writing, many opinions; for opinion in good men is but knowledge in the making.

John Milton

We credit scarcely any persons with good sense except those who are of our opinion.

François de La Rochefoucauld

New opinions are always suspected, and usually opposed, without any other reason but because they are not already common.

John Locke

Singularity in right hath ruined many: happy those who are convinced of the general opinion.

Benjamin Franklin

One must judge men not by their opinions, but by what their opinions have made of them.

Georg Christoph Lichtenberg

His opinions were as pliant as his bows.

Frances Burney

No man ought to be molested on account of his opinions, not even on account of his religious opinions, provided his avowal of them does not disturb the public order established by the law.

Declaration of the Rights of Man by The French National Assembly (1789)

A man's opinions are generally of much more value than his arguments.

Oliver Wendell Holmes, Sr.

There is no greater mistake than the hasty conclusion that opinions are worthless because they are badly argued.

Thomas Henry Huxley

It is only about things that do not interest one that one can give a really unbiased opinion, which is no doubt the reason why an unbiased opinion is always absolutely valueless.

Oscar Wilde

It were not best that we should all think alike; it is difference of opinion that makes horse-races.

Mark Twain

In all matters of opinion our adversaries are insane.

Mark Twain

Refusing to have an opinion is a way of having one, isn't it?

Luigi Pirandello

Opinion is that exercise of the human will which helps us to make a decision without information.

John Erskine

We tolerate differences of opinion in people who are familiar to us. But differences of opinion in people we do not know sound like heresy or plots.

Brooks Atkinson

Pain

An hour of pain is as long as a day of pleasure.

English proverb

Who, except the gods,
can live time through forever without
any pain?

Aeschylus

If you are distressed by anything external, the pain is not due to the thing itself but to your own estimate of it; and this you have the power to revoke at any moment.

Marcus Aurelius

Those who do not feel pain seldom think that it is felt.

Samuel Johnson

Pleasure is often a visitant; but pain
Clings cruelly to us.

John Keats

He preaches patience that never knew pain.

H. G. Bohn

To render ourselves insensible to pain we must forfeit also the possibility of happiness.

Sir John Lubbock

Behind joy and laughter there may be a temperament, coarse, hard and callous. But behind sorrow there is always sorrow. Pain, unlike pleasure, wears no mask.

Oscar Wilde

Pain and suffering do not ennoble the human spirit. Pain and suffering breed meanness, bitterness, cruelty. It is only happiness that ennobles.

W. Somerset Maugham

Pain and death are a part of life. To reject them is to reject life itself.

Havelock Ellis

Pain makes man think. Thought makes man wise. Wisdom makes life endurable.

John Patrick

Man endures pain as an undeserved punishment; woman accepts it as a natural heritage.

Author unknown

Parents

The toil undertaken for a parent should not be remembered.

Sophocles

The joys of parents are secret, and so are their griefs and fears: they cannot utter the one, nor they will not utter the other.

Francis Bacon

We never know the love of our parents for us till we have become parents.

Henry Ward Beecher

Where parents do too much for their children, the children will not do much for themselves.

Elbert Hubbard

Parentage is a very important profession; but no test of fitness for it is ever imposed in the interest of the children.

George Bernard Shaw

It is not enough for parents to understand children. They must accord children the privilege of understanding them.

Milton R. Sapirstein

Romance fails us and so do friendships, but the relationship of parent and child, less noisy than all others, remains indelible and indestructible, the strongest relationship on earth.

Theodor Reik

The ideal of American parenthood is to be a kid with your kid.

Shana Alexander

The world talks to the mind. Parents speak more intimately—they talk to the heart.

Haim Ginott

Wonderful people do not always make wonderful parents.

Abraham Maslow

Parents are the bones on which children cut their teeth.

Peter Ustinov

Patience

Patience is a bitter plant but it has sweet fruit.

German proverb

Patience is the companion of wisdom.

Saint Augustine

Patience accomplishes its object, while hurry speeds to its ruin.

Saadi

All men commend patience, although few be willing to practise it.

Thomas a Kempis

A man must learn to endure that patiently which he cannot avoid conveniently.

Michel Eyquem de Montaigne

How poor are they that have not
 patience.
What wound did ever heal but by
 degrees?

William Shakespeare

Patience and delay achieve more than force and rage.

Jean de La Fontaine

All commend patience, but none can endure to suffer.

Thomas Fuller

Patience is the art of hoping.

Marquis de Vauvenargues

He that can have patience can have what he will.

Benjamin Franklin

Patience is bitter, but its fruits are sweet.
Jean Jacques Rousseau

Our patience will achieve more than our force.
Edmund Burke

The first virtue: patience. Nothing to do with simple waiting. It is more like obstinacy.
André Gide

Patience, n.   A minor form of despair, disguised as a virtue.
Ambrose Bierce

A wise man does not try to hurry history. Many wars have been avoided by patience and many have been precipitated by reckless haste.
Adlai E. Stevenson II

You can't set a hen in one morning and have chicken salad for lunch.
George Humphrey

Peace

A bad peace is better than a good war.
Russian proverb

He knows peace who has forgotten desire.
Bhagavad-Gita

Peace is liberty in tranquillity.
Cicero

The passions that incline men to peace are fear of death, desire of such things as are necessary to commodious living, and a hope by their industry to obtain them.
Thomas Hobbes

'Tis safest making peace with sword in hand.
George Farquhar

Better a lean peace than a fat victory.
Thomas Fuller

It is madness for a sheep to treat of peace with a wolf.
Thomas Fuller

Peace hath higher tests of manhood
Than battle ever knew.
John Greenleaf Whittier

If peace cannot be maintained with honor, it is no longer peace.
Lord John Russell

Peace is better than a place in history.
Justo Pastor Benítez

You may call for peace as loudly as you wish, but where there is no brotherhood there can in the end be no peace.
Max Lerner

Peace is when time doesn't matter as it passes by.
Maria Schell

We are going to have peace even if we have to fight for it.
Dwight David Eisenhower

Arms alone are not enough to keep the peace. It must be kept by men.
John Fitzgerald Kennedy

There is no way to peace. Peace is the way.
A. J. Muste

You cannot shake hands with a clenched fist.
Indira Gandhi

If you want to make peace, you don't talk to your friends. You talk to your enemies.
Moshe Dayan

Philosophy

Philosophy is the cultivation of the mental faculties; it roots out vices and prepares the mind to receive proper seed.
Cicero

The beginning of philosophy is the recognition of the conflict between opinions.
Epictetus

Wonder is the foundation of all philosophy, inquiry the progress, ignorance the end.

Michel Eyquem de Montaigne

There is nothing so strange and so unbelievable that it has not been said by one philosopher or another.

René Descartes

To make light of philosophy is to be a true philosopher.

Blaise Pascal

When one man speaks to another man who doesn't understand him, and when the man who's speaking no longer understands, it's metaphysics.

Voltaire

The first step towards philosophy is incredulity.

Denis Diderot

To be a philosopher is not merely to have subtle thoughts, nor even to found a school, but so to love wisdom as to live according to its dictates, a life of simplicity, independence, magnanimity, and trust.

Henry David Thoreau

Philosophy goes no further than probabilities, and in every assertion keeps a doubt in reserve.

James Anthony Froude

All philosophies, if you ride them home, are nonsense; but some are greater nonsense than others.

Samuel Butler

Philosophy, n. A route of many roads leading from nowhere to nothing.

Ambrose Bierce

A great philosophy is not a flawless philosophy, but a fearless one.

Charles Péguy

The object of studying philosophy is to know one's own mind, not other people's.

William Ralph Inge

There is an enormous need for philosophies to be rethought in the light of the changing conditions of mankind.

Alfred North Whitehead

The great philosophers are poets who believe in the reality of their poems.

Antonio Machado

Pleasure

The pleasure that is safest is the least pleasant.

Ovid

There is no such thing as pure pleasure; some anxiety always goes with it.

Ovid

No pleasure is fully delightful without communication, and no delight absolute except imparted.

Michel Eyquem de Montaigne

Do not bite at the bait of pleasure till you know there is no hook beneath it.

Thomas Jefferson

One half of the world cannot understand the pleasures of the other.

Jane Austen

We may lay in a stock of pleasures, as we would lay in a stock of wine; but if we defer tasting them too long, we shall find that both are soured by age.

Charles Caleb Colton

Most men pursue pleasure with such breathless haste that they hurry past it.

Søren Kierkegaard

The great pleasure in life is doing what people say you cannot do.

Walter Bagehot

There are two things to aim at in life: first, to get what you want; and, after that, to enjoy it. Only the wisest of mankind achieve the second.

Logan Pearsall Smith

A bookworm in bed with a new novel and a good reading lamp is as much prepared for pleasure as a pretty girl at a college dance.

Phyllis McGinley

Enjoyment is *not* a goal, it is a feeling that accompanies important ongoing activity.

Paul Goodman

Mankind is safer when men seek pleasure than when they seek the power and the glory.

Geoffrey Gorer

People seem to enjoy things more when they know a lot of other people have been left out on the pleasure.

Russell Baker

Pleasure is not happiness. It has no more importance than a shadow following a man.

Muhammad Ali

Politics

The good of man must be the end of the science of politics.

Aristotle

Persistence in one opinion has never been considered a merit in political leaders.

Cicero

Politics is such a torment that I would advise every one I love not to mix with it.

Thomas Jefferson

Contact with the affairs of state is one of the most corrupting of the influences to which men are exposed.

James Fenimore Cooper

Politics is the doctrine of the possible, the attainable.

Otto von Bismarck

Politics makes strange bedfellows.

Charles Dudley Warner

Politics is perhaps the only profession for which no preparation is thought necessary.

Robert Louis Stevenson

The politician is an acrobat. He keeps his balance by saying the opposite of what he does.

Maurice Barrès

Politics, and the fate of mankind, are shaped by men without ideals and without greatness. Men who have greatness within them don't go in for politics.

Albert Camus

When the political columnists say "Every thinking man" they mean themselves, and when the candidates appeal to "Every intelligent voter" they mean everybody who is going to vote for them.

Franklin P. Adams

A politician is a man who understands government, and it takes a politician to run a government. A statesman is a politician who's been dead 10 or 15 years.

Harry S. Truman

Politicians are the same all over. They promise to build a bridge even where there is no river.

Nikita Khrushchev

The end of all political effort must be the well-being of the individual in a life of safety and freedom.

Dag Hammarskjöld

Since a politician never believes what he says, he is surprised when others believe him.

Charles de Gaulle

Politics are almost as exciting as war, and quite as dangerous. In war, you can only be killed once, but in politics many times.

Sir Winston Churchill

A political leader must keep looking over his shoulder all the time to see if the boys are still there. If they aren't still there, he's no longer a political leader.

Bernard Baruch

Politics is war without bloodshed while war is politics with bloodshed.

Mao Tse-tung

Experience suggests that the first rule of politics is never to say never. The ingenious human capacity for maneuver and compromise may make acceptable tomorrow what seems outrageous or impossible today.

William V. Shannon

Politics is the art of the possible.

Lyndon Baines Johnson

The difference between the men and the boys in politics is, and always has been, that the boys want to be something, while the men want to do something.

Eric Sevareid

I learned one thing in politics. If you go into it . . . then sooner or later you have to compromise. You either compromise or get out.

Hugh Sloan

Our national politics has become a competition for images or between images, rather than between ideals.

Daniel J. Boorstin

Power

O, it is excellent
To have a giant's strength; but it is tyrannous
To use it like a giant.

William Shakespeare

The sole advantage of power is that you can do more good.

Baltasar Gracián

Let not thy will roar when thy power can but whisper.

Thomas Fuller

In the general course of human nature, a power over a man's subsistence amounts to a power over his will.

Alexander Hamilton

Power is not happiness. Security and peace are more to be desired than a name at which nations tremble.

William Godwin

To know the pains of power, we must go to those who have it; to know its pleasures, we must go to those who are seeking.

Charles Caleb Colton

You shall have joy, or you shall have power, said God; you shall not have both.

Ralph Waldo Emerson

The highest proof of virtue is to possess boundless power without abusing it.

Thomas Babington Macaulay

Power tends to corrupt and absolute power corrupts absolutely.

Lord Acton

The only prize much cared for by the powerful is power. The prize of the general is not a bigger tent, but command.

Oliver Wendell Holmes, Jr.

The possession of unlimited power will make a despot of almost any man. There is a possible Nero in the gentlest human creature that walks.

Thomas Bailey Aldrich

A friend in power is a friend lost.

Henry Brooks Adams

The sense of power is an essential element in all pleasure, as consciousness of defeat is always painful.

John Lancaster Spalding

Our sense of power is more vivid when we break a man's spirit than when we win his heart.

Eric Hoffer

We can't do without dominating others or being served. . . . Even the man on the bottom rung still has his wife, or his child. If he's a bachelor, his dog. The essential thing, in sum, is being able to get angry without the other person being able to answer back.

Albert Camus

The problem of power is how to achieve its responsible use rather than its irresponsible and indulgent use—of how to get men of power to live *for* the public rather than *off* the public.

Robert Francis Kennedy

The real power is to make people say yes to you when they want to say no.

Julian Bond

Praise

He who praises you for what you have not wishes to take from you what you have.

Don Juan Manuel

He who refuses praise only wants to be praised again.

François de La Rochefoucauld

There's no praise to beat the sort you can put in your pocket.

Molière

There can hardly be imagined a more desirable pleasure than that of praise unmixed with any possibility of flattery.

Richard Steele

Be not extravagantly high in expression of thy commendations of men thou likest; it may make the hearer's stomach rise.

Thomas Fuller

Praise, though it be our due, is not like a bank-bill, to be paid upon demand; to be valuable, it must be voluntary.

Colley Cibber

Praise, like gold and diamonds, owes its value only to its scarcity.

Samuel Johnson

Among the smaller duties of life I hardly know any one more important than that of not praising where praise is not due.

Sydney Smith

Applause is the spur of noble minds, the end and aim of weak ones.

Charles Caleb Colton

Expect not praise without envy until you are dead.

Charles Caleb Colton

Pride

Pride is the mask of one's own faults.

Hebrew proverb

Pride goeth before destruction, and a haughty spirit before a fall.

Proverbs 16 : 18

There is but a step between a proud man's glory and his disgrace.

Publilius Syrus

If we had no pride we should not complain of that of others.

François de La Rochefoucauld

It is as proper to have pride in oneself as it is ridiculous to show it to others.

François de La Rochefoucauld

Pride is a kind of pleasure produced by a man thinking too well of himself.

Baruch Spinoza

Pride and grace dwelt never in one place.

James Kelly

The proud hate pride—in others.

Benjamin Franklin

Pride, like the magnet, constantly points to one object, self; but, unlike the magnet, it has no attractive pole, but at all points repels.

Charles Caleb Colton

There are two sorts of pride: one in which we approve ourselves, the other in which we cannot accept ourselves.

Henri Frédéric Amiel

Pride is at the bottom of all great mistakes.

John Ruskin

There was one who thought he was above me, and he was above me until he had that thought.

Elbert Hubbard

Progress

Progress is only possible in those happy cases where the force of legality has gone far enough to bind the nation together, but not far enough to kill out all varieties and destroy nature's perpetual tendency to change.

Walter Bagehot

Every step forward is made at the cost of mental and physical pain to someone.

Friedrich Nietzsche

All progress is based upon a universal innate desire on the part of every organism to live beyond its income.

Samuel Butler

Progress is the realization of Utopias.

Oscar Wilde

Progress needs the brakeman, but the brakeman should not spend all his time putting on the brakes.

Elbert Hubbard

There is no greater disloyalty to the great pioneers of human progress than to refuse to budge an inch from where they stood.

William Ralph Inge

What we call progress is the exchange of one nuisance for another nuisance.

Havelock Ellis

Progress might have been all right once, but it's gone on too long.

Ogden Nash

The ordinary affairs of men proceed if they do not always progress.

Eric Sevareid

The idea of progress is not merely a dream unfulfilled but an inherent absurdity.

Philip Slater

The human mind, in attempting to free itself from the shackles of error, ignorance and superstition, brings about great social and political advances that are properly called progress.

Charles Van Doren

Prudence

No one tests the depth of a river with both feet.

Ashanti proverb

People who live in glass houses should not throw stones.

English proverb

He that fights and runs away
Will live to fight another day.

Old English rhyme

Consider the little mouse, how sagacious an animal it is which never entrusts its life to one hole only.

Plautus

The better part of valour is discretion.

William Shakespeare

Love all, trust a few, do wrong to none.

William Shakespeare

Prudence is but experience, which equal time equally bestows on all men, in those things they equally apply themselves.

Thomas Hobbes

If thou thinkest twice before thou speakest once, thou wilt speak twice the better for it.

William Penn

Distrust yourself, and sleep before you fight,
'Tis not too late tomorrow to be brave.

John Armstrong

Judgment is not upon all occasions
required, but discretion always is.
  Lord Chesterfield

I would rather worry without need than
live without heed.
  Pierre Augustin Cardon de Beaumarchais

Put all your eggs in one basket—and
watch that basket.
  Mark Twain

Prudence is sometimes stretched too far,
until it blocks the road of progress.
  Tehyi Hsieh

Quality

Good things cost less than bad ones.
  Italian proverb

It is quality rather than quantity that
matters.
  Lucius Annaeus Seneca

Things that have a common quality ever
quickly seek their kind.
  Marcus Aurelius

The quality of mercy is not strained;
It droppeth as the gentle rain from
  heaven
Upon the place beneath. It is twice
  blessed—
It blesseth him that gives, and him that
  takes.
  William Shakespeare

We should not judge of a man's merits
by his great qualities, but by the use he
makes of them.
  François de La Rochefoucauld

Quality, without quantity, is little
thought of.
  James Kelly

A man has generally the good or ill
qualities which he attributes to mankind.
  William Shenstone

One shining quality lends a lustre to
another, or hides some glaring defect.
  William Hazlitt

Nothing endures but noble qualities.
  Walt Whitman

It is easier to confess a defect than to
claim a quality.
  Max Beerbohm

Reason

Reason is the wise man's guide, example
the fool's.
  Welsh proverb

Reason commands us far more
imperiously than a master; in disobeying
the latter we are made unhappy, in
disobeying the former, fools.
  Blaise Pascal

Peace rules the day, where reason rules
the mind.
  William Collins

Swift instinct leaps; slow reason feebly
climbs.
  Edward Young

Reason deceives us more often than does
nature.
  Marquis de Vauvenargues

We may take Fancy for a companion,
but must follow Reason as our guide.
  Samuel Johnson

Error of opinion may be tolerated where
reason is left free to combat it.
  Thomas Jefferson

Reason is nothing but the analysis of
belief.
  Franz Peter Schubert

The man who listens to Reason is lost:
Reason enslaves all whose minds are not
strong enough to master her.
  George Bernard Shaw

Logic is one thing, the human
animal another.
  Luigi Pirandello

The golden rule is to test everything in the light of reason and experience, no matter from whom it comes.

Mohandas K. Gandhi

Reason in my philosophy is only a harmony among irrational impulses.

George Santayana

Reason cannot save us, nothing can; but reason can mitigate the cruelty of living.

Philip Rieff

Religion

Pure religion and undefiled before God and the Father is this, To visit the fatherless and widows in their affliction, and to keep himself unspotted from the world.

James 1 : 27

It is when we are in misery that we revere the gods; the prosperous seldom approach the altar.

Silius Italicus

Nature teaches us to love our friends, but religion our enemies.

Thomas Fuller

A life that will bear the inspection of men and of God, is the only certificate of true religion.

Samuel Johnson

Nothing is so fatal to religion as indifference.

Edmund Burke

Every sect is a moral check on its neighbor. Competition is as wholesome in religion as in commerce.

Walter Savage Landor

Men will wrangle for religion, write for it, fight for it, die for it; anything but live for it.

Charles Caleb Colton

There is only one religion, though there are a hundred versions of it.

George Bernard Shaw

The true laws of God are the laws of our own well-being.

Samuel Butler

In my religion there would be no exclusive doctrine; all would be love, poetry and doubt.

Cyril Connolly

It may be that religion is dead, and if it is, we had better know it and set ourselves to try to discover other sources of moral strength before it is too late.

Pearl S. Buck

Nobody can have the consolations of religion or philosophy unless he has first experienced their desolations.

Aldous Huxley

Religion is a candle inside a multicolored lantern. Everyone looks through a particular color, but the candle is always there.

Muhammad Naguib

The cosmic religious experience is the strongest and the noblest driving force behind scientific research.

Albert Einstein

All God's religions . . . have not been able to put mankind back together again.

John Cage

Responsibility

He who weighs his responsibilities can bear them.

Martial

The fault, dear Brutus, is not in our stars,
But in ourselves, that we are underlings.

William Shakespeare

The vast majority of persons of our race have a natural tendency to shrink from the responsibility of standing and acting alone.

Francis Galton

Few things help an individual more than to place responsibility upon him, and to let him know that you trust him.

Booker T. Washington

Responsibility, n. A detachable burden easily shifted to the shoulders of God, Fate, Fortune, Luck or one's neighbor. In the days of astrology it was customary to unload it upon a star.

Ambrose Bierce

To be a man is, precisely, to be responsible.

Antoine de Saint-Exupéry

Man's responsibility increases as that of the gods decreases.

André Gide

Today responsibility is often meant to denote duty, something imposed upon one another from the outside. But responsibility, in its true sense, is an entirely voluntary act; it is my response to the needs, expressed or unexpressed, of another human being.

Erich Fromm

Our privileges can be no greater than our obligations. The protection of our rights can endure no longer than the performance of our responsibilities.

John Fitzgerald Kennedy

Man must now assume the responsibility for his world. He can no longer shove it off on religious power.

Harvey Cox

The great thought, the great concern, the great anxiety of men is to restrict, as much as possible, the limits of their own responsibility.

Giosuè Borsi

It is our responsibilities, not ourselves, that we should take seriously.

Peter Ustinov

Sacrifice

Greater love hath no man than this, that a man lay down his life for his friends.

John 15 : 13

The same god who is propitiated by the blood of a hundred bulls is also propitiated by the smallest offering of incense.

Ovid

To make large sacrifices in big things is easy, but to make sacrifices in little things is what we are seldom capable of.

Johann Wolfgang von Goethe

Without sacrifice there is no resurrection. Nothing grows and blooms save by giving. All you try to save in yourself wastes and perishes.

André Gide

Self-sacrifice enables us to sacrifice other people without blushing.

George Bernard Shaw

Sacrificers are not the ones to pity. The ones to pity are those they sacrifice.

Elizabeth Bowen

The mice which helplessly find themselves between the cat's teeth acquire no merit from their enforced sacrifice.

Mohandas K. Gandhi

Many men have sacrificed everything to errors, and I have always thought that heroism and sacrifice were not enough to justify a cause. Obstinacy alone is not a virtue.

Albert Camus

What do the dangers or sacrifices of a man matter when the destiny of humanity is at stake?

Ché Guevara

Nothing is costly to one who does not count the cost.

Antonin G. Sertillanges

Sacrifice remains the solution of that which has no solution.

Jean Guitton

Service

The charity that is a trifle to us can be precious to others.

Homer

Had I but serv'd my God with half the
zeal
I serv'd my king, he would not in mine
age
Have left me naked to mine enemies.
  William Shakespeare and John Fletcher

To oblige persons often costs little and
helps much.
  Baltasar Gracián

They also serve who only stand and
wait.
  John Milton

I have the consolation of having added
nothing to my private fortune during my
public service, and of retiring with
hands as clean as they are empty.
  Thomas Jefferson

The noblest service comes from nameless
hands,
And the best servant does his work
unseen.
  Oliver Wendell Holmes, Sr.

You must act in your friend's interest
whether it pleases him or not; the object
of love is to serve, not to win.
  Woodrow Wilson

Human service is the highest form of
self-interest for the person who serves.
  Elbert Hubbard

A large part of altruism, even when it
is perfectly honest, is grounded upon
the fact that it is uncomfortable to
have unhappy people about one.
  H. L. Mencken

The pleasure we derive from doing
favors is partly in the feeling it gives us
that we are not altogether worthless.
  Eric Hoffer

To serve is beautiful, but only if it is
done with joy and a whole heart and a
free mind.
  Pearl S. Buck

I expect to pass through this world but
once. Any good therefore that I can do,
or any kindness that I can show to any
fellow creature, let me do it now. Let me
not defer or neglect it, for I shall not
pass this way again.
  Author unknown

Solitude

The earth is a beehive; we all enter by
the same door but live in different cells.
  African proverb

Solitude is the mother of anxieties.
  Publilius Syrus

He never is alone that is accompanied
with noble thoughts.
  Francis Beaumont and John Fletcher

Better be alone than in bad company.
  Thomas Fuller

To dare to live alone is the rarest
courage; since there are many who had
rather meet their bitterest enemy in the
field, than their own hearts in their
closet.
  Charles Caleb Colton

He who does not enjoy solitude will not
love freedom.
  Arthur Schopenhauer

I never found the companion that was
so companionable as solitude.
  Henry David Thoreau

I would rather sit on a pumpkin and
have it all to myself than be crowded on
a velvet cushion.
  Henry David Thoreau

What a commentary on our civilization,
when being alone is considered suspect;
when one has to apologize for it, make
excuses, hide the fact that one practices
it—like a secret vice!
  Anne Morrow Lindbergh

It is in solitude that the works of hand, heart and mind are always conceived, and in solitude that individuality must be affirmed.

Robert Lindner

You find in solitude only what you take to it.

Juan Ramón Jiménez

Solitude is the playfield of Satan.

Vladimir Nabokov

Solitary trees, if they grow at all, grow strong.

Sir Winston Churchill

The person who tries to live alone will not succeed as a human being. His heart withers if it does not answer another heart. His mind shrinks away if he hears only the echoes of his own thoughts and finds no other inspiration.

Pearl S. Buck

Sorrow

It is folly to tear one's hair in sorrow, as if grief could be assuaged by baldness.

Cicero

There is something pleasurable in calm remembrance of a past sorrow.

Cicero

He truly sorrows who sorrows unseen.

Martial

Sorrow breaks seasons and reposing hours,
Makes the night morning and the noontide night.

William Shakespeare

Gnarling sorrow hath less power to bite
The man that mocks at it and sets it light.

William Shakespeare

When sorrows come, they come not single spies,
But in battalions.

William Shakespeare

The pleasure that is in sorrow is sweeter than the pleasure of pleasure itself.

Percy Bysshe Shelley

Two in distress makes sorrow less.

H. G. Bohn

Sorrow makes us all children again.

Ralph Waldo Emerson

When a man or woman loves to brood over a sorrow and takes care to keep it green in their memory, you may be sure it is no longer a pain to them.

Jerome K. Jerome

One cannot be deeply responsive to the world without being saddened very often.

Erich Fromm

Sorrow you can hold, however desolating, if nobody speaks to you. If they speak, you break down.

Bede Jarrett

Soul

If I err in my belief that the souls of men are immortal, I err gladly, and I do not wish to lose so delightful an error.

Cicero

There is a god within each breast.

Ovid

What shall it profit a man, if he shall gain the whole world, and lose his own soul?

Mark 8 : 36

The soul is the mirror of an indestructible universe.

Gottfried Wilhelm Leibniz

There is one spectacle grander than the sea, that is the sky; there is one spectacle grander than the sky, that is the interior of the soul.

Victor Hugo

To think about the soul, to think about it at least once in the confusion of every crowded day, is indeed the beginning of salvation.

Georges Duhamel

Physical strength can never permanently withstand the impact of spiritual force.

Franklin Delano Roosevelt

It is with the soul that we grasp the essence of another human being, not with the mind, not even with the heart.

Henry Miller

We are very strange creatures, so strange that, in my opinion at least, not a philosopher of them all has written the first sentence in the book of the soul.

W. Macneile Dixon

The soul has its time and seasons and will not be forced: that which is its beatitude becomes its bunkum, and bunkum is seen to be beatitude the next day but one.

Stephen Mackenna

State

A prosperous state is an honor to the gods.

Aeschylus

The state exists for the sake of a good life, and not for the sake of life only.

Aristotle

Honest mediocrity is the most suitable condition for states; riches lead to softness and corruption.

Frederick the Great

A state without some means of change is without the means of its conservation.

Edmund Burke

The true wealth of a state consists in the number of its inhabitants, in their toil and industry.

Napoleon I

The state calls its own violence law, but that of the individual crime.

Max Stirner

Thou, too, sail on, O Ship of State!
Sail on, O Union, strong and great!
Humanity with all its fears,
With all the hopes of future years,
Is hanging breathless on thy fate!

Henry Wadsworth Longfellow

When all the fine phrases are stripped away, it appears that the state is only a group of men with human interests, passions, and desires, or, worse yet, the state is only an obscure clerk hidden in some corner of a governmental bureau. In either case the assumption of superhuman wisdom and virtue is proved false.

William Graham Sumner

The State is made for man, not man for the State.

Albert Einstein

The responsibility of great states is to serve and not to dominate the world.

Harry S. Truman

The modern state no longer has anything but rights; it does not recognize duties any more.

Georges Bernanos

Strength

These three things deplete man's strength: fear, travel, and sin.

Hebrew proverb

When strong, be merciful, if you would have the respect, not the fear of your neighbors.

Chilon

It is excellent
To have a giant's strength, but it is
    tyrannous
To use it like a giant.

William Shakespeare

What is strength without a double share of wisdom?

John Milton

We deceive ourselves when we fancy that only weakness needs support. Strength needs it far more.

Madame Swetchine

The strongest man on earth is he who stands most alone.

Henrik Ibsen

That cause is strong which has not a multitude, but one strong man behind it.

James Russell Lowell

Strong men can always afford to be gentle. Only the weak are intent on "giving as good as they get."

Elbert Hubbard

Our strength is often composed of the weakness we're damned if we're going to show.

Mignon McLaughlin

True strength is delicate.

Louise Nevelson

If we are strong, our character will speak for itself. If we are weak, words will be of no help.

John Fitzgerald Kennedy

It is not good to see people who have been pretending strength all their lives lose it even for a minute.

Lillian Hellman

Success

Success abides longer among men when it is planted by the hand of God.

Pindar

Constant success shows us but one side of the world. For as it surrounds us with friends who will tell us only our merits, so it silences those enemies from whom alone we can learn our defects.

Charles Caleb Colton

The way to secure success is to be more anxious about obtaining than about deserving it.

William Hazlitt

Success, as I see it, is a result, not a goal.

Gustave Flaubert

The ability to convert ideas to things is the secret of outward success.

Henry Ward Beecher

All you need in this life is ignorance and confidence, and then success is sure.

Mark Twain

The most important single ingredient in the formula of success is the knack of getting along with people.

Theodore Roosevelt

Virtue we still consider the best goal for others: but for ourselves, success.

Edward Verral Lucas

Pray that success will not come any faster than you are able to endure it.

Elbert Hubbard

There is nothing in the world that will take the chip off one's shoulder like a feeling of success.

Thomas Wolfe

The key to success isn't much good until one discovers the right lock to insert it in.

Tehyi Hsieh

Success is that old ABC—ability, breaks and courage.

Charles Luckman

Nothing recedes like success.

Walter Winchell

I don't know the key to success, but the key to failure is trying to please everybody.

Bill Cosby

Sweat plus sacrifice equals success.

Charles O. Finley

The fastest way to succeed is to look as if you're playing by other people's rules, while quietly playing by your own.

Michael Korda

Suffering

A man who suffers before it is
necessary, suffers more than is necessary.
  Marcus Annaeus Seneca

I reckon that the sufferings of this
present time are not worthy to be
compared with the glory which shall be
revealed in us.
  Romans 8 : 18

He who fears he shall suffer, already
suffers what he fears.
  Michel Eyquem de Montaigne

It requires more courage to suffer than
to die.
  Napoleon I

Suffering is the sole origin of
consciousness.
  Fyodor Mikhailovich Dostoevsky

What really raises one's indignation
against suffering is not suffering
intrinsically, but the senselessness of
suffering.
  Friedrich Nietzsche

Although the world is full of suffering,
it is also full of the overcoming of it.
  Helen Keller

We are healed of a suffering only by
experiencing it to the full.
  Marcel Proust

It is not true that suffering ennobles the
character; happiness does that
sometimes, but suffering, for the most
part, makes men petty and vindictive.
  W. Somerset Maugham

Nothing is more dear to them [men]
than their own suffering— They are
afraid that they will lose it— They feel
it, like a whip cracking over their heads,
striking them and yet befriending them;
it wounds them, but it also reassures
them.
  Ugo Betti

Most people get a fair amount of fun
out of their lives, but on balance life is
suffering, and only the very young or
the very foolish imagine otherwise.
  George Orwell

It is infinitely easier to suffer in
obedience to a human command than to
accept suffering as free, responsible men.
  Dietrich Bonhoeffer

We cannot live, sorrow or die for
somebody else, for suffering is too
precious to be shared.
  Edward Dahlberg

Sympathy

When you live next to the cemetery,
you cannot weep for everyone.
  Russian proverb

As man laughs with those that laugh, so
he weeps with those that weep; if thou
wish me to weep, thou must first shed
tears thyself; then thy sorrows will
touch me.
  Horace

We are so fond of each other because
our ailments are the same.
  Jonathan Swift

Dear honest Ned is in the gout,
Lies rack'd with pain, and you without:
How patiently you hear him groan!
How glad the case is not your own!
  Jonathan Swift

Teach me to feel another's woe,
To hide the fault I see:
That mercy I to others show,
That mercy show to me.
  Alexander Pope

Sympathy is a supporting atmosphere,
and in it we unfold easily and well.
  Ralph Waldo Emerson

The world has no sympathy with any
but positive griefs. It will pity you for
what you lose; never for what you lack.
  Madame Swetchine

Sympathy is the one emotion which seems most perfect as it becomes most animal: in its human aspect it too often lapses into the moralizing grandmother.

John Oliver Hobbes

There is nothing sweeter than to be sympathized with.

George Santayana

When you are in trouble, people who call to sympathize are really looking for the particulars.

Edgar Watson Howe

Pity may represent little more than the impersonal concern which prompts the mailing of a check, but true sympathy is the personal concern which demands the giving of one's soul.

Martin Luther King, Jr.

Nothing is more salutary for those who are in affliction than to become consolers.

Maurice Hulst

Talent

Talent without sense is a torch in folly's hand.

Welsh proverb

No one respects a talent that is concealed.

Desiderius Erasmus

There is no so wretched and coarse a soul wherein some particular faculty is not seen to shine.

Michel Eyquem de Montaigne

There is hardly anybody good for everything, and there is scarcely anybody who is absolutely good for nothing.

Lord Chesterfield

Talent is a gift which God has given us secretly, and which we reveal without perceiving it.

Montesquieu

Talent is a question of quantity. Talent does not write one page: it writes three hundred.

Jules Renard

Talent, I say, is what an actor needs. And talent is faith in oneself, one's own powers.

Maxim Gorki

It takes little talent to see clearly what lies under one's nose, a good deal of it to know in what direction to point that organ.

W. H. Auden

Everyone has a talent, what is rare is the courage to follow the talent to the dark place where it leads.

Erica Jong

Thousands of people have enough talent to become famous. It is the *need* to use it which is lacking.

Katharine Butler Hathaway

Technology

It is said that one machine can do the work of fifty ordinary men. No machine, however, can do the work of one extraordinary man.

Tehyi Hsieh

Electronic calculators can solve problems which the man who made them cannot solve; but no government-subsidized commission of engineers and physicists could create a worm.

Joseph Wood Krutch

If it [automation] keeps up, man will atrophy all his limbs but the push-button finger.

Frank Lloyd Wright

We cannot get grace from gadgets. In the bakelite house of the future, the dishes may not break, but the heart can. Even a man with ten shower baths may find life flat, stale and unprofitable.

John Boynton Priestley

If there is technological advance without social advance, there is, almost automatically, an increase in human misery.

Michael Harrington

Technological progress has merely provided us with more efficient means for going backwards.

Aldous Huxley

Humanity is acquiring the right technology for all the wrong reasons.

Buckminster Fuller

There is unquestionably a contradiction between an efficient technological machine and the flowering of human nature, of the human personality.

Arthur Miller

Technology was developed to prevent exhausting labor. It is now dedicated to trivial conveniences.

B. F. Skinner

We shall have a race of men who are strong on telemetry and space communications but who cannot read anything but a blueprint or write anything but a computer program.

John Kenneth Galbraith

We should now give some real thought to the possibility of reforming our technology in the directions of smallness, simplicity, and nonviolence.

E. F. Schumacher

Any sufficiently advanced technology is indistinguishable from magic.

Arthur C. Clarke

Technology or perish.

John R. Pierce

Thought

Learning without thought is labour lost; thought without learning is perilous.

Confucius

Our life is what our thoughts make it.

Marcus Aurelius

I think; therefore I am.

René Descartes

The secret thoughts of a man run over all things, holy, profane, clean, obscene, grave, and light, without shame or blame.

Thomas Hobbes

The thoughts that come often unsought, and, as it were, drop into the mind, are commonly the most valuable of any we have.

John Locke

Great thoughts come from the heart.

Marquis de Vauvenargues

Thought once awakened does not again slumber.

Thomas Carlyle

Profundity of thought belongs to youth, clarity of thought to old age.

Friedrich Nietzsche

I think that I think; therefore, I think I am.

Ambrose Bierce

One must live the way one thinks or end up thinking the way one has lived.

Paul Bourget

Thinking is the endeavor to capture reality by means of ideas.

José Ortega y Gasset

To think is to differ.

Clarence Darrow

What was once thought can never be unthought.

Friedrich Dürrenmatt

Where all think alike, no one thinks very much.

Walter Lippmann

Time

Time brings all things to pass.

Aeschylus

Time heals what reason cannot.

Lucius Annaeus Seneca

Time ripens all things. No man's born wise.

    Miguel de Cervantes

Gather ye rose-buds while ye may,
Old time is still a flying:
And this same flower that smiles today,
Tomorrow will be dying.

    Robert Herrick

But at my back I always hear
Time's wingèd chariot hurrying near.

    Andrew Marvell

Those who make the worst use of their time are the first to complain of its brevity.

    Jean de La Bruyère

Time is money.

    Benjamin Franklin

Dost thou love life, then do not squander time, for that's the stuff life is made of.

    Benjamin Franklin

Time makes more converts than reason.

    Thomas Paine

There is one kind of robber whom the law does not strike at, and who steals what is most precious to men: time.

    Napoleon I

One always has time enough, if only one applies it well.

    Johann Wolfgang von Goethe

Time deals gently only with those who take it gently.

    Anatole France

Half our life is spent trying to find something to do with the time we have rushed through life trying to save.

    Will Rogers

Killing time is the chief end of our society.

    Ugo Betti

Time is a merciless enemy, as it is also a merciless friend and healer.

    Mohandas K. Gandhi

Time is a storm in which we are all lost.

    William Carlos Williams

Time is not the fourth dimension, and should not be so identified. Time is only a relative observation.

    Buckminster Fuller

Trust

Do not trust the man who tells you all his troubles but keeps from you his joys.

    Hebrew proverb

Trust, like the soul, never returns, once it is gone.

    Pubilius Syrus

Love all, trust a few.

    William Shakespeare

The trust that we put in ourselves makes us feel trust in others.

    François de La Rochefoucauld

A man who doesn't trust himself can never really trust anyone else.

    Cardinal de Retz

Trust thyself only, and another shall not betray thee.

    Thomas Fuller

Trust men and they will be true to you; treat them greatly and they will show themselves great.

    Ralph Waldo Emerson

I prefer to have too much confidence, and thereby be deceived, than to be always mistrustful. For, in the first case, I suffer for a moment at being deceived and, in the second, I suffer constantly.

    Paul Gauguin

No man ever quite believes in any other man. One may believe in an idea absolutely, but not in a man.

    H. L. Mencken

To love means you also trust.

    Joan Baez

Don't trust anyone over thirty!

    Mario Savio

Truth

Every truth has two sides; it is well to look at both, before we commit ourselves to either.

    Aesop

Those who know the truth are not equal to those who love it.

    Confucius

. . . the truth shall make you free.

    John 8 : 32

Truth often suffers more by the heat of its defenders than from the arguments of its opposers.

    William Penn

Truth is no road to fortune.

    Jean Jacques Rousseau

Truth is always strange—stranger than fiction.

    Lord Byron

Truth is mighty and will prevail. There is nothing the matter with this, except that it ain't so.

    Mark Twain

To love the truth is to refuse to let oneself be saddened by it.

    André Gide

We taste and feel and see the truth. We do not reason ourselves into it.

    William Butler Yeats

I don't want any yes-men around me. I want everyone to tell me the truth— even though it costs him his job.

    Samuel Goldwyn

I am quite prepared to admit that, being habitual liars and self deluders, we have good cause to fear the truth.

    Saul Bellow

The truth believed is a lie. If you go around preaching the truth, you are lying. The truth can only be experienced.

    Werner Erhard

Truth is the glue that holds governments together. Compromise is the oil that makes governments go.

    Gerald R. Ford

The truth of a thing is the feel of it, not the think of it.

    Stanley Kubrick

The truth about a man lies first and foremost in what he hides.

    André Malraux

The best mind-altering drug is truth.

    Lily Tomlin

Truth is stranger than fiction, but not so popular.

    Author unknown

Understanding

If you would judge, understand.

    Lucius Annaeus Seneca

Time which diminishes all things increases understanding for the aging.

    Plutarch

Nothing can be loved or hated unless it is first known.

    Leonardo da Vinci

A moment's insight is sometimes worth a life's experience.

    Oliver Wendell Holmes, Sr.

Understanding is the beginning of approving.

    André Gide

Perfect understanding will sometimes almost extinguish pleasure.

    A. E. Housman

We can see through others only when we see through ourselves.

    Eric Hoffer

Understanding a person does not mean condoning; it only means that one does not accuse him as if one were God or a judge placed above him.

    Erich Fromm

Can we understand at all, ever, where we do not love?

Sherwood Anderson

One who understands much displays a greater simplicity of character than one who understands little.

Alexander Chase

To understand is to forgive, even oneself.

Alexander Chase

The pain of leaving those you grow to love is only the prelude to an understanding of yourself and others.

Shirley MacLaine

Valor

Valor and boastfulness never buckle on the same sword.

Japanese proverb

Hidden valor is as bad as cowardice.

Latin proverb

Valor is stability, not of legs and arms, but of the courage and the soul.

Michel Eyquem de Montaigne

The better part of valour is discretion.

William Shakespeare

True valor lies in the middle, between cowardice and rashness.

Miguel de Cervantes

Between cowardice and despair, valour is gendred.

John Donne

It is a brave act of valour to contemn [despise] death; but where life is more terrible than death, it is then the truest valour to dare to live.

Sir Thomas Browne

Perfect valor is to do without witnesses what one would do before all the world.

François de La Rochefoucauld

Immod'rate valour swells into a fault.

Joseph Addison

Wherever valour true is found,
True modesty will there abound.

Sir William Schwenck Gilbert

Valor is a gift. Those having it never know for sure whether they have it till the test comes. And those having it in one test never know for sure if they will have it when the next test comes.

Carl Sandburg

Value

Men understand the worth of blessings only when they have lost them.

Plautus

That which cost little is less valued.

Miguel de Cervantes

We never know the worth of water till the well is dry.

Thomas Fuller

Everything that enlarges the sphere of human powers, that shows man he could do what he thought he could not do, is valuable.

Samuel Johnson

All good things are cheap; all bad are very dear.

Henry David Thoreau

The timid man yearns for full value and demands a tenth. The bold man strikes for double value and compromises on par.

Mark Twain

The value of a thing is the amount of laboring or work that its possession will save the possessor.

Henry George

The world is always curious, and people become valuable merely for their inaccessibility.

F. Scott Fitzgerald

Try not to become a man of success but rather try to become a man of value.

Albert Einstein

Nothing is intrinsically valuable; the value of everything is attributed to it, assigned to it from outside the thing itself, by people.

John Barth

What we must decide is perhaps how we are valuable rather than how valuable we are.

Edgar Z. Friedenberg

Variety

It takes all sorts to make a world.

English proverb

No pleasure lasts long unless there is variety in it.

Publilius Syrus

As land is improved by sowing it with various seeds so is the mind by exercising it with different studies.

Pliny the Elder

To sing the same tune, as the saying is, is in everything cloying and offensive; but men are generally pleased with variety.

Plutarch

Age cannot wither her, nor custom stale Her infinite variety.

William Shakespeare

Variety is the soul of pleasure.

Aphra Behn

Variety's the very spice of life.

William Cowper

For variety of mere nothings gives more pleasure than uniformity of something.

Johann Paul Friedrich Richter

Variety is the mother of Enjoyment.

Benjamin Disraeli

They are the weakest-minded and the hardest hearted men, that most love variety and change.

John Ruskin

Victory

It is no doubt a good thing to conquer on the field of battle, but it needs greater wisdom and greater skill to make use of victory.

Polybius

There is no pain in the wound received in the moment of victory.

Publilius Syrus

All victories breed hate.

Baltasar Gracián

When you have gained a victory, do not push it too far; 'tis sufficient to let the company and your adversary see 'tis in your power but that you are too generous to make use of it.

Eustace Budgell

When in doubt, win the trick.

Edmond Hoyle

The god of Victory is said to be one-handed, but Peace gives victory to both sides.

Ralph Waldo Emerson

Victory at all costs, victory in spite of all terror, victory however long and hard the road may be; for without victory there is no survival.

Sir Winston Churchill

The problems of victory are more agreeable than those of defeat, but they are no less difficult.

Sir Winston Churchill

When you win, nothing hurts.

Joe Namath

When a game is lost, or well on the way to being lost, the bench is quiet and the strong faces grow still and watchful. The only happiness for the proud ones is victory.

Tex Maule

Virtue

The superior man thinks always of virtue; the comman man thinks of comfort.

Confucius

Virtue is more clearly shown in the performance of fine actions than in the nonperformance of base ones.

Aristotle

Virtue is its own reward.

Cicero

Let your every act and word and thought be those of a man ready to depart from life this moment.

Marcus Aurelius

When men grow virtuous in their old age, they only make a sacrifice to God of the devil's leavings.

Jonathan Swift

Virtue and happiness are mother and daughter.

Thomas Fuller

No virtue is ever so strong that it is beyond temptation.

Immanuel Kant

The measure of any man's virtue is what he would do, if he had neither the laws nor public opinion, nor even his own prejudices, to control him.

William Hazlitt

The extremes of vice and virtue are alike detestable; absolute virtue is as sure to kill a man as absolute vice is.

Samuel Butler

Happiness cannot be the reward of virtue; it must be the intelligible consequence of it.

Walter Lippmann

We are more inclined to regret our virtues than our vices; but only the very honest will admit this.

Holbrook Jackson

Whenever there are great virtues, it's a sure sign something's wrong.

Bertolt Brecht

Virtues are generally fashioned (more or less elegantly, according to the skill of the moral couturier) out of necessities.

Aldous Huxley

Woman's virtue is man's greatest invention.

Cornelia Otis Skinner

Virtue can be afforded only by the poor, who have nothing to lose.

Alexander Chase

War

To lead an uninstructed people to war is to throw them away.

Confucius

There never was a good war or a bad peace.

Benjamin Franklin

It is not merely cruelty that leads men to love war, it is excitement.

Henry Ward Beecher

To call war the soil of courage and virtue is like calling debauchery the soil of love.

George Santayana

It is easier to lead men to combat and to stir up their passions than to temper them and urge them to the patient labors of peace.

André Gide

War is like love, it always finds a way.

Bertolt Brecht

War makes strange giant creatures out of us little routine men who inhabit the earth.

Ernie Pyle

I love war and responsibility and excitement. Peace is going to be hell on me.

General George S. Patton, Jr.

After each war there is a little less democracy to save.

Brooks Atkinson

It is fatal to enter any war without the will to win it.

General Douglas MacArthur

Men love war because it allows them to look serious. Because it is the one thing that stops women laughing at them.

John Fowles

War is not madness, war is calculation.

Fredric Wertham

War is not healthy for children or other living things.

From a poster of the 1960's

All wars are popular for the first thirty days.

Arthur M. Schlesinger, Jr.

The military don't start wars. Politicians start wars.

General William Westmoreland

Wealth

Wealth unused might as well not exist.

Aesop

Wealth maketh many friends.

Proverbs 19 : 4

It is easier for a camel to go through the eye of a needle, than for a rich man to enter the kingdom of God.

Matthew 19 : 24

A great fortune is a great slavery.

Marcus Annaeus Seneca

Riches rather enlarge than satisfy appetites.

Thomas Fuller

We may see the small value God has for riches by the people he gives them to.

Alexander Pope

Many a man would have been worse if his estate had been better.

Benjamin Franklin

It is better to live rich than to die rich.

Samuel Johnson

There are men who gain from their wealth only the fear of losing it.

Antoine Rivaroli

It is only when the rich are sick that they fully feel the impotence of wealth.

Charles Caleb Colton

Wealth is the product of man's capacity to think.

Ayn Rand

It is not wealth that stands in the way of liberation but the attachment to wealth.

E. F. Schumacher

Wisdom

Wisdom
comes alone through suffering.

Aeschylus

The fear of the Lord is the beginning of wisdom.

Psalms 111 : 10 and Proverbs 9 : 10

The function of wisdom is to discriminate between good and evil.

Cicero

To wisdom belongs the intellectual apprehension of eternal things; to knowledge, the rational knowledge of temporal things.

Saint Augustine

A short wise man is preferable to a tall blockhead.

Saadi

The fool doth think he is wise, but the wise man knows himself to be a fool.

William Shakespeare

It is easier to be wise on behalf of others than to be so for ourselves.

Francois de La Rochefoucauld

Wisdom rises upon the ruins of folly.

Thomas Fuller

Youth is the time to study wisdom; old age is the time to practice it.

Jean Jacques Rousseau

It is better to have wisdom without learning, than to have learning without wisdom; just as it is better to be rich without being the possessor of a mine, than to be the possessor of a mine without being rich.

Charles Caleb Colton

It is a characteristic of wisdom not to do desperate things.

Henry David Thoreau

It is the province of knowledge to speak and it is the privilege of wisdom to listen.

Oliver Wendell Holmes, Sr.

The art of being wise is the art of knowing what to overlook.

William James

Growth in wisdom may be exactly measured by decrease in bitterness.

Friedrich Nietzsche

It requires wisdom to understand wisdom; the music is nothing if the audience is deaf.

Walter Lippmann

If one is too lazy to think, too vain to do a thing badly, too cowardly to admit it, one will never attain wisdom.

Cyril Connolly

Woman

These impossible women! How they do get around us!
The poet was right: can't live with them, or without them.

Aristophanes

Who can find a virtuous woman? For her price is far above rubies. The heart of her husband doth safely trust in her, so that he shall have no need of spoil. She will do him good and not evil all the days of her life.

Proverbs 31 : 10–12

What one beholds of a woman is the least part of her.

Ovid

One must choose between loving women and knowing them.

Attributed to Ninon Lenclos

What is woman?—only one of Nature's agreeable blunders.

Hannah Cowley

Man has his will—but woman has her way.

Oliver Wendell Holmes, Sr.

Modern invention has banished the spinning wheel, and the same law of progress makes the woman of today a different woman from her grandmother.

Susan B. Anthony

Here's to woman! Would that we could fall into her arms without falling into her hands.

Ambrose Bierce

Woman's basic fear is that she will lose love.

Sigmund Freud

When every unkind word about women has been said, we have still to admit . . . that they are nicer than men. They are more devoted, more unselfish, and more emotionally sincere.

Cyril Connolly

Ah, but what is "herself"? I mean, what is a woman? I assure you, I do not know. I do not believe that you know. I do not believe that anybody can know until she has expressed herself in all the arts and professions open to human skill.

Virginia Woolf

It has been women who have breathed gentleness and care into the harsh progress of mankind.

Elizabeth II

Women are most fascinating between the age of thirty-five and forty after they have won a few races and know how to pace themselves. Since few women ever pass forty, maximum fascination can continue indefinitely.

Christian Dior

Women are like dreams—they are never the way you would like to have them.

Luigi Pirandello

The basic and essential human is the woman.

Orson Welles

It sometimes seems as though woman would not be woman unless man insisted upon it, since she tends so markedly to be just a human being when away from men, and only on their approach does she begin to play her required role.

Florida Scott-Maxwell

The definition of a beautiful woman is one who loves me.

Sloan Wilson

When men reach their sixties and retire, they go to pieces. Women just go right on cooking.

Gail Sheehy

Male and female are really two cultures and their life experiences are utterly different.

Kate Millett

God made men stronger but not necessarily more intelligent. He gave women intuition and femininity. And, used properly, that combination easily jumbles the brain of any man I've ever met.

Farrah Fawcett

Women are not inherently passive or peaceful. We're not inherently anything but human.

Robin Morgan

Whether women are better than men I cannot say—but I can say they are certainly no worse.

Golda Meir

Women's Rights

The history of mankind is a history of repeated injuries and usurpations on the part of man toward woman, having in direct object the establishment of a tyranny over her.

"Declaration of Sentiments" passed at the Women's Rights Convention, Seneca Falls, New York, 1848

Men, their rights and nothing more; women, their rights and nothing less.

Susan B. Anthony

The growing freedom of women can hardly have any other outcome than the production of more realistic and more human morals.

John Dewey

Women are equal because they are not different any more.

Erich Fromm

We cannot reduce women to equality. Equality is a step down for most women.

Phyllis Schlafly

Women, as well as men, can only find their identity in work that uses their full capacities. A woman cannot find her identity through others—her husband, her children. She cannot find it in the dull routine of housework.

Betty Friedan

What I am defending is the real rights of women. A woman should have the right to be in the home as a wife and mother.

Phyllis Schlafly

We are not going to abolish the family. We are not going to abolish marriage. We are not going to abolish the office. But we can change the structure.

Betty Friedan

The world runs better when men and women keep to their own spheres. I do not say women are better off, but society in general is. . . . To say to us arbitrarily as some psychologists and propagandists do, that it is our *duty* to be busy elsewhere than at home is pretentious nonsense. Few jobs are worth disrupting family life for unless the family profits by it rather than the housewife herself.

Phyllis McGinley

Women must be free to determine their own life pattern and their destinies without suffering lifelong guilt for not having lived up to society's or their family's expectations.

Boston Women's Health Collective, *Our Bodies, Ourselves*

I'm the most liberated woman in the world. Any woman can be liberated if she wants to be. First, she has to convince her husband.

Martha Mitchell

A liberated woman is one who feels confident in herself, and is happy in what she is doing. She is a person who has a sense of self. . . . It all comes down to freedom of choice.

Betty Ford

I'm for women's lib, but I don't mind walking three paces behind Jerry.

Betty Ford

Work is not really new for women; what is new for women is the chance to be leaders.

Clay Felker

Any society that stifles the potential of more than one-half of its population [women] is more than prejudiced and discriminatory. It is foolish and wasteful as well.

Charles H. Percy

There is a place for women in the power structure. We don't want so much to see a female Einstein become an assistant professor. We want to see a woman *schlemiel* to get promoted as quickly as a male *schlemiel*.

Bella Abzug

The woman who climbs to a high post and then wants everybody to know how important she is, is the worst enemy of her own sex.

Claire Giannini Hoffman

It's about time women had their say in the laws governing them—laws that for 5,000 years have been made by old men . . . who have long since forgotten what it was like to be young and never knew what it was like to be a woman.

Theodore H. White

It will be a long time before women at all levels, high to low—whatever that means—will be treated as full participants in the jobs they're holding. We should be able to lose our tempers without having it attributed to our gender, be as aggressive as men without being dubbed a shrew. I'd like to get to the point where I can be just as mediocre as a man.

Juanita Morris Kreps

Work

To work is to pray.

Saint Benedict of Nursia

Work banishes those three great evils, boredom, vice and poverty.

Voltaire

I like work; it fascinates me. I can sit and look at it for hours. I love to keep it by me: the idea of getting rid of it nearly breaks my heart.

Jerome K. Jerome

Constant labor of one uniform kind destroys the intensity and flow of a man's animal spirits, which find recreation and delight in mere change of activity.

Karl Marx

No race can prosper till it learns there is as much dignity in tilling a field as in writing a poem.

Booker T. Washington

Work and play are words used to describe the same thing under differing conditions.

    Mark Twain

Anyone can do any amount of work, provided it isn't the work he is supposed to be doing at the moment.

    Robert C. Benchley

Work expands so as to fill the time available for its completion. . . . The thing to be done swells in importance and complexity in a direct ratio with the time to be spent.

    C. Northcote Parkinson

Most people spend most of their days doing what they do not want to do in order to earn the right, at times, to do what they may desire.

    John Mason Brown

He who considers his work beneath him will be above doing it well.

    Alexander Chase

The work that the kids saw around them was so odious, so boring, so worthless that they came to regard WORK as the only dirty four-letter word in the English language.

    Abbie Hoffman

Work should abound in small beginnings and small ends; they console us for the deadliness of middles.

    Oscar W. Firkins

World

The world is a sure teacher, but it requires a fat fee.

    Finnish proverb

The world is nothing but an endless seesaw.

    Michel Eyquem de Montaigne

        All the world's a stage,
And all the men and women merely players:
They have their exits and their entrances,
And one man in his time plays many parts,
His acts being seven ages.

    William Shakespeare

The world is a comedy to those that think; a tragedy to those that feel.

    Horace Walpole

This world, after all our science and sciences, is still a miracle; wonderful, inscrutable, magical and more, to whosoever will think of it.

    Thomas Carlyle

The world is getting better every day— then worse again in the evening.

    Kin Hubbard

The most incomprehensible thing about the world is that it is comprehensible.

    Albert Einstein

The world only exists in your eyes— your conception of it. You can make it as big or as small as you want to.

    F. Scott Fitzgerald

A day like today I realize what I've told you a hundred different times—that there's nothing wrong with the world. What's wrong is our way of looking at it.

    Henry Miller

Forcing the world to adjust to oneself has always seemed to me an honorable life work. . . . That one fails in the end is irrelevant.

    Gore Vidal

The world has narrowed to a neighborhood before it has broadened to brotherhood.

    Lyndon Baines Johnson

Youth

No wise man ever wished to be younger.

    Jonathan Swift

Every one believes in his youth that the world really began with him, and that all merely exists for his sake.

Johann Wolfgang von Goethe

Youth smiles without any reason. It is one of its chiefest charms.

Oscar Wilde

Young men have a passion for regarding their elders as senile.

Henry Brooks Adams

It is better to waste one's youth than to do nothing with it at all.

Georges Courteline

Don't laugh at a youth for his affectations; he is only trying on one face after another to find a face of his own.

Logan Pearsall Smith

While we are young the idea of death or failure is intolerable to us; even the possibility of ridicule we cannot bear.

Isak Dinesen

Youth is a quality, not a matter of circumstances.

Frank Lloyd Wright

Those who love the young best stay young longest.

Edgar Z. Friedenberg

Youth is not chronological age but the state of growing, learning, and changing. . . . All people must be helped to regain the condition of youth.

Charles Reich

It is one of life's injustices that young men must fight the wars that older men begin.

J. William Fulbright

Isn't one of the illusions of youth to believe that you can do absolutely anything?

Henry Miller

It is one of the surprising things about youth that it can so easily be the most conservative of all ages.

Randolph Bourne

Notes about the authors

A

Abzug, Bella Savitzky (1920–), American lawyer, Congresswoman, prominent figure in the women's movement

Acton, Lord (1843–1902), English historian; editor of the *Cambridge Modern History*

Adams, Franklin P. (1881–1960), American humorist, journalist, author, and radio personality

Adams, Henry Brooks (1838–1918), American historian and philosopher

Adams, Joey (1911–), American comedian, radio and TV personality, and author

Adams, John (1735–1826), the second President of the United States (1797–1801)

Addison, Joseph (1672–1719), English essayist, poet, and politician

Aeschylus (525–456 B.C.), ancient Greek writer of tragedies

Aesop, a reputed Greek writer said to have lived from about 620–560 B.C.; considered to be the author of Aesop's Fables

Alcott, Bronson (1799–1888), American teacher, social reformer, and philosopher

Aldrich, Thomas Bailey (1836–1907), American editor, author, and poet

Alexander, Shana (1925–), American journalist, essayist, and TV commentator

Ali, Muhammad (1942–), American heavyweight boxer

Allen, Woody (1935–), American humorist, writer, actor, and filmmaker

Amiel, Henri Frédéric (1821–1881), Swiss philosopher, writer, and poet

Anderson, Robert (1805–1871), American army officer in command of Fort Sumter when it was attacked by the Confederate army

Anderson, Sherwood (1876–1941), American writer

Anouilh, Jean (1910–), French playwright

Anthony, Susan B. (1820–1906), American social reformer and suffragette

Aquinas, Saint Thomas (1225?–1274), European theologian and philosopher

Aristonymus (flourished 5th century B.C.), Greek philosopher and comic writer; member of Plato's Academy

Aristophanes (445?–385? B.C.), ancient Greek comic playwright

Aristotle (384–322 B.C.), Greek teacher, scientist, and philosopher; considered to be one of the greatest thinkers of Western civilization

Armstrong, John (1709–1779), Scottish physician and poet

Arnold, Matthew (1822–1888), English poet, and literary and social critic

Astaire, Fred (1899–), popular American dancer and actor

Athenodorus Cananites (flourished first century B.C.), Stoic philosopher; tutor of the Roman emperor Augustus

Atkinson, Brooks (1894–   ), American drama critic and author

Attlee, Clement Richard (1883–1967), English politician; Prime Minister (1945–1951)

Auden, W. H. (1907–1973), English poet and dramatist

Augustine, Saint (354–430), North African convert to Christianity, theologian, and father of the early Catholic church

Austen, Jane (1775–1817), English writer; often considered to be the first great woman novelist

B

Bacon, Francis (1561–1626), English philosopher, statesman, and author

Baez, Joan (1941–   ), American folk singer; also renowned as a civil rights and antiwar activist of the 1960's

Bagehot, Walter (1826–1877), English economist, journalist, and editor

Baker, Karle (1878–1960), American writer and poet

Baker, Russell (1925–   ), American humorist, journalist, and political commentator

Bakunin, Mikhail (1814–1876), Russian anarchist and writer

Baldwin, James Arthur (1924–   ), black American novelist and playwright

Baring, Maurice (1874–1945), English journalist, military man, novelist, and Russian scholar

Barrès, August Maurice (1862–1923), French novelist, essayist, and politician

Barrie, Sir James Matthew (1860–1937), Scottish playwright and novelist, best known for his play *Peter Pan*

Barth, John (1930–   ), American contemporary novelist

Barth, Karl (1886–1968), Swiss Protestant theologian

Barthélemy, August (1796–1867), French journalist, poet, and political satirist

Bartol, C. A. (1813–1900), American clergyman and religious leader

Baruch, Bernard Mannes (1870–1965), American financier and statesman; advised every President from Woodrow Wilson to Dwight D. Eisenhower

Barzun, Jacques (1907–   ), American educator and scholar

Beaumarchais, Pierre Augustin Cardon de (1732–1799), French playwright and financier

Beaumont, Francis (1584?–1616), English playwright; famous for his collaboration with fellow Englishman John Fletcher

Beecher, Henry Ward (1813–1887), American clergyman and writer

Beerbohm, Sir Max (1872–1956), British essayist and caricaturist

Behn, Aphra (1640–1689) English playwright, novelist, and poet; first English woman to become a professional writer

Bell, Lilian (1867–1929), American fiction writer

Bellow, Saul (1915–   ), American novelist

Benchley, Robert C. (1889–1945), American humorist; works included newspaper articles, movies, radio work, and books

Benedict of Nursia, Saint (480?–543?), Italian priest who founded the Benedictine order of monks and the first monastery in Europe

Benítez, Justo Pastor (1896–   ), Paraguayan diplomat and journalist

Benson, Arthur Christopher (1862–1925), English educator, editor, and scholar

Berdyaev, Nicolas (1874–1948), Russian religious and political thinker, and author

Bernanos, Georges (1888–1948), French novelist

Bernard of Clairvaux, Saint (1090–1153), French theologian and monastic leader

Bernard, Tristan (pen name of **Paul Bernard**) (1866–1947), French novelist and playwright

Berrigan, Phillip (1923–   ), American former Catholic priest known for his anti-Vietnam War activities

Berry, John (1915–   ), American poet and writer

Betti, Ugo (1892–1953), Italian playwright

Bhartrihari (flourished early seventh century A.D.), Hindu poet, philosopher, and grammarian

Bhutto, Zulfikar Ali (1928–1979), Pakistani political leader

Bierce, Ambrose Gwinett (1842–1914?), American short-story writer and journalist

Bismark, Otto von (1815–1898), Prussian statesman; unified the German states into an empire

Boethius, Manlius Severinus (480?–524), Italian translator of Aristotle and author of *Consolations of Philosophy*

Bohn, Henry George (1796–1884), English publisher and translator

Bond, Julian (1940–   ), American black civil rights leader and politician

Bonhoeffer, Dietrich (1906–1945), German theologian whose participation in a plot to kill Hitler cost him his life

Boorstin, Daniel J. (1914–   ), American historian and educator

Borland, Hal (1900–1978), American author and naturalist

Borsi, Giosuè (1888–1915), Italian writer

Bourget, Paul Charles Joseph (1852–1935), French Catholic conservative novelist, playwright, poet, critic, and short-story writer

Bourne, Randolph (1886–1918), American essayist, educational writer, and pacifist

Bowen, Elizabeth Dorothea Cole (1899–1973), English novelist

Bradley, Omar Nelson (1893–   ), American general; commanded the largest armed force during World War II; became the first chairman of the Joint Chiefs of Staff

Bradstreet, Anne Dudley (1612?–1672), American poet; wrote first volume of original poetry in North American colonies

Brecht, Bertolt (1898–1956), German playwright, poet, and theatrical producer; author of *The Threepenny Opera*

Brenton, Myron (1942–   ), American social science writer

Bret, Antoine (1717–1792), French dramatist

Bronowski, Jacob (1908–1974), Polish-born British scientist and author

Brothers, Joyce (1929–   ), American psychologist and author

Brougham, Henry Peter (1778–1868), Scottish jurist, editor, and political leader

Broun, Heywood Campbell (1888–1939), journalist and newspaper columnist; helped organize the American Newspaper Guild

Brown, John Mason (1900–1969), American drama critic, biographer, lecturer, and essayist

Browne, Sir Thomas (1605–1682), English physician and author

Brownell, William Crary (1851–1928), American journalist and literary critic

Browning, Robert (1812–1889), English Victorian poet; most famous for his use of the dramatic monologue

Buck, Pearl S. (1892–1973), American author; won a Nobel prize for literature

Budgell, Eustace (1686–1737), English essayist

Buffon, Comte de (1707–1788), French naturalist; wrote the first comprehensive work of natural history

Burke, Edmund (1729–1797), British statesman, author, and spokesman for conservative opinions

Burney, Frances (1752–1840), English novelist and diarist

Butler, Samuel (1835–1902), English satirical novelist

Byron, Lord (1788–1824), English poet whose life and work embodied the Romantic spirit

C

Cage, John (1912–   ), American composer

Camus, Albert (1913–1960), French writer; associated with existentialist movement

Carlyle, Thomas (1975–1881), Scottish historian, essayist, and social critic

Carrel, Alexis (1873–1944), French surgeon and biologist

Cervantes, Miguel de (1547–1616), Spanish writer; author of *Don Quixote*

Chase, Alexander (1926–   ), American journalist

Chaucer, Geoffrey (1340?–1400), English poet; author of *Canterbury Tales*

Chesterfield, Lord (Philip Dormer Stanhope) (1694–1773), English politician and wit

Chesterton, Gilbert Keith (1874–1936), English poet, novelist, and essayist

Chevalier, Maurice (1888–1972), French-born actor, singer, and dancer

Chilon (flourished sixth century B.C.), Spartan magistrate; one of the Seven Sages of ancient Greece

Chisholm, G. Brock (1896–1971), Canadian psychiatrist

Churchill, Sir Winston Leonard Spencer (1874–1965), English statesman and historian; twice Prime Minister (1940–1945; 1951–1955)

Cibber, Colley (1671–1757), English poet, actor, and dramatist; Poet Laureate 1730

Cicero, Marcus Tullius (106–43 B.C.), Roman orator, philosopher, and statesman

Clark, Kenneth Bancroft (1914–   ), American educator and psychologist

Clark, Willis Gaylord (1808–1841), American poet and journalist; champion of international copyright

Clarke, Arthur C. (1917–   ), British novelist and science fiction writer

Clarke, John (1609–1676), English-born American clergyman and physician

Cleaver, Eldridge (1935–   ), black American author and spokesman for Black Power in the 1960's

Cleveland, Grover (1837–1908), twenty-second and twenty-fourth President of the United States (1885–1889; 1893–1897)

Coffin, William Sloane, Jr. (1924–   ), American clergyman and antiwar activist

Colby, Frank Moore (1865–1925), American editor

Collins, William (1721–1759), English lyric poet

Colton, Charles Caleb (1780?–1832), English clergyman; compiled two volumes of aphorisms

Confucius (551?–479? B.C.), Chinese philosopher

Connolly, Cyril (1903–   ), English author and editor

Conrad, Joseph (1857–1924), Polish-born novelist who wrote in English

Coolidge, Calvin (1872–1933), thirtieth President of the United States (1923–1929)

Cooper, James Fenimore (1789–1851), American novelist

Cornuel, Anne Bigot de (1605?–1694), French woman of letters

Cosby, Bill (1937–   ), American comedian

Courteline, Georges (pen name of **Georges Moineaux**) (1860–1929), French humorous writer

Cowley, Hannah (1743–1809), English playwright

Cowley, Malcolm (1898–   ), American editor and writer

Cowper, William (1731–1800), English poet

Cox, Harvey (1929–   ), American Baptist minister, writer, and educator

Crabbe, George (1754–1832), English poet

Craik, Dinah Mulock (1826–1887), English novelist

D

Dahlberg, Edward (1900–1977), American poet, critic, and novelist

Dangerfield, Rodney (1922–   ), American comedian

Dante Alighieri (1265–1321), Italian poet; author of the *Divine Comedy*

Darrow, Clarence Seward (1857–1938), American criminal lawyer; champion of labor and the oppressed

Da Vinci, Leonardo (1452–1519), Italian Renaissance painter, sculptor, engineer, and inventor

Davis, Jefferson (1808–1889), American military man and politician; President of the Confederate States of America

Dayan, Moshe (1915–   ), Israeli military and political leader

Defoe, Daniel (1660–1731), English novelist, journalist; author of *Robinson Crusoe*

De Gaulle, Charles (1890–1970), French patriot, soldier, and political leader; leader of the Free French forces during World War II; president of the Fifth Republic

Demonax of Cyprus (flourished c. A.D. 100), Greek cynic philosopher

De Quincey, Thomas (1785–1859), English essayist

Descartes, René (1596–1650), French philosopher, mathematician, and scientist

Dewey, John (1859–1952), American philosopher and educator

Dickens, Charles (1812–1870), English novelist of enduring popularity and importance

Diderot, Denis (1713–1784), French philosopher, writer, and editor of the French *Encyclopedia*

Dimnet, Ernest (1869–1954), French abbot, lecturer, and writer

Dinesen, Isak (pen name of **Baroness Karen Blixen-Finecke**) (1885–1962), Danish author

Dionysius of Halicarnassus (died about 7 B.C.), Greek scholar; wrote a history of Rome

Dior, Christian (1905–1957), French fashion designer

Dirksen, Everett McKinley (1896–1969), American politician

Disraeli, Benjamin (1804–1881), English novelist, politician, and Prime Minister (1868; 1874–1880)

Dixon, William Macneile (1866–1945), Scottish writer and poet

Dodson, Fitzhugh (1923–   ), American psychologist

Donne, John (1571?–1631), English poet and Anglican preacher

Dos Passos, John (1896–1970), American novelist

Dostoevsky, Fyodor Mikhailovich (1821–1881), Russian novelist

Douglas, Kirk (1918–   ), American actor

Douglas, William Orville (1898–1980), Supreme Court Justice of the United States

Dreikurs, Rudolf (1897–1972), Austrian-born American psychiatrist and educator

Dryden, John (1631–1700), English poet, dramatist, and literary critic

Duhamel, Georges (pen name of **Denis Thévenin**) (1884–1966), French literary and social critic, poet, and novelist

Dulles, John Foster (1888–1959), American diplomat; Secretary of State under Dwight D. Eisenhower

Durant, Will (1885–   ), American historian, philosopher, and educator

Dürrenmatt, Friedrich (1921–   ), Swiss playwright and novelist

E

Eastman, Max Forrester (1883–1969), American writer, and literary and social critic

Edison, Thomas Alva (1847–1931), American inventor; invented the electric light and the phonograph; improved the telephone, typewriter, motion pictures, electric machines

Ehrenburg, Ilya (1891–1967), Russian poet, novelist, and short-story writer

Einstein, Albert (1879–1955), German-born scientist and creator of the theory of relativity

Eisenhower, Dwight David (1890–1969), American army general and political leader; supreme commander of Allied forces in World War II; thirty-fourth President of the United States (1953–1961)

Eliot, George (pen name of **Mary Ann Evans**) (1819–1880), English novelist

Eliot, T. S. (1888–1965), American-born English poet and playwright

Elizabeth II (1926–   ), Queen of England (1952–   )

Ellington, Duke (1899–1974), American jazz pianist, composer, and band leader

Ellis, Havelock (1859–1939), British author and psychologist

Emerson, Ralph Waldo (1803–1882), American essayist and poet

Epictetus (A.D. 60?–117?), Greek Stoic philosopher

Epicurus (342?–270 B.C.), Greek philosopher

Erasmus, Desiderius (1466?–1536), Dutch priest, scholar, and humanist

Erhard, Werner (1935–   ), American founder of EST, a self-improvement movement

Erskine, John (1879–1951), American novelist

Ervin, Sam J., Jr. (1896–   ), U.S. Senator

Euripides (about 480–406 B.C.), Greek tragic playwright

F

Farquhar, George (1678–1707), English playwright

Fasteau, Marc Feigen (1942–   ), American lawyer and author

Faulkner, William (1897–1962), American novelist and short-story writer; recipient of two Pulitzer prizes

Fawcett, Farrah (1947–   ), American actress

Felker, Clay (1928–   ), American editor and publisher

Felsen, Henry Gregor (1916–   ), American writer

Fiedler, Leslie (1917–   ), American educator, scholar, and literary critic

Finley, Charles O. (1918–   ), American baseball team owner and businessman

Firkins, Oscar W. (1864–1932), American literary and dramatic critic

Fitzgerald, F. Scott (1896–1940), American novelist and short-story writer

Flaubert, Gustave (1821–1880), French novelist

Fletcher, John (1579–1625), English playwright famous for his collaboration with Francis Beaumont

Ford, Elizabeth (Betty) Bloomer (1918–   ), wife of U.S. President Gerald R. Ford

Ford, Gerald Rudolph (1913–   ), American politician; appointed Vice-President under Richard Nixon; after Nixon resigned, became thirty-eighth U.S. President (1974–1977)

Fowles, John (1926–   ), English novelist

France, Anatole (pen name of **Jacques Anatole François Thibault**) (1844–1924), French novelist, critic, and recipient of the Nobel prize for literature

Francis de Sales, Saint (1567–1622), Italian-born religious leader and founder of the Visitation Order

Frankl, Viktor (1905–   ), Viennese-born psychiatrist

Franklin, Benjamin (1706–1790), American philosopher, politician, inventor, scientist, diplomat, writer, printer and statesman; signer of the Declaration of Independence and a leader in the Constitutional Convention

Frederick the Great (1712–1786), Prussian King and military hero

Freud, Sigmund (1856–1939), Austrian physician and founder of psychoanalysis

Friedan, Betty (1921–   ), American author and feminist

Friedenberg, Edgar Z. (1921–   ), American educator and sociologist

Fromm, Erich (1900–1980), German-born social psychoanalyst

Frost, Robert Lee (1874–1963), American poet and four-time recipient of the Pulitzer prize for poetry

Froude, James Anthony (1818–1894), English historian

Fulbright, J. William (1905–   ), American senator; outspoken critic of Vietnam War

Fuller, Buckminster (1895–   ), American designer, teacher, and writer

Fuller, Thomas (1608–1661), English clergyman and author

G

Galbraith, John Kenneth (1908–   ), American economist

Galton, Sir Francis (1822–1911), English scientist

Gandhi, Indira Priyadarshini (1917–   ), first woman Prime Minister of India

Gandhi, Mohandas K. (1869–1948), national leader in India's movement to gain independence from Great Britain

Gardner, John William (1912–   ), American Secretary of Health, Education, and Welfare under President Lyndon B. Johnson

Gauguin, Paul (1848–1903), French painter

Gay, John (1685–1732), English playwright and poet

George, Henry (1839–1897), American social reformer

Gibbon, Edward (1737–1794), British historian

Gibran, Kahlil (1883–1931), Lebanese poet and painter

Gide, André (1869–1951), French playwright, novelist, and recipient of a Nobel prize for literature

Gilbert, Sir William Schwenck (1836–1911), English journalist, humorist, and playwright; collaborated on 14 operettas with Sir Arthur Seymour Sullivan

Ginott, Haim (1922–1973), Israeli-born American psychologist and author

Giraudoux, Jean (1882–1944), French playwright

Girodias, Maurice (1919–   ), American publisher

Glasgow, Ellen (1847–1945), American novelist

Godwin, William (1756–1836), English writer, free-thinker, and social reformer

Goethe, Johann Wolfgang von (1749–1832), German poet, novelist, playwright, best known for the play *Faust*

Goldsmith, Oliver (1730?–1774), Irish-born playwright, novelist, and essayist

Goldwyn, Samuel (1882–1974), American pioneer of the motion-picture industry

Goodman, Paul (1911–1972), American psychotherapist, poet, novelist, essayist

Gorer, Geoffrey (1905–   ), English anthropologist and writer

Gorki, Maxim (1868–1936), Russian novelist, playwright, and autobiographical writer

Gracián, Baltasar (pen name of **Lorenzo Gracián**) (1601–1658), Spanish Jesuit and novelist

Graham, Katharine (1917–   ), American publisher of *The Washington Post* from 1969 to 1979

Granville, George (1712–1770), English politician and statesman

Gray, Thomas (1716–1771), English poet

Greene, Graham (1904–   ), English novelist

Grotius, Hugo (1583–1645), Dutch lawyer, theologian, statesman, and poet

Guevara, Ché (1928–1967), Argentinian-born Cuban revolutionary who became powerful member of Fidel Castro's cabinet

Guicciardini, Francesco (1483–1540), Italian historian and statesman

Guitton, Jean (1901–   ), French scholar and writer

H

Haecker, Theodor (1879–1945), European essayist and critic

Halleck, Seymour L. (1929–   ), American psychiatrist, administrator, and writer

Hamilton, Alexander (1755 or 1757–1804), American statesman and political leader

Hammarskjöld, Dag (1905–1961), Swedish statesman and Secretary-General of the United Nations

Hancock, Henry (1737–1793), American revolutionary leader; president of the Continental Congress; first signer of the Declaration of Independence

Harrington, James (1611–1677), English political philosopher

Harrington, Michael (1928–   ), American lawyer and social critic

Harris, Sydney J. (1917–   ), American columnist, essayist, and author

Hathaway, Katherine Butler (1890–1942), American author

Hazlitt, William (1778–1830), English essayist and literary critic

Heine, Heinrich (1797–1856), German poet

Heinlein, Robert A. (1907–   ), American science-fiction writer

Heller, Joseph (1923–   ), American novelist

Hellman, Lillian (1905–   ), American playwright

Helps, Sir Arthur (1813–1875), English historian

Hemingway, Ernest (1899–1961), American novelist, and recipient of a Nobel prize for literature

Henri, Robert (1865–1929), American painter and teacher

Henry, Patrick (1736–1799), English-born statesman, orator, and leader of the American struggle for independence

Heraclitus (flourished around 500 B.C.), Greek philosopher

Herbert, George (1593–1633), English poet

Heriat, Philippe (pen name of **Raymond Gerard Payelle**) (1898–1971), French novelist, critic, and playwright

Herrick, Robert (1591–1674), English poet

Heschel, Abraham (1907–1972), Polish-born American Jewish theologian and author

Hesse, Hermann (1877–1962), German novelist, poet, and winner of a Nobel prize for literature

Hobbes, John Oliver (pen name of **Pearl Mary Teresa Craigie**) (1867–1906), American-born English novelist and dramatist

Hobbes, Thomas (1588–1679), English philosopher

Hochhuth, Rolf (1931–   ), German playwright

Hodges, Luther (1898–1974), American politician, businessman, and author

Hoffer, Eric (1902–   ), American social philosopher

Hoffman, Abbie (1936–   ), American political activist

Hoffman, Claire Giannini (1904–   ), American bank director

Holmes, Oliver Wendell (1809–1894), American physician, essayist, and poet

Holmes, Oliver Wendell, Jr. (1841–1935), American lawyer and Supreme Court Justice

Homer, ancient Greek poet considered to be the author of the *Iliad* and the *Odyssey*

Hoover, Helen (1910–   ), American naturalist and children's writer

Horace (65–8 B.C.), ancient Roman poet

Housman, A. E. (1859–1936), British poet

Houssaye, Arsène (1815–1896), French novelist, poet, literary critic

Howe, Edgar Watson (1853–1937), American journalist and author

Hoyle, Edmond (1672–1769), English author of rule books for card games

Hubbard, Elbert (1856–1915), American writer, editor, and printer

Hubbard, Frank McKinney (used pen names Abe Martin, Kin Hubbard) (1868–1930), American newspaper writer and humorist

Hugo, Victor Marie (1802–1885), French author

Hulst, Maurice (1841–1896), French Catholic priest and writer

Humphrey, George (1889–1966), English psychologist, educator, and writer

Humphrey, Hubert Horatio (1911–1978), American politician; Vice-President under Lyndon B. Johnson and U.S. Senator from Minnesota

Hungerford, Margaret Wolfe (1855?–1897), Irish novelist

Hutchins, Robert Maynard (1899–1977), American educator

Huxley, Aldous Leonard (1894–1963), English novelist

Huxley, Thomas Henry (1825–1895), English zoologist, lecturer, and author

I

Ibarruri, Delores (1895–   ), Spanish Communist leader

Ibsen, Henrik (1828–1906), Norwegian dramatist

Inge, William (1913–1973), American playwright

J

Jackson, Holbrook (1874–   ), English editor, poet, and author

Jackson, Jesse Louis (1941–   ), American black civil rights leader

James, William (1842–1910), American philosopher

Jarrell, Randall (1914–1965), American poet

Jarrett, Bede (1881–1934), English monk and medieval scholar

Jefferson, Thomas (1743–1826), American politician, third President of the United States (1801–1809), and author of the Declaration of Independence

Jerome, Jerome K. (1859–1927), English humorist, novelist, and playwright

Jiménez, Juan Ramón (1881–1958), Spanish poet; recipient of a Nobel prize for literature

Johnson, Flora (1948–   ), American journalist and essayist

Johnson, Lyndon Baines (1908–1973), American politician; U.S. Senator from 1948 to 1960; thirty-sixth President of the United States (1963–1969)

Johnson, Samuel (1709–1784), English lexicographer, author, poet and essayist

Jong, Erica (1942–   ), American novelist

Joplin, Janis (1943–1970), American rock singer

Joubert, Joseph (1754–1824), French philosopher and writer

Jung, Carl Gustav (1875–1961), Swiss psychiatrist and psychologist, developed analytical psychology

Juvenal (A.D. 60?–130?), Roman poet

K

Kahn, Herman (1922–   ), mathematician and social critic

Kant, Immanuel (1724–1804), German philosopher

Keats, John (1795–1821), English romantic poet

Keller, Helen (1880–1968), American author and lecturer who overcame blindness and deafness

Kelly, James (1855–1933), American sculptor

Kempis, Thomas a. See Thomas a Kempis

Kennedy, John Fitzgerald (1917–1963), American politician; thirty-fifth President of the United States (1961–1963); assassinated while still in office

Kennedy, Robert Francis (1925–1968), American politician; assassinated while campaigning for the Democratic nomination for President

Kerr, Jean (1923–   ), American playwright and author

Kesey, Ken (1935–   ), American novelist

Kettering, Charles Franklin (1876–1958), American engineer and inventor

Khrushchev, Nikita Sergeyevich (1894–1971), first secretary of the Communist Party and premier of the Union of Socialist Republics (1953–1964)

Kierkegaard, Søren Aabye (1813–1855), Danish philosopher and religious thinker

King, Martin Luther, Jr. (1929–1968), American black minister and leader of the civil rights movement

Klee, Paul (1879–1940), Swiss painter

Koestler, Arthur (1905–   ), Hungarian-born novelist and essayist

Korda, Michael (1933–   ), American publisher and writer

Krafve, Richard E. (1907–1974), American industrialist

Krassner, Paul (1932–   ), American editor

Kreps, Juanita Morris (1921–   ), American labor economist and member of the Cabinet under President Jimmy Carter

Krishnamurti, J. (1895–   ), Indian-born religious philosopher

Kronenberger, Louis (1904–   ), American writer, historian, biographer, and editor

Krutch, Joseph Wood (1893–1970), American critic, essayist, and educator

Kübler-Ross, Elisabeth (1926–   ), Swiss-born physician and psychologist

Kubrick, Stanley (1928–   ), American motion-picture director

Kuhlman, Kathryn (1910–1976), American Protestant minister and faith healer

L

La Bruyère, Jean de (1645–1696), French satirist

La Fontaine, Jean de (1621–1695), French poet

Laing, R. D. (1927–   ), British psychiatrist

Lamb, Charles (1775–1834), English literary critic and essayist

Landers, Ann (1918–   ), American author and newspaper columnist

Landor, Walter Savage (1775–1864), English poet and author

La Rochefoucauld, François de (1631–1680), French writer

Lawrence, D. H. (1885–1930), English novelist, essayist, and short-story writer

Lee, Robert Edward (1807–1870), American general and commander of the Confederate Army during the Civil War

Leibniz, Gottfried Wilhelm (1646–1716), German scholar, mathematician, and philosopher

Lenclos, Anne (1620–1705), French society matron and hostess of the most fashionable salon of her day

Lerner, Max (1902–   ), American editor, writer, and educator

Lewes, George Henry (1817–1878), English philosopher and literary critic

Lichtenberg, Georg Christoph (1742–1799), German physicist and satirist

Lincoln, Abraham (1809–1865), American politician; sixteenth President of the United States (1861–1865); refused to let the South secede from the Union; issued the Emancipation Proclamation which freed the slaves in the South; first President to be assassinated in office

Lindbergh, Anne Morrow (1906–   ), American poet and essayist

Lindner, Robert (1933–   ), American religious historian

Ling, Nicholas (flourished c. 1600), British writer

Lippmann, Walter (1889–1974), American journalist, and political writer and philosopher

Livy (59 B.C.–A.D. 17), Roman historian

Locke, John (1632–1704), English philosopher

Longfellow, Henry Wadsworth (1807–1882), American poet

Lowell, James Russell (1819–1891), American poet and essayist

Lubbock, Sir John (1803–1865), English astronomer and mathematician

Lucas, Edward Verral (1868–1938), English publisher, writer, and editor

Luce, Clare Boothe (1903–   ), American editor, playwright, politician, and diplomat

Luckman, Charles (1909–   ), American business executive and architect

Lurie, Alison (1926–   ), American writer

Luther, Martin (1483–1546), German priest, writer, composer, and leader of the Reformation

M

MacArthur, Douglas (1880–1964), American general; directed the Allied victory in the Southwest Pacific during World War II

Macaulay, Rose (1889?–   ), English novelist

Macaulay, Thomas Babington (1800–1859), English historian

Machado Ruiz, Antonio (1875–1939), Spanish poet, playwright, and scholar

Mackenna, Stephen (1888–   ), English novelist

MacLaine, Shirley (1934–   ), American actress and writer

Macmillan, Harold (1894–   ), British Prime Minister (1957–1963)

Maharishi Mahesh Yogi (1911?–   ), Indian religious leader and founder of Transcendental Meditation

Mailer, Norman (1923–   ), American novelist and essayist

Malcolm X (1925–1965), American leader in the black separatist movement

Malraux, André (1901–1976), French novelist

Mann, Thomas (1875–1955), German novelist and winner of a Nobel prize for literature

Mannes, Marya (1904–   ), American journalist and essayist

Manuel, Don Juan (1282–1349?), Spanish prince, general, statesman, and writer

Mao Tse-tung (1893–1976), Communist leader of China from 1949 to his death in 1976

Marcus Aurelius (A.D. 121–180), Roman emperor and Stoic philosopher

Maritain, Jacques (1882–   ), French philosopher

Martial (A.D. 40?–104?), ancient Roman writer

Marvell, Andrew (1621–1678), English poet

Marx, Karl (1818–1883), German philosopher and social scientist whose ideas form the basis of Communist theories

Maslow, Abraham H. (1908–1970), American psychologist

Maugham, W. Somerset (1874–1965), English novelist, short-story writer, and playwright

Maule, Tex (pen name of **Hamilton Bee Maule**) (1915–   ), American reporter, columnist, and editor

Maurois, André (pen name of **Émile Herzog**) (1885–1967), French novelist and biographer

May, Rollo (1909–   ), American psychologist and writer

McGinley, Phyllis (1905–1978), American poet

McLaughlin, Mignon (?–   ), American journalist and writer

McLuhan, Marshall (1911–   ), Canadian professor, writer, and educator

Mead, Margaret (1901–1978), American anthropologist

Meir, Golda (1898–1978), American-born Prime Minister of Israel (1969–1974)

Menander (342?–291? B.C.), Greek playwright

Mencius (372?–289? B.C.), Chinese philosopher

Mencken, H. L. (1880–1956), American critic, editor, and journalist

Menninger, Karl Augustus (1893–   ), American physician, teacher, researcher, and medical administrator

Merton, Thomas (1915–1968), American poet and religious writer

Mill, John Stuart (1806–1873), English philosopher and leader of the utilitarian movement

Miller, Arthur (1915–   ), American playwright

Miller, Henry (1891–1980), American novelist

Millett, Kate (1934–   ), American author and feminist

Milton, John (1608–1674), English poet and political writer

Mitchell, Martha (1918–1976), American public figure; wife of John N. Mitchell, attorney general under President Richard M. Nixon

Molière (1622–1673), French playwright

Monroe, Marilyn (1926–1962), American actress

Montaigne, Michel Eyquem de (1533–1592), French writer and essayist

Montesquieu (1689–1755), French philosopher

Morell, Thomas (1703–1784), English classical scholar

Morgan, Robin (1941–   ), American writer, poet, and feminist

Morris, Wright (1910–   ), American novelist

Mostel, Zero (1915–1980), American actor

Muste, A. J. (1885–1967), American clerygman and pacifist

Myerson, Bess (1924–   ), American governmental official, columnist, and Miss America of 1948

N

Nabokov, Vladimir (1899–1977), Russian-born novelist

Naguib, Muhammad (1901–   ), Egyptian leader in the revolution that ousted King Faruk

Namath, Joe (1943–   ), American football player and entertainer

Napoleon I (1769–1821), French self-proclaimed emperor of France and half of Europe

Nash, Ogden (1902–1971), American humorist and poet

Nehru, Jawaharlal (1889–1964), Indian politician and his country's first Prime Minister

Neill, A. S. (1883–1973), progressive educator

Nevelson, Louise (1900–   ), American sculptor

Nietzsche, Friedrich (1844–1900), German philosopher

Norris, Kathleen (1880–1966), American novelist

O

O'Casey, Sean (1880–1964), Irish playwright

Olmedo, José Joaquín (1782–1847), Ecuadorian politician and poet

Ortega y Gasset, José (1883–1955), Spanish philosopher and writer

Orwell, George (pen name of **Eric Blair**) (1903–1950), English novelist and social critic

Osler, Sir William (1849–1919), Canadian physician and educator

Overstreet, Bonaro (1902–   ), American writer

Ovid (43 B.C.–A.D. 17 or 18), Roman poet

P

Paine, Thomas (1737–1809), English-born pamphleteer, agitator, and writer who had much influence on the leaders of the American Revolution

Parkinson, C. Northcote (1909–   ), American historian and writer

Pascal, Blaise (1623–1662), French religious philosopher, mathematician, and scientist

Paterson, Isabel (1885?–1961), American novelist and book columnist

Paton, Alan Stewart (1903–   ), South African novelist and short-story writer

Patrick, John (pen name of **John Patrick Goggan**) (1907–   ), American playwright

Patton, George Smith, Jr. (1885–1945), American general

Pavese, Cesare (1908–1950), Italian novelist, critic, and poet

Pearson, Hesketh (1887–1964), English writer

Péguy, Charles (1873–1914), French philosophical writer, critic, and editor

Penn, William (1644–1718), English religious leader and founder of the Pennsylvania colony in America

Percy, Charles Harting (1919–   ), United States Senator

Phelps, William Lyon (1865–1943), American educator and literary critic

Picasso, Pablo (1881–1973), Spanish-born painter and the most influential of the modern artists

Pierce, John R. (1910–   ), American electrical engineer and author

Pindar (522?–443 B.C.), Greek lyric poet

Pirandello, Luigi (1867–1936), Italian philosophic playwright

Plato (427?–347? B.C.), ancient Greek philosopher and educator

Plautus (254?–184 B.C.), Roman comic playwright

Pliny the Elder (A.D. 23–79), Roman historical and scientific writer

Plutarch (A.D. 46?–120?), Greek biographer and essayist

Poe, Edgar Allan (1809–1849), American poet, short-story writer, and literary critic

Polybius (204?–122? B.C.), Greek historian

Pope, Alexander (1688–1744), English poet, satirist, and translator

Porchia, Antonio (1886–   ), Italian-born Argentine typographer and writer

Porter, Cole (1891–1964), American songwriter

Prather, Hugh (1938–   ), American author

Priestley, John Boynton (1894–   ), English novelist, playwright, and journalist

Proust, Marcel (1871–1922), French novelist

Publilius Syrus (flourished first century B.C.), Latin mime writer and actor

Pyle, Ernie (1900–1945), American journalist and columnist

Pythagoras (580 B.C.?–?), Greek philosopher and mathematician

R

Raleigh, Sir Walter (1552?–1618), English soldier, explorer, writer, and businessman

Rand, Ayn (1905–   ), American author and social critic

Ray, John (1627?–1705), English naturalist

Redfield, William Cox (1858–1932), American industrialist and politician

Reed, Myrtle (1874–1911), American novelist

Reed, Thomas Brackett (1839–1902), American politician and speaker of the House of Representatives

Reich, Charles (1928–   ), American author and social critic

Reik, Theodor (1888–   ), Austrian-born American psychologist

Renan, Ernest (1823–1892), French historian and religious scholar

Renard, Jules (1864–1910), French writer and playwright

Reston, James (1909–   ), Scottish-born American journalist and editor

Retz, Cardinal de (1614–1679), French cardinal and politician

Reynolds, Sir Joshua (1723–1792), English portrait painter and writer

Richardson, Elliot Lee (1920–   ), American politician and statesman

Richter, Johann Paul Friedrich (1763–1825), German humorist and prose writer

Rickaby, Joseph (1845–1932), English theologian and scholar

Rieff, Philip (1922–   ), American sociologist and writer

Riesman, David (1909–   ), American sociologist, writer, and lecturer

Rilke, Rainer Maria (1875–1926), German lyric poet

Rivaroli, Antoine (1753–1801), French journalist

Rodino, Peter (1909–   ), American politician

Roemer, Michael (1937–   ), American economist

Rogers, Samuel (1763–1855), English poet

Rogers, Will (1879–1935), American humorist, lecturer, actor, and social critic

Roosevelt, Eleanor (1884–1962), wife of U.S. President Franklin D. Roosevelt; active in humanitarian causes

Roosevelt, Franklin Delano (1882–1945), thirty-second President of the United States (1933–1945)

Roosevelt, Theodore (1858–1919), twenty-sixth President of the United States (1901–1909)

Rorem, Ned (1923–   ), American composer and writer

Rousseau, Jean Jacques (1712–1778), Swiss-born French philosopher

Roux, Joseph (1834–1905), French priest and writer

Rowland, Helen (1876–?), American writer

Royce, Josiah (1855–1916), American idealist philosopher

Ruskin, John (1819–1900), English social, literary, and art critic

Russell, Bertrand Arthur William (1872–1970), English mathematician and philosopher

Russell, Lord John (1792–1878), English statesman; Prime Minister (1846–1852; 1865–1866)

Rutherford, Mark (pen name of **William Hale White**) (1831–1913), English novelist

S

Saadi (1184?–1291), Persian writer and poet

Saikaku, Ihara (1642–1693), Japanese writer

Saint-Exupéry, Antoine de (1900–1944), French aviator and writer on aviation

Saint Francis de Sales. See Francis de Sales, Saint

Sallust (86–34 B.C.), Roman historian and politician

Sandburg, Carl (1878–1967), American poet, historian, and biographer of Abraham Lincoln

Santayana, George (1863–1952), Spanish-born philosopher and author

Sapirstein, Milton R. (1914–   ), American psychiatrist and writer

Saroyan, William (1908–   ), American playwright and short-story writer

Sartre, Jean-Paul (1905–1980), French existentialist philosopher

Savio, Mario (?–   ), American political activist of the 1960's

Sayce, Archibald Henry (1845–1933), English clergyman and philologist

Schell, Maria (1926–   ), Austrian actress

Schelling, Felix E. (1858–?), American educator

Schlafly, Phyllis (1924–   ), American author

Schlesinger, Arthur M., Jr. (1917–   ), American historian

Schopenhauer, Arthur (1788–1860), German philosopher

Schubert, Franz Peter (1797–1828), Austrian composer

Schumacher, E. F. (1911–1977), English economist

Scott, Sir Walter (1771–1832), Scottish novelist

Scott-Maxwell, Florida (1883–   ), American-born Scottish writer, psychologist, playwright, suffragist, and actress

Selden, John (1584–1654), English jurist, scholar, and statesman

Seneca, Lucius Annaeus (4 B.C.?–65 A.D.), Roman statesman, author, and Stoic philosopher

Seneca, Marcus Annaeus (54 B.C.?–39 A.D.), Roman rhetorician

Sennett, Mack (1884–1960), American motion-picture director and producer

Sertillanges, Antonin G. (1863–1948), French Roman Catholic apologist and philosopher

Sevareid, Eric (1912–   ), American journalist and TV news commentator

Shadwell, Thomas (1642?–1692), English dramatist and poet

Shahn, Ben (1898–1969), American painter

Shakespeare, William (1564–1616), English playwright and poet

Shannon, William V. (1927–   ), American correspondent and author

Shaw, George Bernard (1856–1950), Irish-born playwright, critic, and essayist

Sheehy, Gail (?–   ), contemporary American writer and journalist

Shelley, Percy Bysshe (1792–1822), English lyric poet

Shenstone, William (1714–1763), English poet

Silius Italicus (25–101 A.D.), Latin epic poet and politician

Skinner, B. F. (1904–   ), American psychologist

Skinner, Cornelia Otis (1901–1979), American actress and writer

Slater, Philip (1927–   ), American sociologist and educator

Sloan, Hugh W., Jr. (?–   ), American businessman and formerly treasurer of the Committee to Re-Elect President Nixon

Smith, Adam (1723–1790), English economist and author

Smith, Alexander (1865–1922), Scottish-born American chemist and educator

Smith, Alfred Emmanuel (1873–1944), American politician

Smith, Logan Pearsall (1865–1946), American essayist

Smith, Sydney (1771–1845), English clergyman, essayist, and wit

Socrates (469?–399 B.C.), Greek philosopher and teacher

Solon (639?–599? B.C.), Greek lawmaker

Solzhenitsyn, Alexander (1918–   ), Russian-born novelist

Sophocles (496?–406? B.C.), Greek writer of tragic drama

Spalding, John Lancaster (1840–1916), American Roman Catholic Bishop

Spinoza, Baruch (1632–1677), Dutch philosopher

Staël, Madame de (1766–1817), French critic and novelist

Stalin, Joseph (1879–1953), dictator of the Union of Soviet Socialist Republics

Stanislas I, King of Poland (1677–1766), Polish monarch (1704–09; 1733–35)

Steele, Sir Richard (1672–1729), Irish-born English writer and essayist

Stevenson, Adlai Ewing, II (1900–1965), American politician

Stevenson, Robert Louis (1850–1894), Scottish novelist, essayist, and poet

Stirner, Max (1806–1856), German philosopher

Stone, I. F. (1907–   ), American journalist, publisher, and editor

Stoppard, Tom (1937–   ), Czechoslovakian-born English playwright

Stravinsky, Igor Fyodorovich (1882–1971), Russian-born composer

Summer, William Graham (1840–1910), American sociologist and economist

Swetchine, Madame (Anne Sophie) (1782–1857), Russian-born French writer

Swift, Jonathan (1667–1745), English author, satirical writer, and pamphleteer

T

Tacitus, Cornelius (about A.D. 55–about 120), Roman orator, politician, and historian

Tagore, Sir Rabindranath (1861–1941), Indian poet and philosopher

Taylor, Henry (1800?–1886), English poet, statesman, dramatist, and critic

Tehyi, Hsieh (1884–?), Chinese educator, writer, and diplomat

Tennyson, Lord, Alfred (1809–1892), English poet and poet laureate

Terence (195?–159? B.C.), Roman comic playwright

Thackeray, William Makepeace (1811–1863), English Victorian novelist

Thomas a Kempis (1380?–1471), German-born medieval religious writer

Thompson, Francis (1859–1907), English poet

Thomson, Virgil (1896–   ), American composer and music critic

Thoreau, Henry David (1817–1862), American writer and essayist

Tillich, Paul (1886–1965), German-born American theologian

Tocqueville, Alexis de (1805–1859), French statesman and political philosopher

Toffler, Alvin (1928–   ), American journalist, writer, and social critic

Tolstoy, Leo Nikolaevich (1828–1910), Russian novelist, short-story writer, and religious and social critic

Tomlin, Lily (1939–   ), American comedian and actress

Torrey, Jesse (1787–1834), American moralist and abolitionist

Toynbee, Arnold Joseph (1889–1975), English historian

Trollope, Anthony (1815–1882), English novelist

Trudeau, Arthur G. (1902–   ), American military man

Truman, Harry S (1884–1972), American politician; thirty-third President of the United States (1945–1953)

Twain, Mark (pen name of **Samuel Langhorne Clemens**) (1835–1910), American novelist, travel writer, and satirist

Tynan, Kenneth (1927–1980), English drama critic, dramatist, author, and playwright

U

Updike, John (1932—   ), American author

Ustinov, Peter (1921–   ), English actor, director, playwright, and author

V

Valéry, Paul (1871–1945), French poet

Van Doren, Carl Clinton (1885–1950), American biographer, editor, scholar, and educator

Van Doren, Charles L. (1926–   ), American scholar and writer

Van Gogh, Vincent (1853–1890), Dutch-born painter

Vauvenargues, Marquis de (1715–1747), French soldier and moralist

Vidal, Gore (1925–   ), American novelist, essayist, and short-story writer

Virgil (70–19 B.C.), Roman poet

Voltaire (pen name of **François Marie Arouet**) (1694–1778), French author

W

Wallace, W. R. (1819–1881), American poet and composer

Waller, Edmund (1606–1687), English poet

Walpole, Horace (1717–1797), English letter writer, author, and Gothic novelist

Warner, Charles Dudley (1829–1900), American author

Washington, Booker T. (1856–1915), American black leader and educator

Washington, George (1732–1799), American general and politician; Commander in Chief of the Revolutionary army; first President of the United States (1789–1797)

Webster, Daniel (1782–1852), American orator, lawyer, and statesman

Weil, Simone (1909–1943), French philosopher

Welles, Orson (1915–   ), American actor and filmmaker

Wertham, Frederic (1895–   ), German-born American psychiatrist, writer, and educator

West, Jessamyn (1907–   ), American author

West, Mae (1892–1980), American movie star

Westmoreland, William Childs (1914–   ), American general; commander of U.S. forces in Vietnam (1964–1968)

Wheeler, Sir Charles (1892–1974), English sculptor, painter, and writer

Whichcote, Benjamin (1609–1683), English philosophical theologian

White, Theodore H. (1915–   ), American journalist, author, and historian

Whitehead, Alfred North (1861–1947), English mathematician and philosopher

Whitman, Walt (1819–1892), American poet

Whittier, John Greenleaf (1807–1892), American poet

Wilde, Oscar (1854–1900), Irish-born author, playwright, and wit

Williams, Tennessee (1911–   ), American playwright

Williams, William Carlos (1883–1963), American poet

Wilson, Angus (1913–   ), English novelist and short-story writer

Wilson, Sloan (1920–   ), American author

Wilson, Thomas (1663–1755), English clergyman

Wilson, Woodrow (1856–1924), American educator and politician; twenty-eighth President of the United States (1913–1921)

Winchell, Walter (1897–1972), American newspaper columnist and commentator

Wolfe, Thomas Clayton (1900–1938), American author

Woolf, Virginia (1882–1941), British novelist and critic

Wright, Frank Lloyd (1867–1959), American architect

Y

Yeats, John Butler (1839–1922), Irish artist; father of poet William Butler Yeats

Yeats, William Butler (1865–1939), Irish poet, dramatist, and recipient of a Nobel prize for literature

Yevtushenko, Yevgeny (1933–   ), Russian poet

Young, Andrew Jackson, Jr. (1932–   ), American minister, civil rights leader, politician, and first black Ambassador to the United Nations

Young, Edward (1683–1765), English poet

Index of authors and other sources

Index of opening words

I